BETWEEN FEAR & HOPE

a decade of peace activism

EDITED BY SONIA SHAH

Fortkamp Publishing Company
Baltimore, Maryland

ISBN#: 1-879175-10-X
Library of Congress Catalog#: 92-071044

Cover photo by Ellen Shub
Text design by David Gerratt, dg graphics

Previously published *Nuclear Times* articles
are reprinted with permission from the authors.

Fortkamp Publishing Company
202 Edgevale Road
Baltimore, MD 21210

To order books: 1-800-43PEACE

Acknowledgements

Grateful acknowledgement to the executive editor of
Nuclear Times, John Tirman, for his direction and support.
Special thanks to James Brogioli for all his help, and
especially to Nancy Stockford, who painstakingly
typed and proofread this manuscript. Finally,
thanks to all the authors who agreed to allow
us to reprint their articles in this book.

Contents

Introduction

IN THE EARLY TO MID-1980S, IN A SHOW OF POLITICAL COMMITMENT AND participation since unheard of, *millions* of Americans protested the nuclear arms race. The massive grassroots reaction to the nuclear arms buildup forced the political establishment to respond and legitimized the now mainstream debates over arms control and alternative security. Yet there are very few historical treatments of the peace movement available.

Too often, the difficult work of change is left undocumented, or at best, spottily recorded. Without accessible historical examples, we are left to continually reinvent the wheel. *Between Fear & Hope*, compiled with an eye toward historical documentation, strives to better this situation. And *Nuclear Times*, as a magazine for and predominantly written by peace activists and scholars, is essential to any proper history of the peace movement in the last decade.

Although the magazine changed hands and formats several times over the years, always evident was a strong sense of support for the goals, if not the tactics, of the peace movement. At times that support has, perhaps, clouded the analysis of the movement. Many articles in this collection were selected because they showed, by their omission, the biases of the movement at the time. Others document the movement straightforwardly or offer analysis and investigation. Thus the collection offers the critical reader a unique opportunity to reflect on the alarmism and elitism that informed the movement—as well as how the work of this community changed public awareness, politics, and the shape of progressive movements in America.

The first chapter—"The Movement Part One: Salad Days 1982-1984"— covers the heyday of the freeze movement during the time of mounting Cold War tensions, a hawkish administration, and a spiraling arms race. Activists managed to put the freeze resolution to a vote in ten states, the District of Columbia, and about 30 cities and counties—the largest referendum on a single issue ever—and won virtually every contest. Freeze activists committed themselves to passing the resolution in the House and Senate, and with growing popular support endorsed a broad platform that included an ambitious electoral effort in 1984, opposition to the deployment of the cruise and Pershing 2 missiles in Europe, and ending the testing of nuclear weapons. Activists agreed that time was of the essence, as nuclear war seemed more and more likely.

The second chapter—"Gaining Ground: How Different Communities Joined the Peace Movement"—documents the growth of the disarmament movement, and how it spread to professional and religious communities. Massive petitioning drives, education projects, and discoveries such as federal coverup of radiation illness in military personnel used as "guinea pigs" in nuclear tests, or accidental radiation contamination at weapons testing sites galvanized diverse communities to join the antinuclear movement. Religious, labor, women's, arts, and academic communities all threw their weight behind the drive for a nuclear freeze, the call for an end to the testing, development, and production of nuclear weapons by the United States and the Soviet Union. The release of nearly 20,000 pages of secret reports on dangerously high radioactive releases at the Hanford nuclear facility and the Chernobyl disaster triggered more focus on the dangers of nuclear weapons production itself. Such events touched off a debate within the environmental movement as to whether to work on disarmament issues, as the connections between global security and environmental viability grew stronger.

Chapter three—"The Cold War: Activists' Interpretations and Responses"—documents activists' interpretations of the Cold War stalemate and its aftermath. In the early 1980s, activists launched citizen diplomacy projects, and started analyzing and attempting to shed anti-Soviet biases. The fear of being branded pro-Soviet permeated their work. But by 1987, activists were talking about how ignorance and intolerance of the Soviets within the movement may have been one of the reasons the Cold War had not been effectively challenged. The chapter ends with an insightful analysis of how the peace movement helped end the Cold War.

Chapter four—"How Alternative Security Was Charted"—provides a sampling of the groundbreaking debate that shaped present arms control discussions. The debate started around 1985, growing stronger and more sophisticated through the end of the 1980s. Theorists discussed no-first-use, alternative defense, nuclear diplomacy, and flaws in the theory of nuclear deterrence. By August 1988, analysts pressed for a stronger United Nations, arguing that multilateral diplomacy would open the doors for alternative defense.

Chapter five—"The Movement Part Two: Transitions 1984-1989"—examines the years from the reelection of President Reagan to the inauguration of President Bush. These articles provide insights into the rocky relationship all social movements have with the electoral system. "This was to have been a watershed year for advocates of a nuclear weapons freeze," said one activist in December 1984. "Instead 1984 turned into a washout." Activists reevaluated tactics that relied on electoral gains and sympathetic politicians, agreeing they needed a more multilayered approach, and that the administration had succeeded in neutralizing the "climate of urgency" that imbued the early 1980s. The Freeze Campaign, for the first time, discussed direct action and civil disobedience tactics, rather than their previous emphasis on legislative and electoral strategies.

In January 1988, the *Nuclear Times* cover story's headline read: "Is There a Peace Candidate? Does It Really Matter?" Activists were more concerned with pushing issues, not politicians. The days of apocalyptic electoral peace campaigns seemed to be over, replaced by a myriad of organizations launching direct action, education, and citizen diplomacy, as well as legislative and electoral projects.

Chapter six—"Access and Image: Representations in the News Media"—examines the history of the peace movement and communications. The prime-time television movie, *The Day After,* sparked an initial surge of media activism: organizers wondered whether millions of prime-time television watchers would join the movement after watching it. Throughout the decade, activists complained about their lack of access to news media, and their collective biases against television in particular. In 1985, a discussion of the lack of news media relations and savvy within the movement sprang up. In 1989, people were still investigating the peace movement's image and how it was used against them. The last article documents the coverage of the peace movement during the gulf war, and introduces new and ambitious media projects.

Chapter seven—"The Academy: the Growth of Peace Studies Programs"—chronicles one of the greatest successes of the peace movement. Articles discuss how public schools taught kids about nuclear weaponry and war, and how peace studies programs grew, were institutionalized, and are now conducted at hundreds of colleges. In the mid-1980s, peace programs in public schools sparked a nationwide controversy. Many in the peace studies field now wonder whether the programs have become so institutionalized as to ignore the impulse for change that sparked them in the first place.

Chapter eight—"The Movement Part Three: Moving On 1990 to present"—assesses the impact of the dramatic world events of late 1989 and the early 1990s: the transformation of Eastern Europe, the end of the Cold War, the Persian Gulf War, and the prospect of a new policy of U.S. intervention in the Third World. In the beginning, activists worked to uncover the hidden environmental and social costs of the Cold War, and turned their attention toward domestic welfare and the peace dividend. The Persian Gulf War shook the peace community, which launched strong, yet ultimately unsuccessful antiwar campaigns. The shock waves of the war are still reverberating in the peace community, as activists struggle to analyze their setbacks and predict the future course of U.S. foreign policy.

The last chapter—"How They Saw It: The Internal Debates"—shows how activists interpreted the movement in their own words. Randy Kehler, David Cortright, Pam Solo, and Daniel Ellsberg, among others, argue about how the movement should have proceeded and why. Kehler, in 1984, advocated uniting different organizations and adopting a common agenda. In late 1988, Solo recommended the adoption of the concept of common security. Nine activists, in a roundtable discussion, reflected on the movement's loss of focus at the end of the decade. After the gulf war, 11 peace leaders assessed what the movement overlooked in its campaign against the war. In the summer of 1991, Cortright consoled peace activists that the community can and will regroup after the devastating let-down of the gulf war.

There are many insights to be gleaned from *Between Fear & Hope*. Each article presents hard-to-find information on the history of the U.S. peace movement from a source committed to peace. As a whole, the book presents a historical overview of the successes and failures of the movement, and perhaps most importantly, provides clues explaining both. We hope it will help those interested in pursuing and analyzing social change—and serve as testimony for the thousands of passionate, committed peace activists who worked diligently for peace during the 1980s.

—Sonia Shah
Managing Editor, *Nuclear Times*
April 1, 1992

ONE

The Movement Part One:
Salad Days 1982–1984

The Last Newspaper Column
By Robert Friedman
October 1982

THE FEDERAL EMERGENCY MANAGEMENT AGENCY, THE BUREAUCRACY IN charge of our nation's civil defense program, has prepared a series of 15 articles to be published in newspapers around the country in the event of a nuclear war. Like other civil defense measures, such as the relocation of urban populations to rural areas, FEMA's media campaign is based on the assumption that the Russians will give us at least a few days warning before launching their missiles. Otherwise, we may never get to read the final installment of the series, the one with the happy ending, headlined, "Would Survivors of Nuclear Attack Envy the Dead? . . . Experts Say 'No.' "

The 15 articles, each about 1,500 words in length, are intended to be kept on file in newsrooms and civil defense offices in anticipation of a so-called "crisis buildup period." They provide helpful hints on how to survive a nuclear attack, including what to do if the bomb drops while you're still on the road (follow the detailed plans for digging a "car-over-trench" fallout shelter); where to go if there's no basement in your house (lie down in the middle of the living room and surround yourself with furniture and dresser drawers filled with dirt); and how to treat early symptoms of radiation sickness (two aspirin every three or four hours). There are also diagrams for a nifty "preplanned snack bar shelter" (a basement wet bar that converts into a well-stocked fallout shelter); tips on fire prevention ("If a nuclear explosion affects your home, go upstairs *immediately* and . . . stamp out burning drapes"); and a handy guide for what to take along on a two-week trip to the nearest fallout shelter ("travel light").

As farfetched as FEMA's syndicated columns may seem, as evocative as they are of an earlier generation of propaganda efforts (recently compiled in the documentary film *The Atomic Café*), civil defense in the age of Ronald Reagan is no laughing matter. The administration is planning to spend $4.2 billion over the next seven years—of which Congress has already approved an initial expenditure of $152 million—on crisis relocation planning. The aim of this program is to convince the Russians that the United States is prepared to fight and survive such a war, but first Washington must convince its own citizens.

This is where FEMA's newspaper series comes in. Implicit in each of the articles is the message that millions, tens of millions, perhaps even a majority of Americans can survive an all-out nuclear attack—if only we are prepared. "A close look at the facts," writes the anonymous author of these pieces, "shows with fair certainty that with reasonable protective measures, the United States could survive nuclear attack and go on to recovery within a relatively few years."

This conclusion, with fair certainty, would have trouble clearing the fact-checking department of any newspaper in a city large enough to be targeted by Soviet missiles. According to recent studies prepared by the Congressional Office of Technology Assessment, the Center for Defense Information, and Physicians for Social Responsibility, survivability in an all-out nuclear exchange is a myth—quite a contradiction to FEMA's contention that Americans "could meet and overcome all the challenges of the post-attack environment." To the extent that the public can be lulled into a false sense of security by FEMA's unabashed cheerfulness, nuclear war becomes *more*, not less likely.

As it happens, most of the American press is not having any. A random survey of newspaper editorials on the administration's civil defense program reveals little enthusiasm for the plan.

With a few exceptions, such as the arch-conservative Manchester, New Hampshire, *Union Leader*, which argued that a strong civil defense effort would "perhaps deter the enemy from mistakenly concluding that we would rather be Red than dead." Most newspapers have displayed open scorn for the crisis relocation plan that lies at the heart of the Reagan program. The *Albuquerque Journal*, a paper not known for its liberal views, called "the insanity of the scenario . . . breathtaking." The *Chicago Tribune* said it couldn't decide "whether to laugh or weep." And the *Houston Chronicle* observed that "we are kidding ourselves if we think that $4 billion worth of studies and blast shelters would do much to sustain life following a nuclear holocaust."

Given this overwhelming negative reaction on the part of the press, FEMA might be better off burying all existing copies of its newspaper columns in strategically located fallout shelters. Down there—where, according to FEMA, a stack of paper 14 inches thick would offer as much protection from fallout as a four-inch block of concrete—they might actually do some good.

Bringing the Bomb Home
By Robert Jay Lifton
October 1982

WE ARE JUST NOW BEGINNING TO REALIZE THAT NUCLEAR WEAPONS radically alter our existence. It is true that none of our actions, problems, or symptoms is caused by nuclear weapons alone. But it is also true that nothing we do or feel—in working, playing, and loving, and in our private, family, and public lives—is free of their influence. The threat they pose has become the context for our lives, a shadow that persistently intrudes upon our mental ecology.

We would hardly expect the influence to be a salutary one, but we have been slow to come to terms with how malignant it is. At the heart of the matter are ways in which the bomb impairs our capacity to confront the bomb. The presence of these mass-killing devices in the world, that is, creates staggering new problems for us and at the same time distorts our thinking and blunts our feeling about precisely these problems.

Our immediate predicament can be summed up by a single word: absurdity. Perhaps existentialist philosophers are correct in their assertion that human existence, in the face of our knowledge of death, has always been absurd. But we live now in a very special realm of absurdity. We are haunted by something we cannot see or even imagine, threatened by something we call "nuclear holocaust."

Our absurdity, then, has several layers. First, there is the idea that organizations of human beings (we usually think of the Soviet Union and the United States, but they are hardly the only ones) stand poised to destroy virtually all of human civilization—destroy humankind—in the name of destroying one another. That is our basic absurdity.

Our second absurdity is the knowledge on the one hand that we, each of us, could be consumed in a moment together with everyone and everything we have touched or loved, and on the other, our tendency to go about business as usual—continue our routines—as though no such threat existed. This is the absurdity of our double life.

A third layer of absurdity has to do with the mind's relationship to the "thing." We simply cannot locate in our images anything like this "nuclear holocaust." Here is the special absurdity of the mind, our struggle with our limited capacity to (in Buber's phrase) "imagine the real." With the appearance of nuclear weapons, doing just that has become uniquely difficult and at the same time a prerequisite for collective survival.

From the standpoint of psychic impact, it does not matter much whether we imagine the end of *all* or merely *most* human life. Either way, we can no longer feel certain of biological posterity. We are in doubt about the future of *any* group—of one's family, geographic or ethnic confreres, people, or nation. The image is that of human history and human culture simply terminating. The idea of *any* human future becomes a matter of profound doubt. In that image we, or perhaps our children, are the last human beings. There is no one after us to leave anything to. We become cut off, collectively self-enclosed, something on the order of a vast remnant. The general human narrative would come to an end, and nothing in that narrative can justify to us or explain the reasons for that end.

This sense of radical futurelessness does not *in itself* cause any of our mental conflicts or aberrations but at the same time influences all of them and colors all that we experience.

Consider the radical new situation between parent and child. Undermined now in that relationship is the fundamental parental responsibility: that of "family security," seeing the child safely into some form of functional adulthood. The parent must now doubt his or her capability of doing just that. And the child must also sense, early on, the parental doubt and associate it with the overall inability of the adult world to guarantee the safety of children. We have, then, beginning evidence of significant impairment to the overall parent-child bond and its balance between protection and love on the one hand, and not just compliance, but inner acceptance of authority on the other. With nuclear subversion of that authority, the ambivalence from both sides, always present in any case, can be expected to intensify and perhaps subvert feelings of love.

The marital relationship itself may well be threatened in another way. The long-term, indeed virtually permanent, commitment traditionally associated with marriage becomes much harder to make in the face of uncertain biological continuity. The permanence of any relationship is thrown into question, and even more so the central function of marriage, which is to provide a reliable institution for the rearing of children. As a result there could be a greater reluctance to marry, increasing ambivalence among married people about the institution and what one gives up in its name, or an increasing need to maintain love relationships outside of marriage. Imagery of extinction, then, could well contribute significantly to recent increases in such phenomena as divorce, experimental substitutes for marriage (people living together in different ways for varying lengths of time), modified marital arrangements and practices involving extramarital relationships, and the decision on the part of married couples not to have children.

Indeed, one may recognize a related uneasiness in attitudes toward work in general. The possibility of nuclear holocaust makes us doubt that anything we do or make will last. I have in mind here the shifts from what was called the "hippie ethos" of the 1960s and the early 1970s, in which most work was to be avoided as meaningless and unpleasurable, to the seemingly opposite attitude during the late 1970s and early 1980s of embracing the safest and best-paying jobs in society (a considerable run on the legal and medical professions, for instance). In both attitudes—and they are clearly related—there is a struggle around the psychic inroads of the new ephemeralism and a quest for either work or cultural substitutes for work that can suggest meaning, pleasure, lastingness.

We are only now emerging from the psychological bondage that has made it so difficult for us to confront the bomb's threat to our existence. At this point we can speak of a turn toward awareness, which could lead to more extensive antinuclear commitment. But awareness is a necessary first step, and that awareness requires that we acknowledge how deeply nuclear weapons have affected every corner of our lives.

Back to "Grassroots"
By George Palmer with Michael Kazin and Steve Burkholder
October 1982

WITH CONGRESS TURNING ITS BACK, AT LEAST TEMPORARILY, ON A nuclear freeze, supporters of a moratorium on the nuclear arms race are returning to the "grassroots"—where, they have said all along, the real strength of the movement lies.

This fall, voters in 10 states, the District of Columbia, and at least 30 cities and counties around the country—representing one quarter of the nation's population—will have a chance to vote yes or no on the nuclear freeze. Taken together, this will be the largest referendum on a single issue in the country's history, and when the final votes are counted this November, it will be much clearer just how strong and effective the fledgling antinuclear movement really is.

In November, freeze resolutions will appear on ballots in California, New Jersey, Rhode Island, Michigan, Arizona, Oregon, Montana, Massachusetts, and North Dakota. Chicago, Philadelphia, Denver, and Miami will vote on the freeze. On the other end of the population scale, so will little Kearny, Nebraska (population 21,149), and Izard Country, Arkansas (10,768).

In Wisconsin, the first state to vote on the freeze, the resolution carried by an overwhelming three-to-one margin. More than 800,000 people turned out to vote on the measure, which was included on a state primary ballot September 14.

The referendum was not placed on the November ballot because of a compromise reached by the Wisconsin legislature when it voted on the measure. Republican legislators demanded the earlier date in return for their votes, figuring it would give backers less time to drum up support among the electorate.

During the weeks before the vote, the Reagan administration sent State Department officials into Wisconsin to argue against the freeze. One of them, Christopher Lehman, director of the department's office of strategic nuclear policy, sounded what will probably be the administration's theme song this fall, when he told Wisconsinites that the measure would "freeze the balance of power in a position of Soviet advantage" and would "undercut" administration attempts to negotiate an arms agreement with the USSR.

In the weeks preceding the vote, freeze supporters—among them Senator Alan Cranston of California, retired Admiral Eugene Carroll, Jr., of the Center for Defense Information in Washington, D.C., and Helen Caldicott, of Physicians for Social Responsibility—also visited Wisconsin to make public appearances. Ben Senturia, referendum coordinator for the Nuclear Weapons Freeze Campaign in St. Louis, Missouri, spent two days at state Freeze Campaign headquarters in Madison helping the state committee arrange for speakers and prepare for the final days of the campaign.

Senturia says he expects Wisconsin to be a preview of campaigns in other states. "Because of the magnitude of this thing, with 26 percent of the population involved, I expect the administration to take this very seriously, just as they did the vote in Congress."

The nuclear freeze movement—which, in its most basic form, calls for a halt to the testing, development, and production of nuclear weapons by the United States and the Soviet Union, followed by negotiations to reduce the nuclear arsenals of both countries—has been called a popular movement without precedent in American history. Since the spring of 1981, when a scattering of New England town meetings voted to endorse a resolution drawn up by military analyst and peace activist Randall Forsberg, it has been endorsed by 232 city councils, 446 New England town meetings, 51 county councils, and the state legislatures of Massachusetts, Oregon, Connecticut, Vermont, Maine, Minnesota, Wisconsin, Hawaii, Delaware, Iowa, and New York.

According to a May New York Times poll, 87 percent of the population favors a nuclear freeze that would give neither the United States nor the Soviet Union a military advantage.

However, the freeze movement has also suffered its setbacks. In June, the Senate Foreign Relations Committee turned down a freeze resolution sponsored by Senators Edward Kennedy of Massachusetts and Mark Hatfield of Oregon, preventing the measure from reaching the Senate floor. And in August, the House of Representatives, after intense lobbying by the Reagan administration, voted against a similarly worded freeze resolution. The crucial vote, on the administration's version of a freeze, which would have allowed a buildup of nuclear forces prior to negotiations, was 204–202.

So for now, advocates of a nuclear freeze are pinning their hopes on the November vote—not just on the referenda, but on a number of congressional races that pit backers and opponents of the freeze against each other. "This movement is strong enough to weather a defeat in Congress," says Randy Kehler, national coordinator of the Nuclear Weapons Freeze Campaign.

Of the 10 state referenda, four of them—in Wisconsin, Massachusetts, New Jersey, and Rhode Island—were put on the ballot by a vote of the state legislature; the other six are the result of initiative petition drives. Although they are all basically alike in calling for an end to the nuclear arms race and reductions in numbers of nuclear weapons, they differ slightly from state to state. In Wisconsin, the resolution called upon the U.S. government "to work vigorously to negotiate a nuclear weapons moratorium and reduction." In California, the resolution requires the governor to write to the president and the state's congressional delegation requesting a nuclear freeze along the lines of the one proposed by Kennedy and Hatfield. Montana's freeze resolution includes a phrase expressing opposition to the MX missile, which the administration has said it may base in the state. North Dakota's calls for a multilateral, rather than a bilateral freeze.

And, as might be expected in a political movement that has sprung from scores of local groups with only a minimum of direction from national organizations, the campaigns that got the resolutions on the ballots have been as varied as the states themselves.

The following is a brief rundown on the eight states that will be voting on freeze referenda this November:

• **California:** By far the largest number of votes that will be cast on a freeze resolution this November will be in California, with its diverse population of 24 million. There, in one of the broadest coalitions in the state's history, feminists have joined with Roman Catholic bishops, black ministers with corporate lawyers, and Berkeley radicals with both of Ronald Reagan's daughters. To get the resolution on the ballot, supporters collected more than three quarters of a million signatures. As befits a state of this magnitude, the California freeze campaign has also had the largest budget. By September, the campaign had spent $1 million and it expects to raise another $500,00 to $1 million by November for what promises to be a bruising battle with administration forces.

According to a Mervin Field poll, taken in late April, 64 percent of the population in California favored the freeze. Support, said the pollster, "cuts across most ideological, partisan, geographic, ethnic, educational, and other demographic lines." A later poll suggests the vote will be much closer.

• **New Jersey:** On June 10, New Jersey Governor Thomas Kean, a Republican, signed the legislation that put the freeze referendum on the ballot. Furthermore, he said he intended to vote for it. The passage and signing of the bill was the culmination of three months of lobbying by freeze committees in each of New Jersey's 40 legislative districts.

The debate in the state senate took place a matter of days after President Reagan's Eureka, Illinois, speech, in which he proposed that the United States and USSR reduce their ICBMs by one third. Resolution sponsors anticipated a heated debate and a close vote.

In the end, however, the bill passed the senate by a vote of 30–0, and the assembly by 70–2. There have been no statewide polls but a recent poll in populous Bergen County found 87 percent in favor of a nuclear freeze.

• **Massachusetts:** Up to the last minute, it appeared that Massachusetts's freeze referendum would never get out of the state legislature. Although both houses approved freeze resolutions in July, it was necessary for a conference committee to iron out the differences between the two versions. And with the September deadline for getting on the November ballot fast approaching, Speaker of the House Thomas W. McGee was refusing to appoint conferees, thus effectively killing the measure.

Political pressure broke the logjam. On September 20, 200 freeze supporters gathered outside the State House to protest McGee's inaction. About the same time McGee also received a letter signed by 12 of the 14 members of the state's congressional delegation urging him to reconsider. On September 22, a conference committee met and approved a freeze resolution calling for a "nuclear weapons moratorium," and on the following day, just hours before the deadline, both houses voted to put it on the ballot November 2.

• **Arizona:** Two political novices in Tucson, Nancy Carroll and Sister Gail Britanick, can take much of the credit for the appearance of the freeze resolution on Arizona's ballot. After Carroll returned from the freeze campaign's national convention in Denver last February, they put together a volunteer organization and started a petition drive. "All the politicians we talked to told us there wasn't enough money or time to do it," says Carroll. Yet, within 90 days, they collected 74,000 signatures, far exceeding the 54,000 required to place the measure on the state ballot. Total cost for the campaign, which operated out of Carroll's basement: $1,000.

Arizona's churches were instrumental in the petition drive. The state's three Catholic bishops all gave public support. Bishop Thomas O'Brien of the Phoenix Diocese distributed 1,000 petitions to all his parishes with instructions on how to collect signatures. Tucson's bishop, Manuel Moreno, sent a letter to each congregation urging parishioners to support the freeze initiative. The state's Presbyterian, Episcopalian, and Methodist churches also endorsed the drive.

The most vocal opposition so far has come from the *Arizona Republic* in Phoenix, which editorialized against the "mush-heads" and "communist dupes" who wanted to stop building nuclear weapons. The state's other major daily, the *Tucson Star*, has supported the campaign.

• **Michigan:** In Michigan these days, if you want to find a lot of people in one place, go to the unemployment office. In fact, says freeze organizer Michael Betzold, "unemployment offices proved to be one of our best petitioning spots."

To get the resolution on the state's ballot required 229,000 signatures. When organizers presented their petitions to state officials in May they had 385,000, all collected in a four-month period.

In early January, the *Detroit Free Press* published an article by Betzold, in which he described his own personal terror of nuclear war and suggested a freeze initiative in the state. "Immediately volunteers just came out of the woodwork," says Betzold. Churches and labor unions contributed volunteers. One Sunday in March was dubbed "Signature Sunday," and parishioners were asked to sign petitions as they left services.

A poll conducted in Detroit this August by the *Free Press* and a local television station found 40 percent in favor of the freeze resolution outright, 31 percent in favor only if they were convinced that there is military parity between the United States and the Soviet Union. This suggests that the final outcome is still in doubt, but freeze organizers say they will try to win over the decisive 31 percent by hammering at the economic side of the issue—that the arms race costs jobs in hard-pressed Michigan.

• **North Dakota:** In North Dakota, the smallest of the initiative states, with a total population of 652,000, campaign workers had to gather 13,000 signatures for the referendum to get on the ballot. They turned in over 16,000.

The task was easier in some respects than in other states because there is no voter registration in North Dakota. (Anyone over 18 who has lived in the state for 30 days is eligible to vote.) "We were amazed at how easy it was," says freeze worker Marv Mutzenberger of Bismarck. "We could have gotten 30,000 signatures if we'd had to. The national office said they had a little money if we needed it. We didn't need it."

Volunteers for the petition drive came from various peace groups as well as the Catholic, Methodist, and Lutheran churches. The sponsoring committees for the initiative include representatives of the state's electrical cooperative; Sam McQuade, a beer distributor; Thomas Clifford, president of the University of North Dakota; former Republican national committee member, Gerridee Wheeler; and three Republican state legislators.

• **Oregon:** Freeze workers in Oregon collected 112,000 signatures in about 10 weeks this spring, more than twice the number needed to put a referendum on the ballot. In Portland alone last May, more than 8,000 volunteers circulated petitions.

The initiative was filed with state officials by U.S. Representatives Jim Weaver and Les AuCoin, and the petition drive was coordinated by their staffs. Volunteers came from the Audubon Society, Friends of the Earth, the Sierra Club, and Physicians for Social Responsibility, as well as traditional peace groups.

At the center of the campaign has been the Ecumenical Ministries of Oregon, which includes the Catholic Church and 11 Protestant denominations. Member churches appointed a person in each congregation to collect signatures. One Portland woman collected 1,100 signatures at her church on a single Sunday.

Freeze organizers say support for the campaign has been so broad that they have had trouble keeping up with events. Julie Williamson, who works out of Representative AuCoin's office in Portland, says her office has stopped planning freeze activities altogether: "There isn't any need. So many groups are active in the freeze right now that we're just acting as an information clearinghouse, just trying to let everyone know what everyone else is doing."

• **Montana:** In early 1981, amid talk in Washington about basing part of the MX missile system in Montana, John McNamer, a cattle rancher who lives about 60 miles north of Missoula, started circulating petitions around Missoula to protest the government's plan. In August, encouraged by the success of his private petition drive, McNamer joined forces with the Montana Network for Nuclear Disarmament, and the Montana freeze initiative was born.

By December 1981, before most other freeze groups had even formed, 11,000 Montanans had signed freeze petitions. In the end, although only 18,000 signatures were required, organizers turned in a total of 32,453—representing one out of every 25 residents of the state.

"We've been mad about nuclear weapons for a long time now," says freeze worker Deb Thomas in Missoula. As she points out, 200 of the nation's 1,000 Minuteman ICBMS are based in Montana. "We've been waiting for the rest of the country to catch up with us."

If this sounds strange to outsiders, the fact is that Montana has a recent history of dissent on nuclear-related issues. In 1978, Montana voted in a state referendum to prohibit construction of nuclear power plants without a majority vote of the population. Two years later, they voted not to allow nuclear waste to be stored in the state.

"The core of the issue in Montana right now is the MX," says freeze staffer Mike Kadas, who recently won the Democratic nomination for a seat in the state legislature running on an anti-MX plank. "But for us it's just a foot in the door to begin discussing broader disarmament issues. We're going to be discussing them between now and November."

The Montana freeze campaign has spent about $1,000 so far, collected by charging admission at dances and raffling off a turkey and a lamb donated by John McNamer.

• **Rhode Island:** Rhode Island's referendum emerged from the state legislature by a lopsided vote of both houses. It is supported by Governor J. Joseph Garrahy, a Democrat, and by all four members of the congressional delegation.

The freeze campaign, which was begun by the state American Friends Service Committee and Women for a Non-Nuclear Future, now has a full-time coordinator, Jim Moran. Freeze workers are busy canvassing neighborhoods to identify freeze supporters and make sure they are registered to vote in November. Although there have been no polls, organizers expect the referendum to pass.

Moran says the local campaign got a big lift in August, when the *Providence Journal* ran a front-page story about a new Pentagon study for fighting a "limited" nuclear war. The headline read:

PENTAGON STRATEGISTS ENVISION VICTORY
WITH LOSS OF NO MORE THAN 20 MILLION LIVES

"We got more of a reaction to that than to anything we could have done ourselves," says Moran. "A lot of people who were concerned but more or less dormant came forward and got involved with the campaign."

Moran says the Rhode Island freeze campaign hasn't encountered any organized opposition to date, but he expects that to change before November. "So much of it is out of our hands," he says. "For example, Reagan could go on national TV the night before the vote and say that negotiations in Geneva are about to turn a corner and that a nuclear freeze would tie the administration's hands.

"All we can do," says Moran, "is be ready."

Freeze Sets Daring Strategy
By David Corn
March 1983

WHEN RANDY KEHLER TOOK TO THE STAGE TO CONVENE THE THIRD annual convention of the Nuclear Weapons Freeze Campaign last month in St. Louis he called for "a unified national strategy that will carry us forward." But Kehler, national coordinator of the campaign, also reminded his audience of 650 freeze activists from across the country that "the controversy that may be engendered as we work through these difficult decisions is not only inevitable, it is natural and very healthy."

Two days later, the conference presented a new strategy for the campaign. After a series of debates on policy and tactics the delegates reaffirmed their commitment to passage of the freeze resolution in the House and then in the Senate. But they also endorsed a far-reaching platform that seeks to test, as well as increase, the campaign's political clout. To the campaign's agenda they added an ambitious electoral effort in 1984, opposition to the deployment of the cruise and Pershing II missiles in Europe, and suspension of funds for the testing of individual nuclear weapons systems—on the condition that the Soviets display restraint.

Hard decisions had been made, and, above all, a strong sense of unity had been maintained. But while the conference concluded with the adoption of a platform that seemed to be supported by all, tensions within the movement were evident throughout the weekend. As Kehler noted, it was healthy controversy, that of a movement that is growing and stretching. But it also showed that as the campaign moves further from symbolic actions and enters the political arena, the decisions facing it will become even harder.

The Stakes Are Higher

Throughout the weekend, February 4–6, differences and disagreements surfaced as delegates and the campaign's leadership grappled with the central question: Where does the freeze go from here? That has been the question at each of the national freeze conferences, but this year, many participants observed, the specific issues that were debated required a greater amount of sophistication.

"The questions at this conference," says Pam Solo, chair of the campaign's strategy task force, "had a higher degree of political and strategic importance. The decisions were more complex. The relevant information was more detailed.

And the political realities were coming from many more directions and layers."

With the campaign's recent success, Kehler noted at the close of the conference, "suddenly the ante has been raised, the stakes are higher." This sense of urgency—in part due to the pending deployment of the Euromissiles and the imminence of the 1984 elections—pervaded the gathering. "I feel, almost viscerally, that the level of concern and anxiety is rising about the decisions we make," Kehler added.

In the final plenary session on February 6, the delegates, representing 47 states and 225 congressional districts, adopted a strategy paper that had been carefully pieced together during the weekend in a series of meetings attended by delegates and campaign leaders. As a general statement of principle, the campaign declared, after much disagreement over precise wording, that until the U.S. government proposes a bilateral freeze to the Soviet Union, it will "urge the U.S. Congress to suspend funding for the testing, production, and deployment of U.S. nuclear weapons, calling upon the Soviet Union to exercise corresponding restraint . . ."

This policy includes several specific strategies—each aimed at achieving a bilateral freeze. As a legislative option, the delegates approved a call to attach amendments to the funding bills of new warheads and weapons systems, which will cut off funds for testing, as long as the Soviet Union refrains from testing a comparable weapon. "It is intended as a choke point, where we get to choke off not merely the testing, but the production and deployment of these weapons systems, to challenge the Soviet Union, and to get our congressmen on record," Randall Forsberg, author of the original call for a freeze, told the conference. U.S. weapons affected by this would include the MX, the Trident II missile, ground- and submarine-launched cruise missiles, and the B-1 and Stealth bombers.

The conference also adopted a legislative strategy intended to halt the deployment of cruise and Pershing 2 missiles in Europe, now scheduled for December 1983. If the United States and the Soviet Union cannot reach an agreement that will cancel deployment of these missiles, the campaign "will support a year's delay in the production and deployment of these U.S. missiles, in order to give negotiators more time to negotiate." To this end, the campaign will try to attach amendments to appropriation measures for these missiles, freezing funds for a year. (The campaign also called for substantial reductions in Soviet intermediate-range missiles targeted on Europe.)

From Mandate to Policy

A point raised again and again throughout the convention—during strategy meetings, in informal discussions among delegates, in keynote addresses by Forsberg, Helen Caldicott, and others—was the need to develop a political strategy aimed at influencing the 1984 elections. This is the tactic perhaps most in line with the campaign's theme for 1983: "From Popular Mandate to Public Policy." In fact, as Christopher Paine of the Federation of American

Scientists points out, the delegates were ahead of the leadership on this issue.

Delegates at the final plenary session adopted an amendment from the floor that was more strongly worded than the proposal offered by the campaign's strategy task force. Calling Project '84 one of its "highest priority goals for 1983," the conference declared it would work to "elect in 1984 a President and Congress who will actively support the freeze." Throughout the weekend delegates discussed various electoral strategies that included the direct endorsement of candidates, electing freeze delegates to the national nominating conventions, and providing volunteer support to pro-freeze candidates. A newly formed task force will consult with local affiliates and then draft a set of recommendations.

The freeze campaign also expanded its scope by endorsing a series of other measures. It opposed the expansion of U.S. and Soviet facilities designed to make plutonium and tritium for nuclear warheads, as well as increasing the rate of production of such material. The delegates endorsed Jobs with Peace Week (April 10–16) and the Martin Luther King 20th Anniversary March on Washington (August 27). They supported a call for nationwide pro-freeze demonstrations, to be held October 7–8 (in part a sign of solidarity with the European peace community, which is planning demonstrations for later in October). Noting the link between economic and military security, the delegates passed a strongly worded resolution critical of Reagan's economic policies. They also called for a task force to promote education on nuclear weapons in the Pacific and for a campaign to oppose "U.S. nuclear weapons collaboration with South Africa."

"Many of these resolutions are signs of political sophistication," notes Mike Jendrzejczyk of the Fellowship of Reconciliation. "People have accused the freeze of being too white and middle-class and not sensitive to coalition building, the economy, and racism. The strong endorsement of the King march and the economic resolution shows this is not true."

A Critical Debate

With its 1983 strategy, the freeze campaign has drawn up a game plan with political teeth. Most speakers and participants emphasized repeatedly that 1983 is the critical year. And it was this feeling—that time is indeed short—that was perhaps most responsible for maintaining unity.

But delegates at the third convention had to rise above many differences to unite behind a common strategy. Many of the issues raised during the debates that preceded adoption of the campaign's 1983 strategy—not only in formal sessions, but during meals and late-night ad hoc meetings—were important and are likely to come up again.

Perhaps the biggest debate was on the wording of the general statement of principle that urged for a "cut off" of funding for nuclear weapons, while "calling upon" the Soviet Union to exercise corresponding restraint.

According to delegates who attended the strategy sessions that led up to the final plenary, there was much discussion on the "calling upon" phrase. Some delegates wanted to make the suspension of U.S. funds *contingent* upon Soviet restraint. This would make the essence of the freeze campaign a tit-for-tat policy. In other words, the campaign could then *only* advocate measures that had a specific Soviet corollary. For example, the campaign could only call for a U.S. weapons system to be stopped if the Soviets would halt a similar system. Some delegates noted that this might prevent the campaign from opposing the development of the cruise missile because the Soviets do not have a corresponding missile.

Throughout the convention this was a sensitive issue. Most delegates emphasized the need to develop a strategy that would, above all, preserve the bilateral nature of the campaign, and some believed that the wording of the general statement of principle would leave the campaign open to charges of unilateralism—that it will work to reduce the U.S. nuclear arsenal, regardless of Soviet activity.

When the final plenary convened, the first question off the floor concerned changing the wording to include a contingency clause. But as Helena Knapp, cochair of the plenary, explained, the "calling upon" language was designed to be broad, so as to include many specific strategies, some of which would call for contingent Soviet action. But one delegate complained that the statement of principle would be misinterpreted and that "you can't explain it to the vast public." His move to substitute a contingency clause was soundly defeated by the crowd, which resembled a miniature political party convention.

During the whole conference the problem of interpretation was often raised. Would aspects of the new strategy be taken as a unilateral stance? During strategy sessions, some delegates said that they thought opposing deployment of the Euromissiles without tying it to a Soviet move might be regarded as a unilateral action. But Kehler argued that the campaign "must enact interim restraints to make sure the arms race on both sides does not hurtle forward, producing and deploying weapons that will undermine the possibility of a bilateral freeze." He emphasized at the end of the conference that the strategy remained "rigidly bilateral" and that every activity proposed by the campaign was seen as a step toward a bilateral freeze.

Despite Kehler's assurances, some outside observers, including the *Washington Post*, the *Chicago Tribune*, and Richard Perle, assistant secretary of defense for international security policy, immediately proclaimed that the freeze campaign was drifting toward unilateralism. "It was unfortunate that the 'calling upon' language wasn't explained better," says Jendrzejczyk. "The problem is that it *has* to be explained."

Remember Mom

Another issue raised during strategy sessions has more tangible consequences for the campaign. As campaign strategy becomes more sophisticated, some delegates maintained, it might become harder to win grassroots support. The campaign had to come up with a strategy that would take into account the intricacies and complexities of Capitol Hill, yet be comprehensible to the campaign's supporters.

During his keynote address at the start of the conference, retired Admiral Gene LaRocque, director of the Center for Defense Information, urged the delegates to arrive at a strategy that is "sound, simple, and recognizably achievable." The value of the freeze, LaRocque said, is that his 87-year-old mother could understand it. The next day, while the campaign's leaders and delegates struggled to develop the 1983 strategy, the issue of preserving the freeze's simplicity was raised constantly. "I keep thinking of Gene's 87-year-old mother," Kehler commented during a dinner break.

"An attempt to lobby or rouse support for dealing with a particular weapons system would be terribly complicated and hard for people to understand," one delegate noted during a Saturday morning strategy session. "The problem with this strategy," another one said, "is that you need Jeremy Stone [director of the Federation of American Scientists] to explain it." Another delegate complained that using a phone tree for implementing parts of the new strategy would be hopeless. "The people on the other end of the phone," she added, "would not know what we are talking about."

But by the end of the conference, few delegates were complaining. Any reservations they previously had were overwhelmed by the spirit of goodwill that dominated the convention.

"Coming to this conference was spiritually uplifting," said a delegate from Boulder, Colorado, on the final day of the weekend. "You're out there often feeling you're involved in a lone struggle, but then you come here, meet all the others who are working with you, and feel a part of a movement that stands a good chance of success."

But does that mean that delegates caught up in the spirit of the occasion ended up avoiding some of the tough questions? Pam Solo doesn't believe so. "There was not a glossing over by any means," she observed afterward. "What was written and passed was responsive to what people had said through the entire weekend."

A Winnable Freeze

Will the new strategy work? As the campaign's agenda for a winnable nuclear freeze expands, it must prepare to work on several fronts, all of which might not be victorious. This may make it more difficult for the movement to maintain its focus and its momentum. And one disarmament lobbyist says he believes the campaign's new legislative strategies were developed without taking the realities of the Hill into consideration. These tactics are aimed for the most part at the appropriations committees, which, he notes, will not be receptive to the campaign's attempts to tack qualifying amendments on weapons appropriations bills. But he was clearly expressing a minority opinion at the conference.

Targeting individual weapons systems (particularly the cruise and Pershing II missiles), establishing itself not as a third party but as a "third force" in the 1984 elections—these are new steps for the campaign. And to achieve a freeze they are logical steps. If the president will not negotiate an end to the arms race, the campaign will press Congress to legislate arms control. And it will work to place in power those politicians who will actively support a freeze.

At the same time, the freeze campaign is seeking to expand its outreach and educational programs. Nothing will succeed without further support from the grassroots—that was the note sounded throughout the weekend. As the strategy of the freeze campaign becomes more sophisticated and complex, more broad-based educational work will be needed. The campaign is taking some bold steps—to the delight of nearly everyone who attended the convention. But it must remain careful not to place too much distance between its advanced guard and the grassroots.

Following the conference, the campaign's top priority is passage of the House resolution, which is expected to come up for a vote this month. To insure success, the campaign is staging freeze lobby days, March 7–8. Thousands of activists from across the nation will converge on Congress to lobby for the freeze. With 178 sponsors now, the resolution is expected to pass. But the campaign is trying to achieve a veto-proof margin of victory—two thirds of the House. From there it will take the resolution to the Senate, where the fight will be more difficult.

Though the campaign is stretching, flexing its political muscle, and taking on new issues, its focus remains fixed on the bilateral, verifiable, and comprehensive freeze. That is the movement's strength, Kehler noted repeatedly. In his opening remarks to the convention, he introduced the delegates to a traditional black spiritual that was the clarion call for both the abolitionist movement of the 19th century and the civil rights movement of the 1950s and 1960s. He declined to sing the song, but recited the song's chorus: "Keep your eyes on the prize, hold on, hold on."

Later that evening, when Dorothy Cotton, a close associate of Martin Luther King, Jr., presented her keynote address, she began with a powerful rendition of the song that brought the audience to its feet. Two days later, Kehler and a group of delegates opened the final plenary session by singing the song. The verses had been changed to reflect the specific issues relevant to the freeze campaign. But the chorus remained the same: "Keep your eyes on the prize, hold on, hold on."

Test Ban Wins Support
By Douglas Lavin
August 1984

AT THE NEVADA TEST SITE ON FEBRUARY 15 THE GROUND CAVED IN following a nuclear test, killing one worker and injuring 13 others. A test blast on May 1 at Yucca Flat caused the earth to rumble, raised dust storms in the desert, and made skyscrapers sway in Las Vegas, about 80 miles away. For most Americans, however, nuclear testing is a subterranean issue, out of sight and out of mind. But many in the arms control community are now attempting to raise the issue up from underground.

In fact, as groups press for a ban on nuclear testing, some hope to make it one of the most important issues for the movement in the months ahead and in 1985. David Cortright, executive director of SANE, for example, sees a moratorium on nuclear testing and approval of a comprehensive test ban treaty (CTBT) as an effective first step towards a freeze. The Center for Defense Information held a meeting with most of the top church and arms control groups in Washington in June as a first step in forming a coalition on this issue. Those who advocate making a CTBT the legislative priority for the movement reason that it is the most politically achievable, and that it lays the groundwork for other antinuclear objectives, such as a freeze or a "quick freeze."

A comprehensive test ban treaty has been a U.S. policy objective since President Kennedy's administration when atmospheric tests were halted. But in 1982 President Reagan suspended test ban negotiations because of verification difficulties. Test-ban advocates counter that recent advances in seismic monitoring and a Soviet decision to allow on-site inspection mean that all but the smallest underground blast could be verified. The CTBT could become an electoral issue this fall, since the Democratic presidential candidate favors a CTBT.

Greenpeace and its 400,000 supporters are pursuing a two-pronged fight for a CTBT, with legislative work on Capitol Hill and direct action at the Nevada Test Site, an empty stretch of desert in southern Nevada pockmarked by hundreds of tests the United States has conducted there since 1951. Greenpeace and other antitest groups, such as the Center for Defense Information, Physicians for Social Responsibility, and the Environmental Policy Institute, lobbied consistently for Senate Joint Resolution 29, which was written by Senators Edward Kennedy and Charles Mathias. The nonbinding resolution was recently turned into an amendment to the defense authorization bill, at which point it picked up an influential cosponsor, Senator Charles Percy, who, according to Greenpeace's Disarmament Director Eric Fersht, had been "an obstacle" to the amendment when it was in the form of a resolution.

The amendment, which was passed in the Senate 77–22 on June 20, called for the president to "propose to the Soviet Union an immediate resumption of negotiations toward . . . a verifiable Comprehensive Test Ban Treaty," and to seek Senate approval for the Threshold Test Ban and the Peaceful Nuclear Explosions treaties. (Those treaties created a 150-kiloton limit on the yield of underground nuclear explosions and are observed by both the United States and the Soviet Union, although not ratified by the United States.) Fersht called the margin of victory in the Senate "amazing"—it exceeded by ten votes the minimum vote necessary to ratify a CTBT in the Senate. The amendment's counterpart in the House is sponsored by Representatives Jim Leach and Berkley Bedell.

David Martinez of San Francisco's Gold Gate Alliance thinks Congress should go further. Last winter Martinez sent a draft resolution to his representative, Barbara Boxer, which called for the United States to end warhead testing immediately and challenge the Soviet Union to do the same (like a "quick freeze," except without the call for a freeze on deployment). Martinez's original version was reworked and introduced by Boxer and Representative Nicholas Mavroules of Massachusetts earlier this year as House Joint Resolution 441, but it lacks the support of key House leadership, and may not make it out of committee.

A moratorium on testing is the only way to prevent negotiators from "holding talks until doomsday," says Martinez. Other activists are forcing the issue by going to court and taking direct action at the test site. Janet Gordon, coordinator of Citizens Call, a Utah group based near the test site, is less concerned with legislation than with the medical problems of locals who have been exposed to radiation from atmospheric tests conducted in the 1950s and leaks from underground tests conducted since then. "I don't see any need for a moratorium," says Gordon. "They could sign a treaty in five minutes if the will was there." Citizens Call, together with groups such as Downwinders, whose members live downwind from the test site, are pressing the government to pay compensation to those afflicted with cancer associated with radioactive fallout. Gordon cites a May federal district court ruling that found the government negligent and blamed fallout from nuclear weapons tests for nine cancer deaths as an important first. (Judge Bruce Jenkins awarded $2.66 million in damages.) This decision—the first to link low-level radiation to cancer in court—should affect hundreds of similar suits if it is not overturned on appeal.

Other groups working in the test site region are Greenpeace and the Lenten Desert Experience, a religious group composed mostly of Franciscans that held its annual Lent vigil at the test site last April. The vigil, which included a blockade and a call for a 30-day test moratorium, resulted in 61 arrests, but no charges. The action prompted the group to change its name to Nevada Desert Experience and to begin planning a weekend action this fall before the elections.

Greenpeace members have blocked roads leading to the test site, and have stumped security forces by entering and camping out on the site for five days. This spring Greenpeace, which started in 1971 as a movement to stop nuclear testing at the Amchitka test site in Alaska, helped organize a cross-country tour to publicize a new group, International Alliance of Atomic Veterans. The tour culminated at the Nevada Test Site with a dramatic Memorial Day ceremony dedicated to servicepeople who were exposed to radioactive blasts in military experiments. "It's very likely we'll do a direct action [at the test site] this fall," says Nevada Greenpeace staffer Stephen Rohl, noting that Greenpeace is considering occupying public land near the test site and eventually may try to install a seismic monitor there to keep track of underground testing (if funding is available). Its campaigns to save whales and baby seals have sometimes placed Greenpeace's test-ban efforts on the back burner, but in the past two years the Greenpeace Disarmament Campaign has become one of the organization's top priorities and receives about one third of Greenpeace's total budget," says Eric Fersht.

Meanwhile testing continues at an increasing rate. Seven tests have been announced so far this year. The Department of Energy, which conducts the tests, has requested $638 million for FY85—up from $388 million in FY84—for test site operations alone. The total Department of Energy request for testing-related activities is close to $3 billion. These figures have led some activists to concentrate on Congress's budgetary authorization power as a way to stop warhead tests. "We need more than a resolution which says we support a comprehensive test ban treaty," says SANE's David Cortright. "We need a series of legislative steps that will begin to cut off funding."

TWO

*Gaining Ground: How Different
Communities Joined the Peace Movement*

Bishops' Next Move: Nuclear Ban?
By Thomas C. Fox
November/December 1982

WITH THE RELEASE, ON OCTOBER 26, OF THE SECOND DRAFT OF A PAS-
toral letter on nuclear weapons, a committee of Roman Catholic bishops has
placed the challenge of peace, for the first time, at the very center of Catholic
faith and action. This challenge, if met in even a partial way by the nation's 50
million Roman Catholics, could change the political climate in America for years
to come.

The statement by the bishops is by far the most complete and authoritative
condemnation of the nuclear arms race ever issued by the Catholic hierarchy.
What is emerging among the bishops, although not yet in final form, is a new
commitment to Christian pacifism, adapted to the realities of the nuclear age.
The Catholic Church in this country is lining up with traditional "peace
churches," such as the Quakers and Mennonites. The significance of this shift
for Catholics, and for the nation as a whole, may be monumental.

The release of the 105-page draft of the pastoral letter, entitled *The Challenge
of Peace: God's Promise and Our Response*, made front-page headlines around the
country. The media focused on the bishops' moral reservations about "the
deterrence policy of our nation," and their opposition to new weapons systems,
such as the MX missile, which improve first-strike capability. The bishops, it was
widely reported, called for "immediate, bilateral, verifiable agreements to halt
the testing, production, and deployment of new strategic systems" and expressed support for "deep cuts" in the arsenals of the superpowers.

But the pastoral letter is more than just another official denunciation of the
arms race. In calling upon Catholics to consider the moral implications of the
arms buildup, the document redefines what it means to be an active Catholic in
America today. The bishops are, in essence, developing a new theology of
peace, and calling upon the church, and society as a whole, to become engaged
in the process.

"We are called to move from discussion to witness and action," the bishops wrote, in responding to critics who argued that they should stay out of politics.

Pastoral letters are occasionally drawn up by the hierarchy of the church in an effort to apply church teachings to moral issues facing Catholics. Church leadership has been methodically working on the nuclear weapons statement since November 1980 when a five-member bishops' committee was formed, headed by Archbishop Joseph Bernardin of Chicago. (The committee includes a peace activist, Thomas Gumbleton of Detroit, and a military vicar, John O'Connor.) When the committee first met, Bernardin was archbishop of Cincinnati, but last summer he was appointed archbishop of Chicago, making him the head of the largest Catholic diocese in the nation. This appointment gave the committee's work more clout.

The five men and their staff met more than a dozen times in the past 18 months. They interviewed scores of moral theologians, peace activists, military authorities, and policymakers within the Reagan administration. Secretary of Defense Caspar Weinberger told the committee that "the burden of proof must fall upon who would depart from the sound policies of deterrence which have kept the peace for so long."

The bishops issued the first draft of their letter in June and requested responses. More than 700 comments were sent to the committee. In a letter to the bishops, Weinberger wrote that their views might weaken America's deterrent strategy, thereby making nuclear war more likely. William Clark, Reagan's national security adviser, told the bishops in another letter that their condemnation of America's first-strike resolve could invite war in Europe. The bishops' statement, he said, could lead "the Soviets to believe that Western Europe was open to conventional aggression."

To the surprise of many observers, inside and outside the church, the second draft of the letter, circulated at the end of October, was even more critical of the arms race than the first. This draft was debated in Washington, D.C., at the National Conference of Catholic Bishops, November 15–18, but it will not be revised and voted on until some time next year. Major revisions are not expected.

This final statement will be more than symbolic. It will call on priests, Catholic educators, religious leaders, and peace and justice committees within the Church to make all Catholics aware of the contents of the letter, and enact programs that will resist further arms escalations and work for serious disarmament. It is likely to offer support for civil disobedience. "Nonviolent resistance," the bishops wrote in the second draft, "deserves a serious place in any positive theology of peace."

The bishops have not confined themselves to abstractions. The pastoral letter specifically condemns retaliatory strikes and any use of nuclear weapons aimed at population centers. The statement further condemns *any* first-strike use of nuclear weapons—even if NATO forces were being overrun by Soviet forces in Europe. The bishops repeatedly stated that the boundary that separates conventional and nuclear war must never be crossed. "We find the moral responsibility of beginning nuclear war not justified by rational political objectives," they said. The bishops also denounced any measures that might limit human involvement in the decision to fire a nuclear weapon—an apparent reference to "launch on warning" systems.

The bishops issued directives to ordinary citizens as well as policymakers. They warned military personnel that it was immoral to "carry out orders or policies deliberately aimed at killing noncombatants." And they called on men and women employed in defense plants to take a hard look at this line of work.

While the bishops denounced the production, use, and threatened use of nuclear weapons, they stopped short of condemning their outright possession. Until now the church hierarchy has accepted the argument that these weapons may, in fact, deter war and save lives. The bishops' letter, however, offers a "strictly conditioned" acceptance of elements of the U.S. deterrent system only so long as "progress toward a world freed of the threat of deterrence" is being pursued through arms control and disarmament.

Within this acceptance lies a veiled threat. The bishops may come to condemn the very possession of nuclear weapons, if the weapons remain an integral part of the U.S. defense system and if meaningful negotiations toward disarmament do not take place. To stimulate these negotiations the bishops recommend unilateral U.S. disarmament initiatives, but they have not spelled them out. The bishops said that they "cannot at this time" require Catholics who work in weapons plants to quit their jobs, but added: "Should we become convinced that even the temporary possession of such weapons may no longer be morally tolerated, we would logically be required to consider immoral any involvement in their manufacture."

How will lay Catholics respond to the bishops' message? No one knows for sure. Many conservatives probably agreed with one prominent Catholic, columnist William F. Buckley, Jr., when he offered this rebuke to the bishops: "To say our possession of the nuclear bomb is marginally justifiable is to say, in effect, that 37 years without a world war is marginally justifiable." Michael Novak of the American Enterprise Institute, another leading lay Catholic writer, has pointed out that "the bishops have encouraged Catholics to question the government, and inevitably Catholics are also going to question the bishops . . . The more [the bishops] leave behind the Gospel and the more private judgment they get involved in, the more they are just like every other citizen."

But Catholic peace ranks have swelled in recent months. Nearly half of the 348 U.S. bishops have signed in support of the nuclear freeze. A Catholic peace organization, Pax Christi USA, has quadrupled in size in two years; 56 bishops belong to the group. Archbishop Raymond Hunthausen of Seattle has called on people to refuse to pay 50 percent of their federal income tax—the portion that goes for defense spending. Bishop Leroy Matthiesen of Amarillo, Texas, has suggested that those in his diocese should not work at a local nuclear weapons plant. Meanwhile, lay Catholics, priests, and nuns are spearheading acts of nonviolent resistance against weapons policy and weapons manufacturing.

Some analysts familiar with church policy have openly worried that a serious split in Catholic ranks was almost certain as a result of the bishops' action. But after reading the second draft of the letter last month, many have observed that the document could rally wide support because of its strong grounding in theology, and because, as one Catholic nun who is active in the peace movement put it, "survival is, after all, a conservative issue." Catholic peace activists are likely to be somewhat disturbed that the hierarchy has not unequivocally condemned the possession of instruments of massive death.

The debate among Catholics extends beyond U.S. shores. Catholic bishops in Europe are also examining their nations' roles in the arms race and have been keeping an eye on the U.S. Catholic hierarchy, before issuing final judgments. The final draft of the bishops' letter, to be issued next year, will not only shape the Catholic conscience in the United States but will set the tone and standards by which the Catholic Church worldwide will consider this pressing issue, with potentially enormous consequences.

"Guinea Pigs" Fight Coverup
By Howard Rosenberg
November/December 1982

MORE THAN 50 FORMER U.S. SERVICEPEOPLE WHO PARTICIPATED IN atmospheric nuclear tests in the 1940s and 1950s, gathered in Arlington, Virginia, recently to trade medical stories, argue about the nuclear freeze, and assess their current legal status. Once, they carried America's banner onto the battlefields of the Cold War, vaporizing imaginary enemy troops with actual atomic bombs. Now, in an ironic twist that some of them still find difficult to reconcile, the U.S. government has become their enemy.

An estimated 250,000 soldiers, sailors, pilots, and marines took part in atmospheric nuclear tests in Nevada and the South Pacific between 1945 and 1963, often marching into highly radioactive zones to prove that U.S. troops were willing and able to fight a nuclear war. Thousands of these veterans now claim they are sick and dying as a result of their exposure to the atomic fallout. The government insists there is no connection.

In the four years since the founding of the National Association of Atomic Veterans, or NAAV, dozens of bills have been introduced in Congress, investigations have been launched by federal agencies, and scores of lawsuits have been filed in courts around the country. Yet little has actually come of the effort by these men to secure recognition of their plight. The proposed legislation has been bottled up in committee, the lawsuits are in limbo, and the investigative reports continue to pile up on bureaucrats' desks. As E. Cooper Brown, the group's general counsel, puts it, "We are in danger of becoming an organization of widows and orphans instead of veterans."

At the convention in Arlington in mid-September, veterans from 21 states and all points on the political and economic spectrum discovered they had more in common than their shared experiences. After a heated debate they voted to endorse the call for a mutually verifiable, bilateral freeze on the production and testing of nuclear weapons. The vote marked a dramatic turning point for the organization. Having risked their lives for their government, many members were reluctant to support a measure they saw as defeatist—or, worse—treasonous. But to the majority the freeze resolution represented an undeniable reality: despite the rhetoric of nuclear war planners, the atomic veterans know from firsthand experience that in nuclear war there will be no winners, only losers. And the losers are all around.

One of them is John Smitherman, president of the NAAV, a double amputee afflicted with a rare disorder known as acute lymphadema. The day after the convention, Smitherman led a brigade of atomic veterans in a lobbying assault on Capitol Hill. Among the representatives he visited was Senator Alan Simpson, Republican of Wyoming and chair of the Veterans Affairs Committee. It didn't take long for Simpson to agree to hold hearings early next year on the question of whether significant information had been deliberately withheld from the veterans.

"John," the senator said when Smitherman removed a towel draped over his left arm, "you could move a stone."

Smitherman's left arm is a puffy mass that looks like the creation of a Hollywood special-effects wizard. Along its length distended veins run in bas-relief. At its end shapeless digits curve downward, permanently clenched. Because his lymph system is unable to purge his body of biochemical wastes, toxic fluids accumulate in his extremities. He has already lost both his legs, which were amputated when they swelled to five times their normal size. Now, the wastes collect in his left arm.

Half a dozen times Smitherman has filed claims with the Veterans Administration, and half a dozen times his claims have been denied. Smitherman observed two atom bomb tests in the South Pacific in 1946, but the government says his exposure to radiation is unrelated to his illness. And VA doctors recommend only one course of treatment for his ever-swelling arm—cut it off.

In desperation Smitherman traveled this summer to the People's Atomic Hospital in Hiroshima for medical help. "The Japanese treated me real well," he says in a quiet Southern drawl. "I got the same treatment as the *hibakusha* get— you know, the survivors of the atom bombings. They concluded that the lymphadema was definitely radiation-related." But in spite of the Japanese wealth of knowledge about radiation injuries, the only treatment doctors could suggest was the predictable one: amputate the arm.

Understandably, Smitherman resists the advice of doctors. He has only one good arm and hand now. If his left arm is amputated, and the disease follows the pattern it always has, his only remaining limb would be the next to go. But as long as he can get around—he steers a motorized wheelchair with a small joystick near his right hand—he plans to use his energies on behalf of the atomic veterans.

The hearings called by Senator Simpson represent a small victory for the NAAV, which has been chipping away at what it believes is a massive government coverup. Under the leadership of Wanda Kelly, the widow of an atomic veteran from Burlington, Iowa, the organization has grown in the past four years from a dream envisioned by a dying man to a national movement of 8,000 members.

Orville Kelly, Wanda's husband and the founder of NAAV, died of cancer in 1980 at the age of 49. He had witnessed 21 atom bomb tests at Eniwetok atoll and was convinced the blasts had dealt him a death sentence. In the years before he succumbed to cancer, Kelly fought vainly to win compensation from the Veterans Administration for what he insisted were military-related injuries.

In part because of Kelly's intensive research and widespread attention he received in the media, a number of investigations were launched by federal agencies and Congress. The Defense Nuclear Agency concluded that more than 90 percent of the servicepeople exposed to radiation during atomic tests received a dose of less than one rad, and only a handful received more than five rads, the allowable occupational exposure for nuclear workers. Therefore, the DNA insisted, the maladies of atomic veterans could not possibly be related to radiation exposure.

But there were other opinions. In 1980 a congressional subcommittee charged that the federal government had deliberately concealed the dangers of radiation from people living near the Nevada Test Site in the 1950s and the 1960s. In a report entitled "The Forgotten Guinea Pigs," a House Interstate and Foreign Commerce subcommittee concluded that the Atomic Energy Commission was more concerned with developing nuclear weapons than with protecting the public from injury. "All evidence suggesting that radiation was having harmful effects," the report noted, "was not only disregarded, but actually suppressed."

The committee recommended "prompt and adequate compensation" for civilian victims of the tests, but made no mention of the soldiers involved. Other evidence subsequently revealed that film badges in use during atom bomb tests were sadly inadequate, that monitoring was sometimes not even done, and that soldiers were often ordered to march dangerously close to ground zero. Yet, despite this mounting evidence, Kelly and other atomic veterans were stymied.

The main obstacle is a Supreme Court decision known as the Feres Doctrine, under which servicemen and their survivors are prohibited from suing the government on grounds of negligence for injuries sustained while in the armed forces. NAAV's legal efforts to circumvent the Feres Doctrine have met with mixed success. One lawsuit, challenging the guidelines used by the VA in determining claims, resulted in a new set of guidelines, but those, too, were considered inadequate by the organization.

As for the VA, it has never conceded a causal relationship between radiation exposure and cancer. Last year Congress passed a bill, over the Pentagon's objections, ordering the VA to offer priority treatment to atomic veterans. But even this small victory has been pyrrhic. The VA hospitals are not properly equipped or staffed to provide the necessary care and treatment for some radiation-related diseases. And no provision is made for caring for the genetically defective offspring of these men.

One clear benefit of the legislation, however, was that it laid out the Pentagon's position for all to see. While the House was considering action on the bill late last year, William Howard Taft IV, the defense department general counsel, sent an urgent and private letter to Representative G.V. "Sonny" Montgomery, chair of the House Committee on Veterans Affairs.

The bill, wrote Taft, "creates the unmistakable impression that exposure to low-level ionizing radiation is a significant health hazard when available scientific and medical evidence does not support that contention. This mistaken impression has the potential to be seriously damaging to every aspect of the Department of Defense's nuclear weapons and nuclear propulsion programs. The legislation could adversely affect our relations with our European allies, impact upon the civilian nuclear power industry, and raise questions regarding the use of radio-active substances in medical diagnosis and treatment."

Taft's message was clear. The veterans themselves are inconsequential, their deaths are meaningless, and their sacrifices only incidental. What was, and is, important to the Pentagon is maintaining the illusion that there is such a thing as a safe level of radiation exposure—an illusion that, if made believable enough, will help convince people that a nuclear war can be fought and won.

The Next Step: Acting on Faith?
By Thomas C. Fox
February 1983

THE RELIGIOUS COMMUNITY IN AMERICA, WHICH HAS GROWN DRAMA-tically hostile to the arms race, is now at a critical juncture, and the direction it takes may shape the peace movement—and the churches—for years to come.

The nation's religious leadership must decide if they will place their resources behind their words. If they do, and there are budding signs they might, they will clash with U.S. policies in a confrontation with widespread and profound implications. If they do not, many observers feel, the peace movement will lack the breadth and support to alter the path leading to nuclear confrontation.

The peace movement has ebbed and flowed through more than three decades of opposition to U.S. and Soviet nuclear arms policies: First, the "Ban the Bomb" days of the 1950s, then the antiwar years of the 1960s and early 1970s, and now the astonishingly successful nuclear freeze campaign of the early 1980s. The religious community has been active in each of these movements, but as theologian Harvey Cox has pointed out, "the strength of declarations made by the mainstream churches [today] is really unprecedented." Richard

Deats, executive secretary of the Fellowship of Reconciliation, points out: "The center of peace activism used to be the college campuses. Today it seems to be the religious community."

Why is the religious community so critical to the peace movement of the 1980s? Among all who participate in the movement no other single element can offer the base and the legitimacy that religious leadership can provide. None other can reach so many people so intimately. And none is as uniquely positioned to change attitudes toward warfare, or to articulate a new moral vision. In the end, this latter ability may be the most crucial in determining if there will be a nuclear war.

"The churches have said the right thing," says Rose Lucey, a former board member of the San Francisco-based Ecumenical Peace Institute. "They have put the peace issue up front. But the critical question remains: Will they back up their words with church resources?"

After more than three decades of working for peace, Lucey is quick to point out, the churches have failed to adequately educate their members on how to *make* peace. Lucey feels that church leaders must start working immediately to help individuals who would face severe sacrifices should they quit a job in the defense industry, withhold federal income taxes, or engage in civil disobedience.

"If we are going to really redirect our society and wean ourselves from a military-oriented economy," Lucey says, "then many individual sacrifices will be required. Will the churches be there to cushion the blows?"

John M. Swomley, Jr., president of the Methodist Peace Fellowship and a teacher of Christian ethics at St. Paul School of Theology in Kansas City, Missouri, is critical of churches that have passed resolutions defending conscientious objectors, while doing little to support the COs once they state their claims. "Why the silence?" Swomley asks.

On the other hand, there is growing talk in some churches of raising money to help support those who leave jobs in the defense industry. Leroy Matthiesen, a Catholic bishop in Amarillo, Texas, established a fund in 1981 after he suggested that Catholics in his diocese consider leaving their jobs at the Pantex plant, the final assembly place for all nuclear weapons in the United States. Tens of thousands of dollars in donations poured in from throughout the country.

The growing tax resistance movement was partly inspired by Archbishop Raymond Hunthausen of Seattle who, in July 1981, called upon those in his diocese to consider withholding one half of their federal income tax payments in protest against the arms buildup. In the wake of Hunthausen's statements, contributions to his diocese from its members have grown substantially. Recent statements by members of the Reagan administration, who say they will crack down on tax resisters, indicate that Washington is concerned. Many religious figures, including Swomley and Philip Berrigan, are calling for a show of resistance this spring through acts of "non-collaboration," including withholding taxes on April 15. Will the religious leadership back such steps? Will they support tax resisters, such as Hunthausen, who face federal indictment and imprisonment?

On the whole, the church leadership has not kept up with activists within the denominations, Swomley notes. "It's been said that for every bishop who is speaking out, there are several nuns with pins," he says. Religious women in America have been at the forefront of peace and justice advocacy and have served as the conscience of much of the rest of the church.

The Old and the New

It was not always so easy to create change from congregation up. "In the 1960s we went to jail alone," Daniel Berrigan has said. "Now there are bishops at our side and Jesuits putting up bail."

Once prodded along this road by the activists, church leaders begin to speak out, lending legitimacy to grassroots peace activities. Eventually, many of those who fill the pews begin to trust the activists, and the ranks of peace organizations grow.

Included among the groups that have focused on the arms race have been the traditional "peace churches," the Mennonites, Quakers, and Church of the Brethren. But in addition, mainstream Protestant churches, including the Episcopal Church, the American Lutheran Church (which is both politically and theologically conservative), and the Presbyterian Church have denounced the current arms buildup. In 1981 the National Council of Churches issued a strong resolution in support of a bilateral nuclear freeze, and called upon member organizations to direct their resources to educating on behalf of the freeze. The Union of American Hebrew Congregations has strongly backed the freeze.

While the Washington, D.C.-based Sojourners, and their founder, Jim Wallis, have spearheaded peace activities among evangelicals, the most important evangelical convert to the peace movement has been Billy Graham, who experienced a change of heart two years ago and unexpectedly began to call for disarmament in his Crusades. Graham said that he felt he had a "responsibility" to speak out for peace. By doing so he outraged many of his political friends but he has made the idea of disarmament respectable among many evangelicals. "I believe in risks for peace," Graham has said.

Lessons from Vietnam

How did the religious community come to embrace, and inspire, the new peace movement? Jim Rice of Sojourners refers to "an outpouring of spirit, even more than Reagan's provocative stance, that has caused the revitalization of the peace movement." Like so many others, religious groups and leaders were influenced by what Bill Price of World Peacemakers calls "the miracle of the European peace movement," which is led largely by church activists.

But no assessment of the peace movement can be undertaken without recalling the Vietnam War, the opposition to it, and its influence on the movement today.

From 1965 to 1975—almost one third of the Atomic Age—peace activities in the United States focused on Vietnam. There could be little discussion of nuclear issues while children were being napalmed. By removing national attention from the nuclear issue while a new generation of weapons was quietly being introduced into the arsenals of the superpowers, the Vietnam War gave weapons-boosters a ten-year grace period.

But Vietnam also taught the movement many critical lessons, among them that religious denominations could work effectively together across church lines. There was a time, as late as the mid-1960s, when "ecumenism" was solely the work of theologians studying scripture and church documents in an attempt to justify bringing the denominations closer together. Vietnam ended that. Religious distinctions—and denominational rivalries—faded away during planning sessions for peace marches. Prayer vigils were held in whichever church had the space. Ecumenism, in practice rather than in theory, was born.

This forging of concerns has lasted until today, and has greatly affected the nature of many churches—the ways they look at themselves, each other, and the world. Members of the Catholic, Protestant, and Jewish organizations alike are all working to apply simple biblical notions to a world seemingly bent on self-destruction. And within all of these denominations and groups, religious distinctions are essentially irrelevant.

The common commitment is to a more equitable and peaceful world. What has emerged in the 1980s within the peace movement is a new linkage, often missing during the 1960s, of peace and economic issues. This marks a new maturity as well as a new challenge for the churches. Ironically, President Reagan, by means of his budget proposals to boost defense spending at the expense of social programs, helped establish this link. A growing number of churches, such as the Quakers and the Mennonites, are now researching the effects and benefits of converting the U.S. economy from militaristic to peaceful business.

The Catholic Church's bonds to Central America have also served to educate key members of many denominations. Last month over 300 religious leaders in America—including 22 bishops, several heads of Protestant denominations and nine rabbis—signed a message denouncing the Reagan administration's policies in Central America. It was not until 1971, very late in the Vietnam War, that the bishops condemned U.S. involvement. But ten years later a new generation of bishops has emerged and many are determined to halt further U.S. military aid to El Salvador.

The "Third Awakening"?

There appears to be a significant religious revival occurring in many U.S. churches as they get deeper into the disarmament issue. Joe Holland of the Washington-based Catholic think tank, the Center of Concern, calls this the

"Third Great Awakening in America." The first religious revival, he says, led to a social protest against Britain and finally to revolution in the 13 colonies. The second, he says, launched the struggle against slavery. Now the third revival, Holland believes, is moving the nation to revolt against those "who have come to control our government and threaten the nation with nuclear war."

How does this revival affect the churches themselves? Many religious-minded people who contemplate the arms race are eventually forced to ask themselves a very basic question of faith: Where do I place my ultimate trust—in the nuclear umbrella or in God? Consequently, within the churches there is increasing talk of "nuclear idolatry," deeper examination of the scriptures, and a renewal of faith.

Will the new activism divide the church and ultimately prove counterproductive? Divisions are indeed likely but those who support peace initiatives argue that division itself is a sign of life and it is better to be alive than to be irrelevant. Even if only a small portion of those who claim religious beliefs follow the initiatives being taken by church leadership, the impact will be substantial. Regardless of how many follow, it is essential, peace proponents argue, that religious leaders articulate moral teachings as they understand them, no matter how "secular" they seem.

Asked recently whether he favored disarmament by the United States—irrespective of a Soviet reduction—Thomas Gumbleton, auxiliary bishop of Detroit and head of Pax Christi USA, answered: "Yes. When you make judgments about what is morally right or morally wrong, you can never base your judgment on what someone else does. You teach your children not to steal because it is wrong. You don't say, 'Don't steal unless you see somebody else stealing.'"

Should the churches now go on to actively confront what many of their leaders have called the greatest moral peril of our time—the nuclear arms buildup—and if they commit their resources and full energies to reversing this buildup, then they will undoubtedly transform themselves in the process, and possibly, change the course of history.

Movement Looks for the Union Label
By Bruce Shapiro
April 1983

WHILE ON VACATION IN ENGLAND TWO YEARS AGO, LARRY FRANK FOUND himself in a pub drinking with workers from the nearby Lucas Aerospace plant. Frank, a Los Angeles-based labor organizer who has run campaigns for several major unions, was startled to learn that the workers at the plant had drawn up a plan to retool their company, which had been involved primarily in military production, so that it could manufacture more socially useful products.

When Frank returned home he began working to organize labor against what author Seymour Melman calls "the permanent war economy." He is chair of Southern California Unions for a Nuclear Weapons Freeze—one of a small but growing number of labor organizations around the country actively involved in the nuclear disarmament campaign.

Since last summer, labor participation in the nuclear freeze movement—though mostly low-key—has rapidly increased. At least 16 major unions and labor organizations have officially endorsed the call for a bilateral freeze. Several unions have freeze education campaigns. Central labor councils—county-wide union coalitions—in a number of states have backed the freeze and military budget-cutting initiatives. The grassroots Jobs with Peace Campaign, aimed at redirecting government spending, has attracted broad labor support.

All this activity marks a significant change for much of the labor movement, which since World War II has largely been guided by the rule of thumb that military spending creates jobs. The shift has not come easily. Many union members still adhere to the traditional guns-equals-jobs view. Under Lane Kirkland's leadership, the AFL-CIO opposes a nuclear freeze and urges an increase in defense spending. The stricken American economy has forced even progressive unions to look first at short-term bread-and-butter issues.

Labor has not had an entirely comfortable relationship with the largely white, middle-class nuclear freeze movement. It is a problem both sides acknowledge; they are actively seeking to bridge the gap. Freeze organizers say there is growing recognition of the central role labor must play in bringing about any political solution to the arms race. And unions, though often reluctant to enter coalitions, have begun throwing their support behind freeze-related projects.

Jobs and the Freeze

Unions have a variety of motivations for their alliance with the freeze movement. For some traditionally liberal organizations, such as the Amalgamated Clothing and Textile Workers Union, participation in the campaign was almost a reflex.

For many unions, particularly those with members in the defense contracting work, joining the freeze movement was a deliberate outgrowth of a longstanding and immediate concern: jobs. The International Association of Machinists , for example, under the leadership of its president, William Winpisinger, has been openly critical of military spending for years, even though some 85,000 IAM members work for military contractors. Plagued by shifts toward high-technology weaponry and increased subcontracting abroad, the Machinists have found that greater military spending has not brought greater prosperity.

In fact, it has brought the opposite. "For every new military contract," says Lou Kiefer, an IAM organizer in the Hartford, Connecticut, area, "we see fewer jobs." Forty percent of the Machinists in Kiefer's District 91 have military-related jobs, mostly at seven plants owned by United Technologies. Today—even though the corporation tripled its defense contracting revenues over the

1970s—that number has dropped to 20,000. In 1978 the IAM commissioned what organizers such as Kiefer had long suspected: Machinist employment was falling in almost direct proportion to the rising military budget. During the 1970s the number of skilled journeyman machinists decreased by 76,000 nationwide.

But if the issue of jobs helped bring the IAM and other unions close to the freeze movement, the same specter of unemployment has pushed another important progressive union—the United Auto Workers—into keeping its distance. Historically a critic of defense spending, the UAW in the past year has been markedly mute. Although still on record as opposing higher defense spending, UAW President Douglas Fraser sided with Lane Kirkland against a nuclear freeze, reportedly because he does not want to jeopardize Kirkland's support for proposed auto-content legislation. He beat back a freeze resolution in his own union, and will not discuss the issue even with close allies.

Opposition to the freeze from Kirkland and the AFL-CIO executive council is more than symbolic. According to published reports, Kirkland at least once threatened to revoke the charter of a district labor council if it endorsed the freeze. His office reportedly even lobbied to have the word "Peace" removed from the "Jobs, Peace, and Freedom" rally planned for August 27 to mark the 20th anniversary of Martin Luther King's historic March on Washington, D.C.

The persistence of unions in publicly defying Kirkland marks a significant historical departure for the normally monolithic AFL-CIO. Several of the unions most outspoken in favor of the freeze, such as the American Federation of State, County, and Municipal Employees and the United Food and Commercial Workers Union, are among the largest in the federation. Even more dissent on military spending is reportedly building at the local level. The American Federation of Teachers and the Communications Workers of America, for example, endorsed the freeze despite opposition from their own presidents.

An Uneasy Alliance

Despite this new wave of antinuclear sentiment among unions, however, there is still a gulf between labor and other elements of the nuclear freeze movement. Organizers from community peace groups and union locals say they have had an uneasy alliance, sometimes because peace activists have been unresponsive to the special interests and problems of labor, and often because freeze campaigners are unaware of the basic structure and workings of unions.

Even progressive unions, such as the IAM, contain opposition within their ranks, explains Steve Daggett of the Coalition for a New Foreign and Military Policy, which works closely with the IAM and other unions. "In the past there has not been a lot of sensitivity to this," adds Daggett. There has also been some insensitivity to job issues, acknowledges Gene Carroll, labor coordinator for the National Freeze Campaign and a former ACTWU organizer. "People have not always talked about, for instance, income security for defense workers displaced by a nuclear weapons freeze," admits Carroll.

Some union organizers are also put off by what they see as the arrogance of middle-class disarmament campaigns. "Lots of people are trafficking in our problems," says Dick Greenwood, a special assistant to IAM president Winpisinger, "but what we need are solutions." Greenwood, who acts as his union's liaison with the National Freeze Campaign, says he is particularly frustrated by the sometimes slow, coalition-style decision-making process adopted by the movement—very different from that of labor.

"You go to these meetings," he says, "and everyone's got their own thing—all those autonomous organizations—you talk, talk, talk. It's almost a group grope." His union's members, he says, are facing an immediate economic crisis and "we don't have time for those things—we need results." He adds, "I'm not knocking any of those organizations, but it's not always enough."

Greenwood is also skeptical of extremely decentralized efforts such as Jobs with Peace. "They think you can sit at the local level and be the tail that wags the dog," he says. "But you've got to have a centralized system for channelling resources and coordinating activity. You're up against corporations which are all over the map. General Dynamics is not just in Groton, Connecticut [where Trident submarines are built]." The IAM's own antimilitary spending program combines national studies with worker education and a grassroots network of shop committees to deal with issues such as economic conversion—retooling military-based industries and factories for other purposes. The union has also backed conversion legislation on the state level.

The National Freeze Campaign, for its part, is making a concerted effort to bridge the gap. Partly this is a matter of political necessity; many key members of Congress are from regions heavily dominated by labor. But in large part, says Gene Carroll, it stems from the realization that "labor support for stopping the arms race exists and is growing, but this support is coupled with everyone's awareness of the economic survival question."

Bridge Building

In February 1982, the national conference of the Freeze Campaign created an economic issues task force, including representatives from a number of unions. The task force is trying to generate enough labor support to drive the Kennedy-Hatfield freeze bill through Congress. Over time, the group plans a wide-ranging education campaign on the economic effects of the arms race and alternatives.

Last month the task force released its first publication, *The Freeze Economy*, a comprehensive handbook on economic and labor issues. Prepared by the Mid-Peninsula Conversion Project in Mountain View, California, it contains both background information and organizing strategies—including advice on working with unions. Significantly, the book comes with letters of endorsement from the presidents of five major unions.

Given all this bridge-building, it seems likely labor's role in the disarmament movement will continue to grow. "Our people understand what we're talking about," the IAM's Dick Greenwood says. "It's not like the good old days of World War II." Says California's Larry Frank, "There has been much more support from labor than we could have hoped for. The atmosphere is different now from even three years ago. Labor is in the trenches, under attack. There are new people in union leadership, and they're looking around to see who else is in the trenches with them, who their allies are."

Still, optimism about a flood of labor support for the antinuclear weapons movement should be tempered with caution. "It is true," says Gene Carroll, "that we have a long way to go in building a broad and deep working-class component among freeze supporters." The current AFL-CIO leadership, for instance, is unlikely to change its position in the near future.

Labor support will probably remain parallel to the antinuclear weapons movement rather than be absorbed into it, observers agree. "The freeze movement has its own agenda, and we in labor have ours," says Larry Frank. For unions and the labor movement, the struggle to end the arms race remains indelibly colored not just by prospects of long-term survival, but by the pressure of tomorrow's job.

From Earth Mother to Expert
By Suzanne Gordon
May 1983

IN THE LATE 1960S, AT THE HEIGHT OF THE MOVEMENT TO END THE WAR in Vietnam, a large group of antiwar activists withdrew in protest from a number of antiwar groups. Fed up with doing the "scut-work" of political organizing and providing a support system for the superstars who dominated the movement and the media debate, these activists challenged the power relationships that prevailed both inside the peace movement and society at large. The protestors were women, of course, and the movement they helped create was modern feminism.

Now, two decades later, feminism has altered the lives of many women both in the United States and across the globe. Women are now taking leadership positions in the new peace movement that is struggling to rid the world of nuclear weapons and war.

The fact that women are active peace campaigners is not a new phenomenon. When it comes time to advance emotional arguments against war and the arms race, women are thought to be "natural" advocates of peace. According to many women and men, the old question of biology still plays a part: as givers of life women are the symbolic guardians of human and planetary existence.

Unfortunately, this role of "peace mother" has often limited both women's effectiveness and the extent of their participation in antiwar movements. When it comes time to leave passion aside and discuss the "real" issues—military strategy, economics, international relations, and political policy—women are often asked to yield the floor to the legitimate experts, to let men take over and "really give peace a chance."

In the past women could do little to counter male domination: they had been effectively barred from developing expertise in so-called masculine fields. But today, some of the new peace movement's most influential experts and organizers are women.

As grassroots organizers, women have been instrumental in the freeze campaign and in protesting the deployment of missiles in Europe. As disarmament experts, women such as Alva Myrdal and Randall Forsberg have promoted viable negotiating formulas that have been adopted by major political constituencies. As weapons and arms control experts, women such as Mary Kaldor and Jane Sharp have helped transform the strategic debate. And as political leaders, Petra Kelly of Germany and Luciana Castellina of Italy—among many others—have fought for peace in legislatures and parliament.

Women have indeed changed. The question is, has the world they inhabit changed with them? Do women have a special role to play in the new peace movement and does the peace community and the world at large recognize and respect their considerable contribution and expertise?

Grit, Grace, and Dragon Ladies

Marjorie Tuite, director of Citizen Action for Church Women United and the president of the National Assembly of Religious Women, argues that women bring "grit and grace" to the movement. "They bring the staying power," says Tuite, a 50-year-old Dominican nun who has just returned from a visit to Greenham Common in England and Comiso in Sicily, "and a willingness to take risks. Because earth consciousness is woman consciousness, they have a special understanding of what it means to have the earth raped by the insertion of missiles. Women," she concludes, "just aren't conditioned to the militaristic mindset to which men are conditioned."

Tuite, furthermore, believes that women necessarily expand demands raised by the peace movement. "The key question is whether peace is possible in a patriarchal society," she observes. "I'm not sure, but one thing I do know is that women can't fight just for peace. Because of our experience we know that we must also change the power equation in society if peace is to be attained."

Cora Weiss, codirector of the Riverside Disarmament Project, and a longtime peace campaigner, does not attribute women's role in the peace movement to biology. She does, however, believe women's subordinate position in a male-dominated society helps them grasp the fact that a society that wages "war" at home—against the poor, women, and minorities—will eventually wage war against all human and planetary life.

Weiss herself became involved in the peace movement when she realized that nuclear weapons and weapons-testing put children in direct jeopardy. "When President Kennedy was shooting the A-bomb into the air like firecrackers," she recalls, "I learned that you could test the amount of radioactive fallout by measuring its presence in the teeth of kids who drank milk with strontium 90 in it. After my infant daughter lost her first tooth, I put 25 cents under her pillow for the tooth fairy, and took the tooth to be tested. That got me really scared and I joined Women's Strike for Peace and suddenly found myself marching in front of the White House in white gloves and high heels."

Although Weiss is emphatic about women's central importance, she is careful to point out that women and men must be in this struggle together. "Only the bomb doesn't discriminate in this world," she observes. "It's going to take us all with it, and we must all form a powerful movement for change."

While Weiss, Tuite, and many others emphasize the motivating force of femininity and feminism, other women attach less importance to this factor.

"I mainly see myself as a representative of the labor movement and a representative of people fighting for peace and equality, whether it is equality of working people or minorities or women," says Judith Pratt, a three-term New Mexico state legislator and national coordinator of the National Peace Caucus of State Legislators. "My main battle is to fight for peace and the working person."

Jane Sharp, a British expert on the history of arms control and visiting scholar at the peace studies program at Cornell University, also finds the "grit and grace" argument less than convincing. "I'm just not sure how special women are," Sharp says. "If, for example, you get a man and a woman who are experts in arms control, I don't think you would find their expertise colored by their gender. Indeed, you'd find many 'dragon ladies' in the arms field. They aren't for peace, they're for war. Women heads of state—Mrs. Thatcher or Mrs. Gandhi, for example—aren't particularly benign. When I hear talk about woman as nurturers, I just feel uncomfortable. I think men are just as often nurturing."

All a Matter of Talk

No matter what their position on women's "special" qualifications, most women activists do agree that women have a harder time being taken seriously than do men.

Carolyn Roberts, a minister of the United Church of Christ and the peace advocate for the United Campus Christian Ministry at Stanford University, feels that at public meetings "men dominate the discussion. I find that men tend to jump into a debate and take an active role, even if they're not experts. They feel freer to participate as a means of self-education. Women, I think, feel that they get educated by listening, not by participating. I tend to do that when I'm unsure of an area being discussed." Roberts says she spends a good deal of time boning up on the issues so that she will feel more confident in public discussions.

"Women aren't only nurturers," Cora Weiss says, "they're experts as well. But you wouldn't know it if you go to 60 percent of the conferences being given. They're male-dominated." She cites as one example the recent University of Pennsylvania Forum Toward Preventing Nuclear War. Of 47 leading participants only six were women.

"What happens," says Randall Forsberg, director of the Institute for Defense and Disarmament Studies, and founder of the Freeze Campaign, "is that about 50 percent of all conferences and public debates include virtually no women or only a token woman." Forsberg cites the first Physicians for Social Responsibility Program on the Medical Consequences of Nuclear War as a perfect illustration. "When PSR organized the meeting, they had no women speakers at all," Forsberg charges. "Several women on the PSR steering committee complained and said they'd quit if women weren't represented.

"So PSR called me and asked for names of prominent women. I offered several, and they were rejected because they weren't well enough known to attract journalists. When I suggested that this superstar syndrome trapped women in a vicious cycle—that is, women aren't asked because they're not prominent enough and they're not prominent enough because they're not asked—I was reminded that the purpose of PSR was to end nuclear war. That, the PSR representative told me, was the group's most important task, and if it was watered down by fighting another battle [the battle of the sexes], we wouldn't win."

Forsberg says she has found this kind of attitude to be far more prevalent in groups that are new to the peace movement than in older, more established peace groups.

And, like so many other women, she says she frequently encounters blatant discrimination outside the peace community. "Once you move outside the peace movement," she says, "you find that many people believe that men are more knowledgeable about military forces and strategies and economic and foreign policy issues and that we should look to men to inform us about these matters."

This pattern of discrimination is evident, says Forsberg, within foreign policy and political elites and in the press. "When I'm giving a public speech alone there is no problem," Forsberg continues, "but I find that if I'm debating before a general audience or conference, or in the media, with a member of the military establishment, he'll be looked at with the expectation that he, a man, will be far more knowledgeable than I am."

Ironically, many women experts and organizers say that the military establishment takes women far more seriously than do politicians or the public. "People in the military recognize very quickly that I know a great deal about military forces and military strategy," says Forsberg.

Cora Weiss and Jane Sharp point to the National Security Institute for Women, held in Washington, D.C., on March 30–31, as further proof of the military's awareness of the "female threat."

With the defense budget being debated in Congress, the Pentagon invited to the conference many friendly forces—defense department employees, female military officers, and Gold Star Wives, among others—as well as some defense critics and arms control experts. The 250 women who attended heard a succession of defense luminaries, including Caspar Weinberger and Jeanne Kirkpatrick, most of whom gave simplified presentations accompanied by patronizing jokes and asides to "you ladies." The speakers seemed shocked by the response.

"It was incredible to watch," says Jane Sharp, who attended the conference. "These guys didn't know what hit them. Women challenged their views of history, their figures, and their strategies. At a reception following the program, men came up to us and said they were surprised because 'you girls have really done your homework.'"

"The Pentagon," Weiss points out, "thinks women are a threat. If they didn't they would never have put on such a show for women only."

Exploding the Myths

That a male-dominated society should discriminate against women is, of course, not surprising. Indeed, Mary Kaldor, Britain's foremost female peace activist and scholar, believes that male-dominated institutions don't reserve their contempt for women only—they treat the entire peace movement with the kind of disdain generally reserved for women.

"If you listen to the male, military establishment's arguments against the peace movement, you realize that they view the movement rather like they view women," Kaldor says. "They say we're well-intentioned but misguided and muddle-headed people who really don't know what we're talking about. They say we're utopian dreamers, idealists, too emotional, not rational. What they do is try to feminize the movement so they can dismiss it."

Fortunately, both the peace movement and the women who are some of its most hardy advocates are fighting back. The disarmament movement has proven that it is a force for social and political change. And within it, women insist that the struggle for acceptance and for an end to war are not—as some would argue—separate and unequal battles.

As Cora Weiss argues, "This movement is about exploding myths. It's about exploding the myth that we need nuclear weapons and that we thrive in a militarized economy. And it's about exploding the myth that only men are able to fully solve our problems and formulate the terms of the debate."

On the Road for Disarmament
By Renata Rizzo
July 1983

"COME AND JOIN US! COME JOIN THE PARADE!" MEMBERS OF THE BREAD and Puppet Theater stand in front of the Plymouth Congregational Church in downtown Syracuse, New York, some handing brightly colored banners and flags to curious passersby, others blowing into homemade flutes and whistles.

"This is what's best about Bread and Puppet," says troupe member Richard Norcross. "Being out on the street, we hit everyone and everything."

A few minutes later a rag-tag ensemble of people—on stilts, carrying streamers, and dressed in the vividly symbolic sculpture-puppets that have, for 20 years, been the hallmark of the troupe—start their ten-minute parade to Hanover Square. Papier-maché washerwomen, garbagemen, and huge white cloth birds dance to the whimsical dixieland music of the Bread and Puppet Band. And the people of Syracuse are bewildered.

"What are they doing?" a woman carrying several shopping bags asks a friend, who replies, "I think it's to do with something *nuclear*." Greg Pitel, a young businessman, doesn't think that disarmament is possible. "There's enough communism and war overseas," he adds. "We don't need it here." But Debbie Callahan is worried about her six children. "I want the world to be around when they grow up," she says. "They're scared, and I want to reassure them."

The parade, now considerably lengthened by fascinated children with parents in tow, reaches Hanover Square, where an audience of 200 has gathered.

The people in Hanover Square are about to become part of the first PAND (Performing Artists for Nuclear Disarmament) Spring Caravan, a group of more than 60 performers who toured upstate New York from April 14 through May 15, visiting Brockport, Rochester, Ithaca, Albany, Syracuse, and a dozen smaller towns. Traveling in nine trucks and one brightly painted bus, and performing on college campuses, in churches, synagogues, parks, cafes, community theaters—and straying from the "mainstream" circuit, the Clinton Correctional Facility in Dannemora, New York, and the Onondaga Indian reservation outside of Syracuse—the Caravan artists reached thousands of people with their antinuclear message.

"We took all of this on with absolute naiveté and an innocence that was preserving—it allowed us to do what otherwise couldn't be done," says Florence Falk, writer, organizer, and president of PAND. "After all," she adds, "this really was an absurdly massive undertaking."

PAND's inception dates back to December 1981. After discussing the idea with members of the Talking Band theater group, Falk arranged a meeting, held in Robert Jay Lifton's apartment in Manhattan. Nearly 100 people attended, and the decision was made to create an organization around the caravan idea.

PAND's inaugural rally was held on April 5, 1982, when it made clear its intention to unite the performing arts community and its audiences in a sustained and practical effort to bring about worldwide nuclear disarmament. The New York PAND chapter now has 1,000 members, with directors that include Harry Belafonte, Susan Sarandon, Andre Gregory, and David Byrne. Additional PAND chapters have been established in Seattle, Atlanta, Baltimore, and Portland, Oregon, and PAND International, formed in February, has chapters in five European countries, and Australia.

The Spring Caravan became the cornerstone project of PAND in New York, demanding herculean efforts from the staff and the Caravan artists. "Do you know what it means to assemble 65 performers, six theater pieces, and a dance group and put them on the road?" Falk asks.

The Grassroots of Syracuse

Jim Clark is the managing director of the Syracuse Stage, a large glassy building that houses two theaters—the Archbold, with a seating capacity of 510, and the Experimental, with 212 seats. Clark is simultaneously answering phones, dealing with his staff, and trying to find the Bread and Puppet Theater's lunch, yet he welcomes a visitor into his office with the same crisp, professional energy that characterizes the organization he runs.

"When we first heard about the PAND Caravan," he says, "what immediately perked our interest was the caliber of the theater groups—all of them are representative of the best in experimental theater—and we rarely see that kind of work in Syracuse. Two months later Charles Tarzian [the Caravan's producer] sent us more details, and some reviews, and I became even more interested."

Clark contacted Parker Brown, a local tax attorney "who was wearing a big freeze button at one of our openings" and who, with his wife Amanda, had formed a neighborhood freeze group. The Browns worked on the disarmament side of the issue, while Clark contacted members of the arts community, and a model grassroots coalition was formed.

Betty Ann Kram, the coordinator and only paid member of the coalition, worked for nine months to bring the Caravan to Syracuse for four days. "The beauty of our coalition was that the members had no prior contact with each other—we have people who voted for Reagan, we have people from all over," Kram says. "This is the kind of issue that transcends political barriers." With a steering committee of ten people, Kram's coalition raised $5,600 to cover promotional and rental fees, found housing for all of the PAND performers and staff, printed 65,000 publicity fliers, and organized potluck suppers for the artists.

"Lots of people would assume that the people who donated money for this were all left-wing radicals, but really, that's not the case," says Betty Wiles, fundraiser for the coalition. "We've got some of the pillars of the community in this—doctors, lawyers, political conservatives."

The Syracuse Coalition seized the opportunity to educate theatergoers. At each of the 15 Caravan performances, dozens of pamphlets from freeze and peace organizations were on hand. In addition, every program contained a two-page insert with step-by-step instructions for becoming an active member of the peace movement. Weeks before PAND's arrival in Syracuse, Jim Clark distributed the coalition's publicity fliers to 12,000 Syracuse Stage subscribers. "One guy was really angry that we were welcoming this type of theater to the Stage," says Clark, "but I think part of the point of art is to stir up and not just entertain."

The Caravan received extensive media coverage while in Syracuse, with local television crews at every outdoor Bread and Puppet festivity, and theater critics at the evening performances. An editorial in the May 11 issue of the city's *Post Standard* urged Syracuse residents to attend the Caravan's performances, expressing an attitude that was not, however, universally shared. Syracuse Common Councilor Edward Nowakowski, referring to the grant given to the Caravan by the New York State Council on the Arts, said that there is "no excuse for spending money from taxpayers to fund a group with an antigovernment stance." And Anthony Bouscaren, professor of political science at nearby Lemoyne College, called the PAND Caravan "a bunch of dissenters." When asked if he planned to attend any of the PAND events, Bouscaren was adamant: "Heavens, no! I wouldn't be caught dead there! Would I go to a Nazi show?"

The Caravan Lineup

Ollie Clubb, a soft-spoken political science professor at Syracuse University who teaches a course on disarmament, is addressing an audience of 100 people after the Talking Band's production of *Soft Targets* at the Experimental Theater.

"One of the most important things that this play was about is assuming responsibility," Clubb says. "Once you begin to do the kinds of things depicted in this play, you can reach other people who are terrified of nuclear war, but who just put it out of their minds."

A man's hand goes up. "How is it that artists, creators, can deal with the subject of extinction?" he asks. Paul Zimet, director of *Soft Targets*, replies, "We turn it around and think about what is precious in life. We wanted to make a piece that wasn't just about the horrors of war, but about what was worth preserving."

Another question: "How can you reach the people that really need to hear your message? All of *us* are already sympathetic." Zimet answers, "I think the important thing is to give energy to each other. This is hard work, discouraging work and frightening work, and if our play gave back some energy to encourage people to go out and continue, then that's enough."

● ● ●

JoAnne Akalaitis drops into a chair in her dressing room as an audience of 200 files out of Syracuse's Civic Center Theater, bringing to a close the last PAND performance of Mabou Mines's *Dead End Kids—A History of Nuclear Power*. Incorporating film, dance, electronic sound effects, and displays of magic, the production—so highly technical that it was staged only in Albany and Syracuse—is relentlessly cerebral. Before the PAND tour, Mabou Mines visited Toronto, Philadelphia, Minneapolis, Milwaukee, and Seattle with *Dead End Kids*, and the show enjoyed a long run in Manhattan. "We're not trying to make things easy for the audience," Akalaitis says. "We refuse to condescend to them. If the play is baffling, it's more stimulating."

While some of the artists on the Caravan have made nuclear issues an integral part of their lives, the bottom line with Akalaitis is theater. "We are not trying to reach a specific audience, we're aiming for theatrical excellence," says Akalaitis.

"We're not trying to do an antinuclear *Chorus Line*." But a nationally distributed film version of *Dead End Kids* will, she says, "provide a perfect opportunity to spread the word."

. . .

"I wanna go on wakin' up, and cookin', and doin' hair, and lovin' my husband," says the southern beautician Loretta in a monodrama created, written, and performed by Rebecca Wells at the Plymouth Congregational Church in Syracuse before 70 people. *Permanent Wave* is the story of Loretta's nuclear awakening. The issue hits home when she hears a "lady doctor" describe what a nuclear holocaust would do to hair. Loretta writes a concerned letter to President Reagan, admonishing him, "if nothing else, please—think of your looks."

Wells, raised in Louisiana as a "southern belle," now lives in Seattle, where she established a PAND chapter, conducts nuclear awareness workshops, and tours Seattle schools as part of a nuclear education program. She has enjoyed the audience contact while on the Caravan. "The people feel they can talk to me because I do a piece that's so hands-on," Wells says. "It's non-intellectual, non-leftist, and outside of the liberal, college-educated world that so many of us live in. What I found on the Caravan is that people really want to talk—they hope you have some answers, some sort of hint on how to get at what's important."

. . .

Comedian Paul Zaloom stands in front of the capacity audience in the Syracuse Stage's Sutton Pavilion, dressed as a civil defense buff in coveralls and cap plastered with badges. In his one-man show, *Do It Now*, Zaloom, choking on patriotic enthusiasm, summarizes helpful hints gleaned from FEMA nuclear evacuation plans. "Question: What about the pets?" Zaloom asks. Well, since pets are not included in the emergency plan, FEMA advises leaving them at home "with an adequate supply of food and water."

The comic pores over newspapers and magazines to find topics for his shows because he feels that nuclear reality is far more interesting than anything he can invent. "Take the FEMA plan," Zaloom says. "It's so ludicrous, so insanely crazy, that it's a goldmine for a comic."

Zaloom has been to virtually every town on the Caravan tour. "The right-wing calls us gloom and doom freaks, and they're right," he says. "We need humor and lightness in our ranks. Sure, we're reaching people who are generally sympathetic to the cause. But are they *active*? I think a lot of people who saw the Caravan who weren't doing anything will now become activists. To me, that's the best part of our work. People decide to act on ideas that we've generated—how much more creative can you get?"

. . .

Over 150 people in the Experimental Theater are on their feet, applauding wildly for the 13 dancers on stage. "What a fantastic way for the Caravan to end!" Betty Ann Kram says. "I'm euphoric." Among the people crowding to the stage to talk with the dancers is Pat Rector, a local activist. "Seeing those bodies on stage, moving so splendidly, really drove home the beauty, the vulnerability, and the threat all at once," she says.

The Caravan Dancers came together when Dancers for Disarmament, a Manhattan-based group, was asked to form an ensemble for the PAND venture. Their program of seven dances deals mainly with the issue of nuclear war. "This is the first time I've been able to find a place to be active politically," says troupe member Myrna Packer. "We were angry about the issue, and now we can attack it through something we love and do best."

Although there have been problems—the dance group lacks a director, and some performers feel that they've given up considerable career momentum in order to be part of the Caravan—the members do not doubt their effectiveness. "It's wonderful to see how moved people are by our work," dancer Carey Erikson comments. "I think that dance somehow allows ideas to break through, almost on an unconscious level."

• • •

What will happen to the Caravan now that the New York state tour is over? "There is clearly the intention to have a second incarnation of the Caravan," says Falk, who is eager to connect with other PAND chapters and set up regional tours.

But changes will be made. At a meeting in New York City on May 18, PAND artists and board members agreed that the next Caravan should be less ambitious; not only would a smaller Caravan be less expensive (the $100,000 tour left New York PAND $30,000 in the red), but the problem of several groups "competing" against each other for audiences in one community would be eliminated as well. Attendance at several shows, especially on college campuses, was poor. And communication between PAND staff members and local organizers—so well coordinated in Syracuse—was far less effective in other cities.

In keeping with the gypsy-like nature of the Caravan, many felt the low-tech, go-anywhere style of the Bread and Puppet Theater, Paul Zaloom, and Rebecca Wells would be particularly appropriate for future projects. And community outreach will be a priority next time around. Greater efforts will be made to perform for schools, blue-collar workers, and, in particular, minority communities. In order to facilitate this, PAND members are thinking of expanding their focus to include issues such as racism and U.S. intervention in the Third World countries. PAND would like to assemble a full-time staff to conduct extensive research of potential "host" communities, so that working links with local disarmament groups could be made well ahead of time.

The PAND members gathered for this post-mortem meeting—some visibly exhausted, others critical—nonetheless share a strong sense of a job well done. "I think we managed to avoid the didacticism that threatens so many political organizations," says producer Tarzian. "We've reached people by affirming, by doing. We went beyond abstracts to *action*."

His words bring to mind one last Syracuse scene: a rainy day, a lake, and a group of PAND performers and Syracuse organizers. Rick Wallace, company manager for the tour, raises his glass of wine in a toast. "All through this tour, there has been powerful inspiration, both for the communities we visited and the artists themselves. We can use that inspiration to move forward now. I really feel that—in Syracuse especially—we accomplished all that we set out to do."

"We didn't stop nuclear war!" someone shouts.

Wallace looks up. "Maybe not," he says, quietly. "But we're working on it."

The Bomb at Home
By Robert Alvarez
July/August 1986

LIKE HIS NEIGHBORS WHO FARM THE VAST SEMI-ARID EXPANSES NEAR THE Columbia River in eastern Washington, Tom Bailie was not one for giving speeches. It wasn't easy for him to climb up to the podium of the high school auditorium at the "Hanford, the Public Health, and the Law," symposium in Spokane, Washington, particularly since he wasn't invited. As the tall, wiry, grey-haired Bailie introduced himself as a "Hanford downwinder," a Department of Energy official on the stage assumed a stone-like expression and glared down at his notes. The DOE public relations people in the audience also looked uncomfortable, since they had worked hard to prevent this kind of unpleasant surprise.

But this wasn't a time for social niceties. It was just three days after the world learned that the nuclear reactor core at Chernobyl was spewing radiation into the atmosphere some 10,000 miles away in the Soviet Union. That Tom Bailie's farm is a few miles away from an operating reactor, similar in design to the one burning up at Chernobyl, was good enough reason for him to crash the meeting.

Bailie spoke of growing up near DOE's Hanford facility, the world's oldest nuclear explosive production complex and now the nation's largest and most problem-plagued nuclear and toxic waste dump site. In December of 1949, when Bailie was two years old, the government deliberately released about 5,500 curies of radioactive iodine into the atmosphere, according to papers made public only recently. The intensely radioactive cloud deposited fallout on the farms of Bailie's family and neighbors and traveled as far as Spokane, 125 miles to the northeast. Although this "planned release," which may have been part of a radiation warfare experiment, was over 460 times larger than the official estimate of leakage from the Three Mile Island reactor accident, the exact reasons for this experiment remain a classified military secret.

While Bailie was growing up, Columbia River water passed through the cores of as many as eight Chernobyl-type reactors as coolant, returning to the river with enormous amounts of radioactive contamination. A few miles downstream, Bailie's unsuspecting family swam in the river, irrigated their crops with this water, and ate radiation-contaminated food.

Well before Bailie learned about Hanford's operating history from the almost 19,000 pages of secret reports released earlier this year, he knew that there was something terribly wrong. He and his neighbors refer to the stretch of farmland just downstream from Hanford as "death mile." Only one in 10 farms along "death mile," where Bailie and his family live, have escaped cancer.

"This week the nations of the world have condemned Russia for its silence," Bailie concluded. "Is its crime any greater than what has been done to us? Is its silence for three days worse than Hanford's silence for 40 years?"

These are difficult times in eastern Washington for the U.S. nuclear weapons industry, which is definitely not used to being challenged by local citizens. It is, perhaps, even more difficult for the people of this conservative part of the state, who for more than 40 years never questioned what went on at Hanford. They are now facing a different kind of "unthinkable" of the nuclear age—the distinct possibility that in making the very nuclear weapons that are supposed to protect them, the U.S. government is willfully destroying ever-widening tracts of their homeland, and may be spawning a human health legacy of major proportions.

To a significant extent, the situation at Hanford is a microcosm of a growing national crisis surrounding the DOE's nuclear weapons production and testing complex. It is a crisis that could have a major impact not only on the human environment but also on the size and scope of the nuclear arms race in the 1990s and beyond.

Discreet Charm of the DOE

With over $24 billion in physical assets and an annual budget now in excess of $8 billion, the energy department's nuclear weapons production industry would rank among the top tier of the "Fortune 500" corporations. The design, production, and testing of nuclear warheads involves over 150 facilities and employs about 115,000 people. DOE's weapons sites are operated under contract by Rockwell International, Martin Marietta, DuPont, Westinghouse, Monsanto, and other companies. The amount of land occupied by weapons facilities is "equal to the size of Delaware and one-and-a-half times the size of Rhode Island," according to General William Hoover, a former DOE official.

DOE's budget for producing key ingredients of nuclear explosives such as plutonium, tritium, and highly enriched uranium has quadrupled between 1980 and 1984, from $486.2 million to $1.864 billion. The increase is crucial to implement the Reagan plan to build as many as 13,000 new nuclear warheads over the next decade.

Although the Reagan era has brought major funding increases, the DOE's weapons program still faces very serious problems stemming from its failure to modernize. "The majority of the Nuclear Material Production plants are over 25 years old," the FY86 DOE congressional budget request declares, "and have considerable age and deterioration. Some equipment is obsolete and/or replacement parts are unavailable."

Because it has operated in strict secrecy and has been self-regulating for over four decades, the DOE's nuclear weapons program has not, until recently, been subject to the same kinds of pressures for change as the commercial nuclear industry. Despite huge sums being spent for refurbishment of weapons material plants, DOE cannot afford to meet state-of-the-art health and safety standards without causing serious disruptions in warhead schedules or accumulating staggering costs that could dramatically alter the economics of nuclear arms production.

In addition, the DOE has not changed in over 40 years the basic way large amounts of intensely radioactive and toxic wastes are generated and stored. Eighty million gallons of high-level radioactive wastes have accumulated in carbon steel tanks, and hundreds of thousands of gallons have already leaked into the environment at Hanford and Savannah River. "An explosion involving a DOE high-level nuclear waste tank would make Bhopal look rather minor," says Dr. Arjun Makhijani, an engineer and professor at the Capitol Institute of Technology in Maryland.

If such an accident were to occur, private contractors would be *exempt* from liability under the Price-Anderson Act even if the accident stemmed from their gross negligence. Without outside incentives for safety, contractors at DOE sites, says Fred Christensen, a former nuclear safety engineer at the Savannah River Plant, will continue to run government nuclear plants "like a bank that has never had to face the bank examiner and knows he will never show up at the door."

The Wasteland

Concerns over how DOE is managing its nuclear operations have prompted members of Congress representing districts near DOE weapons plants to introduce legislation calling for sweeping regulatory changes. Representative Ron Wyden, a Democrat from Portland, Oregon, is a leading advocate for independent regulation at DOE sites. He justifies his legislation on the grounds that the manufacture of nuclear weapons is "the largest, most ultra-hazardous industry of its kind in the world" and should not be left to a bureaucracy that places production above all else.

Taking away the department's self-regulation, argued nuclear weapons analyst A.T. Peaslee in a 1981 report by the DOE's Los Alamos National Laboratory, could "effectively curtail nuclear weapons production" in this country. "The key to successful realization" of DOE's nuclear explosives buildup, said Peaslee, is to maintain self-regulation in order "to preclude the delaying and harassing tactics of opponents of nuclear power, nuclear weapons, big business, modern technology, and so forth."

Of particular concern to communities near DOE plants are revelations about DOE's radioactive and toxic waste management practices, which are brutally simple: Soil, groundwater, and surface streams are used as disposal media for billions of gallons of contaminated process liquids and solid wastes. For instance:

• At DOE's Oak Ridge, Tennessee, Y-12 weapons component plant, some 2.6 million pounds of mercury were deliberately passed into the environment.

• Over ten tons of mercury mixed with organic solvents and radioactive wastes were dumped in shallow burial pits at the Savannah River Plant. Wastes contaminated with plutonium were buried at the site in cardboard boxes until 1984.

In the wake of these disclosures, nearby communities are now reexamining their priorities and in some instances are opposing additional nuclear activities. In the past year, a proposed $2 billion nuclear spent fuel interim storage facility at Oak Ridge, Tennessee, has been turned down by elected officials throughout the state. Despite the permanent layoff of 800 workers at the Oak Ridge site in the spring of 1985, area Representative Marilyn Lloyd finds that her constituents are "struggling desperately to diversify their economies . . . in an effort to become less dependent on Department of Energy programs."

There is also a growing militancy among workers at weapons plants over health and safety. Last fall, workers at the DOE's Fernald, Ohio, uranium processing plant successfully struck for a formal commitment to clean up the site and to refuse dangerous work.

With a major part of the nuclear weapons workforce over 40 years of age, many "old-timers" are becoming worried about contracting cancer and not receiving compensation. According to several internal DOE studies released last year, they have good reason to be worried. Studies of groups of DOE nuclear workers at over 20 sites, underway since 1964, are finding significant cancer death and incidence rates.

By forcing DOE to internalize the real costs of meeting today's health and safety standards, the economic benefit of nuclear deterrence is not looking as good as it did in the 1950s when it was sold to the public as the cheapest way to keep the peace. Over the next few years, DOE is planning to spend almost $870 million for environmental protection, mainly at sites where citizens have expressed vocal demands. Citizen pressure has also helped add over $700 million in FY87—an additional 30 percent—to the costs of making nuclear explosives, in the form of nuclear waste cleanup funds. These costs, DOE concedes, will continue to go up.

Along with involuntary expenditures have come disruptions in production schedules. At the Savannah River Plant, the South Carolina Department of Health and Environmental Control delayed the startup of a plutonium production reactor for two years, even though the Reagan administration warned that this action would hurt national security by delaying weapons schedules.

Surprisingly, Congress, while not stopping a single major nuclear weapons system, has over the past decade enacted several laws giving states and independent agencies the power to regulate environmental protection at DOE weapons sites. These laws, DOE has loudly complained, have put national security decisionmaking, to a growing degree, into the hands of citizens.

There is little disagreement about the impact these laws will have, reports *Engineering News-Record*, a magazine of the construction industry: "Combatants on both sides say that the groundwork is set for a major redirection of the nuclear weapons program in the United States."

The War at Home

The Reagan policy of accelerated weapons production is on a collision course with the nation's growing environmental ethic. Last year, leaders of 10 national environmental organizations representing wide political views concluded that "a race between the superpowers to amass more nuclear explosives poses serious health and environmental problems . . . the federal government should immediately reevaluate nuclear weapons production policies with regard to their effect on health and the environment. A similar proposal should be made to the Soviet Union." Their recommendation calling for a "mutual and verifiable moratorium on the production, testing, and deployment of nuclear weapons" is based to a large extent on the conclusion that nuclear weapons are simply too costly and dangerous for our society to make.

This unique way of coming to grips with nuclear weapons strikes a chord for many Americans who have not been active in promoting arms control initiatives. Instead of dealing with nuclear weapons primarily within the context of U.S.-Soviet relations, activists living near bomb plants are more concerned with the relationship between the U.S. government and its citizens.

Ironically, the very regions that host DOE weapons facilities, where campaigns like the nuclear freeze made few inroads, are the areas where the antinuclear ethic is the strongest. "By only emphasizing the dangers of nuclear war, it's as if nuclear freeze supporters fell into a silent consensus with the proponents of nuclear weapons," says Janet Gordon, director of Citizen's Call, a southern Utah group seeking compensation for radiation victims of nuclear fallout and an end to nuclear weapons testing. "They both act like there are no real dangers to nuclear weapons unless they are used in a war with the Russians. The government has been waging nuclear war near our homes for over 35 years now."

Groups Form United Fronts:
Coalitions and Mergers Stir Debate
By Alex Miller
September/October 1986

"IT'S THE FIRST TIME THE GROUPS HERE HAVE GONE BEYOND SAYING 'we're all in this together,'" says Don Skinner, state coordinator of Citizens for a Nuclear Free Oregon, one of several groups representing an array of nuclear interests that are working cooperatively with environmental groups to pass three statewide ballot initiatives in November. But Oregon is not alone. Across the nation, groups have formed coalitions to work on specific campaigns, coordinate events or strategies, and present a more unified voice to the news media and the public.

These coalitions frequently take the form of umbrella organizations that oversee a loose federation with participation on an ad hoc, volunteer basis. In some cases, however, groups with specific, well-established identities (such as freeze or Central America groups), have disappeared or broadened their focus by merging into larger organizations with wider peace and justice agendas.

Does the grassroots coalition-building activity open the door for a similar evolution at the national level, such as the proposed SANE/Freeze merger? And if coalition building leads toward a broader focus, is the antinuclear weapons movement destined to become a multi-issue "peace" movement, with impetus coming from the roots on up?

Urge to Merge

Unification efforts, once rare, have become commonplace.

• With a paid, part-time staff member, 15 participating organizations and a combined membership of roughly 20,000, the Colorado Coalition for the Prevention of Nuclear War is one of the most successful statewide coalitions. It was instrumental in getting the Denver City Council to pass a test ban resolution, and is now coordinating a series of events called "Decision '86/National Security in the Nuclear Age."

Beginning with a symposium on September 12–13 organized by the Women's International League for Peace and Freedom, the two-month "Decision '86" program consists of numerous speakers and events around the state, including a televised debate between congressional candidates. The events are being organized and cosponsored by coalition groups, which include the Colorado Council of Churches and local chapters of the League of Women Voters and the Lawyers Alliance for Nuclear Arms Control. The three-year-old coalition is itself hosting an event in early October with former CIA director William Colby. The coalition functions as a loose, umbrella structure, says Liz Moore, the coalition's vice president and founder. "Each organization retains its own agenda and sovereignty. It's like a federation of states."

• By contrast, in Nebraska, the state's five largest peace-related groups recently merged to form Nebraskans for Peace (NFP). Three of the five were formerly freeze affiliates, one opposed deployment of the MX missile, and the fifth was a 15-year-old peace and justice organization whose name was adopted by the new group, which now has 2,500 members. Unlike most coalition efforts, these groups actually joined to form a single new entity—so that when the merger occurred last February the individual groups disappeared.

"Initially the groups here had focused on politics within the state," says Larry Zink, state coordinator of the new NFP. "It became clear to us, though, that to be more effective we needed to focus on Congress, and that requires a statewide network." The new NFP has a broad agenda that includes a nuclear weapons freeze, nonintervention in Central America, antiapartheid work and the farm crisis.

It took over a year of discussion to complete the merger, but most activists there support the change. "We tended to be isolated from each other," says Marylyn Felion, who was a freeze group director in Omaha. "Now there is a feeling of solidarity."

But some Nebraskan peace activists raise questions about the benefits of a merger. Marilyn McNabb, a former board member of the old NFP, wrote in the group's newsletter that pre-merger discussions had centered on *how* to merge the groups, not *whether* to do it.

The new NFP has been slowed because of time spent on the merger. "It [the merger] has taken a fair amount of leadership and energy to bring about," says Zink. "The momentum of the movement here has suffered from it. But I'm confident in the long term that we'll rebound."

• In Ohio, the state Freeze Campaign funds and manages the Peace Clearinghouse, which helps coordinate Ohio peace groups. The board of directors of the Ohio Freeze, which includes representatives of Physicians for Social Responsibility, Women's Action for Nuclear Disarmament, the Catholic Commission of the Columbus diocese, and other participants, directs the project.

"When we go to donors and they see a single organization supporting all the peace groups in the state," says Helen Seidman, president of the Ohio Freeze, "their eyes light up and they take out their checkbooks." The clearinghouse gets frequent coverage on the wire services, who consider it newsworthy for coordinated protests to take place in several cities on the same day.

Launching the project had its difficulties, however. Local groups in Ohio were reluctant to spend staff time working on a cooperative effort, or to share their donor lists. "It's ironic," says Seidman, "that the protection of turf is somewhat like the nationalism that fuels the arms race." Organizing difficulties aside, she feels that the project can play an important role by providing a "bird's eye view" on the state so that resources can be channelled to areas where they're most needed.

Operation Cooperation

The coalition efforts in Colorado, Oregon, Ohio, and Nebraska comprise only a small part of the growing cooperation among peace groups across the country. Active coalitions have been organized in Rhode Island, Washington state, Texas, Florida, Connecticut, North Carolina, and other states. There are a number of local professionals' coalitions as well, coordinated out of a national office in Washington, D.C.

Some coalitions address single issues, such as the Coalition for a Nuclear Free Harbor in New York City, which is fighting the Navy's plan to base nuclear-capable ships on Staten Island (and has swung seven local representatives to its side recently). In others, peace groups have been reaching beyond their peers to join with other types of groups. Boston-area SANE, for example, recently worked with labor unions at the Quincy Shipyard in Massachusetts to promote economic conversion and save jobs after General Dynamics closed its facility there.

But it is not clear that all of this alone will lead to a broad-based peace and justice movement. Many Freeze groups have significantly broadened their focus, but the professionals' groups and coalitions, and many of the umbrella groups stick narrowly to the nuclear weapons issue. Several observers suggest that the professionals' groups cannot adopt a broad, left-wing foreign policy position for fear of alienating their more conservative members.

And skeptics abound. Damon Moglen, medical outreach coordinator for Physicians for Social Responsibility (PSR), argues that many groups freely endorse broader issues or coalitions, but when staff time and money are involved their commitment dries up. "In truth, a lot of these coalitions are about as deep as the paper they're signed on to," says Moglen. Many other activists commented that often when a campaign or event ends so does cooperation.

Coalition building has not been without its growing pains and failures. To avoid "turf" problems, organizers of the joint initiative effort in Oregon made specific agreements among themselves on who would petition where, and the roles of the various groups. Commitment to a coalition can also be problematical. In Montana, peace groups working with organizations representing farmers and low-income citizens on a set of initiatives only gathered about one sixth of the signatures necessary to be placed on the November ballot. "In the end we never really pulled together a true coalition," says Butch Turk, who coordinated the campaign.

In Maryland, which had been touted for months as a cooperation test site by the SANE/Freeze Commission, a communications breakdown has hurt relations between the Freeze and SANE there. According to Maryland Freeze Coordinator Kye Briesath, SANE members began organizing among local groups associated, albeit loosely, with the state Freeze. One such group recently became a SANE chapter—which Briesath didn't learn about until reading the group's newsletter. (SANE never consulted her.) Briesath is now advising local Freeze groups not to become SANE chapters until the national unity process is completed. Maryland, however, is not the only location to experience merger pains. Chris Pelly, field coordinator at the Freeze Campaign's national office in Washington, D.C., wrote a letter in late June to the head of the Northern Virginia Freeze, a group that was considering affiliating with a nearby SANE chapter. The letter, which was published in the group's newsletter, advised the Freeze not to affiliate with SANE. David Cortright, executive director of SANE, called for a meeting with Freeze leaders to discuss the concerns raised by Pelly. The result: SANE agreed not to approach local Freeze groups until the national unity debate is resolved, and the Freeze sent a letter to its local groups saying that the national organizations had agreed that affiliation should not take place until after the unity process was finalized. "If each local affiliation signs a different agreement, it will make it harder to unify the two groups in the end," Pelly says.

At another SANE/Freeze test state, however, local groups are getting the jump on the national unity commission. The New Jersey state Freeze office recently merged into New Jersey SANE, and will continue to coordinate local New Jersey groups through a nominally autonomous Freeze network. According to Michael Immerso, director of the New Jersey Freeze network, and now a SANE staffer, the move to combine the two groups began before the national unity plan was announced. The Freeze had almost always worked out of the SANE office, and the groups realized that their efforts were overlapping, especially in fundraising.

Immerso feels the New Jersey solution would be a good model for other states, or even the national groups, to follow. The organization draws on the canvass and political strength of SANE, while continuing to support the grassroots disarmament organizing of the Freeze. "It's a question of tactics," says Immerso. "Let's say 60 percent of the Freeze supporters already belong to existing local organizations. Do you create another membership group out of nothing, or do you consolidate with the groups that exist?" In New Jersey, at least, the answer seemed obvious.

The Ultimate Threat to the Environment?
Should National Environmental Organizations
Work on Disarmament and Peace Issues?
By Jeff Johnson
July/August 1987

IN JUNE, THE SIERRA CLUB'S 410,000 MEMBERS RECEIVED A MAIL BALLOT asking them to vote on an issue that has long been a stone in the hiking boot of "the Club," as its friends like to call the nation's oldest environmental organization.

The issue is nuclear war. Or rather how great the Sierra Club's commitment to opposing nuclear weapons should be.

The resolution specifically earmarks one percent, or $150,000, of the Sierra Club's yearly membership income to lobby and campaign for "preventing nuclear war/ending the arms race." The Club annually spends this amount on each of a half dozen "national priority" campaigns.

The vote is the result of a petition drive by a minority of Club members who are attempting to side-step the board of directors and force the Club to commit resources and assign a full-time lobbyist to work on this thorny issue.

The issue is not a new one for the organization. Since 1969, when it opposed nuclear bomb tests in Alaska, the Sierra Club has publicly opposed nuclear weapons. In fact, within the last few years the Club has made the issue a priority. Its efforts, however, have consisted of occasional mailings and infrequent lobbying. The group has never put its full weight behind a concerted campaign. And now a growing number of members want to do more.

For philosophical, environmental, and even spiritual reasons, activists in the Club and other environmental organizations are picking up the peace banner, especially at the local level. Some believe that environmentalists could fill voids within the national peace and disarmament movement, others argue that a union between peace and environmental activists is a logical development, while others say the disarmament movement's strategy of lobbying for test bans and arms control is bankrupt and that it should adopt other ways to effect change.

The Sierra Club's vote may be a barometer of the environmental community's willingness to embrace peace issues. And its outcome may shape the kind of relationship the peace and environmental movements—clearly two of the largest progressive movements in the United States today—will have in the future. But it is doubtful the vote will put the issue to rest.

The Sierra Club controversy may beg the question: Does it make sense for the Club, or any national environmental group for that matter, to move onto the peace movement's turf?

Two staff members of national peace organizations wondered aloud—and anonymously—if the peace movement needs the environmental movement right now. In their view the peace movement seems strong, well-funded, and is doing well on its own. Environmentalists, they believe, already have their hands full with a federal administration unwilling to enforce environmental laws and industries crying for greater access to natural resources.

Moreover, representatives from most environmental groups, such as the National Audubon Society and the National Wildlife Federation, are wary of moving in the direction the Sierra Club is considering. They defended their organizations' refusal to go beyond endorsing disarmament policy.

"There is actually a counter-pressure," said Jan Beyea, an Audubon senior staff scientist. "Peace groups ignore issues that we place a high priority on— habitat preservation and wildlife protection—and so there is pressure put on us to stick with what no one else does.

"One big movement is doomed to failure. We all operate as individuals. I may do work on disarmament issues and someone else may do work on habitat, but this does not imply people should adopt a group-love approach.

"People in the environmental movement should be reminded that they should be working on peace issues—as individuals, not as groups," Beyea said.

Agreeing but disagreeing was David Lewis, legislative director for the Physicians for Social Responsibility.

"On the local level [peace and environmental groups] do work together if for no other reason than because it's often the same people in both groups," he said. "But the Sierra Club has activists in districts where a lot of peace groups do not have much strength, and activists in those areas could make a difference. On a lot of [disarmament] votes, the margin is very small.

"The Sierra Club is an amazing organization. It has a wealth of resources. It has contact with an enormous number of people and a great set-up here in Washington," he said. "A Sierra Club staff person working with us could be an incredible help."

Peace On and With the Earth

One of the chief proponents of making nuclear war issues a Sierra Club priority is David Brower, the silver-haired, 74-year-old sage of the environmental movement.

"Nuclear war is the ultimate environmental threat to the Earth," declared Brower, speaking from his home in Berkeley, California. "If we don't have peace on and with the Earth soon," he said, "then the two movements better get together or we are going to have neither."

Brower, who minces few words in his support for the Sierra Club resolution on nuclear weapons, was the only board member to sign a statement supporting it.

"The Club has good policies: It wants to reduce funding for Star Wars, wants to get a comprehensive test ban treaty through, it doesn't want destabilizing weapons," Brower explained. "It has a good many policies, but until this is put in a priority list and gets staff time and publications, its 400,000 members won't have a chance to mobilize."

Brower concluded by citing the battle over Jimmy Carter's plan to deploy the MX missile in the Southwest in the late 1970s as a prime example of how a unified front can win. The Sierra Club and other national and local environmental groups together with disarmament organizations and a range of citizen's groups could all agree on one thing—no MX missile.

Fighting the MX

Chad Dobson, codirector of the National Campaign to Stop the MX, coordinated the efforts of organizations from the disarmament and environmental movements.

Dobson, a psychologist by training, is from Utah. He now works in Washington, D.C., as a consultant to groups on peace and international environmental issues.

Looking back, Dobson called Carter's plan to deploy missiles on trucks constantly shuttling around Nevada and Utah an "absolutely off-the-wall thing that no one could buy except a general in Washington. These states did not vote for Carter and as far as he was concerned there was nothing out there."

Despite the craziness of this teamster's dream, Utah's Democratic Governor Scott Matheson supported the plan.

Dobson was working at a television station when he obtained a map laying out the details of the MX-basing plan.

"Looking at the map, everything that wasn't a mountain was going to be a missile race track," he recalled. "To get environmentalists on board, all you had to do was send them a map.

"Environmental groups such as the Sierra Club and FOE saw [the MX campaign] as a land-use issue," he said. We put together a coalition of Native Americans, women's organizations, cattlemen, ranchers, peace people, and environmentalists. We got to know each other."

The coalition learned from military briefing reports that the water necessary to make the tons of concrete would drain the arid state dry. "They had no idea where the water was going to come from," Dobson continued. "It hit Indians, ranchers, anyone concerned about losing water and land, but the clincher was when the Mormon Church came out against it.

"We looked at early church teachings, about the land growing and becoming beautiful, but instead [Utah and Nevada] had become dumping grounds for the military-industrial complex. The church didn't move out here to take the place and turn it into a dumpsite.

"Then, in an Easter message the Mormon Church came out against the weapons system. Matheson turned around too."

It was a two-year fight, Dobson said, and its success depended not only on support from environmental and peace groups, but also on local political leaders who could make connections between issues such as spending for war and spending for day care, which were necessary to bring in groups less directly affected by MX deployment.

For Dobson the MX campaign demonstrates what he calls the "trickle-up theory" in which national groups such as the Sierra Club agree to support a campaign only when their local activists become deeply involved.

Homeporting

The success of the MX campaign is not lost on Anne H. Ehrlich, author, Stanford University biologist, and chair of the Sierra Club's National Committee on the Environmental Impacts of Warfare.

Ehrlich does not support the resolution mandating the antinuclear weapons lobby because it goes outside the normal priority-setting process. But she adds that it would be "lovely" to have the money "awarded" to the antiweapons campaign if it is seen as "necessary and there were useful places to put it."

Listening to Ehrlich speak, one hears Dobson's trickle-up theory working its way through the Sierra Club over "homeporting," the U.S. Navy's plan to base nuclear-weapons-carrying ships at 13 ports around the country.

Ehrlich said local chapters have been "bombarding" her committee with material explaining the issue and seeking support, an effort she applauds.

"There is room in the whole system to bring in the environmental arguments on peace," Ehrlich said.

One of the Navy's planned nuclear weapons homeports is Staten Island in New York City, where Shira Flax, a marketing analyst for an asbestos abatement company, lives.

Flax first became active with the Sierra Club in opposing the Navy's plan, and now she is the Club's volunteer, antinuclear weapons lobbyist. She occasionally works with members of the Professionals' Coalition, an organization of Washington, D.C., groups, which includes representatives of Physicians for Social Responsibility, Federation of American Scientists, Educators for Social Responsibility, Union of Concerned Scientists, Common Cause, and others that lobby on peace issues. Because the Sierra Club is not a member of the Professionals' Coalition, Flax says she usually works through coalition organizations.

Flax, like David Lewis of PSR, believes that the Club's influence with southern Democrats and moderate New England Republicans, whom she says are not normally part of the peace movement, is strong.

"On Hatfield-Kennedy [test ban legislation], we have a board member calling [Sen. Robert] Packwood's office, another calling senators from Florida, we're networking with other Club activists," she said. "We've talked to congressional representatives from some parts of the country who tell us this is the first time they have had extensive talks with arms controllers."

Several years ago, Flax said, broad coalitions made up of community groups, local environmental and peace organizations, and some labor unions began working to stop homeporting in areas near large cities, such as Everett, Washington, San Francisco, and New York City. She said people were worried about bay pollution from harbor dredging projects, the effects that paints and sand- blasting materials used on ships could have on sea life, as well as the problems inherent in storing nuclear weapons in cities that millions of people call home.

But Flax said organizing was restricted to West and East Coast cities, and little attention was paid to other homeport areas in Alabama, Florida, Mississippi, and Texas—until a few months ago.

"The Sierra Club people in those areas were worried about taking this on—it makes them out as being too leftist," Flax said. "But they are good citizens. They testified at hearings. They pointed out the environmental problems from the paints, the dredging wastes, and the coastal management mitigation efforts they feel are inadequate. And they are very concerned that the Navy hasn't addressed the possibility of nuclear hazards.

"Sierra Club members took a low profile [and] asked for an adequate environmental impact statement. They wrote letters, which they expected the Navy to answer. But the Navy feels it can come in and walk all over people, and it really antagonized our members."

Flax pointed out that a similar situation developed last year when Sierra Club members in Ohio complained about severe contamination problems at Department of Energy nuclear weapons production facilities in Ohio.

"Oddly enough, no environmental or peace groups seem to be mobilizing members around this," Flax said.

Both the Natural Resources Defense Council and the Environmental Policy Institute have supplied technical support by suing and providing expert testimony concerning these facilities' violations of environmental law, she said. But neither organization has a membership base.

"We're trying to get the Sierra Club with its ability to do constituency work with Congress to get involved in this," Flax added.

New and Strange Alliances

Like the MX basing plan in Utah and Nevada nearly a decade ago, Reagan's military buildup over the last six years has made many enemies in different parts of the country.

Along with attempting to provide new ports to base nuclear-weapons-carrying ships, the president's attempt to revive dilapidated DOE nuclear reactors shut down 20 years ago has generated concern and anger from a range of opponents— environmentalists, community activists, labor unions, and peace groups. But according to Robert Alvarez, director of the Environmental Policy Institute's Nuclear Project, none of the national peace or environmental organizations have taken on the administration's plan in any coherent way.

Alvarez noted that a few environmental organizations such as Greenpeace and NRDC have tried to put together coalitions to look at environmentally unsound DOE weapons-making facilities. But most of the activities have come from local groups near facilities that produce plutonium, highly enriched uranium, and tritium at places such as the Feed Material Production Center at Fernald, Ohio; the Savannah River Plant near Aiken, South Carolina; the Hanford facility in eastern Washington; and the Oak Ridge Reservation in Tennessee.

Alvarez talks of "potentially new and strange alliances," between labor unions, environmentalists, and church, community, and peace groups that have taken place in locations where arms control advocates have made few inroads in the past—southern Ohio, South Carolina, Utah, Nevada, and eastern Washington.

He points to a one-day strike at Fernald, where unions and environmentalists were able to work together, as an example of such an alliance. He now works with Atomic Trade Labor Council leaders at Oak Ridge who, he said, "ten years ago would have kicked my ass if they saw me walking down the street."

While he worries that both peace activists and environmentalists are missing an opportunity to halt environmental pollution and curb the proliferation of nuclear weapons, he reserves most of his criticism for the peace and disarmament movement.

"There is an implied consensus between the arms control advocates and the nuclear weapons industry in this country," Alvarez said, "that the dangers of nuclear weapons production and development in times of peace are negligible and should not be included in arms control objectives. The record shows this is dead wrong."

Over the last year, due to dangerous operating conditions, leaks into soil and groundwater, and other problems, DOE has shut down its plutonium generating reactor at Hanford, halved plutonium production at Savannah River, and closed four research reactors at Oak Ridge. DOE has also been lambasted by Congress, the General Accounting Office, and the National Academy of Sciences for conditions at its weapons production facilities.

The problem of hazardous waste at DOE and Department of Defense plants is enormous. At one site, Rocky Mountain Arsenal in Colorado, the DOD is investigating 224 hazardous waste sites, each of which may be as dangerous as sites on the commercial Superfund list.

Overall, the DOD estimates that cleanup of closed hazardous waste sites could cost $10 billion, which critics say is a conservative figure. DOE officials say a partial cleanup at Hanford alone could top $17 billion. By comparison, Congress, over Reagan's strong objections, set aside $10 billion for cleanups at nonfederal sites under Superfund's five-year program.

Despite suits, environmental laws, and angry members of Congress, DOE—with justice department support—has fought to limit the Environmental Protection Agency's and state regulators' power to enforce environmental laws at its facilities. Both in this session of Congress and the last, bills have been introduced to require DOE to comply with federal environmental laws.

DOE's historic position that nuclear weapons production cannot be regulated by any other agency, coupled with Reagan's decision to reopen antiquated reactors, has focused greater attention on DOE facilities.

"We're talking about 1950s-era reactors that have not undergone any significant upgrading," Alvarez said. "What you are seeing today is Congress cutting back on the Reagan agenda, not for arms control reasons, but for economic reasons.

"Last year, for the first time since 1980, Congress actually cut nuclear weapons production spending in order to enhance nuclear waste cleanup. Hanford's plutonium production operation has been shut down over health and safety issues and Congress is debating whether Hanford should be producing plutonium at all."

Alvarez estimates that for every dollar spent producing nuclear weapons, 43 cents is spent managing its nuclear waste.

He urges organizing around this environmental issue and making sure it is clear that the "true costs" of U.S. weapons production are identified—the increased environmental dangers and health risks, and the money spent to clean it up.

"This is a way for ordinary citizens to have control over this industry in ways that actually that have a limiting effect on the program. It's not tied to the Cold War dynamic. We are talking about environmental safety and health. We're not talking about relationships between the Soviet Union and the United States, but relationships between a government and its citizens."

No fan of electoral politics, Alvarez called faith in electing a "good guy to run the country about the same as a roll of the dice" and sending letters on arms control to Congress "about the same as sending something into a black hole."

Anti-DOE Coalitions

Alvarez pointed to a collage of local groups and chapters of national organizations that organized around DOE production sites.

Some groups, such as the Hanford [Washington] Education Action League provide strictly educational information, believing as Larry Shook, a HEAL spokesperson put it, "These are matters to be decided in the democratic process by the public." HEAL's three-person staff works full time running public forums, filing Freedom of Information Act requests, and doing research to make the public more aware of DOE's operations.

Other groups are more advocacy-oriented. The Energy Research Foundation, located in South Carolina near the DOE's Savannah River Plant, has filed law suits in conjunction with the NRDC, the Georgia Conservancy, and the League of Women Voters to force the facility to comply with federal laws.

Frances Hart, who founded the Energy Research Foundation in 1980, warns that DOE is seeking funds to build a new production reactor to generate plutonium and tritium, which would be built to more rigid environmental specifications. She said South Carolina politicians want the plant because it would create new jobs with higher wages.

"There are few unions in the area and few jobs," she said. Her organization gets little support from the people living near the facility.

She stresses that her group walks a narrow line in South Carolina.

"We are just an environmental group. We're not against nuclear war per se; we just don't like the mess they make when they make the bombs," she added with a quiet chuckle. "Does that make sense or not? It does if you live in South Carolina."

The "Issue" Marketplace

Steve Rauh, longtime Sierra Club activist and editor of the San Francisco Bay Area chapter's monthly newspaper, the *Yodeler*, is one of the primary movers in the petition drive to get the Club's board to assign full funding to the antinuclear arms program. He compares environmentalists who do not address the environmental consequences of militarism with economists who conduct cost-benefit analyses of nuclear energy without considering the costs of high-level nuclear waste disposal.

"If the Sierra Club's mission is to preserve the Earth, and it doesn't address the single most phenomenal threat to the planet or try to reduce the needs for militarism by establishing a better relationship to the Earth, then it really isn't addressing the preservation of the Earth and the environment," Rauh said.

Rauh is a founder of the Peace and Environmental Project, which grew out of a coalition of organizations that sought to get strong environmental planks added to the 1984 Republican and Democratic platforms. Now the project is doing educational work for schools and organizations, relating nuclear war to a broad range of effects on society.

For Rauh, the concerns underlying the Sierra Club's election run far deeper than hiring a lobbyist to promote arms control.

"I've come to object to the word 'issues,'" Rauh said. "What we tend to do is treat life and death matters as issues, which you then pick and choose between. There is a marketplace of issues. You sell issues to members, and you acquire new members if you pick the right ones to sell. We don't see the relationship between them. They're symptoms of a society gone berserk."

Rauh would like to see the Sierra Club work to develop a "moral obligation" to protect the Earth, to develop "people-to-people, worldwide environmental restoration projects," and at the same time fight to enforce environmental laws, protect the forests—the traditional environmental actions the Club has carried out.

"I worry that what we are doing is preserving a corner of an institutionally viable relationship to Congress and ignoring our moral obligation to the Earth."

To a degree, Chad Dobson, the former anti-MX organizer, echoed Rauh's concerns.

"When you start at any place and look deeply enough, it all relates to everything," Dobson said. "We need leaders who understand these links and can articulate them.

"For instance, how are the rainforests important to the peace movement? The destruction of the world's rainforests is tied hand-in-glove to international debt, which is destabilizing Africa and putting pressure on us to support and maintain stable dictators. We are part of a downward spiral moving the world toward less security. The environment and peace movements are clearly tied to this. We have got to quit making these artificial separations.

"We cannot have national security if the rest of the world is starving to death and we're arming ourselves to the teeth."

THREE

The Cold War:
Activists' Interpretations and Responses

Avoiding the "Probable" War
An Interview with George Kennan
November/December 1982

GEORGE KENNAN, A FORMER AMBASSADOR TO MOSCOW, PULITZER PRIZE winner, and diplomatic historian at the Institute for Advanced Study in Princeton, is one of the most remarkable public servants America has produced in this century. He has distinguished himself with the forthright clarity of his views, which have persistently been ahead of their time.

Kennan came into prominence in the antinuclear weapons movement in the spring of 1981 when he received the Einstein Peace Prize. He said at the time that only "a bold and sweeping departure" from present military and political trends could go to the heart of the problem of the buildup of nuclear arsenals. He called for an immediate 50 percent across-the-board cut in the strategic arsenals of both the United States and the Soviet Union. Kennan's latest book is The Nuclear Delusion *(Pantheon, 1982).*

The following interview was conducted by Yorick Blumenfeld, who has written extensively on nuclear issues. It is extracted from many hours of conversation, which have been condensed into George Kennan: A Critical Voice, *an hour-long documentary produced for PBS, and scheduled to be shown nationally in January. (It was shown on WNET in New York in October 1982.) Most of the interview published here is from material not included in the program.*

NT: *How do you now feel about the state of Soviet-American relations?*

Kennan: I do think that we are on a collision course at this time with the Soviet Union.

I believe that because I don't see in the statements and positions of our own government any hope or likelihood of any development other than a military one. The slogan of the moment seems to be simply to build up, to continue to build up, military strength indefinitely, and to hope to get from them some sort of capitulation, or perhaps to achieve the disintegration of the Soviet government.

NT: *You don't feel, then, that the proposed American buildup could redress or tilt the balance of power?*

Kennan: I don't know of any theory concerning action and interaction in the field of weaponry which has been more blown, which has been more disproven by experience, in the last decades than the theory that you can only get disarmament if you arm so greatly that the other fellow becomes afraid of you and says, "Oh dear, now I must make an agreement because he's arming so greatly." It works, of course, exactly the other way, and this has happened time after time after time.

Of course, there are those who believe this is a conflict to the death and that it has to end with the utter demise of one system of government or the other. I do not see it that way. I think that reflects a zero-sum psychology.

NT: *How do you feel about such public comparisons of Soviet and American strength?*

Kennan: I deplore it. One hundred years ago it would have been regarded as highly offensive and unacceptable to talk about military plans and to mention another country by name as the target against which those plans were to be implemented. Now this is being done every day. It represents a deterioration of the whole quality of discussion of international relations.

In the course of this past year there have been literally hundreds of items in the American press, items originating from responsible officials of the government, sometimes even highly placed officials of the armed services, in which there have been speculations of what the Soviets could do to us in a war and what we could do to them and what we would propose to do to them when a war comes. Every one of these discussions conveys in a subtle way the implication that we view this war as not only probable, but as the overriding prospect of our relations with the Soviet Union.

NT: *Repeatedly I have heard the question asked at meetings: "But how can you trust the Russians?" How would you respond to this?*

Kennan: This is a meaningless question, because there is no such thing as abstract trust. You can trust somebody for something, trust them to do something, but you can't just trust them in the abstract. I think you can trust the Soviet government to follow what they think are their own interests as they see them.

I have always maintained that the Soviet government will, normally, live up to its undertakings provided that these are absolutely specific, don't go into questions of motive or use highfalutin terms like "peace-loving" or "democratic." If the agreements merely say, "This is what you will do and this is when you will do it, and this is what we will do and when we will do it," and if then you show a serious interest in the observance of these agreements, the Soviet government, in my experience, will do likewise.

NT: *But aren't our suspicions of this regime in the Kremlin justified?*

Kennan: I recently had occasion to say that cynicism, too, can be exaggerated. We should remember, after all, that Brezhnev has repeatedly and publicly declared that they will not be the first to use nuclear weapons and they will never use them against a country which does not have them. But this has been greeted with the usual total cynicism in Western circles. I think that is quite wrong.

We cannot be such perfectionists that we say, "Well, we cannot be absolutely sure that they believe what they say, therefore we can't pay any attention to it." You can't live that way. There is always an element of insecurity in life. And the greatest conceivable insecurity comes from the quest for total security.

NT: *Do you believe there has been a change of outlook on the part of the Kremlin gerontocracy?*

Kennan: Well, the statements that have been forthcoming both publicly and privately from Moscow within the last year or so convince me that there has been a firm and very serious decision there that there is no way in which their vast nuclear armory possibly could be used to their advantage.

It is important to recognize that the Russians have committed themselves to the renunciation of first use. They have done it unilaterally. They have done it publicly. They have done it with every evidence of meaning it. We are the ones who have dragged our feet.

NT: *Hasn't their commitment to secrecy been a big obstacle in the way of coming to agreement with them?*

Kennan: Yes. One of the most unfortunate aspects of their passion for secrecy is that it permits a very serious overestimation of their military capabilities. They don't like the tensions to which these exaggerated impressions of their strength give rise. On the other hand, they prefer to have other people believe they are very strong.

NT: *But hasn't this backfired for the Russians?*

Kennan: This whole great discussion of rearmament and further armament in the U.S. goes back to the impressions we have had of Soviet strength. We can't be quite sure, because of their secrecy, how correct our impressions really are. If you try to make an estimate of what the Russians have in a certain category of weaponry, you come up with a minimum and a maximum estimate. And there's a good distance between them. Well, then, this information is revealed, most often leaked, to the press and the public—and usually it is the maximum estimate which is leaked.

NT: *Why is that?*

Kennan: Partly, this is for reasons of prudence on the part of the respective intelligence services, who don't want to get caught underestimating Soviet strength. Therefore they use the larger figure. But partly, I think, they are always having difficulty getting as much money as they want, and they think that the more frightening you can make the Soviet defense establishment appear, the better chance you'll have of getting appropriations.

NT: *Don't you believe that the technological arms race has an impetus of its own?*

Kennan: One of the things that people are gong to have to understand is that any weapons race between great military powers begins to take on a momentum of its own which is entirely detached from the original political differences that may have divided them. So they don't need to have any specific issues about which they disagree; the mere fact that both are arming becomes in itself the overriding issue of their relationship and tends to take over.

The tremendous momentum of military competition is not just true today. It was true a hundred years ago. It played a part in the origins of World War I. There were few real issues between Russia and Germany before the first World War, yet these two powers were carried into disastrous conflict, disastrous for both of them, simply by this sort of momentum.

NT: *Do you believe the negotiations now going on in Geneva could put a stop to this arms race?*

Kennan: The pattern of negotiations of START, like those of SALT I and SALT II, are not a way out of the nuclear weapons race; they are part of it.

I do not believe we can afford to spend six or seven years negotiating a new agreement, as has been suggested by this administration's timetable. The nuclear balance as it exists today is unstable, precarious. It is in great danger of being undermined by new technological developments, such as the cruise missiles.

NT: *What do you think is the best approach to halt the nuclear arms race?*

Kennan: I believe that there are a number of good ideas in the wind. I prefer a series of reciprocal, unilateral actions which don't commit anybody, which don't require ratification by a legislative body. I would like to see, first of all, the abandonment of the option of first use. Then, of course, a freeze is better than an unlimited building up, but it's not enough. I have personally suggested an immediate 50 percent cut, without any more haggling, in long-range strategic weapons. Even that would not be enough.

NT: *What size cuts are you suggesting?*

Kennan: I have felt for many years that the present levels were far beyond anything which could be explained by any rational motives of national defense. I should think that something between 10 and 20 percent of the present arsenal would suffice for deterrence.

NT: *You don't seem highly enthusiastic about a "freeze."*

Kennan: I see the freeze merely as meaning that we must stop at the present levels of armament. I should think that it would be easier, if a freeze existed, to then negotiate about the starting point for deep cuts. If there is no freeze, you're always going to have the argument about where it is that you are starting from. So from that point of view, I'm all for it.

NT: *What is your reaction to the plans for the buildup of civil defense in the U.S.?*

Kennan: I think it would be perpetrating an indefensible deceit upon the American people to allow them to think that there was any way, if these nuclear warheads started falling, they could be saved, or anything worth saving could be saved in this country.

NT: *But haven't the Russians built up their civil defense programs?*

Kennan: There's been a lot of discussion recently that the Russians must be planning to fight a nuclear war because they've installed such a tremendous and effective civil defense system. I think this is mostly nonsense. That the Russians have such a system on paper, I don't doubt. They have such plans for the same sort of reasons, I suppose, that we do. But if you have a nuclear war, these shelters are not going to mean a thing. I know of nobody who has lived in Russia who has ever seen any evidence that this civil defense system is more than a pretense.

NT: *Do you feel threatened by the prospects of nuclear proliferation?*

Kennan: I think time is running out on us. We must simply do something to remove this danger from all the peoples of the northern hemisphere. Until we Americans rid ourselves of the option of first use, we are never going to be able to prevent proliferation into the hands of others, many of whom may be far less responsible and more likely to use nuclear weapons for frivolous purposes.

NT: *What advice do you have for those who want to lessen the dangers of nuclear war? What can they do?*

Kennan: I think they can participate, of course, in peaceful demonstrations. But they can also study, learn how to argue, learn why they believe what they believe not just emotionally, but intellectually, and then they can try to increase their influence as citizens in public affairs.

The public discussion taking place in this country is not yet an intellectual argument. It is important that those in Washington understand not just that people are indignant and upset, but *why* they are upset. If this government were persuaded to take action to reduce nuclear weaponry only because it was afraid of a mass movement whose motives it didn't understand, if it did it unwillingly, it wouldn't do it very well. I distrust efforts by governments dictated solely by the intimidation of a public opinion which is neither shared nor understood. The problem is how to make government respond in a determined and effective manner.

Having said that, I do believe that the public discussion of the problems presented by nuclear weaponry now taking place in this country is going to go down in history as the most significant any democratic society has ever engaged in . . . provided, of course, that history is to continue at all and does not itself fall victim to the sort of weaponry we have been discussing.

Citizens Back Detente from Below
By Rima Shore
June 1984

RUSSIA. LAND OF BURLY, VODKA-GUZZLING MEN AND LONG-SUFFERING women. Of heartless KGB operatives and mindlessly patriotic schoolchildren . . .

"We are all drowning in clichés and stereotypes," says Alexander Sakharov, who, until renouncing his Soviet citizenship three years ago, was a Washington-watcher for the Soviets at the Institute of USA-Canada Studies. Now he studies U.S.-Soviet relations in Berkeley at Peace and Common Security, which sponsors an ongoing project on nuclear crisis risk reduction. "Soviets think that America is dominated by military-industrial warmongers," Sakharov says. "Americans have a grotesque picture of Russia. When people talk about evil empires and evil people, this is dehumanizing. When they talk about the evilness of the system, it is the same. After all, people made the system.

"You cannot love an adversary, but you cannot hate a partner. Our long-term interests are the same. That's where the activity should be."

Increasingly that's where the activity is. After months of asking "What about the Russians?" in films, booklets, and at conferences, antinuclear groups are starting to institute ongoing Soviet programs. Exchange groups are expanding their efforts. And Soviet studies in academia are growing. As official relations between the United States and the Soviet Union have soured and arms talks have broken off, citizen diplomacy—or "track-two" negotiation between the superpowers—has flourished.

An impressive new newsletter, "Surviving Together," published by the Friends Committee on National Legislation and the Institute for Soviet-American Relations, chronicles this area of growing activity. Every issue reports on dozens of organizations that are "reweaving the torn fabric of Soviet-American relations."

But while these citizen efforts to establish what E.P. Thompson has called "detente from below" are laudable, can they really accomplish much in the absence of a thaw at the top?

Being There

Organizations that foster face-to-face meetings between people on the street—Main Street and Lenin Prospect—are growing in number and in scope. Groups as diverse as Ranchers for Peace, Athletes United for Peace, and International Physicians for the Prevention of Nuclear War have hosted or visited their Soviet counterparts. Religious groups, including the National Council of Churches and the Baptist Church, are increasingly active in exchanges. Physicians for Social Responsibility will be sending its first large group—45 members—to a total of seven Soviet cities this June. The Federation of American Scientists, in addition to its own exchanges, now presses members of Congress to visit the Soviet Union (only about 125 representatives and 52 senators have done so).

The involvement of the Fellowship of Reconciliation in exchanges, according to Executive Director Richard Deats, grows out of concern "that there is so much fear and paranoia and exaggerated feeling about the Soviets that disarmament will be impossible." Working closely with groups such as the Women's International League for Peace and Freedom, FOR organizes visits with the goal of building a "constituency of people who have been there," Deats explains.

But not everyone committed to humanizing relations with the Soviets can hop a plane for Moscow. As a result, much of the activity in this field is aimed at those who cannot go.

Sister Cities International has established links between Seattle, Houston, Oakland, Jacksonville, Baltimore, and Detroit and six Soviet cities. Through the Pairing Project, an Oregon-based spinoff of Ground Zero, Americans from more than 1,200 communities have sent detailed descriptions of their hometowns to people across the Soviet Union. Only four of the communities have received responses, but the Soviet Friendship Society in Moscow has heard from at least 89 communities interested in taking part. This indicates that most of the towns are clearing their responses with Soviet officials first, according to Earl Molander, director of the Pairing Project. Next year, with the Project's help, residents from some of the American communities may visit their "twin" towns in the Soviet Union.

To educate other people who haven't "been there," FOR is fostering more human images of the Soviets through a classroom-to-classroom swap of essays and art, and a poster series depicting what Daniel Berrigan has called "forbidden faces"—portraits of Soviet citizens who are neither commissars nor soldiers.

Other stay-at-homes have pioneered the application of satellite technology to bring Soviets and Americans closer together. Nancy Graham of ISAR, which is coordinating activities among groups active in satellite communication, calls these efforts some of the most promising in the track-two arena because of their potential for reaching large audiences in both countries. Several simulcasts have taken place, but received little news media coverage. The Esalen Soviet-American Exchange program was instrumental in bringing together a Soviet rock group in a Moscow studio and American musicians in Los Angeles for a split-screen jam session as part of the U.S. Festival last year. Other simulcasts included a children's film festival and a discussion among Soviet and American scientists last November of the biological consequences of nuclear war. The new Town Meeting of the Planet project, based in New York, proposes to bring citizens from abroad to Lawrence, Kansas, to discuss the nuclear threat; thousands of others around the world would take part through a closed-circuit satellite hookup.

New York-on-Volga

Track-two initiatives in the midst of chilly official relations are not a new phenomenon.

It was 22 years ago that Dan James, then an advertising executive, drafted a plan by which Americans, including relatives of lawmakers, would take up residence for a time in the Soviet Union, and Soviets would live temporarily in the United States. The arrangement was conceived as one possible deterrent to nuclear war.

James called it the Hostages for Peace plan. It attracted some press, but the hostage concept proved too threatening to achieve much popularity. It has been revived in another form in California, where Representative John Vasconcellos has proposed a "Soldiers for Peace" program, involving the exchange of 100,000 Americans and 100,000 Soviets.

James's Peace Hostage Foundation became the Citizen Exchange Corps, and began sending groups of Americans from all walks of life to meet with their Soviet counterparts. (James has left CEC and is now working on the TOP project.)

Ten years ago, there were few organizations in this field. The American Friends Service Committee was one. People to People International was organizing goodwill tours to the Soviet Union. The International Research and Exchanges Board was operating its program for scholars and professionals, as it does today.

But it was difficult to spark interest in private initiatives in Soviet-American relations, and it was not easy to raise money. Many urged leaving diplomacy to the diplomats. There were threats from extremist organizations, visits from the FBI, and many weeks without paychecks.

Today such harassment is almost nonexistent, according to leaders of several groups. And Michael Brainerd, who directs CEC (now known as the Citizen Exchange Council), says that "the USSR is more accessible to foreigners than ever, and more forthcoming about offering programs with real content." He points out that official cultural exchanges, such as those sponsored by the United States Information Agency, and trade group visits have declined over the last decade, while private, citizen groups have become more active. "They've stepped into the gap," Brainerd says. "Imagine what relations would be like without this."

CEC has more than a dozen exchange visits scheduled in 1984. While CEC is the largest organization of its kind, it shares the field with many other groups, such as Bridges for Peace, Promoting Enduring Peace, the Esalen Soviet-American Exchange, and the USA-USSR Citizens' Dialogue.

Professional groups have gotten into the act as well. After an unusually productive exchange, members of the Lawyers Alliance for Nuclear Arms Control and the Association of Soviet Lawyers recently composed three detailed working papers and a joint statement calling for "the preservation, strengthening, and development of the existing legal basis of U.S.-Soviet relations."

Benina Berger, a family therapist from the San Francisco area who traveled to the Soviet Union last September with a delegation from the Association of Humanistic Psychology, saw the trip as a way to begin to grasp "the feelings, thoughts, and intuitions of the Soviet people, not just their similarities with Americans." Through official and unofficial meetings with Soviet psychologists, and with people on the streets and in shops and restaurants, she believes they made a step in the direction of breaking down "the enemy concept, which is based on a lack of knowledge."

One professional from the arms control community who recently returned from the Soviet Union says that until her visit she thought exchanges were "nice" but basically "a waste of time." Now she says she sees "the intrinsic value in getting-to-know-you. I learned something I didn't know: that the fear and distrust of the Soviet Union expressed here are exactly mirrored there. Like people here, they interpret the *rhetoric* of leaders as *policy*."

Politics and Propaganda

Clearly, Soviets and Americans are getting together, at least on the citizen level. About 40,000 Americans traveled to the Soviet Union in 1983—many fewer than in the mid-'70s, when tourism (and detente) peaked, but far exceeding the 13,000 who went in 1980, in the aftermath of Afghanistan. And about 8,000 Soviets per year have been coming to the United States.

But what are they talking about? Thinking back to my own experience with citizen exchange groups, I recall acting as an interpreter for many warm, spontaneous conversations between Americans and Soviets in informal and formal settings. But I also remember some gruesome meetings with local official peace committees and friendship societies, where practiced American-greeters sometimes put our tourists on the defensive with well-rehearsed challenges, and where Americans let our hosts know that they didn't believe a word they were hearing.

Alexander Sakharov believes that "peace missions" may have less impact than visits that stress professional exchange. "Discussions of the nuclear threat cannot break the wall between the two cultures," he argues. In fact, he adds, the Soviet Union uses the threat to justify further stiffening of the system. "Americans have the mistaken impression," he says, "that if the Soviets knew more about war, they would be better, act better. But the Soviets already know more about war."

How can citizen groups improve the dialogue? Better coordination among the dozens of groups involved in Soviet-American exchanges might help. Several leaders of these groups say they welcome more contact but others (off-the-record) say they are reluctant to join forces because of the pro-Soviet leanings of some purportedly "apolitical" groups.

But the sheer number of initiatives may baffle the Soviets. "There is a tendency on the part of Americans to create 5,000 peace projects," comments Clinton Gardner of Bridges for Peace, "each ready to save the world, each one a power center: town twinning, satellite communications, exchange visits. . . . Over there, they're amused and delighted, but they can't absorb it all."

Is citizen diplomacy getting anywhere? In the short run, not far enough. Certainly face-to-face contact makes a difference, but in the absence of massive exchanges, the number of Americans and Soviets who trade places remains too small to have an immediate, significant effect. In this sense, satellite linking—affording exposure to the diversity of each other's culture—is potentially a more powerful tool.

But in the long run, activists say, there *is* hope. "The issue is educational," says Ground Zero's Theo Brown, who believes that a more human view of the Soviets will ultimately move officials towards warmer ties. A recent report commissioned by the W. Alton Jones and Kettering Foundations concluded that new media and educational projects were badly needed "if we are to go beyond the 'gee whiz, they're people just like us' phase to a more realistic understanding of the enormous differences in culture and values between our two countries."

Grant Pendill, assistant director of the American Committee for East-West Accord, has been involved in Soviet-American exchanges since Arms of Friendship in 1957. He calls citizen diplomacy "a long, slow process, an investment in the future, not a means towards rapid change." Of the hundreds of Soviets he has introduced to Americans over three decades, a great many belong to the generation that is only now moving into positions of power in the Soviet Union. If contact with the adversary does indeed translate into saner policy, this investment may soon begin to pay off.

Beyond the Cold War:
Can America Shed 70 Years of Anti-Sovietism?
By George Perkovich
January/February 1987

"HOW CAN YOU TAKE A POSITIVE STAND ON AN ISSUE THAT THE SOVIETS happen to support without making your work ineffective?" Susan Alexander, executive director of Educators for Social Responsibility, sounds perplexed as she poses the question that many others have stumbled over without answering. "There is so much anti-Sovietism and you can get damaged by it if you're perceived as pro-Soviet. People act as if you're either pro-Soviet or anti-Soviet— as if it's so black and white. I'm certainly not pro-Soviet. The Soviet system is repressive and this matters to me. On the other hand I'm not comfortable with all the connotations of being anti-Soviet."

Alexander's dilemma is profound, and it is widely shared. The problem of "anti-Sovietism" confronts anyone working to end reliance on nuclear weapons and war as instruments of national security.

Anti-Sovietism is difficult to define. It is more than a reflexive hatred of the Soviet Union, but how much more?

Is it anti-Sovietism or realism when someone strongly criticizes a specific policy or practice of the Soviet Union, such as the invasion of Afghanistan or the use of psychiatry as a means of stifling dissent? Is it anti-Sovietism or pragmatism when an individual or group chooses not to publicly challenge Cold War ideology for fear of being labeled pro-Soviet?

While encapsulating American attitudes in one term—"anti-Soviet" or "pro-Soviet"—ignores the nuances, it nevertheless conveys in shorthand the tendency toward *intolerance* or *indulgence* of the Soviet Union that operates in our culture. A third term, "not-soft," may be coined to connote the widespread reluctance to deal with the Soviet issue for fear of being deemed "soft on the Russians" or an "apologist."

In the late 1980s, it is imperative that Americans reexamine their attitudes toward the Soviet Union and the role the Cold War plays in the world. Economically, ecologically, and technologically, the world has become stunningly interdependent. Ozone depletion, deforestation, terrorism, Third World debt, the thorough interaction of capital on world markets, nuclear waste, nuclear accidents, and ultimately the threat of total annihilation in nuclear war demand international or multilateral responses. A bipolar, Cold War world view predicated on conflict and unilateralism seems to deepen these problems, not solve them.

Reevaluating attitudes toward the Soviet Union has gained particular urgency in the past two years. Despite the peace movement's successes, the Reagan administration and Congress have continued to cling to Cold War arguments at a time when the Soviet Union shows real signs of wanting to demilitarize and "de-ideologize" superpower relations and international politics, and make dramatic concessions on nuclear weapons issues.

The new generation of Soviet leaders appears to recognize that the Cold War was an anachronistic attempt to readjust (or maintain, for the USSR) the results of World War II, and that the threats to security in the modern era are so different that only forward-thinking can help make us safe. Many Europeans, such as Helmut Schmidt, have urged the United States to accept the reality that economics—not ideology or weaponry—is the source of security.

Finally, the American public, awakened and informed by the peace movement, and alarmed by a silo-rattling president, is beginning to feel the need for a new, "pragmatic, live-and-let-live" attitude toward the USSR, according to the pollsters Daniel Yankelovich and John Doble.

Yet despite the indications that we are on the cusp of a new era, the leadership needed to take the United States into the post-Cold War epoch has not emerged. The peace movement has remained diffident. The Freeze Campaign always "lacked a strategy for taking [Cold War ideology] on directly," says one of its founders, Pam Solo. And the movement today, notwithstanding some discrete educational and exchange programs, appears undecided on whether and how to proceed toward a new American understanding and policy toward the Soviet Union.

Head-on or End Run?

The movement's failure to take the lead in reorienting America's Soviet policy has stimulated some vigorous internal questioning. Two related themes run through these discussions: Has the movement unwisely ducked the Soviet issue, mistakenly thinking arms reductions and Soviet-American relations are separable problems? And is "anti-Sovietism"—ignorance and intolerance of the Soviets—*within* the movement one of the reasons why the Cold War has gone largely unchallenged?

Dr. Bernard Lown, cofounder of the International Physicians for the Prevention of Nuclear War, stepped into the breech in a powerful speech at the annual Physicians for Social Responsiblity meeting last March. "The people who have been most committed in struggling against the consequences of the Cold War are unwilling to oppose its premises," Lown said, referring to the peace movement.

Suzanne Gordon, who has written about (and been allied with) the movement for years, argued in the November 1986 issue of the *Progressive* that "Soviet-phobia is found . . . in the peace movement as well as in the Pentagon. . . . A number of the more 'liberal' arms-control groups . . . seem to have concluded that they can best exert their influence by catering to conventional anti-Soviet biases."

Others, such as Anne Cahn, director of the Committee for National Security, feel that "if anything, some segments of the peace movement bend over backwards not to accuse the Soviets of anything."

Caught between potential assaults from the right or the left, the movement has been paralyzed when it comes to devising and promoting a shared analysis of the Soviet Union and a policy toward it. As a participant in one of the regular meetings of peace organization directors in Washington, D.C., recently put it, "the group acknowledged the problem anti-Sovietism posed to a number of policy stances, but did not try to address it head on. Instead they went forward as if the whole anti-Soviet/pro-Soviet issue would take care of itself."

The movement's "Soviet problem," and what to do about it—work around it or tackle it directly—stands as a paramount issue as activists and analysts grapple with the question, "Where do we go from here?" In order to begin to answer this question, it is first necessary to explore the forms "anti-Sovietism" takes in different segments of society, and the myriad reasons for it.

Easy To Be Hard

There are common roots to all the branches of anti-Sovietism in America. And it is psychologists such as Jerome Frank, John Mack, and Steven Kull who seem to have exposed these roots most clearly.

Mack, a Harvard psychiatrist and Pulitzer Prize-winning author, diagnoses America's anti-Sovietism as an "ideology of enmity." Mack writes that "the ideologies of enmity are oversimplified ways of looking at complex political relationships, so that all evil intention and behavior is seen as residing in the other; aggression and destructiveness committed by one's own nation is made invisible, or justified and rationalized. Responsibility for the predicament is found elsewhere."

This need for an enemy has always existed in the United States no less than in Russia. Regrettably, the Soviet Union has done plenty to justify America's primal fear and contempt for that nation, just as the United States has helped solidify Soviet fears of it.

"It's not hard to be anti-Soviet," says Marshall Goldman, associate director of Harvard's Russian Research Center. "It's hard not to have adverse reactions to the Soviet system when you've dealt with it."

The legacy of Stalin's murderous collectivization and great purges is imprinted on America's mind, as is the domination of Eastern Europe, anti-Semitism, the psychiatric torture of a handful of dissidents, and so on. Though the Soviet system today differs dramatically from the Soviet system in Stalin's era, and is likely to become more open under Gorbachev's leadership, scholars and peace activists who visit the Soviet Union are often frustrated and angered by the Soviets' reluctance to share blame for the arms race or discuss Soviet secrecy, among other issues.

Thus, in both the recesses of our memory, and in current Soviet reality, there is much that impels Americans toward anti-Sovietism.

The Entertainment Industry and the News Media

The psychological source of anti-Sovietism no doubt flows into, and is expressed by, the news media, specialists, politicians, the public, and the peace movement. Nevertheless, the entertainment industry provides the most graphic evidence of the malady.

Recent movies such as *Rambo, Red Dawn, Invasion USA, White Nights,* and next month's ABC miniseries, *Amerika* (to name only a few), are brutally straightforward assaults on reality that dehumanize the Soviets and portray murderous violence against Russians as the heroic triumph of good over evil. The number of these films and television commercials using an anti-Soviet motif, has increased dramatically during the Reagan era, and testifies to the underlying willingness of Americans to see the Soviet Union as the source of all evil.

The news media present a more complicated picture. Many activists, like Bruce Birchard, codirector of the American Friends Service Committee's Disarmament Program, believes "there is a strong anti-Soviet bias in the way the U.S. media cover the Soviet Union." Dennis McAuliffe, associate editor of the *Washington Post Weekly,* acknowledges that much of the media's treatment of the Soviet Union is often "misleading." By focusing on dissidents and the many problems of Soviet society, the press gives Americans a very skewed picture of life there.

Perhaps the most insidious form of anti-Sovietism is that which dismisses Soviet government statements and proposals as worthless propaganda. The media dismissed, with prejudice, Mikhail Gorbachev's January 1986 proposal to cut strategic nuclear weapons by 50 percent, eliminate intermediate-range nuclear weapons from Europe, extend the Soviet moratorium on testing, and seek to destroy all nuclear weapons by the year 2000. Yet Gorbachev's proposal is nearly identical to the deal President Reagan agreed to in Reykjavik, before differences over the Strategic Defense Initiative came into play. Had the press taken the January proposal seriously, it is likely the implications of such dramatic arms reductions would have been thought out before Reykjavik, avoiding the panic that ensued after it was over.

Besides traditional American anti-Sovietism, what lies behind the news media's failure to provide a sound, contextual understanding of the Soviet Union? Discussions with editors and writers indicate that anti-Sovietism *per se* is less a factor than is commonly thought. Instead, the news media's peculiarities as an institution explain much of the flawed treatment of the USSR. Ignorance, timidity, laziness, and the general inclination to be negative are primary causes of "bad press," and the Soviet Union is only the prime victim among many.

"It is impossible to underestimate the ignorance of most news editors on the subject" of the Soviet Union, comments Michael Janeway, former editor of the *Boston Globe*. This ignorance, among other things, keeps editors and reporters mired in the traditional American way of seeing the Soviet Union and biases them against "anyone who suggests any change for the better" in the Soviet Union, according to Raymond Garthoff, a leading Sovietologist and a senior fellow at the Brookings Institution.

Jerry Hough, a Soviet expert at Duke University, places much of the blame for the press's coverage of the USSR on correspondents in the Soviet Union who rely on American or other Western diplomats as sources for their stories. These reporters thus relay the "administration line" from Moscow back to the United States.

Given the institutional habits of the news media, which are both causes and effects of massive public ignorance of foreign societies, it is no wonder Americans don't really know much about the Russians. Any attempt by the peace and arms control communities to remedy inadequate media coverage of the Soviet Union must start by realizing that the problem is the news media as an institution, not just the news media as "anti-Soviet."

Specialists

The problem of anti-Sovietism takes a different form in the expert community of Sovietologists and arms controllers. While there is a range of opinions in the field, the overall attitude is revealed in a saying sometimes passed between specialists: "The more you know about the Soviet Union, the more you dislike it."

If anti-Sovietism among specialists were purely a function of their detailed knowledge and understanding of the Soviet system there would be no grounds for criticism. This, however, is not the case. The tone, and the political line, specialists take are often affected by how they imagine their peers or powerful officials will perceive them. Usually the incentive is to take a hard line on the Soviet Union.

Brookings's Raymond Garthoff describes the situation this way: "Certainly there is a general tendency in the field of Sovietology to be cautious even in expressing the view that the Soviets have an interest in peace—that they don't want war. Because there's a fear of being considered naive or an apologist, and that does inhibit what people tend to say. So there is caution in saying things in public for fear of being pro-Soviet."

The potential for gaining appointed political posts also impels specialists to err on the side of anti-Sovietism when writing or speaking for attribution. More than one Sovietologist has remarked that Zbigniew Brzezinski's writing on the Soviet Union, for example, reflects the political landscape of Washington more than that of Moscow. The same tendency exists among lesser-known specialists hoping their day in power will come soon.

But all the pressures are not anti-Soviet, as Harvard's Marshall Goldman points out. "I know people who won't criticize the Soviet Union in their work because they worry the Soviets won't give them visas if they do," says Goldman. This reluctance to criticize parallels a tendency among peace movement leaders who worry that raising human rights issues will turn the Soviets against them.

Showing that Soviet actions cut both ways, Goldman reveals that his 1983 book, *USSR in Crisis,* was more "explicit" in its descriptions of the failings of the Soviet system than it would have been had not the Soviets denied *his* visa application just prior to his writing the book. Goldman, one of the most accessible and considerate Sovietologists, says forthrightly that he "would have put more modifiers" on negative words if he hadn't been angered by the Soviets and felt he had nothing to lose once they denied his visa.

Perhaps the most consequential bias in the expert community has less to do with hostility toward the USSR than with a shying away from fundamental questions. "The expert community [inside and outside government] will not get above third-order questions," says Michael MccGwire, a senior fellow at Brookings and a specialist on the Soviet military. "You're taught to think of budgets and technological abilities . . . but not higher order questions, like what is the *nature* of the relationship between the superpowers," and what are the Soviets' deepest interests.

MccGwire's own conclusions after asking first-order questions? "The image of a nation pursuing a 'relentless buildup' to support a quest for world military domination," he says, "is fundamentally inaccurate. The evidence does not support the hypothesis."

Whether or not MccGwire's conclusion is correct, the bias against exploring, in tandem, Soviet intentions and capacities is pervasive and significant. This bias stems from fear of being labeled "pro-Soviet" and from the dominance of worst-case thinking among specialists, especially those dealing with military matters.

MccGwire believes that worst-case thinking has "closed Western policy-makers' minds to the possibility of changes in Soviet policy that could be in Western interests. Serious Soviet proposals [have been] discarded as propaganda, and valuable opportunities missed." MccGwire argues that this mode of thought has been especially costly in arms control where "the West focused on an exaggerated Soviet threat and its own vulnerabilities, thus blinding itself to the evidence that the Soviets have such serious interest in reducing nuclear arsenals that they are willing to make major concessions to reach an agreement."

Many commentators have connected the prominence of worst-case thinking, and the deep prejudice against the Soviet Union, to the powerful role of Eastern European émigrés in the expert community. Poles such as Richard Pipes, Brzezinski, Adam Ulam, Seweryn Bialer, the Hungarian Edward Teller, and numerous Russian émigrés have strong and deep animus towards the USSR that, though justified by their personal experiences, keeps them from being open-minded.

Despite the forces pulling many specialists away from open-minded analyses, a *sufficient* number of experts on the Soviet Union and arms control manage to perceive the shortcomings and outrages of the Soviet system and at the same time remain encouraged by the prospect of developing more cooperative, businesslike relations with Moscow.

Experts like Garthoff, Hough, and MccGwire at the Brookings Institution, Edward Warner at the Rand Corporation, Alexander Dallin at Stanford, and Matthew Evangelista at the University of Michigan, to name a few, are capable of talking and writing about the Soviet Union evenhandedly. These specialists generally view both superpowers, to varying degrees, as self-interested, often ignoble, and usually insecure actors on a stage surrounded by distorting mirrors.

"My basic premise is that the Soviets are very difficult people to work with, but you can do it," says Michael Krepon, a specialist on arms control compliance with the Carnegie Endowment for International Peace. It is to experts with this perspective that the media, the peace movement, and political leaders should turn for guidance in analyzing and understanding the Soviet Union.

Policymakers and the Selling of the Cold War

While politicians and government officials often wear their anti-Sovietism like a badge of honor, they are not inclined to expose the systematic efforts the government has taken to foster Cold War attitudes and anti-Sovietism among the American public. Documentation of massive "brainwashing" campaigns is now extensive. The United States government (along with the press and the public) were averse to communist "Russia" from the beginning, as the American invasion in 1920 and the nonrecognition of the Soviet government until 1933 attest. But American state-sponsored enmity was really unleashed after World War II.

NSC 68, the secret government study overseen by Paul Nitze that elaborated the policy of containment in 1950, helped set the hysterical tone of Cold War anti-Sovietism: "The Soviet Union, unlike previous aspirants to hegemony, is animated by a new fanatic faith, antithetical to our own, and seeks to impose its absolute authority over the rest of the world."

The noted historian of the Cold War, John Gaddis, reports that in order to sell an immensely expensive foreign policy to the public and Congress, the state department undertook, in the words of Edward Barrett, then assistant secretary of state for public affairs, a "psychological scare campaign." The purpose of this campaign was to frighten the public into supporting huge increases in defense spending to meet the ominous (and largely fabricated) Soviet threat.

Dean Acheson, then secretary of state, quaintly described this government propaganda as being "clearer than the truth." The same willingness to promote exaggerated fear and antipathy toward the Soviet Union is evident in NSC 162/2, written in 1953, and in who-knows-how-many other documents not yet published.

In the late 1970s and early '80s, the Committee on the Present Danger successfully propagated Cold War anti-Sovietism. As Richard Pipes wrote in *Commentary:* "CPD had much influence on public perceptions of the Soviet threat, with the result that voters soon took a more favorable view of increased defense expenditures and a more critical one of SALT II, which CPD selected as its particular target."

Most recently, Seymour Hersh detailed, in his book *The Target is Destroyed,* how the Reagan administration knowingly used the shooting down of KAL 007 as an opportunity to spawn hatred of the Soviet Union.

The scandal of these "scare campaigns" is not that they were "anti-Soviet" but that they were not based on reality, and were intended not to educate but to deceive the public. Psychologists remind us of the danger of this tactic. John Mack quotes the Nazi, Goering: "The people can always be brought to the bidding of its leaders. That is easy. All you have to do is tell them they are threatened with attack and denounce the pacifists for lack of patriotism and exposing the country to danger."

Public Opinion

Considering the systematic attempts to stir American hostility toward the Soviet Union it is a wonder that public opinion is as mixed as it is.

The public is of two minds when it comes to the Soviet Union. It tends to vacillate between an image of the Soviets "as people just like us," and one that sees them as "evil, corrupt, and immoral," according to Bob Beschel, a research fellow at the Harvard Center on Science and International Affairs, who specializes in American perceptions of the Soviet Union.

In numerical terms, Beschel says that even "at the height of good relations you have 20 to 25 percent of the people who are solidly and deeply anti-Soviet." He says that another 10–15 percent of the population unwaveringly desires better relations with the Soviets. "And the remaining majority," Beschel concludes, "tends to shift on the basis of presidential leadership."

As of 1984, the majority believed that "the Soviet Union is an aggressive nation both militarily and ideologically, which presses every advantage, probes constantly for vulnerabilities, interprets every gesture of conciliation and friendship as weakness, fails to keep its promises, cheats on treaties, and, in general, gets the better of us in negotiations by hanging tough," according to pollsters Daniel Yankelovich and John Doble.

Today, Tony Wagner, director of The Public, The Soviets, and Nuclear Arms project at the Public Agenda Foundation, summarizes public attitudes this way: "They distrust the Soviets, but they're uneasy with their distrust." Public Agenda's extensive program to develop policy options on nuclear arms and U.S.-Soviet relations attempts to understand the paradoxical nature of American public opinion toward the Soviets. Based on the foundation's preliminary work and numerous other polls, it is clear that the public's anti-Sovietism is not as thoroughgoing as might be expected.

But Wagner, Beschel, and others emphasize that the decisive midsection of public opinion has no interest in being *friends* with the Soviets. "The idea is not friendship, but pragmatism," says Wagner. "It's almost like managers with labor—'we've got to get along with these guys even if we don't like it.'"

To bring the Cold War to a close, or at least encourage public distaste for it, anyone interested in improving Soviet-American relations, Wagner believes, must "respect" that the "public's distrust" of the Soviets is "rooted in a clear need for strong defense, but is not based on hostility or fear."

Wagner suggests that "business" metaphors may be ones that the public can increasingly relate to. Community leaders around the country, sounded out by Public Agenda, echo Margaret Thatcher's notion that "we can do business" with Gorbachev and the Soviets, he reports. Doing business implies a certain amount of wariness and selfishness, paired with recognition that mutual interests exist and can be acted upon for significant gains—on both sides.

The public also seems open to calls for dealing with the Soviets as we now deal with China, says Wagner. American attitudes toward China are relatively free of ideology and, along with government policy, focus instead on economics and the desire to promote stability in Asia.

It is important to understand, Wagner explains, that unlike Congress and the peace movement, the public thinks "long-term" about the problem. "The public," he says, "wonders where a policy based upon open distrust and enmity will lead us in 20 years. They believe we have to see if there is a way out of the climate where the relationship is based solely on distrust"—and threats of mutual destruction. One of Public Agenda's next projects is to explore public visions of alternative relationships between the superpowers in the 21st century.

The parameters within which public opinion can be moved, however, are significantly determined by the Soviet Union itself, and the extent that Soviet actions offend American sensibilities. Beschel believes that a solid core of anti-Sovietism always remains and can quickly be activated if the Soviets act in a terrible way or the American leadership chooses to wage a campaign to highlight the Soviet threat.

While Wagner, Yankelovich, Doble, and Beschel see the potential for reorienting American attitudes towards the USSR, it must be remembered that polling on the Soviet Union is relatively thin, and public ignorance is enormous. If this ignorance can be supplanted by information cast within central metaphors such as "doing business" with the Soviets, a way out of the Cold War may be found. But if ignorance played upon by metaphors of evil and expansionist militarism, the Cold War is resupplied with the public support it needs. In other words, when the buyer is as unaware of the facts as the American public is, packaging matters most.

The Peace Movement

The Soviet issue is an urgent problem for the American peace movement, both internally and as a matter to be reckoned with in its efforts to mold public opinion and influence policymakers.

A cursory conclusion is that most activists are relatively uneducated about the Soviet Union and share the general public's abhorrence of many facets of the Soviet system—especially its human rights practices—but is convinced that the United States must commit itself to more businesslike relations with Moscow.

The primary difference between this outlook and the broader public's lies in the peace movement's deeper, steadier belief that relations *can* and *must* be improved, and that moving in this direction poses little danger to the United States. More than the public, the peace movement is prepared to rely on the United States's capacity to verify any agreements with Moscow, and to take seriously the Soviet Union's apparent desire to curb the arms race and get on with more pressing economic matters.

This generally positive attitude—by no means a consensus view especially among organization leaders—still contains all the various strains of "anti-Sovietism" (broadly defined), including uninformed condemnations of the Soviet Union and fear of being labeled as pro-Soviet by an anti-Soviet public and news media. Yet, as Sayre Sheldon, president emerita of Women's Action for Nuclear Disarmament, argues, this view also reveals a healthy "new realism," a willingness to think critically about both the United States and the Soviet Union, and at the same time struggle for improved relations *between* them.

Proponents of this type of realism are not embarrassed to point out that it is pragmatic. "If you're dealing with a congressman who's hard on the Soviets and thinks you're soft on them, such as Les Aspin," observes WAND's Sheldon, "you don't challenge his views on the Soviets, but start with budgetary issues."

One reason why this quick-to-be-criticial, slow-to-be-positive stance toward the USSR is pragmatic is the history of red-baiting in the United States that had its contemporary manifestation in 1982–83.

Reader's Digest, in October 1982, spearheaded the right-wing assault on the peace movement with an article by John Barron entitled "The KGB's Magical War for Peace." The article alleged, among other things, that "little more than two miles from the White House, the KGB helped organize and inaugurate the American 'nuclear freeze' campaign." President Reagan deepened the attack with speeches repeating Barron's argument.

For some, the brief red scare that followed affirmed their reluctance to challenge assumptions about the Soviet Union. Others, who were committed to addressing the fallacies of Cold War thinking, stood up to the assault, but at a substantial cost of time and energy. "We didn't play into it or disown our politics," recalls former Freeze Campaign leader Pam Solo. "We didn't slip into anticommunism. We dealt with the accusations directly."

For every person who stood up to the assault, however, another person probably became more inhibited. The scare dramatically affirmed some activists' beliefs that it makes sense not to do anything that even *appears* pro-Soviet in American society, given the domestic political liabilities and their own opposition to the Soviet system.

Anne Cahn of the Committee for National Security acknowledges that this inhibition extends to a reluctance to challenge the assumptions of the Cold War. "Largely as a consequence of red-baiting," she says, arms controllers and pro-arms control congress members "are afraid they'll be called 'soft on communism'" if they openly question Cold War ideology.

It is this strain of anti-Sovietism—the reluctance to take on the unjustifiable premises of the Cold War—that frustrates some leaders in the peace movement, such as Bernard Lown and Pam Solo.

"For a while the implicit assumption was that you can have an end to the arms race and carry on the Cold War, too," Solo says. She now concludes that the two are incompatible. "The peace movement needs to develop a more independent mind about [international politics] and not be captive to Cold War ideology."

Yet, despite the soundness of Solo's recommendation, and Bernard Lown's charge that "American peace movements, with but few exceptions, have diligently avoided addressing the distortion and the caricaturing of nearly every aspect of Soviet society," some left-flank critics go too far the other way. In Anne Cahn's words, there are people in the peace movement who "fail to hold the Soviets accountable" for behavior that violates human rights and other international norms by which the Soviets have agreed to abide.

Many who have been caught up in the skirmishes over the movement's attitude and policies towards the Soviet Union now conclude that the issue has become too polarized, and as a consequence it has become difficult to reach consensus on the need to replace Cold War thinking with a more global, objective assessment of the natures of American and Soviet societies and the threats each of them pose to international security.

Whether the movement can resolve the issue of internal "anti-Sovietism"—ignorance and intolerance of the Soviets and excessive fear of red-baiting—so that it can effectively address societal misperceptions of the Soviet Union is uncertain. Yet by putting the issue openly on the table, Lown, Gordon, Solo, Wagner, Cahn, and others have satisfied one necessary precondition for getting beyond it.

Hard Sell

At this post-freeze/post-Reykjavik juncture it seems that the peace movement can move in one of two directions in its Soviet policy.

Political tacticians such as John Marttila and Tom Graham, who produced the public opinion study on arms control commissioned in 1985 by WAND, suggest that the movement should concentrate on the public desire for arms reduction, publicly challenge the Soviet Union on human rights, and *not* attempt to address anti-Sovietism head on.

"It's counterintuitive, but maybe correct, that public attitudes towards the Soviet Union have much less to do with attitudes towards nuclear reductions than people think," Graham says. By trying to remedy anti-Sovietism, the movement "may be barking up the wrong tree," he concludes, based on his public opinion studies. It may be unnecessary, and in any case is exceedingly difficult, to supplant and replace Cold War attitudes in America, Graham and Marttila believe.

This strategy has, in fact, already taken hold in most arms control organizations working on Capitol Hill. "We in the arms control community have a real problem," explains John Isaacs, legislative director of the Council for a Livable World. "The policies we advocate quite often parallel Soviet policies. This means we have to distance ourselves even more from the Soviet Union, because to be seen as Soviet dupes is death in this country."

Isaacs believes that activists should continue to work from their strength—significant support among the public for arms control. "When you're talking about Soviet-American relations you're working from weakness," he believes. "The way to *get* improved relations is to get arms control."

Opponents of this strategy, however, point out that it fails to recognize that as soon as significant progress towards arms reduction is made, the organized anti-Soviet, anti-arms control community will probably exploit the public's contempt for the Soviet Union and torpedo an arms pact, just as the Committee on the Present Danger sabotaged SALT II.

"The whole premise of our project," says Public Agenda's Tony Wagner, "is that it is a serious mistake not to connect Soviet-American relations with nuclear arms reductions." To be successful, Wagner believes, efforts to reduce arms must deal simultaneously with the public's insistence on "strong defense and deterrence" and the public's view of the threat posed by the Soviet Union, which motivates the call for a strong defense and deterrence. "The Freeze dealt only with the fear of nuclear weapons," says Wagner. "That was the root of its failure."

Expressing the interrelatedness of public attitudes toward defense and the Soviet Union, however, does not explain how to bring about change in either. This is especially true when the attitudes are so paradoxical, and based on general ignorance of what constitutes deterrence and what is the true nature of the Soviet threat. What could be more challenging than to satisfy vague desires for arms reductions and reduced spending while still providing strong defense and deterrence, all in an atmosphere of distrust of the Soviet Union *and* hope that relations would improve between the superpowers?

Still, there is a way to begin. "The Cold War was sold to the American people," Pam Solo says, "and it can be unsold." Wagner concurs. "The public," he believes, "is looking for new national leadership that would seek openings and overtures to the Soviet Union, as we did with China, rooted in continued reliance on military strength but with the hope of putting relations on more cooperative ground in the long term."

A number of disparate, small-scale projects are underway to take Americans beyond the Cold War and anti-Sovietism. Many of these efforts fall into the category of "humanizing the Soviets": exchanges of people, art, and letters; space bridges; films and videotapes of slices of Soviet life; proposals for joint scientific missions to Mars, and more.

Other projects concentrate on promoting the intellectual understanding of the Soviet Union and U.S.-Soviet relations that Americans must have if they are to support (or demand) leaders who will seek to "do business" with the Soviets. Organizations such as the Committee for National Security, the Institute for Soviet-American Relations, Educators for Social Responsibility, the American Friends Service Committee, the Aspen Institute for Humanistic Studies, and the Center for Psychological Studies in the Nuclear Age devote many of their resources to educating the public and leaders about the Soviet Union.

Interestingly, most of these efforts are the products of individuals or small educational organizations. Major organizations with lobbying arms, such as SANE, the Freeze, the Council for a Livable World, WAND, and Physicians for Social Responsibility have no "Soviet" programs, or very limited ones. Together or alone, these organizations have been unable or unwilling to develop and promote a "Soviet policy," a platform describing what the U.S.-Soviet relationship should look like.

The task of leading the United States out of the Cold War and into "businesslike" relations with the USSR is so daunting that political and media leaders cannot be expected to blaze the trail themselves. Clearly, the major peace or arms control organizations must lead the way, and then encourage political and media representatives to follow.

Goodbye Good Guy-Bad Guy

Fortunately, there is evidence that progress on a new course can be made. Leaders of many of the largest peace and arms control organizations appear to recognize the necessity of dealing with the "Soviet issue" and getting beyond the "good guy-bad guy" syndrome to develop a far-reaching analysis of the Soviet Union that transcends both the unjustified indulgence and intolerance of the Soviets that has hampered work to date.

Many seem to recognize the need for a hardheaded, independent analysis of international affairs and the adoption of standards and goals to which all governments would be held accountable. From such a platform, individuals and organizations would criticize and pressure *all* states that violate the principles the movement supports—including human rights—and support states when they act in accord with the standards. Thus, as Pam Solo and SANE's Executive

Director David Cortright suggest, Americans should be willing to speak out when the Soviet Union violates human rights guaranteed by its constitution and its signature on international agreements, just as Americans should commend Soviet initiatives in other areas, such as the test ban moratorium. Rather than blind partisanship or nationalism, what Solo, Cortright, Bernard Lown, and others are calling for is a commitment to open-mindedness and evenhandedness regarding all governments. It is these attributes that the Cold War has corrupted.

This effort to get beyond the Cold War will require engagement of the media and expert communities, as well as political leaders. To begin, organizations, or coalitions of organizations, could engage the counsel of those specialists who deeply understand the Soviet Union and see the need and opportunity to do business with it. Position papers could be developed and published through the press.

Perhaps more importantly, as the Committee on the Present Danger showed, appointments could be made with editorial boards across the country to spread the views of these highly regarded specialists from the Brookings Institution, Stanford, Princeton, and so on. Since ignorance more than anti-Sovietism may be behind inadequate coverage of the USSR, a well-planned "media education campaign" could succeed. The fact that press coverage of China changed dramatically in a short time should encourage this effort.

Among political elites, a similar educational project could be undertaken. The Congressional Roundtable on U.S.-Soviet Relations and the Aspen Institute's project to educate 25–30 congressional policymakers about the Soviet Union could be augmented, or surpassed, by a Washington-based effort enlisting leading specialists in the area.

John Marttila may be right. "Education about the Soviet Union," he believes, "is such a massive undertaking that only the president or the networks can do it. Any shift would require probably the better part of a generation." But the peace movement has pushed one reluctant president to Iceland, and could persuade others to reappraise timeworn prejudices. In any case, the last five years make it clear that there is little choice but to try.

Toxic Travels:
Inside the Military's Environmental Nightmare
By Seth Shulman
Autumn 1990

HEADING SOUTH ON ROUTE 421, SOMEWHERE PAST THE TINY HOOSIER town of Versailles (pronounced VerSAYLes), lies the U.S. Army's Jefferson Proving Ground. This southeastern corner of Indiana is beautiful American heartland, with miles of rolling pastures and cornfields, situated near the Ohio and Kentucky borders. But here, as in many locales around the nation, an ominous, toxic legacy has surfaced to threaten us all. The question, still very much unanswered, is whether we can successfully meet the daunting challenge this legacy presents.

Arriving at this spot by car, the first thing you notice is the fence: an eight-foot tall, rusting chainlink topped with barbed wire. It seems normal enough at first for a military facility, but as it clings unbroken to the road's edge for mile after mile, past Ripley County, through Bryantsburg and Belleview, the fence's length—and the size of the facility it protects—begins to sink in. Enclosed behind this uninviting 48-mile perimeter is 100 square miles of Indiana that will likely remain closed off forever: an area more than four times larger than Manhattan permanently isolated from human contact like a quarantine victim with a contagious and terminal disease.

The disease afflicting this vast chunk of Indiana is military toxic contamination.

For its size and quality of contamination, Jefferson Proving Ground presents an unparalleled environmental dilemma, but the facility's problems are not unique. Hidden from public view and largely unfettered by environmental regulations, the U.S. armed forces have left a shocking and varied legacy of contamination at virtually every military installation in the country and at hundreds more bases around the world.

Because of its vast size, the U.S. military continues to rank among the world's largest generators of hazardous wastes, producing nearly a ton of toxic pollutants every minute. Despite recently begun "waste minimization" programs, the military continues to dump large quantities of deadly chemicals improperly—with little oversight or public accountability.

Today, hazardous wastes are suspected of contaminating more than 20,000 sites on land currently or formerly owned by the U.S. military. At these locations, millions of tons of military toxins have fouled many hundreds—if not thousands—of square miles of soil and polluted air and groundwater in communities across the country, and undoubtedly at hundreds of overseas bases as well.

The obstacles to environmental restoration are formidable, and not the least of them is money. Between the wastes from the energy department's nuclear production facilities and those of the Pentagon's bases, the job is now expected to cost several hundreds of billions of dollars.

A Shocking Legacy

After more than a year of research, I have caught only a glimpse of the total picture. But my toxic travels lead me to believe, as some in the Pentagon and the Department of Energy are now beginning to acknowledge, that the toxic legacy left by our nation's military infrastructure constitutes the largest and most serious environmental threat this country has ever faced.

At Jefferson Proving Ground, the army has tested huge quantities of conventional munitions since World War II. After 50 years of discharging some 23 million rounds of ordnance, the army has littered the vast site with more than 1.5 million unexploded bombs, mines, and artillery shells. Some of the ordnance, buried as deep as 30 feet below the surface, are white phosphorus shells that officials at the facility say are certain to ignite if ever exhumed. Other bombs explode unexpectedly from time to time; many more surely would if the army tried to remove them. JPG, as the facility is known locally, is also home to low-level radioactive contamination, toxic sludge, and pesticide residues, but overshadowing all other environmental problems are the unexploded bombs.

If the weather is clear, as it was upon my arrival at JPG this spring, you can immediately hear and feel the facility at work, even in a speeding car. The sounds are those of the modern battlefield: explosions as loud as thunderclaps, but deeper, and accompanied by ground-shaking tremors similar to the aftershocks of an earthquake. Later, at an official briefing, Col. Dennis O'Brien, the facility's commander, explains that JPG tests 85 percent of the army's conventional munitions and currently fires some 80,000 rounds annually—nearly one every minute when the facility is operating.

Colonel O'Brien, a stocky combat veteran of Vietnam wearing camouflage fatigues, says that the truth about the unexploded ordnance (or "UXO" in army-speak) is that "nobody has a clue how much stuff we have downrange." In addition to the estimated 1.5 million unexploded rounds, the army now acknowledges that another 6.9 million bombs and shells buried at the facility may also have "explosive potential." Not surprisingly, much of the huge complex is strictly off-limits.

JPG's environmental problems were placed in clear relief recently when the base became one of 86 military installations around the country Congress ordered shut in the first round of base closures. Astonishingly, the military's base closure commission overlooked JPG's millions of unexploded bombs in its cost calculations. The commission budgeted roughly $30 million to shut the facility, which they figured would cover decontamination of JPG's buildings. Then, the commission said, the base's land could be sold to nearby farmers for $25 million and the army would almost break even.

Since the base closure order became final in 1989, a new picture has emerged. Now, it seems, a complete cleanup may be too dangerous and destructive to conduct, not to mention prohibitively expensive. To remove all the bombs, most of JPG's 100 square miles of wooded and bombed-out land would have to be stripped down to a level 30 feet below the current surface, using special armored bulldozers.

Aside from the issue of where the contaminated earth would go, the job is almost unthinkable in magnitude, and environmentally devastating. One estimate projects the cost of such an undertaking at $13 billion. A report commissioned by the state of Indiana determined that even a more limited cleanup could cost as much as $5 billion, and still the facility would not be safe for unrestricted human contact. To complicate matters further, it remains unclear whether JPG can qualify for cleanup dollars from the federal Superfund, because unexploded ordnance is not normally considered by the Environmental Protection Agency as hazardous waste.

Hazardous waste or not, though, the dangers of unexploded ordnance are fatally clear. At a former military artillery range in San Diego County, California, two children were reportedly killed in 1983 when an old, unexploded artillery shell accidently went off a few yards from their home. Fifteen years prior to the incident, the military had sold the land as surplus property and transferred it to housing developers after completing two separate cleanup efforts at the site.

In many ways, JPG is emblematic of the nation's military toxic mess. The military toxic burden is a figurative minefield, just as JPG is a literal one. Like JPG, the larger military toxic waste problem is vast—a nightmare of almost overwhelming proportion. And like JPG, the vast military toxic problem lurks behind a fenced and guarded perimeter, waiting, politically at least, to explode.

The Hidden Reality

To date, none of the energy department's production facilities have been decontaminated, and Pentagon cleanup efforts have been completed at less than 2 percent of those waste sites identified on current and former military installations. Some of the remaining 98 percent of the sites, like Jefferson Proving Ground, already seem destined to become "national sacrifice zones," written off by the government and left to contaminate our country for generations to come.

Rampant secrecy has allowed the military to withhold information for years, even in the face of documented evidence that neighboring residents were endangered. And secrecy continues to mar the military's cleanup program. Almost all of the statistics presented here emanate from the military; there is virtually no other source. The Pentagon, for instance, prefers to discuss its record in terms of individual toxic waste sites rather than contaminated installations. The hidden reality is that cleanup has actually been completed at only a handful of installations—four as of the government's last reporting. Three of these installations had relatively minor environmental problems to begin with.

In truth, most of the military's vaunted cleanup efforts underway or planned for the near term are temporary measures, primarily intended to prevent the contamination from spreading. These "interim actions" include the construction of alternative water supply and treatment systems. Sometimes when contamination has been found in neighboring wells, the military has simply dug deeper wells in the same spot and categorized it as part of their cleanup program.

Despite the military's best efforts to obscure it, we remain in the midst of little more than a counting phase at this point in the military toxic debacle, and the numbers continue to rise. The military's roster of toxic sites has tripled since 1986. Even between the two most recent annual reports—for 1988 and 1989—

the military discovered more than 5,000 new suspected sites at its installations, the bulk of them at army bases.

The real military toxics story, however, does not lie in empty overview numbers or bureaucratic documents, but in individual cases involving specific people and circumstances. Each local military toxic battle exhibits its own distinct features, but most share important aspects as well. The lumbering complexity of military bureaucracy and its penchant for secrecy during the environmental assessment and cleanup process are common complaints. The public is too often "informed of" rather than involved in the decision-making process over cleanup procedures at their local facility, usually after community health has been threatened.

Concerned neighbors of military sites worry about the environmental threat they face, but they also fear the stigma of dropping property values and lost jobs if too much noise is made about the contamination, or if their local military facility, like JPG, is forced to close. What these communities often do not realize is that their struggle is simultaneously being reenacted in many other locations.

In a National Governors' Association report issued earlier this year, the states' executive officers expressed a collective outrage at the federal government's "blatant disregard" for its own environmental laws. They also lambasted a "hamstrung" EPA that is "forced to sit by as basic environmental statutes and regulations are routinely ignored" by the military and other federal facilities.

"Virtually every state has within its borders federally owned or operated facilities with environmental violations and compliance problems," the report noted, adding that the U.S. government's facilities around the country operate "at health and environmental standards below the standards it mandates for private firms." The report addressed all federally owned facilities, but it singled out two agencies as the worst federal offenders of all: the Department of Defense and the Department of Energy.

A Pattern of Abuse

By almost all accounts, the military's treatment of the environment has improved notably over the past several years. Nevertheless, the impact of these changes has only begun to register nationally. Military facilities continue to lag far behind their corporate counterparts in their compliance with environmental regulations, earning them a record as the nation's worst violator of hazardous waste laws. Despite the military's current rhetoric, their cleanup record to date is dismal, displaying an unprecedented pattern of environmental abuse and neglect that spans generations, as the following examples attest.

• **Picatinny:** At the Picatinny Army Installation in New Jersey, levels of the cancer-causing solvent trichloroethylene (TCE) were found in groundwater migrating off the base at levels 5,000 times drinking water standards. The army has known of the contamination since 1976, but the public learned about it only this year from a local newspaper report. Today, 14 years after the contamination was discovered, the Picatinny facility is proposed for inclusion on the

EPA's roster of the nation's most dangerously contaminated facilities. But the army's final study of the pollution is still not completed.

• **Lakehurst:** Nearby, at New Jersey's Lakehurst Naval Air Station, a 1983 navy report documented that 3.2 million gallons of cancer-causing aviation fuel and other toxic substances had polluted an aquifer that provides tap water for most of southern New Jersey. Three different tests indicated levels of toxic substances as high as 10,000 times above levels the state considers safe. The navy's report was not made public until two years later—after the local press had independently investigated the contamination. Lakehurst has yet to be cleaned up.

• **Cornhusker:** At the Cornhusker Ammunition Plant in Nebraska several years ago, an army spokesperson defended the base's decision not to notify nearby residents that their drinking wells were contaminated with dangerous levels of explosive compounds. "We didn't want to get them overly anxious," he said. Consequently, the army waited until 1984—a full year later—to go public with this information, even after three separate tests showed definitively that the installation's chemicals contaminated some 800 private wells. In recent years, residents have been provided with municipal water, piped in at the government's expense, and the army has incinerated more than 40,000 tons of soil at the facility. But the underground plume of polluted water has never been cleaned up, and probably never will be.

• **McClellan:** With a total of 167 separate toxic waste sites, McClellan Air Force Base in Sacramento, California, ranks as one of the most contaminated installations in the country. Much of the waste comes from solvents the air force routinely uses to spray down its planes. For decades, they drained the chemicals directly into the ground. But the military also admits to the presence of high levels of degreasers, PCBs, acids, low-level radioactive waste, and other contaminants.

The McClellan facility is one of the first bases where the local community organized to fight the contamination. Over 23,000 residents depend on the groundwater for domestic and agricultural use, and some won hookups to an alternative water source. A preliminary water treatment facility has been installed at the base to prevent the migration of contaminants off the base. Despite the community's many small and precedent-setting victories, however, the air force says it has completed its cleanup effort at only one of McClellan's 167 toxic sites, and finished its final study of only 17 sites. In fact, at less than half of the base's various contaminated sites has the air force even begun its remedial investigation.

• **Hanford:** At the energy department's notorious Hanford Nuclear Reservation in the southeastern corner of Washington state, one million gallons of high-level liquid radioactive waste have reportedly leaked from underground tanks. And more than a half-million curies of radioactive materials have been released into the atmosphere, exposing at least 13,000 residents to dangerous levels of radiation. The energy department kept the sanctioned airborne emissions secret for 40 years. The information was discovered only after local residents fought for the release of over 19,000 pages of government documents from the facility.

The cost to clean up Hanford's radioactive and mixed toxic wastes is now estimated at a staggering $57 billion, more than four times greater than the energy department's entire budget for fiscal year 1989. In addition, much of this effort still remains technically unresolved; planners have no idea how to clean up the leaking and potentially explosive tank farm. Even if such solutions were found, no permanent dump site yet exists for this high-level nuclear waste.

• Aberdeen: Three officials at the army's Aberdeen Proving Ground in Maryland were convicted last year for "flagrant violations" of the state's hazardous waste laws in an unprecedented criminal trial. Drinking water wells for some 35,000 residents lie within a few miles of the facility. In just one documented incident in 1985, 200 gallons of acid spilled into a local stream that flows into the Chesapeake Bay. State environmental officials described the facility, which develops and tests equipment including chemical munitions, as "a Pandora's box of potential sources of contamination." Workers at the facility are known to have dumped poisons including napalm, arsenic, cyanide, and chemical nerve agents into the ground at the facility, but so far, the army has begun only limited, interim cleanup efforts at the installation.

• Otis: State epidemiological data continue to reveal increased levels of cancer and other diseases among residents of western Cape Cod in Massachusetts, and a link between the health effects and environmental practices at the neighboring Otis Air Force Base is gaining scientific and government support. Residents have complained for more than a decade about environmental practices at the base. Air force personnel have dumped millions of gallons of aviation fuel into the sand, contaminating a shallow aquifer that upper-Cape Cod residents depend upon for drinking water.

Routine open-air burning of toxic artillery propellants and many other illegal environmental practices at the base have amplified the problem. The U.S. Geological Survey documented as early as 1984 that a plume of contaminants, including solvents and volatile organic componds, had migrated off the base and toward the nearby town of Falmouth. Alternative sources of water have been provided to a limited number of residents at the air force's expense, but no official cleanup action has begun at the base.

Standard Operating Procedures

These cases provide only a sample of the overall military toxic picture. They are not isolated incidents. Rather, they represent local pieces of the devastating environmental costs of our nation's ceaseless preparation for war. Furthermore, they don't take into account the contamination at overseas U.S. bases, land formerly owned by the military, and private military contractor sites.

Where, exactly, do these hazardous wastes come from? The first key to understanding the military toxic waste legacy is an appreciation of the defense department's huge scale. The bloated size of the military is often expressed in terms of its $300 billion yearly budget or its two million enlisted personnel, but the scale can be illustrated in other ways as well.

The emerging story of military toxic waste reveals a picture of the defense department as a vast industrial enterprise. It purchased, for example, over 200 billion barrels of oil for military use last year—enough, by one estimate, to run the nation's entire public transit system for 22 years. The armed forces are believed to have some 40,000 underground storage tanks to hold oil and other chemicals, and many of these tanks are known to be leaking. When the military sold off a tiny fraction of its "surplus" hazardous materials over the last few years, even this share was worth hundreds of millions of dollars.

Add to the vast scale of the defense department an appraisal of its mission. The Pentagon's war preparations generate hazardous materials through innumerable facets of its daily work. The overwhelming majority of these hazardous by-products are not the result of some devious, errant base commander dumping toxic wastes illegally after dark. Rather, the bulk of the military's toxic wastes originate from decades of standard daily operating procedures. Many practices have been changed to meet environmental regulations; many others continue unaltered since World War II, and even earlier.

These standard procedures are used for developing, producing, testing, storing, and modernizing the military's conventional weapons as well as its nuclear and chemical arsenals. Cornhusker and other army ammunition plants have caused some of the military's worst environmental problems—mostly from explosive compounds disposed of improperly. But Jefferson Proving Ground gives more than ample illustration that the environmental problems associated with conventional munitions do not come only from their production.

In addition to the military's weaponry, however, huge quantities of waste are generated through the construction and maintenance of military equipment. Each branch of the armed forces maintains a huge fleet of vehicles, tanks, planes, or ships, all of which require the routine use of hazardous materials. In this regard, the different branches of the military have their own problems. Daily operations, such as vehicle and airplane maintenance, generate enormous quantities of toxic waste oils, fuels, solvents, and degreasers. The air force, at sites in dozens of states, has pervasive problems associated with its historically indiscriminate use of solvents to clean its planes. Virtually every air force base is contaminated with solvents, most notably TCE—seen decades ago as "a miracle solvent" and known today as a carcinogen.

The navy has a wide array of toxic problems, including the improper disposal of wastes, residues, and by-products from the specially designed—and highly toxic—paints used on ships and submarines. All the armed services conduct electroplating and other heavy industrial practices that generate heavy metals and acids. And many specialized aspects of the military's mission, such as the development of chemical weapons or high-tech materials, generate even more exotic wastes.

Eastern Europe in the USA

The prevalence of the military toxic waste problem is due largely to the military's penchant for secrecy and the lack of outside oversight of its practices. Ammunition can be made and planes cleaned in ways that minimize environmental effects. We know this because our nation demands it of private industry.

Yet, while the private sector was on a steep learning curve during the environmentally conscious 1970s, the military remained exempt from public scrutiny and historically considered itself above existing environmental laws. "We're in the business of protecting the nation, not the environment," one base commander told Maryland residents in 1984. In some ways, the results of U.S. military practices are akin to the unregulated environmental atrocities perpetrated in many parts of Eastern Europe.

A troubling aspect of the current situation is that the U.S. justice department has consistently held that the EPA cannot enforce environmental regulations at other federal agencies, such as the defense department.

Instead, the Pentagon has been left to police itself. The enfeebled EPA has had to gradually list military sites on its Superfund National Priority List and arrange for so-called "interagency agreements" in which the Pentagon, at its discretion, agrees to abide by the nation's environmental laws. As Rep. Mike Synar (D-OK), a major player in the military toxic debate, has said, "Justice has basically tied the EPA's hands."

To the agency's credit, the EPA has listed or proposed 90 Pentagon sites on its Superfund list, and more are expected. Already, the number listed or proposed has almost doubled since September 1988. Twenty interagency agreements between the EPA and the Pentagon had been signed as of the defense department's most recent report, but twice that number remain tangled in negotiations.

Needless to say, the emerging picture is troubling. "What good does it do to protect ourselves from the Soviets," an exasperated Sen. John Glenn (D-OH) asked his colleagues last year, "if we poison ourselves in the process?"

Spoils of War

Travels for work and pleasure have taken me to many spots around the world where the haunting and palpable memory of war lingers. On the tiny Pacific island of Peleliu, where one of the bloodiest battles of World War II was fought, rusted hulls and bombed-out bunkers left by Japanese and American troops still dot otherwise pristine beaches. No casual visitor here could avoid contemplating the brutal past their presence conjures up.

Few experiences, however, prepared me for the more hidden consequence of war I was to witness at the army's Rocky Mountain Arsenal on the outskirts of

Denver. To me, its lasting image is more potent than books full of data about military contamination.

For decades, some of the most deadly chemicals known have been dumped on the arsenal's land, including lethal by-products of nerve and mustard gas production. The contaminants have conspired to lend the facility its dubious distinction as home to the most toxic square mile on earth. Upon my visit, in the spring of 1988, David Strang, a 15-year veteran of the arsenal who then directed its technical operations division, drove me past a large gray factory complex. Now boarded up and condemned because of their contamination levels, the buildings had been the major site of army production of chemical weapons since World War II.

Continuing our tour past the complex, Strang's pickup truck followed a long, straight road through the center of the facility. Beside the road, stretching ahead to our right, lay the factories' dumping grounds—known euphemistically as Basins A through E—each one now just a huge hollow of burnt-out earth.

The row of dump sites, each the size of a small lake, visibly mark the arsenal's history. At the far end, hundreds of yards across the road, lay the unforgettable sight of the most recent dump—Basin F. Because it had been lined with asphalt, unlike its neighbors, the 93-acre Basin F still displayed its noxious contents: nearly 9 million gallons of aquamarine-colored toxic sludge. Only at the sight of Basin F did the horror of the other now-empty dump sites come into perspective. Only then, before this phosphorescent toxic lake, nestled beneath the Rocky Mountains, could I begin to fathom the arsenal's poisonous underground plume, nearly the size of the entire 26-square-mile facility, migrating inexorably northwest, contaminating groundwater on the edge of Denver and threatening the health of neighboring residents.

Since my visit, the sludge from Basin F has been sucked into large holding tanks, and the residue has now been piled into a huge mound. But the memory of the deadly chemical lake—and its five ghostly predecessors—will always remain for me as a haunting symbol of war's insidious toxic legacy, one as powerful as any I've seen.

Today, only a skeleton crew remains at Rocky Mountain Arsenal. The facility's mission—to manufacture munitions to protect us against a foreign enemy—has now ceased. In the name of defending our national security, however, Rocky Mountain Arsenal has created a different kind of threat to our land, water, air, and to our health.

Beth Gallegos, who lives near the arsenal, was called a "hysterical housewife" in 1985 when she formed a small group called Citizens Against Contamination to address community concern about high levels of solvents and other contaminants that had been found in her town's water. As Gallegos recalls, the group first met opposition not just from the army, but from the EPA, the state health department, and the local water board. Many local officials, she says, were "totally irate" over the concerns her group raised. "At one early meeting,"

Gallegos recalls, "the head of the local water board drank a big glass of the water to try to prove that nothing was wrong."

When a thousand people attended a meeting about the situation in December 1986, Gallegos says things began to change. Soon the army would make one of its very first admissions that they were "a contributor" to off-base water contamination. Now a rudimentary water treatment plant has been built at the edge of the facility to try to catch the deadly contaminants before they migrate into the town's water, but a multibillion-dollar cleanup still lies ahead.

Unquestionably, the site presents daunting costs and technical challenges. With such a variety of lethal contaminants to contend with, it is unclear how to handle the polluted groundwater or the estimated 16 million cubic yards of contaminated soil. The most likely scenario calls for much of the soil to be piled into a huge lined landfill at the arsenal, turning a secret dump site into a legally sanctioned one. The army continues to insist that it will restore the area for unrestricted use, but given the difficulties involved, many observers believe that Rocky Mountain Arsenal, like the Jefferson Proving Ground, lies in jeopardy of being permanently closed off as another national sacrifice zone.

Coming Home

While planning a visit to a military toxic site in a western state some time ago, I spoke to an official from the U.S. Army Toxic and Hazardous Materials Agency. "Why travel all the way out there," she said, trying lightly to deflect attention from the site I hoped to investigate, "the army has a similar problem right in your own town." Although I did not alter my travel plans, her remark stuck with me, and with a colleague, I soon took up her unintended challenge to investigate my local military site.

Granted, my local facility, the Army Material Technology Laboratory in Watertown, Massachusetts, does not compare in scope to Jefferson Proving Ground or Rocky Mountain Arsenal. But as we researched the arsenal, one of the 86 bases Congress slated to close, I learned that 19 separate suspected toxic sites, my backyard's portion of the nation's 20,000, lie less than a mile from my home.

The army dumped toxic and low-level radioactive wastes at this facility, and it continues to burn so-called "depleted" (but nonetheless radioactive) uranium tailings regularly through a smokestack immediately adjacent to an elderly housing complex. Cleaning up this small facility is expected to cost taxpayers as much as $100 million. Compared to many sites, though, we are fortunate: some $50 million has already been pledged toward the effort.

My toxic travels have taught me much about the nation's military toxic waste problem. But with some sort of poetic justice, the contamination at my local facility has been at least as instructive. With help from the local environmental group, we fought a precedent-setting battle to make the army pay for an independent technical consultant to advise us as the cleanup process inches forward. We lost the fight, but earned new allies in the process. Local officials are now so wary of the bungled cleanup assessment, that our town has decided to spend tens of thousands of dollars to hire an independent technical advocate.

As depressing as the overall military toxic picture may be, there is more than a glint of hope as an increasing number of communities around the country begin to fight back. With lessening world tensions and growing public concern for the environment, Congress has also begun to address the military's toxic troubles more responsibly. Currently pending legislation would increase both funding for cleanup and accountability in the environmental restoration process. What is needed now is to blow the lid off the military's decades of secrecy about its toxic problems, and to force greater participation by the public and civilian federal and state agencies, such as the EPA, in the cleanup process, wresting it away from the hands of the military.

Sadly, the chances are good that you too live near a military base. Your community's air and drinking water may also be threatened. Like me, you may justifiably feel anger and outrage about the military's sorry stewardship of your neck of the woods. My outrage remains, but my own struggle against military contamination in my neighborhood has taught me that, with increased public scrutiny and a shrinking military infrastructure, we may be able to change current military practices and ensure a careful and thorough cleanup process.

How We Helped End the Cold War
(And Let Someone Else Take All the Credit)
By David S. Meyer
Winter 1990–91

PEACE ACTIVISTS NEED TO CLAIM CREDIT FOR THEIR ROLE IN ENDING THE Cold War and reshaping the prospects for peace and democracy worldwide. In 1989 we saw that the Eastern bloc was far from monolithic, that its real threat to Western Europe was always overstated, and that policies of conciliation and detente created more space and motivation for reform than a strictly military version of containment. All these revelations should vindicate what peace activists have been arguing for decades, but cold warriors are taking the bows and, more significantly, shaping the current debate.

What Ronald Reagan once called the "evil empire" now produces heroes for American consumption like Vaclav Havel, Lech Walesa, and Mikhail Gorbachev. The arms control process has been revived and firmly institutionalized in East-West relations. Meanwhile, here in the United States, despite the expensive and dangerous military action in the Persian Gulf, the general consensus is that the size and cost of the military must be cut. And despite President Bush's strenuous opposition, a serious debate about the scope and nature of U.S. foreign policy interests and approaches seems inevitable.

The peace movement has been working to push events in the direction of detente since the beginnings of the Cold War, yet just when it seems to be winning, the movement is barely visible, either in contemporary politics, or in the contested debate about history. As a result, the movement and its important role in ending the Cold War have been ignored.

Republican supporters of the Reagan-era military buildup claim that their efforts forced the Soviet Union into submission. Most Democrats are hardly more insightful, arguing that it was the long bipartisan application of containment that made the expansion of the Soviet empire impossible, eventually spurring the reforms of the past few years. Left-wing critics of the Cold War have suggested that the reforms were solely the result of processes within the Soviet Union, particularly the ascension of Mikhail Gorbachev to power.

These explanations all have substantial problems. First, there is no evidence to support any of them. Second, and more immediately relevant, they all lead us to make misjudgments about policy in the future. Left-wing critics underestimate the influence external pressure has on the processes of reform. By denigrating the role of U.S. policy in stalling reform in both the East and West, they suggest that military policy is essentially unimportant and that reevaluating and remaking policy is important only for domestic reasons. The Democratic and Republican perspectives overestimate the importance of U.S. military strength by contending that the United States can force other nations to initiate internal reforms by applying external pressure. The best future policy for the United States, in this view, is essentially more of the same.

In fact, although reform in the Soviet bloc was domestically based and motivated, a posture of conciliation from the West gave Eastern reformers room to operate. American and West European peace activists applied pressure on their own governments to allow the possibility of a new detente and Soviet reform, and constrained the Carter-Reagan military buildup. They built a domestic constituency of support for arms control, forcing their governments to revive the process. Through a network of international citizen-level contacts, peace activists drew attention to Eastern reformers and dissidents and provided them with support. They created a political climate in the United States that forced government officials to respond to the Soviet Union's steps toward detente and reform. Unless we recognize and claim our influence, however, the debate about the future will be left to those who brought us 45 years of Cold War. We need to begin by recalling our history.

Peace Movements and Policy

The relative consistency of post-World War II U.S. military policy masks the political conflicts underlying it. Indeed, for the past 40 years peace movements have reined in the very worst aspects of the arms race, preventing an even more bellicose U.S. posture. Since the dawn of the nuclear age, small groups of people have consistently opposed both the strategy and the conduct of the arms race.

Persistent peace organizations fall roughly into two camps: one opposes nuclear weapons and militarism in general, is distrustful of institutional politics and traditional arms control measures, and supports unilateral initiatives to stop the arms race; the other believes in using conventional politics and international agreements to manage the arms race. The disarmers and arms controllers continue their work in good times and bad. Rarely, however, have they worked together extensively in the context of broader public concern and popular mobilization. These two groups have been able to join forces only when there has been a public atmosphere of crisis about the arms race. During these times, they have built new organizations, put forward strong demands, commanded mainstream attention, and, on occasion, even influenced policy.

Immediately after World War II, a movement led by scientists who were involved in developing the first atomic bombs called for the international control of nuclear weapons. Although quashed by the red scare and McCarthyism of the 1950s, they left in place the organizations that would serve as a base of support for subsequent movements.

By the late 1950s, a broader peace movement resurfaced, focusing on the dangers of atmospheric nuclear testing. Mobilizing around public fear of radioactive fallout, the peace movement called for a ban on nuclear testing. Responding to this public concern, President Kennedy created the Arms Control and Disarmament Agency and negotiated the Limited Test Ban Treaty. The treaty, which banned only atmospheric testing, fell short of what most activists wanted. But it substantially improved the international climate and lessened the dangers of radioactive fallout. After President Kennedy, Soviet General Secretary Nikita Khrushchev, and British Prime Minister Harold Macmillan signed the treaty, the peace movement fragmented—partly in response to its partial victory and as a result of more immediately pressing issues, particularly the struggle for civil rights and the war in Vietnam.

The movement to stop the war in Vietnam was certainly the most volatile and broadly based of the post-World War II peace movements. Although the war dragged on even as the movement grew, popular opposition convinced Lyndon Johnson not to seek reelection in 1968. Citizen activism constrained President Nixon's early plans to escalate militarily in Vietnam, and helped end the draft.

At the end of the 1960s, a smaller peace coalition reemerged. Composed of scientists, dissident strategists, and local activists, the movement concentrated on stopping new technological innovations that threatened to accelerate the arms race, particularly multiple-warhead nuclear missiles (MIRVs) and antiballistic missiles (ABMs). Working primarily through Congress, the movement succeeded in pressuring President Nixon to redefine the mission and siting of ABM systems. Instead of deploying large systems near major cities for population defense, Nixon limited the ABM's mission to the defense of American missile fields. This change meant that ABM systems were deployed in rural North Dakota rather than suburban Chicago, and then only for a few months in

1974. This success resulted from an alliance between strategists who doubted the utility of ABM, scientists who questioned its viability, and local activists who opposed it in any case.

The peace movement never won total victories. Even constrained, the war in Vietnam continued, while arms control served to manage rather than end the arms race. Nuclear testing moved underground and increased after the Limited Test Ban Treaty was signed, and MIRVs became a critical aspect of both U.S. and Soviet nuclear arsenals. The ambiguity of their achievements often leads activists to doubt their influence altogether, but clearly the situation would have been much worse without their efforts.

Freezing the Arms Race

Activists have used opposition to a particularly dangerous aspect of nuclear weapons policy to mount broad-based campaigns challenging the basic tenets of government policy. They have won moderations in policy, but certainly not an end to the arms race. The freeze campaign followed the same basic pattern, emerging when the arms race became more expensive and threatened to become more dangerous.

The idea of a bilateral freeze had circulated periodically throughout the 1960s and 1970s. A freeze represented a simple, verifiable, confidence-building first step toward arms control and disarmament. The freeze proposal contained in Randall Forsberg's "Call to Halt the Arms Race" was different from earlier versions in one critical respect: Forsberg envisioned the freeze not only as an arms control position, but also as the centerpiece of a popular campaign. In December 1979 she proposed the freeze as a strategy for organizing opposition to President Carter's military buildup. The freeze won early support from several pacifist and disarmament groups, but had a difficult time making inroads among arms controllers. Resurrecting SALT II then appeared possible, and without a mass base, activists were unable to command political attention.

Organizers took the freeze proposal to the Democratic national convention in New York during the summer of 1980, but both the Kennedy and Carter campaigns worked to keep it off the convention floor. When Carter won the party's nomination and promised more aggressive and expensive foreign and military policies, the situation appeared desperate for activists. Carter had already withdrawn SALT II from Senate consideration; issued a presidential directive, PD-59, which codified plans for an extended nuclear war; begun plans for deploying the MX, Trident II, Pershing II, and cruise missiles; and commenced a large increase in military spending.

In November 1980, things got much worse. Ronald Reagan, running far to Carter's right, won the presidency in a landslide. For the only time in his career, Reagan's coattails brought enough Republicans into office to win Republican control of the Senate for the first time in nearly 30 years. The ousted senators included some of the strongest arms control advocates in Congress, and they were replaced by conservative Republicans who were either hostile or indifferent to arms control. On the eve of the 1980 election, more than one third of the electorate reported that they feared that Reagan would lead the United States into war. The November returns were both dispiriting and terrifying, as Reagan promised to "rebuild" what he saw as America's neglected military forces.

There was, however, one bright spot in the otherwise dismal electoral returns. In western Massachusetts, a nuclear freeze proposal won 59 percent support in three state senate districts, all of which had supported Reagan for president. In one stroke, the election demonstrated a potential soft spot in Reagan's popular support, the domestic appeal of the freeze proposal, and a tactic for exploiting both.

The freeze quickly won broad support in public opinion polls, town meetings, and state and local referenda throughout the country. Without visible alternatives or leadership from government, arms control groups and congressional supporters now flocked to the freeze. The movement demonstrated clear political support useful for political campaigns and fundraising, and at its height included an exceptionally broad range of political activity. These included civil disobedience and direct action, lobbying and campaign contributions in Congress, large demonstrations, and broad educational programs, all of which continue in some form today. The freeze campaign was the only viable antinuclear game in town, and it made substantial inroads in both the Democratic and Republican parties.

Political Responses

In 1983 the House of Representatives overwhelmingly passed a nonbinding nuclear freeze resolution, and the following year the Democrats nominated a candidate who ostensibly embraced the freeze proposal. Even more significant, the Reagan administration was compelled to respond to the broad concern about nuclear weapons the freeze demonstrated. Reagan refused to allow the movement to demonize him and his policies. He and his administration backed away from the cavalier rhetoric about nuclear warning shots, recallable missiles, improvised fallout shelters, and limited nuclear wars that had characterized the early years of his administration and animated the movement. Instead, they learned the prudence of guarded language about options and flexibility.

The administration engaged in a propaganda war to rob the freeze of the political space it commanded. One ploy involved playing on fears of the Soviet Union by accusing the Soviets of chemical warfare and treaty violations. At the same time, the administration reopened arms control talks with the Soviet Union, proposing treaties such as the zero-zero proposal for intermediate nuclear forces in Europe and the Strategic Arms Reduction Treaty. The proposals called for deep (and what the administration hoped would be unacceptable) cuts in the Soviet arsenal, in exchange for modest reductions in U.S. deployment plans.

The final piece of the Reagan political strategy was the Strategic Defense

Initiative. On March 23, 1983, Reagan abandoned talk of prevailing in nuclear war and instead asked Americans if it wouldn't be "better to save lives than to avenge them." Taken together, the administration's approach prevented the 1984 election from serving as a referendum on Reagan's nuclear policy. Reagan proclaimed his mammoth reelection landslide a mandate for arms control, and ironically, he was right.

The Reagan who campaigned in 1984 was substantially different from the one who took office in 1981. In January 1984, Reagan had announced his intention to resume arms control negotiations with the Soviet Union. He was defensive about his failure to meet with Soviet leaders, promising to do better in his next term. He no longer spoke of "winnable" nuclear wars. Indeed, he memorized and frequently repeated the phrase "nuclear war cannot be won and must never be fought." Between the freeze campaign and his own Star Wars plan, Reagan had become convinced that the system of mutually assured destruction was morally intolerable. Importantly, this all took place well before Mikhail Gorbachev ascended to power in March 1985.

Domestic Containment

The president's conscience was not the only constraint on policy. The peace movement gave new meaning to the policy of containment. Essentially, it limited the president's policy options, making further escalation and hostility politically untenable. Although the movement had become far less visible, it was now entrenched in American institutions. The organizations that supported the freeze continued their own activities, working to build a knowledgeable and effective opposition.

Freeze-supported political action committees made some $6 million in contributions to the campaigns of arms control supporters in 1984, and somewhat more in 1986, when they helped bring Democrats back into control of the Senate. The arms control caucus in Congress was stronger, better educated, and more aggressive than ever. The House of Representatives pushed for restraint in military spending, antisatellite weapons development, research on Star Wars projects, and deployment of first-strike weapons such as the MX missile. Congress also consistently pressed for more active pursuit of arms control. Legislators had good reason to be more concerned about nuclear weapons and arms control, since freeze groups remained active locally and held representatives accountable to the wishes of their districts.

Activists around the country developed peace studies programs at high schools and universities, staged community education forums, and generally raised the national level of nuclear awareness. Political leaders could no longer count on ignorance or apathy about nuclear issues among their constituents. They had to be more aware themselves, and more responsive.

As a result of raised awareness and activism in both Congress and public opinion, Reagan's initial approach to nuclear weapons and foreign policy was no longer possible. The president could not effect further increases in military spending or nuclear capabilities, and he could not abandon arms control or ignore any signs of willingness to negotiate or moderate from the East. When Gorbachev accepted the zero-zero proposal for nuclear weapons in Europe—a proposal the Reagan administration designed to counter the peace movement—Reagan had no alternative but to negotiate.

New International Politics

While the peace movement prevented the Reagan administration from pursuing some policy options, activists also encouraged alternative approaches. Most importantly, peace activists in the West and the East looked beyond their governments to develop a new peace process. The peace movement in America worked to build transnational alliances with antinuclear movements in Western Europe and human rights groups in the East. Dissidents in both blocs found they had common cause in pressuring their governments to be more receptive to change.

Peace groups such as the American Friends Service Committee in the United States organized speaking tours for European activists, clearly showing that support for U.S. or NATO policy was far from uniform. Americans were made to consider the wishes of the people in allied countries as well as their governments. The European and American movements nourished each other, as activists found encouragement across the Atlantic. They also worked to form alliances with unofficial peace and human rights groups in Eastern Europe and the Soviet Union. In doing so, they brought public attention to the cause of dissidents in the East, encouraging the process of reform from below in both blocs.

The peace movements of the West forced the governments of the East to respond to their own dissidents. Publicity strengthened the reformers and human rights activists, helping to establish a powerful and legitimate alternative outside of government. This "civil society" served as the base for democratic reforms within Eastern Europe; these dissidents now hold government positions in Czechoslovakia, Hungary, and Poland, where the peace movements were strongest.

These new connections served as a political advantage for all of the involved groups, and they also helped spread ideas and alternatives across national borders. An approach like "nonoffensive defense," a strategy to minimize the possibility of surprise attack that was researched and developed primarily in West Germany, spread beyond national borders into activist discussions. It ultimately found its way into Gorbachev's speeches and a number of arms control proposals. Similarly, notions of "common security" now creeping into official discussions were developed as alternatives by dissidents.

The work remaining is to define and implement these new approaches to security. The events of the past few years have demonstrated the power of committed activists in both the West and the East, and have also alerted governments to the dangers of ignoring their own citizenries.

History has not ended, however—contrary to the claims of conservative analysts. Despite the last wave of reforms, there is little reason to believe that governments will respond to the needs and wishes of their citizens unless pressured to do so. The peace movement's successes in the past, now more than ever, represent a challenge for the future.

FOUR

National Security:
How Alternative Security Was Charted

Short-term Plans, Long-range Visions
By Katherine Magraw
March/April 1986

EFFORTS TO ENVISION A MORE SECURE WORLD, AND TO DESIGN PLAUSIBLE ways of getting there, are naturally welcomed, at least in theory, by everyone. What is remarkable is how difficult—for different reasons—this task appears to be for activists and analysts alike, and how relatively little emphasis has been placed on this pursuit.

"The propensity for academics to avoid the big issues is more or less limit-less," says Stephen Van Evera, managing editor of *International Security*, a policy-oriented journal produced by Harvard University and the Massachusetts Institute of Technology. And Pam Solo, a veteran leader of the Freeze Campaign, points out: "It is a cultural problem of the American peace movement to emphasize process over substance."

There are many fledgling efforts now under way, however, in both the analyst and activist camps to redress these failings.

Activist Vision

At the Freeze Campaign's national conference last November, its long-range planning subcommittee was charged with the task of defining a "long-range vision of security and America's role in the nuclear-armed world" over the course of this year. "We once thought we didn't need to deal with the political complexities of the nuclear arms race because we had this technical fix," explains Pam Solo. "Now we all know we have to think in terms of long-range strategy that seeks to change the political debate by offering an alternative vision of the future."

SANE is one of the few activist organizations that has adopted a detailed, long-term program. The SANE board this past fall unanimously adopted a proposal to "move beyond the war system to the peace system," submitted in the form of a three-page paper by Marcus Raskin entitled "Disarmament and Common Security." Raskin's vision is based on the 1961 McCloy-Zorin agreements, and calls for the disarmament of all nuclear and conventional forces in three five-year phases. Adoption of the Raskin proposal, SANE's David Cortright says, means that SANE will no longer support "incremental arms control, such as SALT II, which is part of the war system" and "is unlikely to ever put our resources into a single weapons campaign like the MX again."

Other groups are talking of "redefining" national security to include not just military power but economic and educational strength, as well as better relations with the Soviets and the Third World. The current debate over military spending is giving these organizations—which range from Business Executives for National Security to the Coalition for a New Foreign and Military Policy— a timely point of departure from which to suggest positive alternatives to continuing the arms race. (More on this in the next issue of *Nuclear Times*.) Yet leaders of these groups admit that while they have outlined positive steps along a path to a safer world they have not described in detail what that world might look like.

"We don't need to have the all-encompassing vision set out just yet," argues Eric Fersht, disarmament director at Greenpeace. "We have to work on developing the right approach based on familiar American themes and values."

Academic Interest

Will activists searching for new approaches to achieving real security find them among the academics and experts in the national security field? Typically, the work of security experts has been inaccessible to activists and oriented towards policymakers or maintaining the status quo.

And those academics who *are* concerned with describing what a different world could look like have not been closely involved with like-minded activists. Gordon Adams, a former academic and now director of the Defense Budget Project, comments that "while their [experts'] vision can inspire people, it rarely has anything to do with politics because they don't particularly *care* how we get from here to there."

A survey of work being done by security analysts outside of government, however, reveals a widening range of ideas for increasing global security. This is due in part to disillusionment with arms control negotiations and increased awareness of the possibility of inadvertent nuclear war.

A vulgarized form of deterrence theory once dominated thinking in the "liberal" universities and think tanks. It excluded as irrelevant all that was extraneous to weaponry. This view is now giving way to one that acknowledges the importance of the political relationship between the superpowers. The assumption that the two blocs are in a state of permanent war, and will forever remain so, is weakening its hold as specialists from disciplines other than international relations and security studies enter the field.

Any historian will tell you that the Cold War will surely come to an end, one way or another. But until now national security experts trained in the "realist" school of political science, which admits little room for cooperation between rivals in a bipolar world, have been hesitant to grant that possibility much credence.

What follows is a survey of a number of dominant ideas concerning nuclear policy and the superpower relationship coming from established academics and experts. Not all are visionary. They were chosen to illustrate strong tendencies and trends in this field and are grouped along a rough continuum that runs from improving the status quo to looking beyond the nation-state.

Improve the Status Quo

A common position among many security experts is that the United States should "enhance deterrence and stability" through selective modernization and arms control, improve ways to manage U.S.-Soviet interaction in crises and avoid actions that could be provocative or destabilizing.

The path to greater security requires neither a restructuring of forces or doctrines, nor a substantial reorientation of the U.S.-Soviet relationship, argues the Harvard University Project on Avoiding Nuclear War. On the contrary, project members argue, deviations from our current posture, such as a no-first-use declaration, a freeze, and efforts to deploy a defense shield for cities, could all have dangerous consequences.

Now the Avoiding Nuclear War group is investigating what may lie "beyond deterrence." However, Fen Hampson, former coordinator of the project, reports: "It's fair to say we have really flopped around a lot." One member concurs: "The problem is, no one in the group really believes that the [superpower] political relationship can ever change."

Crisis Stability and Improving Command and Control

Over the past year or so, the vulnerability and performance of nuclear command and control under attack, and the problems of maintaining civilian control over nuclear forces in a time of crisis, have become two popular areas of study. Recent books by Daniel Ford, Paul Bracken, and Bruce Blair contain ominous warnings about the unreliability and unmanageability of the command and control system. They also provide devastating arguments against the need for further modernization of nuclear weapons.

A crisis stability project sponsored by the American Academy of Arts and Sciences, and headed by Kurt Gottfried of Cornell University, will be publishing a book in mid-summer. According to principal project member Bruce Blair, a guest scholar at the Brookings Institution, the project will offer some policy recommendations, such as removing forward-based tactical nuclear forces and taking nuclear weapons off alert. But it will not directly address the U.S.-Soviet relationship or U.S. doctrine.

"I know that crisis stability is not a theme that can appeal to an activist movement because it is too esoteric," says Gottfried. "And it isn't necessarily the most fruitful approach to enhancing security. But, as a physicist, this is where I can contribute. And crisis stability is important, because crises may well occur even though neither side wants it or can control it."

Far-reaching Changes in the U.S. Nuclear Posture

Morton Halperin, director of the Center for National Security Studies in Washington, D.C., and former deputy assistant secretary of defense, is working on a proposal to move the United States toward a posture of no-first-use and no-early-second-use. The proposal, which will appear in book form this fall, is based on the conviction that the U.S. policy of first use of nuclear weapons substantially increases the risk of nuclear war by giving nuclear weapons a mission other than deterring their use by others.

Under Halperin's plan, *all* nuclear weapons—or "explosive devices," as he refers to them—would be disengaged from the military forces. A finite number of these "devices" would be placed in a separate force under strict presidential control. "The fundamental mistake we've made is to view nuclear explosive devices as 'weapons' and to integrate them into our forces and base our planning and commitments on using them as instruments of foreign policy," Halperin explains.

Halperin's proposal was prompted by his desire to provide an answer to people who ask what can be done to significantly reduce the risk of nuclear war. His proposal does not depend on, or necessarily lead to, a change in the political relationship between the superpowers; the United States (and the Soviet Union if the proposal were to be bilateral) would still be free to intervene in whatever conflicts they wanted.

A quite different approach has been mapped out by Randall Forsberg, director of the Institute for Defense and Disarmament Studies in Cambridge, Massachusetts, and author of the "Call to Halt the Nuclear Arms Race." Forsberg reasons that the only way to reverse the nuclear arms race "is to make conventional war so unlikely that those who support large nuclear forces for conventional deterrence will no longer consider them necessary." The key step toward eliminating the prospect of conventional war is for both superpowers to renounce intervention. "Intervention," Forsberg says, "is the single most important factor of the superpower relationship."

Her proposal consists of six bilateral steps starting with a freeze and followed by a renunciation of intervention and reductions in conventional and nuclear forces in a phased, long-term process. "By gradually confining the role of conventional military forces to defense, more and more narrowly defined," Forsberg has written, "we can move safely toward a world in which conventional forces are limited to short-range, defensive armaments, in which international institutions provide an effective nonviolent means of resolving conflicts, and in which nuclear weapons can be abolished."

Several programs for complete disarmament have been put forward. Jonathan Schell, for one, has called for an "abolition movement." There is a consensus among experts, however, that complete disarmament is not realistic given that the knowledge and resources for manufacturing nuclear and conventional weapons is inherent in advanced technological societies. Many analysts also believe that disarmament, in itself, is not the means to a different world, it is the *product* of changes that are themselves the means—changes in our relationship to the use of military force, changes in domestic politics, and changes in the relationships between nations.

Transforming the Relationship Between the Superpowers

It may take a historian to force a national security expert to consider ways to cease the Cold War. The prominent American historian John Gaddis will try to do just that at a conference he is hosting this April at Ohio University entitled "Resolving Soviet-American Differences: How the Cold War Might End." Robert Jervis, Randall Forsberg, and Walter Rostow are among the six speakers.

Far short of addressing head-on the question of the permanence of the Cold War, a number of academics are investigating ways in which the U.S.-Soviet relationship could evolve that would, at a minimum, increase the level of trust and cooperation between the two nations. Among the most distinct approaches to this problem:

• Several analysts are presenting a strong argument that the United States needs to increase efforts to understand Soviet perceptions. Columbia University's Robert Jervis, whose work has pioneered principles in political psychology, says that "unless statesmen understand the ways in which their counterparts in the Soviet Union see the world, their deterrence policies are likely to fail." Furthermore, Jervis says that the cultivation of positive perceptions on both sides should be fostered by regular communication and agreements. "The general political atmosphere changes the world," he explains. "If you think the world can stay at peace, we are more likely to stay at peace. If you believe war is inevitable then initiating war might make sense."

• A second approach focuses on the practice of negotiation. Harvard law professor Roger Fisher's program, the acknowledged pathmaker in this field, identifies and teaches techniques for negotiation and conflict resolution that maximize mutual benefit in any dispute—from squabbles in the schoolyard to arms control negotiations. A company spawned by the program holds an annual training session for NATO officials and may meet with U.S. and Soviet officials in Vienna this summer.

• A means to achieve more far-reaching change, yet still within an apolitical framework, is suggested by the work of Robert Keohane, a political scientist at Harvard. He argues that changes in the world economy are causing nations to become increasingly dependent on one another, and more apt to adopt global perspectives in their search for solutions to national problems. Keohane's main contribution is to highlight the importance of intergovernmental institutions —such as the International Monetary Fund—that operate across national frontiers and could, under certain conditions, play a decisive role in promoting cooperation among governments.

Joseph Nye at Harvard is one of the few researchers to apply Keohane's work on economic security to questions of national security. But Keohane's theme of interdependence is common to most visions of global security and world order. Studies in world order postulate changes in the relationships between nations that go far beyond anything mentioned here. This field draws on a long tradition, but much of the work is not seriously regarded by the mainstream.

Robert Johansen, senior fellow at the World Policy Institute (formerly the Institute for World Order) in New York City, explains that this is because it has traditionally relied on legal and institutional structures—now discredited by the example of the United Nations and other bodies—and has not paid sufficient attention to the process of *realizing* a world order. The current work is more concerned with uncovering values and norms, as well as suggesting near-term policies, that can point society in the right direction.

Changing Norms and Values, Challenging Assumptions

Princeton University's Richard Falk, the unofficial "dean" of world order studies, emphasizes the need for the creation of new values and norms. "At this stage, blueprints of alternative world order systems are not very important," Falk says. "What is most needed is a new tradition of citizenship based on the values of peace, economic well-being, human rights, and ecological balance. Such a citizen will challenge the logic of war and seek to reinvigorate democracy so that society can control the state rather than the other way around."

Johansen has elaborated on the perspective of "global humanism" in his work, and has used that perspective to interpret the conduct of U.S. foreign policy. Work such as this—what little there is—corresponds closely to the needs voiced by activists and educators (and organizations such as Beyond War) to redefine national security around different themes, values, and assumptions.

Researchers are producing work all the time that could be useful in any public education campaign intended to question some of the key assumptions of U.S. foreign policy, claims *International Security*'s Stephen Van Evera. One example he cites is the presumed vulnerability of Western Europe to a Soviet attack. Two recent *International Security* papers by defense analysts Barry Posen and John Mearsheimer "conclusively and factually debunked the myth of the Soviet threat to Western Europe," Van Evera contends. The trouble is, he says, "the 'left' is not nearly so efficient as the 'right' in getting such studies translated for public consumption, repeated by the media, and broadcast."

Help may be on the way, however. A new project, led by Richard Barnet at the Institute for Policy Studies, will develop educational materials to help average citizens analyze basic security issues and encourage them to consider long-term alternatives to present nuclear policy.

As the range of work done by analysts continues to widen, the possibilities for collaboration with activists look more promising. Many in both camps cite the remarkable job the "New Right" has done over the past decade in promoting a vision of a future using both academic and activist skills. George Rathjens of

M.I.T., chair of a new group of academics, researchers and activists called Exploratory Project on the Conditions of Peace, says his inspiration for the group is the Committee on the Present Danger.

Any activist/analyst collaboration reinforces the relationship between ideas and action, between long- and short-term strategies. "I believe it is important to have a whole range of steps which can be implemented in the immediate future," says Robert Johansen. "But those immediate steps should have some connection with a long-range vision so that people implementing them know that those steps in and of themselves are not sufficient. If they don't, then those steps are simply band-aids."

No-First-Use Debate Widens:
Lawyers, Study Group Consider New Policies
By Susan Subak
March/April 1986

THIRTY LEGAL SCHOLARS MET IN WASHINGTON, D.C., LAST NOVEMBER to discuss no-first-use. The same month, citizens in Boulder, Colorado, passed a ballot initiative calling for a change in this country's first-use policy. And during the past two years thousands of people attending Council for a Livable World conferences have heard experts expound on the subject.

Until recently, the no-first-use debate was confined to academic and policy-making circles. Opinion polls showed that from 70 to 80 percent of the American public believed that no-first-use was *already* U.S. policy. Now it appears that interest in the no-first-use issue is growing in both analyst and activist circles.

"People are beginning to understand that the question of no-first-use is as important as the proposal for a nuclear weapons freeze," explains Morton Halperin, former deputy assistant secretary of defense. Halperin belongs to a working group of analysts who are studying the issue. Recently he helped organize a no-first-use educational project in Washington, D.C., as part of the Center for Education on Nuclear War. "Much too much time has been spent on debating what weapons should be built," Halperin says, "rather than on the fundamental question of when nuclear weapons are to be used, and to what purpose nuclear weapons are to serve other than to deter."

After simmering for almost 20 years, the no-first-use controversy came to a boil in the spring of 1982 when McGeorge Bundy, Robert McNamara, Gerard Smith, and George Kennan—now known as the "gang of four"—published an article in *Foreign Affairs*. They argued that a no-first-use policy may be desirable because it could preclude an irrational initiation of nuclear war and alleviate Soviet fears that the United States was gearing up for a war-winning capability. They attributed the current first-use policy to "an antiquated security guarantee" to Western Europe that was made at a time when the United States had a monopoly on nuclear weapons.

Their proposal was immediately attacked by a gang of four Germans—Karl Kaiser, Georg Leber, Alois Mertes, and Franz-Josef Schulze—who said that a no-first-use policy would indicate that the United States was softening its commitment to defend Western Europe, and would therefore make a conventional attack more likely.

The White House and the Pentagon responded to the proposal with an adamant defense of the status quo in Europe. Even the Catholic bishops, in their pastoral letter, said that a first-use policy might help to deter war. Walter Mondale, during his election bid in 1984, said that no-first-use was unworkable.

The original gang of four, however, have continued to meet, often over dinner, and have joined up with six other experts interested in the issue (not all of them advocates of no-first-use). A year and a half ago these ten individuals formed a working group on no-first-use that is finishing up an extended study of the question.

The working group includes, in addition to Halperin and the original quartet, William Kaufmann of Harvard University, John Steinbruner of the Brookings Institution, Leon Sigal of Wesleyan University, Richard Ullman of Princeton University, and Paul Warnke, former chief SALT II negotiator. They are extending the debate to consider a no-first-use policy in the southern hemisphere, and are exploring proposals that could make a Soviet attack on Europe less likely.

While the Soviets declared a no-first-use policy in 1982, they have not implemented it with strategic changes. The United States should execute a no-first-use policy unilaterally, some members of the working group believe. "The no-first-use issue is something that we can change on our own within negotiating an agreement," says Halperin. Beyond a declaration, the policy would entail restructuring U.S. military forces: the MX, which could be useful in a first-strike scenario (and is also vulnerable to a first strike), would be withdrawn, and nuclear weapons would no longer be deployed near the front lines in Europe. "The Europeans tend to oppose a no-first-use declaration but support the policy issue of removing nuclear weapons from the front lines," says Halperin.

Much of the working group's new research demonstrates that nuclear weapons deployed in Europe could actually reduce the chances that the United States would win a conventional war. "It's a zero-sum game," says Madalene O'Donnell, the project coordinator for the working group, "since Congress imposes a ceiling on military forces in Europe. When nuclear weapons, such as ground-launched cruise missiles, are brought in, conventional forces are sent home."

The question of how a conventional war could escalate into a nuclear war has also drawn the interest of the international and constitutional law community. "There is a fair amount of consensus in the legal community that the threat to use nuclear weapons first violates the Nuremburg Principles, which are binding on the United States," says Daniel Arbess, executive director of the Lawyers' Committee on Nuclear Policy in New York City. "Escalating to the use of nuclear weapons during a conventional war would mean using forces disproportionate to the threat—which is a war crime," Arbess adds.

Thirty constitutional lawyers, convened by the Federation of American Scientists and the Lawyers Alliance for Nuclear Arms Control last November, discussed whether a proposed statute to change the country's first-use policy followed the spirit of the U.S. Constitution.

Most of the legal experts endorsed the statute as constitutional. The proposal, put forth by FAS Director Jeremy Stone, would ban the first use of nuclear weapons, and leave up to a congressional leadership committee the decision to rescind the ban. In the event of a conventional war, Stone argues, there should be time for a congressional committee to meet to discuss the possibility of using nuclear weapons. The assembled experts agreed that since the Constitution gives the president the responsibility to use any weapons to answer a surprise attack on the United States, he may use nuclear weapons second, but in other circumstances only Congress has the right to decide whether to use nuclear weapons.

Objections came from Robert Turner and John Norton Moore, both senior fellows at the Center for Law and National Security in Charlottesville, Virginia. They argued that nothing in the historical record suggests that the founding fathers wanted to impede the president's power to resist a war thrust upon the United States. Despite this dissent, Stone, who thought up the statute, he explains, while taking a shower in 1971, says he was pleased at the outcome. He is planning to hold another meeting, this time with "a second culture"—strategists—to discuss how questions of international politics, defense strategy, and the feasibility of passage relate to the proposal.

Beyond the Bomb ...
Imagining a Nonnuclear Defense
By Mark Sommer
March/April 1986

PROTEST HAS LONG BEEN THE ANTINUCLEAR MOVEMENT'S STRONG SUIT. Opponents of the nuclear arms race have always known far better what is wrong with present policies and strategies than with what they would replace them. This is understandable. Present policies are all too real and specific, while proposed alternatives are at best untested hypotheses. Yet this emphasis has left the movement at a critical disadvantage in reaching a public interested in solutions rather than problems—with what *will* work rather than with what does not. Opponents of the arms race have allowed themselves to be cast in the roles of nay-sayers. They have not yet developed a compelling image and design of their own.

During the past several years, this longstanding imbalance has begun to come aright. A new era of invention has arrived. Recognizing that the better ideas that might take us beyond the bomb will never be invented by those with their fingers on the button, a growing variety of researchers in North America, East and West Europe, and elsewhere have been designing and envisioning alternative ways of achieving security in which armed force no longer plays a central role.

What is new and in fact revolutionary in the work of these alternative theorists is that they have begun to consider the achievement of peace as more than mere wishing, as at least partly a challenge of deliberate design. As military strategists have so long and systematically planned for war, so these thinkers are beginning to plan for peace. Working in isolation from one another and largely without financial resources, these researchers have been sketching strikingly similar designs for their peaceable worlds and the likely transitions to them.

There is as yet no integrated vision of a world beyond the bomb. Even to assert that such a world is possible is, in these times, a profoundly transformative act. What we have at the moment is a kaleidoscope of images and designs that nonetheless bear a certain familial resemblance.

What follows is a look at just a few of many promising ideas.

Alternative Defense

The past few years have seen the emergence, first in western Europe and more recently in the United States, of a new body of thinking somewhere between arms control and disarmament.

A number of theorists have begun to ask themselves whether and how a defense might be fashioned that doesn't depend on threats and yet doesn't threaten one's own security. These researchers have sought to draw a distinction between destructive and protective capabilities, between defense as attack and defense as the capacity to repel attack. Variously termed "nonprovocative defense," "defense without offense," and "just defense," they all call for:

• greatly reducing our reliance on nuclear weapons, both strategic and tactical;

• greatly increasing our reliance on weapons more useful for defense than offense, making ample use of recent advances in defensive weapons technologies like precision-guided munitions;

• developing strategies strong in the defensive mode and deliberately weak in the offensive to signal adversaries that they need not fear attack but that they will not succeed if *they* attack;

• confining defense to the territory of one's own nation and eschewing claims beyond one's borders.

The most comprehensive effort to translate these principles of a nonthreatening defense into the circumstances of a single nation has been the Alternative Defence Commission's Defence Without the Bomb, a detailed plan for a Britain without nuclear weapons. In the United States, Dietrich Fischer has developed a general theory for a nonprovocative defense in his recent book, *Preventing War in the Nuclear Age.*

Alternative Security

While alternative defense theory confines itself to the hardware and strategies of military defense, an alternative security system includes a broad spectrum of nonmilitary initiatives.

By an integrated foreign policy of economic incentives, diplomatic initiatives, development assistance, and participation in global institutions—and by a domestic policy that emphasizes a robust but nonexploitive economy, an equitable distribution of wealth, and a vital social culture—a system of alternative security creates an environment in which military defense is no longer an overwhelming preoccupation.

Norwegian peace researcher Johan Galtung has devised a four-part system of alternative security uniting military and nonmilitary elements:

• "transarming" from an offensive to a purely defensive military posture (as in Switzerland);

• decoupling from superpower alliances;

• cultivating a sound and self-reliant economy, a healthy ecology, and an equitable and stable social system;

• enhancing one's usefulness to would-be adversaries, thus assuring that the rewards of peace always remain greater than the potential spoils of war.

Disarmament

Although there is no dearth of good ideas about how to dispose of the arsenals that now so burden us, none of them appear to possess a compelling motivation to bring them into being. An exception, perhaps, is the strategy of independent initiatives. First proposed nearly a quarter of a century ago by psychologist Charles Osgood, GRIT (Graduated Reciprocation In Tension-Reduction) sought to harness the momentum generated by one side's carefully measured movements in the direction of peace as a means of inducing—and if necessary, pressuring—its adversary into reciprocal gestures.

The Soviet Union's nuclear test moratorium and proposal for phased nuclear disarmament by the year 2000 demonstrate the continuing potential of an initiative strategy. But it also reveals its limitations, for in the absence of support from an informed and aroused public the responding government may dismiss the initiative without incurring any serious political cost.

Nonviolence

Nonviolent action likely has more to offer than any other tradition towards the resolution of the nuclear conundrum. Nonviolent defense has been under development by a small but determined community of researchers for a quarter of a century. As proposed by its foremost theorist, Harvard University's Gene

Sharp, "civilian-based defense" elevates what has historically been a purely ad hoc resistance to tyranny and invasion into a formal strategy. Basing its strength on the seldom recognized truth that all political power ultimately depends on the cooperation or acquiescence of the governed, civilian-based defense seeks, by a variety of broad-based, unified resistance strategies, to withdraw that consent and thus undermine even the most oppressive invader. "There are no white flags of surrender in civilian-based defense," Sharp has written, and this prospect is designed to deter invasion.

During the past several years, the Netherlands, Sweden, Belgium, and France have sponsored small-scale feasibility studies of nonviolent defense. In West Germany, the Green Party has adopted "social defense" as its proposed alternative to current dependence on NATO and nuclear weapons. None of these studies or proposals envisions abandoning military defense, now or ever. All view nonviolent defense as supplementing, rather than supplanting, the military component. But Gene Sharp views such modest beginnings as an opening wedge through which more significant transformations may one day pass.

What I see in this and much other evidence is an implicit consensus of perspective amid a variety of approaches: common defense in place of unilateral offense and a multilayered mutual security based on strategies of nonviolence. One of the richest traditions in alternative thinking is that it is not an ideology— at least, not yet. And we can be thankful for that. When there are too few options on the table and too few in the public mind, it is our first order of business to propagate new choices, to initiate a season of benign invention.

Real Security:
What Is It? How Can We Get It?
By Greg Mitchell
May/June 1986

RONALD REAGAN'S LOOSE TALK ABOUT FIGHTING AND WINNING A nuclear war helped inspire a worldwide disarmament movement in the early 1980s. Antinuclear activists loudly identified what they were *against,* but the effectiveness of this negative message as a political organizing tool has been limited. Now the president is giving the peace movement an opportunity to describe what it stands *for.*

Reagan sells "Star Wars." What is the movement's alternative to mutual assured destruction? Reagan sends war planes to the Middle East, and gunships to Central America. What is the movement's definition of "vital interest," its vision of "national security"? Reagan throws so much money at the Pentagon that two senators from his own party concoct a devastating deficit-cutting scheme. Where does the movement think federal money should be spent?

Slowly, fitfully, sometimes altogether reluctantly, longtime critics of the nuclear arms race, American adventurism abroad, and excessive military spending are realizing that they will never make much progress, politically or with the American public, until they are perceived as standing *for* something—even if it's something so vague (for now) as "real," "true," "common," or "mutual" security. The popularity of Star Wars, and rising public sentiment against intervention and military spending, have created for progressive forces the opportunity (which may be fleeting indeed) to finally provide what the Rocky Mountain Institute's Amory Lovins calls "the critical missing link in the peace movement."

Atmospheric Pressure

A Gallup Poll, released in mid-April, revealed that the war system's window of vulnerability has opened a bit. It showed that for the first time in years the majority of the public believes that nuclear parity exists between the superpowers. In an almost perfect reversal from five years ago, 47 percent now believe we are spending too much on the military, and only 13 percent too little. And Gallup found that the average American believes that fully 37 cents out of every dollar spent on the military is "wasted." On this latter point there was no significant difference between the views of Republicans, Democrats, and independents.

Americans may not yet agree with Kenneth Boulding's recent assessment: "National defense is now the greatest enemy of national security." But after a decade under siege—first from the right, and now from the left—traditional notions of national security may be losing credibility in the center. James Reston, the *New York Times* columnist, actually seemed to be on top of a developing story when he wrote not long ago: "Nicaragua is merely a symbol of a much deeper confusion over the true interests of our nation. It has to do with the conduct of our affairs at home and abroad, not merely with the news of the day but with the history of the Republic—its values and priorities, and the future of our children. . . . A debate on what constitutes 'the national interest' is long overdue."

Reston may not envision a radical reexamination or redefinition of national security. But in admitting that something has gone awry with U.S. policy and budget priorities—and in suggesting that our national security is not what it's cracked up to be (even under a popular, saber-rattling president)—he and other mainstream commentators are helping to create an atmosphere for theoreticians, analysts, and activists to rush forward with *their* visions of real security, and the means of attaining it. They are starting to do so.

And they are doing it in a most savvy and positive way. During the past year, several pollsters and media experts have told peace movement leaders that they have to find a way to appeal to "traditional American values." What is more traditional than the belief in national security? And what constitutes national security is now up for grabs. So you have business executives citing Eisenhower's attack on the military-industrial complex, and you have the Women's International League for Peace and Freedom vowing to "reclaim national security" (they want a two-year cut of $146 billion in the Pentagon budget, for starters).

Security, after all, has a hard ring to it, compared with the mellow sound of "peace" or even "arms control." If you couch it in terms of security you can propose "reorienting our armed forces toward true defense" (as SANE has)—or all sorts of other provocative things. Peace groups have lately called for: pulling troops out of Europe in a staged process; ending Third World intervention; eliminating all funds for the Rapid Deployment Force; cancelling all new nuclear weapons and unnecessary conventional arms. "Do we really need ten divisions of the U.S. Army in West Germany?" asks Erica Foldy of the Coalition for a New Foreign and Military Policy. "Do we need two more aircraft carriers—for what war? Where?"

Thinking Positive

But that's more negatives. What do the advocates of real security stand *for*?

"We must move toward more positive messages that connect nuclear disarmament with the quality of life we envision in this country and around the world," says Diane Aronson, executive director of Women's Action for Nuclear Disarmament.

"Real security," says Representative Edward Markey, "depends upon progress in arms control, developing a quality national educational system, insuring the prosperity of the civilian economy, and a rebuilding of America's cities and infrastructure."

"We and the Soviets must recognize that a state of common peril exists," asserts the American Friends Service Committee. "The answer is for both governments to develop a policy of 'common security.' The basis for a common security policy is that neither superpower can increase its own security at the expense of the other."

Sentiments such as these are often accompanied by specific policy suggestions: Real security means military readiness, not military hardware, so raise military pay. Real security means moving troops to defensive positions, so reduce foreign deployments. Real security means upgrading verification and crisis control technology, so spend money on that, not on modernizing nuclear weapons. Real security means maintaining a strong economy, not a bloated military, so redirect research and development funds from the Pentagon to the private sector. Real security means preventing the development of new Soviet weapons, not creating a Strategic Defense Initiative to try to destroy new Soviet weapons, so enact a bilateral freeze. And so on.

Certainly, there is nothing new about progressive groups criticizing military spending, and providing a long list of domestic programs (from food stamps to environmental protection) that deserve a bigger piece of the pie. And intellectuals like Marcus Raskin have floated ideas about new national security systems for years. What's different now is the pervasiveness of the real security rhetoric and the arrival of so many ambitious projects aimed at turning rhetoric into action. A brief sampling to show the diversity of some of the current endeavors:

• Five years ago, Richard Barnet wrote an important book called *Real Security*. Now he has initiated a major project at the Institute for Policy Studies that will develop material and run workshops to bring "alternative views" of national security to peace, church, and labor groups. "Most U.S. policies," Barnet says, "are based on assumptions that have not been examined for years. They are the sacred cows of American politics." Reaction from the groups so far? "Absolutely phenomenal, across the board," Barnet reports.

• Amory Lovins's Rocky Mountain Institute, long an innovator in energy policy, has launched a Redefining National Security program. It will take account of "new and emerging resource realities," according to Lovins, to determine what makes people really secure. "Today," says Lovins, "the U.S. projects power around the world to protect access to vital and indispensable raw materials at the same time that advances in science and energy are making those resources obsolete." For example, one year's spending on the Rapid Deployment Force, if put into programs to weatherize buildings, Lovins points out, "would about eliminate the need for U.S. oil imports" (thereby eliminating the RDF's mission).

• Arthur Kanegis, former media director of the Center for Defense Information, is attempting to put together a Hollywood blockbuster that would show the world under a new security system in the year 2020. He wants to tap the same vein struck by "We Are the World" and enlist some of the top actors, screenwriters, and filmmakers to bring the project, *Future Wave*, to a mass audience. Paul Newman, Jane Alexander, and Martin Sheen, among many others, are serving on the advisory board, and Arthur C. Clarke, the author of *2001*, has agreed to be a script consultant, beaming in story ideas via modem from his home in Sri Lanka. Kanegis promises a film with "new kinds of heroes and heroines and new ways of overcoming conflict—a positive vision of a world secure from nuclear catastrophe, with mechanisms for averting war."

Ark Communications Institute in Bolinas, California, alone, is producing this year two books, several radio shows, a spacebridge, and a resource guide, all based on redefining national security. The World Policy Institute is taking the findings from its Security Project and briefing political candidates. WAND has gone so far as to officially add an alternative reading of their own name—"Women's Action for a *New Direction*." On April 15 it issued a press release denouncing the U.S. bombing of Libya, and stressing WAND's commitment to "seek new directions in U.S. foreign and national security policy." This would have been unthinkable one year ago.

The Real Thing

The wisdom of tossing one quarter of a trillion dollars at the Pentagon and calling it "national security" is highly debatable, says Howard Morland, of the Coalition for a New Foreign and Military Policy, "but serious debate on it has never taken place."

That's changing now. But how sustained will that debate be? When Physicians for Social Responsibility took up the military budget battle this spring for the first time, it beat the real security drum, but one top PSR staffer in Washington, D.C., admits: "Our alternative vision is still, basically, 'arms control.' Long-term visions just don't sell in this town. You come off as a crackpot."

But the appeal, and the challenge, of real security *is* real, and it will be with us for some time. "Every political candidate I've come across the past two months," reports SANE PAC Director Jerry Hartz, "has been talking about national security and the military budget." Grassroots activists are pressing their national leaders to come up with new, inspiring, and unifying themes for the movement. SDI is rushing ahead, Gramm-Rudman is holding firm, polls show that the public continues to call for harnessing the military. Ronald Reagan has not given us real security—and yet, he has.

The Psychology of Threats:
A Debate on the Use of Nuclear Diplomacy
July/August 1986

MUCH OF THE DEBATE ABOUT NUCLEAR DETERRENCE HAS CENTERED ON questions of whether it has really worked, and what it could possibly be replaced with. William Kincade, who is completing a collaborative project at the Carnegie Endowment for International Peace on the psychology of deterrence, has introduced what he believes is a more interesting question: How did we arrive at our current policy, and what does our theory of deterrence leave out or include that we don't recognize? He concludes that, starting in the 1950s, plain old deterrence began to assume a less sensible form. The new "dogmatic" brand of deterrence attempted not merely to impede *a Soviet attack, but to* compel *certain responses from the Soviet Union. This type of deterrence-plus-compellence, Kincade believes, can be seen in the administration's current efforts to develop SDI in order to coerce the Soviets into curbing arms competition.*

Kincade holds that the theory behind the deterrent and compellent form of nuclear threats was developed without essential insights of psychological knowledge. In their research, he and his colleagues examine the effects of this omission. In the following discussion, which took place in Washington, D.C., recently, Kincade pit his research findings on the use of nuclear coercion in foreign policy against those of Morton Halperin, an expert on U.S. nuclear doctrine, who is completing a book that analyzes from a different perspective the efficacy of nuclear threats as a tool in American foreign policy. Kincade's study, Edge of War: The Psychology of Nuclear Deterrence, *cowritten with Stephen M. Sonnenberg, a psychiatrist and psychoanalyst, will be published by Yale University Press in 1987.* Nuclear Fallacy: Dispelling the Myth of Nuclear Strategy, *by Morton Halperin, will be published by Ballinger Press in late 1986.*

Kincade: The Western theory of nuclear deterrence developed in the 1950s in response to perceptions of a Soviet Union on the march and, partly, to the Soviet acquisition of nuclear weapons, which gave a new meaning to their perceived expansionism. The deterrence that evolved, which I call *dogmatic* deterrence, attempts to influence Soviet behavior through implicit or explicit threats and sometimes rewards. The newer and more elaborate principle differs from what I call *axiomatic* deterrence, or the time-honored principle that military preparedness will cause potential aggressors to be inhibited.

Dogmatic deterrence and "compellence" involve the use of nuclear forces—their deployment, operation doctrine, numbers, and performance—to change Soviet behavior. The Soviets have also used the same dimensions of nuclear forces in attempts to influence the policy of the United States.

In its crudest terms this policy was based on the notion that the response to a credible threat is either "fight or flight." When confronted with the probable horrors of nuclear exchanges, the USSR would choose "flight" and acquiesce to tacit or explicit Western demands. Different specialists gave different weight to the carrots and to the sticks, but there was considerable unanimity on the efficacy of nuclear threats in constraining Soviet behavior.

Few of those involved in the development of deterrence theory had training in or knowledge of psychology or allied fields. Many of the analysts worked at the Rand Corporation and other research centers. Among the important intellectual influences were economic theory, game theory, and systems analysis. Even at the time of its initial elaboration, dogmatic deterrence encountered some skepticism and reservations, especially among social scientists and clinically oriented specialists in psychology. These dissenting voices, however, had little or no material effect. There was no national debate on deterrence.

I'll just mention one, of many, problems with dogmatic deterrence: A threat often leads to a counterthreat that sustains a recurring cycle of coercive actions. In fact, you should *count* on the other country overreacting to the threat. You should count on there being either an immediate, or over a longer period, counterthreat, much as people now expect the bombing of Libya to increase rather than decrease the amount of terrorism.

Halperin: I think we need to have an image of international politics and how it *really* works in our heads in order to deal with these specific questions.

International politics is generally thought of as something like two people exchanging threats and promises and interacting with each other. I believe it's much more like a situation in which you have a football field and a soccer field side by side. The people on each field are concentrating on their [own] game, and every once in a while somebody kicks the ball into the wrong field. Nobody knows quite what to do with this other ball. They have a little discussion about that and finally kick it back into the other field. The process that goes on between nations is, I would argue, much closer to that than the model that is usually in our heads—two people or two small groups interacting. One vital question is to try to understand to what extent is`individual or small group behavior really relevant to the way that nations behave.

Kincade: But nations are governed, especially in connection with the nuclear policy, by individuals. In their response to threats we see very strong parallels at the general public or leadership level to what you would get in research at the individual or small group level. It is people who are making or supporting policy.

Halperin: It may be true that John Foster Dulles reacts to threats in the same way that college students in a small group would. But the question is, what follows that?

In my manuscript [*Nuclear Fallacy*] I am arguing that the major problem with nuclear forces is not that we don't take account of psychological insights of how nations really behave, but that we are trying to use the threat of the use of nuclear weapons to advance our interest in deterring conventional wars. We use nuclear explosive devices as if they were credible weapons of war and that substantially increases the risk of nuclear war. That probably comes not from some misunderstanding of what motivates people but a decision to try to use these things as weapons of war.

The major question is how we should behave in relationship to the Russians so as to reduce the risk of getting into a crisis and so that if we get into a crisis we can get out of it. It is in that process that one should be trying to interject insights and psychological analysis rather than in the theory of deterrence.

Kincade: What accounts for some of our differences is that you're focusing on crises, and my focus has tended to be, not on deterrence as a response to crisis, but deterrence as an ongoing policy, a kind of general, sometimes rather vague threat that hangs over everybody's head, and is given a certain additional sharpness in order to deter rather vague contingencies, like a Soviet move into Western Europe. Frequently U.S. and Soviet leaders have also taken advantage of the particular characteristics of their forces to raise the threat level in order to change adversary behavior. They have used either deployments or numbers or performance characteristics to try to sharpen the threat against their adversary.

Halperin: I don't think that's necessarily true. The Russians did dangerous things when the nuclear balance was adverse to them [before parity] and did not do dangerous things when the nuclear balance was not adverse to them. It's as if they were following the rule, "push while I'm weak so that the opponent does not realize that I'm not stronger than he is."

Kincade: The analysis that Paul Nitze has repeated again and again—and he's a man of great experience and sophistication—about the Cuban missile crisis makes precisely the point that it was the efficacy of our threat of our nuclear weapons [superiority] that made Khrushchev back down. And that has become part of our national security mythology and is even accepted by most liberals. I think what we're trying to do with our project is to use both psychological and behavioral [analysis] and point out that there are a number of reasons for thinking that another interpretation of the Cuban missile crisis may be better than the very simple "nuclear threats work."

Halperin: I agree with you. All I am saying is that you should not ever expect to get evidence so sound that it totally sustains . . .

Kincade: My contention, and here we get into what cannot be proven, is that Khrushchev thought that the U.S. reaction [to the installation of Soviet missiles in Cuba] would be, "Well he's got us where he wants us, we're going to have to make concessions." Instead, there was a rather hysterical reaction, both within the international leadership and amongst the public, and so the Soviets miscalculated because of a very crude understanding of the psychology of threats.

Halperin: I think the Russians underestimated not how people respond to threats, but the domestic politics of that issue. If Kennedy had said that the missiles don't make any difference, which is absolutely the right response if the game was international power, he would have spent the rest of his term in office trying to explain why he allowed the Russians to push him around and it would probably have cost him his reelection.

To put it another way, if you knew that Khrushchev was going to do this [put missiles in Cuba], and you had ten minutes to explain to him what [America's] likely response was going to be, would you spend that ten minutes talking about bureaucratic and domestic politics in the United States, or how individuals react to threats? I would spend the time talking about bureaucratic politics.

Kincade: I think what we have here is two analyses that head in the same direction and what I want to do is to force all of Mort's observations into my psychology-dominated paradigm and he wants to force all of my psychological insights into his domestic-politics dominated paradigm.

But I find that if I simply say that the Cuban missile crisis was not a case of deterrence, but a case of compellence—that it was not a case of inhibiting the Soviet Union from doing something, it was changing their course after it had been set—the flashbulbs go off and people suddenly see things in a very different light.

Halperin: Again I would say that misunderstanding the psychological consequences of what you think you're going to do is much less important than . . .

Kincade: Let's take Richard Perle. It seems to me that he almost epitomizes the kind of person who believes strongly that a good, intense threat is all the Soviets understand, so let's threaten them more and more and one of these days they'll finally say, "Oh my God, I'm just so impressed with the United States that I'm just going to roll over and give up."

Halperin: . . . What I'm saying is that human beings are constantly looking for ways to express their psychological needs without being locked up, and that politics is the place where you can do that because there is no statement you can make about Soviet behavior and about deterrence that can lead you to getting locked up because you're crazy. Policymakers, like most of the rest of us, are playing out their deep psychological needs because nobody knows how to prove that their ideas are wrong.

And if you come, say, to Mr. Weinberger, and say to him, "Do you understand that the way that people respond to threats is with counterthreats and not backing down? His response to that is going to be, "I know as much about how human beings behave as you do, and I know people back down, and you don't."

Kincade: I disagree that just because politics is where we all work out our innermost psychological motivations—which I think is an interesting idea, and may well be true—does not vitiate my view as a source for understanding where some of the problems with deterrence may lie.

A New Agenda:
Common Security is the First Step on the Road to Disarmament
By Bruce Birchard and Rob Leavitt
November/December 1987

THE SEARCH FOR A VISION TO REENERGIZE THE PEACE MOVEMENT BEGAN three years ago, just after the 1984 election. The Nuclear Freeze Campaign had succeeded in slowing President Reagan's massive nuclear buildup and forced his administration to resume arms control talks with the Soviet Union, talks that recently yielded agreement on a modest intermediate nuclear forces (INF) treaty. However, the freeze was not regarded as a serious proposal by the arms control elites and their supporters in Congress and the news media.

When it became evident that Congress and President Reagan would not implement a freeze, it became obvious to activists that the freeze had lost its power to mobilize public support. The Reagan election landslide, the new official rhetoric supporting arms control, and the escapist fantasy of Star Wars took the steam out of the movement. Rethinking was essential.

As part of its current rethinking, the peace movement needs to develop appropriate and effective long-term strategies and near-term priorities.

Nuclear disarmament is not a sufficient long-term goal for the disarmament movement. Governments will not abolish all nuclear weapons without major changes in domestic and foreign policy. Resistance and protest, although essential, will not be enough. Peace advocates must also develop policy alternatives to the present militarized course. We must address the political dynamics that drive the arms race: the Cold War, the push to control the world's resources and markets, and domestic political and economic dynamics. We cannot rely on the Democratic Party or arms controllers to initiate radical policies, so we must begin the process ourselves.

A "common security" policy provides an alternative to nuclearism, militarism, and interventionism. This concept was initially developed by the Independent Commission on Disarmament and Security Issues, chaired by the late Swedish Prime Minister Olof Palme. The commission argued that, given the destructiveness of nuclear and conventional military forces today, as well as the enormous social and economic costs of militarism, nations must recognize that they cannot increase their own security at the expense of their potential enemy's security. The commission stated, "Only through cooperative efforts and policies of interlocking national restraint will all the world's citizens be able to live without fear of war and devastation."

The major elements of a common security program should include:

• An end to military intervention in the affairs of other nations and a global delegitimization of the use of military force for anything other than self defense.

• Drastic restructuring and reductions in the offensive capabilities of conventional weapons and military forces, restricting them to narrowly defined defensive postures and capabilities.

• Substantially reduced tensions between NATO and Warsaw Pact countries, which would enable East and West to improve their social and economic relations; a dissolution of the military blocs; and a withdrawal of superpower military forces from their borders.

• Dramatic reductions in the global burden of military spending, permitting these resources to be devoted to socioeconomic development abroad and economic reconstruction at home.

• Strengthened international and regional institutions of peacekeeping and cooperation, including the United Nations and the World Court, which would expand nonmilitary mechanisms for negotiations, conflict resolution, and problem solving of global issues.

• Robust international standards of national self-determination, human rights, civil liberties, and basic economic rights, with effective nonmilitary mechanisms of enforcement.

• The elimination of all nuclear weapons and nuclear weapons production facilities worldwide.

We deliberately list nuclear disarmament last because we believe that the abolition of nuclear weapons will not be achieved until great progress has been made in the other areas. Nations will not give up their "ultimate deterrent" until their leaders are convinced that the world has become "safe enough" to do so. We urge the disarmament movement to put common security on the top of its agenda.

Adopting a common security agenda would have several benefits. The broader focus on the creation of a just, demilitarized global security system could help unite a broad range of peace and justice organizations and many new constituencies. It could provide clear incentives to groups concerned with federal budget priorities; self-determination in the Third World; human rights in South Africa, the Soviet Union, and Eastern Europe; better East-West relations; Third World development; and strengthening the United Nations. A common security framework would move us away from a bipolar, U.S.-Soviet conception of the world and toward a more global concern for justice and peace.

Within the United States, a common security program demonstrates that the peace movement is concerned about the risk of conventional war, which is a major obstacle to nuclear disarmament. It enables the movement to take a "proactive" stand. And it offers the possibility of dramatic reductions in world military spending, which would free human and economic resources for economic reconstruction in the United States and development in the Third World.

Implications

Adopting a common security approach would have serious implications for the peace movement. One critic has asked, "What are we supposed to do, hit the streets with 'Common Security Now' banners?" Not quite.

To begin with, commitment to common security principles will necessitate the development of a sophisticated communications strategy to reach important constituencies.

The movement must develop a more realistic understanding of the Soviet Union and its allies. It must develop and promote a principled position on human rights in Eastern Europe and the Soviet Union that is consistent with movement positions on human rights in the rest of the world and avoids knee-jerk anticommunism.

Activists will need to increase their cooperation with other elements of the U.S. peace and justice movement. The principles of common security can provide a framework that unites work against U.S. intervention in Central America and other parts of the world with the struggle against apartheid in South Africa and against military bases and nuclear facilities around the world. To confront a world military system and create a stable, disarmed peace, activists must reach out to groups not considered part of the peace movement in the past to create an international movement for common security.

And finally, the movement must develop an organizing strategy that understands the way powerful institutions within the United States oppose change.

Making It Happen

To begin the process of putting common security into action, we suggest the movement pursue three activities: education and consciousness raising, national policy campaigns, and citizen peacemaking initiatives.

Internal education comes first. We need to set aside the time to explore issues related to common security. We should borrow from the new educational programs developed by the Alternative Defense Network of the Institute for Defense and Disarmament Studies and the Institute for Policy Studies' Real Security Education Program. We must be able to articulate complicated ideas, concerns, and proposals.

Public education and consciousness-raising efforts would attempt to provide a larger, common security perspective to immediate issues, and to take up new concerns. The current debate over the elimination of U.S. and Soviet short- and medium-range missiles might be a good place to begin. A common security education effort would stress the dangers of remaining nuclear weapons in Europe, the possibility of shrinking, not expanding, conventional forces in Europe, and the new grassroots efforts linking peace and human rights activists in both Western and Eastern Europe to end the bloc system.

A movement for common security would also take the offensive on national policy, developing its own policy proposals and creating a new style of lobbying. Appropriate policy initiatives might include the creation of an international satellite monitoring agency to verify arms reduction agreements independently of the superpowers, restructuring NATO forces into a nonnuclear, defensive force, and persuading the major powers to outlaw direct military intervention in the Third World.

A nonintervention regime, as outlined by Randall Forsberg, is a good example of a common security policy proposal. Designed as a step toward ending military intervention, the proposal is a plausible, verifiable step. Because the proposal is multilateral, it could gain wide support, promote national self-determination, and nonmilitary means of conflict resolution.

Lobbying for common security would differ from lobbying as we now know it. We would be more involved in promoting a positive agenda. A program initiated in Rhode Island, the "Peace Mission," is one example of this new kind of lobbying. A coalition of peace groups supports an ongoing lobbying effort with the congressional representatives. Such groups could devote half of their sessions with representatives to discussion of long-term trends in the arms race, the common security perspective, and innovative initiatives to move toward common security.

The third area of common security work, citizen peacemaking, is the most open-ended. In "Making Peace Here and Now" (*Fellowship*, January/February 1987), Andrea Ayvazian and Michael Klare argue that the movement must initiate our own peacemaking projects. The Witness for Peace efforts in Nicaragua and the Natural Resources Defense Council seismic monitoring project, which would help monitor a ban on nuclear weapons testing, are two examples of citizen peacemaking.

Municipal foreign policies, a more official kind of citizen peacemaking, also hold great promise for expanding a common security agenda. Establishment of sister city projects with communities from the Soviet Union, China, and Nicaragua; divestment of public funds from firms doing business in South Africa; development of peace curricula for local high schools; providing incentives for firms to convert from military to socially useful projects; and becoming nuclear free zones are all policies that promote common security.

These initiatives can open new lines of communication, mobilize new constituencies, and build coalitions at home and abroad. We do not simply propose that individuals and organizations currently committed to work on nuclear disarmament issues take up everything else. That would be folly. But we do hope that we can all accelerate our attempts to work more cooperatively by supporting each other's specific struggles and by uniting under an overarching program of common security. The concept and principles of common security can provide us with a positive political program that could lead to the eventual abolition of nuclear weapons and the dramatic enhancement of the true security of all the world's people.

Does Deterrence Work:
People Don't Behave the Way the Theory Says They Should
By Robert Schaeffer
January/February 1988

"THE PRACTICE OF DETERRENCE BY THE UNITED STATES IS UTTERLY primitive," says Cornell University Peace Studies Director Richard Lebow, because it fails to appreciate the psychological factors that affect the behavior of politicians and diplomats.

Deterrence is the theory used to guide U.S. and Soviet nuclear policy. As Richard Betts, a defense policy analyst at the Brookings Institution in Washington, D.C., describes it, deterrence is a way of telling a potential adversary: "If you do this bad thing, we'll kill you. If you don't do it, no problem."

From the American point of view, a "bad thing" is aggression, such as a Soviet invasion of Western Europe or a dramatic change in the global status quo, and the threat to "kill" an adversary is backed up with a ready-to-use arsenal of nuclear weapons. Because deterrence attempts to preserve the status quo and not "coerce the opponent into concessions," which he would describe as "compellence not deterrence," Betts says the theory is a "conservative doctrine."

Lebow would not quarrel with this description of deterrence: "Deterrence—the use of threats to persuade an adversary not to attack—has been around since time immemorial." What's different, he says, is that before states acquired nuclear weapons, "people used to be able to convince themselves that they could win if deterrence failed. Now they can't."

It is the failure of deterrence that concerns Lebow and his colleagues Columbia University political science professor Robert Jervis and University of Toronto political science professor Janice Stein. In their book of essays, *Psychology and Deterrence*, Lebow, Jervis, and Stein examine cases where deterrence has failed. They find that it is the peculiar behavior of politicians in difficult circumstances that caused deterrence to fail. This behavior cannot be explained by the theory, nor can the failure of deterrence be blamed on the faulty implementation of deterrence policy. Instead, the actions taken, which frequently result in war, are the result of psychological factors that undermined the deterrence policy of adversary states.

The behavior of leaders in a crisis can be described as foolhardy and irrational. But given the circumstances facing leaders at the time, their actions can also be understood as resulting from what Lebow calls "motivated" and "unmotivated biases," which are common to sober and rational leaders as well as adventurous ones.

"Unmotivated biases" are what psychologists call the mental shortcuts people take when processing information in a complex, stressful environment. Simply put, unmotivated biases result in the phenomenon of "jumping to conclusions."

Leaders frequently draw conclusions based on partial information before being fully apprised of a developing situation. This leads to errors of judgment and miscalculation, which can be disastrous in a crisis.

When people interpret events to conform with their own pre-existing ideas, or when they refuse to listen to ideas that do not conform with their own views, psychologists say they are acting on the basis of "motivated biases." In popular terms, these people are guilty of "wishful thinking." As Jervis says, "People are taken by surprise because they can't process contrary information. In 1941, U.S. leaders could not believe that the Japanese would attack. And in 1973, the Israelis couldn't believe that the Egyptians would launch a surprise attack across the Suez canal. In both cases, information to the contrary was ignored."

U.S. and Israeli leaders did not think they would be attacked because they could not believe a weaker opponent would initiate a war it would doubtless lose. What U.S. and Israeli leaders did not understand is their adversary's psychology: when faced with a stressful and intolerable situation, many people would rather act badly than not act at all.

Because leaders are subject to errors of motivated and unmotivated bias, they can act in ways that a rational theory of deterrence would not predict. "Deterrence," says Jervis, "is a theory of states as rational actors." But because they are biased, they do not always act "rationally."

Lebow agrees. "Deterrence theory assumes that policymakers make a rational cost calculus before taking the initiative. We find that they convince themselves that they will succeed despite information to the contrary."

Based on their study of a variety of cases, the authors of *Psychology and Deterrence* find that deterrence fails as a result of psychological factors even where the conditions for a credible deterrence policy exist. As Jervis says, "The capability and readiness to wage war does not necessarily deter war."

Deterrence Doesn't Fail

Proponents of deterrence theory argue that the work of Lebow, Jervis, and Stein does not undermine the theory in any fundamental way. Proponents have drawn several lines of argument to defend deterrence and repel its critics.

Writing in *International Security*, John Orme, a professor at Oglethorp University in Atlanta, takes issue with Lebow's interpretation of incidents that demonstrate the "failure" of deterrence. Orme argues that a more accurate interpretation reveals that in each of the cases used by Lebow in his book *Between Peace and War*, "Deterrence failed to deter . . . because of the absence of one of the standard preconditions for its successful operation [commitment, credibility, and capability]; not the irrationality of the challenger."

Although Betts thinks Lebow, Jervis, and Stein's historical scholarship is generally sound and agrees with much of their criticism of deterrence, he cautions, "We have to be careful about drawing too many analogies between cases involving nuclear weapons and ones that involve conventional weapons." Betts points out that the critics rely heavily on an examination of conventional conflicts, many prior to the advent of nuclear weapons, and says, "You have to be careful how far you take it."

A second line of defense is that, by and large, deterrence works. Criticism based on historical case studies and interpretation of psychological factors at work in a crisis does not really change this, according to George Quester, professor of government and political science at the University of Maryland. "Lebow looks at the 'failures' of deterrence," Quester says. "But deterrence doesn't 'fail' when you look nuclear weapons in the eye. I think it's quite remarkable how well deterrence has worked."

Quester is reluctant to describe the examples Lebow, Jervis, and Stein use as "failures" of deterrence. "Would it not be more careful, when considering a crisis that led to war, to begin by saying only that 'deterrence did not occur?'" he asks in a forthcoming paper.

A final line of defense is that there is no alternative to deterrence, or that deterrence is just fine. "What alternative do we have?" Quester asks rhetorically.

Betts is more adamant. Whether or not deterrence "fails"—either for psychological reasons or because the policy is badly applied—Betts believes it is a necessary policy: "There are a range of problems where you *need* to threaten your opponent. There are countries that might attack you if it weren't for deterrence."

Deterrence and Reassurance

Jervis concedes that there is a "real problem generalizing from nonnuclear to nuclear cases. The psychological pressures are the same, but there are a lot of counterpressures in the nuclear cases." But he defends comparative historical research: "At a minimum, these cases are illustrative. Many of them can happen again."

As for the argument that deterrence works generally, Jervis agrees with Quester that U.S.-Soviet deterrence "is more robust than it was in the past. That leads me to be optimistic generally, even though I worry about how deterrence can break down."

Lebow agrees that "general deterrence" between the United States and the Soviet Union works pretty well: "The character of superpower relations and the reality of mutually assured destruction makes people cautious, which is good." But while deterrence in general works, deterrence in practice is bad: "Deterrence leads to counterforce and escalation-dominance strategies. These strategies make war more likely by creating arms races and confirming each country's suspicions of the other. As a way to manage conflict, deterrence has been a disaster."

Although critical of it, neither Lebow or Jervis is willing to discard it. "We don't call for abandoning deterrence," Jervis says, "but we want a better instrument of statecraft."

According to Jervis and Lebow, this improved "instrument" would combine deterrence with "reassurance." "You need to combine the two," Jervis says.

"You have to make sure the other side has a tolerable future, which requires a degree of empathy. States often don't understand how their actions threaten other states. You need both, which is extremely difficult and has been neglected by policymakers."

Betts does not think reassurance should be added to deterrence: "I see more costs associated with reassurance policies than they [Lebow and Jervis] do. My work on surprise attacks suggests that the victims thought their opponents needed to be reassured. Stalin tried to reassure Hitler. It didn't work. This makes me careful about the costs of deterrence."

Lebow disagrees with Betts: "Deterrence theory assumes that resorts to force are opportunity-based. Hitler aside ["Hitlers are very rare," he writes elsewhere, and Hitler could not have been successfully deterred *or* reassured, he argues], the evidence shows that leaders adopt risk responses only when they feel weak.

"Deterrence is like a dam. Deterrence theorists assume that a dam should be strong, and if there is the slightest crack, the onrushing water will inundate the valley below. We think that the relevant problem is not just the crack, but the height of the water behind the dam, which can be managed intelligently. You have to reduce the water pressure on the dam *and* make the dam strong to prevent disaster."

For a Stronger U.N.:
Multilateral Diplomacy is the Key
to Open the Doors for Alternative Defense
By Robert Johansen
July/August 1988

MANY U.S. OFFICIALS AND POLITICAL PUNDITS ARE BEGINNING TO acknowledge, at least in rhetoric, what might be called the first principle of alternative security: that the United States cannot increase its security at the expense of its adversaries' security. Ignoring this principle, by building more threatening weapons for example, only prompts Moscow to deploy more dangerous weapons against the United States, encourages nonnuclear countries to reject nonproliferation efforts, and stimulates Washington's rivals to counter U.S. military influence wherever they can. Yet despite rhetorical acceptance of this first principle, the Reagan administration and Congress have not shown interest in limiting the U.S. arsenal to nonthreatening weapons. Why?

The answer lies not in any difficulty of finding the right formula for a non-offensive defense. The real problem is that the United States and other governments have not *wanted* to limit themselves to defensive weapons. Both the Carter and Reagan administrations built weapons such as the MX and Trident D-5 even though they increased the threat to the Soviet Union and did nothing to reduce the vulnerability of U.S. defenses. Similarly, the United States maintains offensive conventional capabilities in every corner of the world, even where its adversaries are incapable of mounting an attack on the United States.

Most countries claim that their military forces are defensive. U.S. officials, for example, say that U.S. strategic nuclear forces and interventionist conventional capabilities are aimed at defending against the Soviet Union and other adversaries.

But this self-justifying approach to the unilateral use of violence is becoming increasingly impractical. If Washington can unilaterally decide that the use of force in Vietnam and Central America is justified, Moscow can likewise unilaterally decide that force can be used in Afghanistan and Eastern Europe, and Havana can claim a right to support insurgencies in the Caribbean. Iraq unilaterally decided to attack tankers belonging to Iran and other countries. Iran then decided to respond by mining the Persian Gulf and attacking those who have helped Iraq continue the war.

These self-justifying judgments about the use of force are what now obstruct efforts to limit armed forces to self-defense. But there is a way to counter them: through the collective views of many governments. Multilateral diplomacy provides the only available procedure for reinforcing norms against the unilateral use of force. Through successful peacemaking and peacekeeping, multilateralism can reduce the major powers' reliance on force.

The United Nations represents the clearest model and yet a disappointing embodiment of multilateralism: its 159 member nations agree in principle to the Charter ban on aggressive uses of force, but it has fallen far short of its potential for limiting violence. There are two areas, however—peacekeeping and global monitoring—where increased multilateral action under U.N. auspices could enhance U.S. and worldwide security. A more serious commitment by the peace movement to promoting these activities could help open a path toward non-offensive defense.

Peacekeeping

Ad hoc U.N. peacekeeping forces have succeeded in dampening conflicts in a half dozen historical cases. In Cyprus in the early 1960s, U.N. forces helped contain conflict between Greeks and Turks. U.N. forces interposed themselves between Egyptian and Israeli forces after the 1956 Suez conflict and in the 1970s after the Yom Kippur War. They quieted a brief civil war in Lebanon in 1958 and tried again in the late 1970s, with less success.

These experiences have demonstrated the promise of U.N. peacekeeping. But they also illustrate the institutional weaknesses that hamper its effectiveness. There are a few basic changes, however, that could correct those weaknesses.

First, the United Nations needs a permanent transnational police force, so that it could, in times of crisis, immediately deploy a highly trained, integrated force. Second, U.N. peacekeepers should be individually recruited from among volunteers throughout the world, rather than being drawn from member countries' armed forces. These changes would give U.N. peacekeepers an even stronger reputation for reliability and political impartiality, which in turn would make countries more willing to rely upon U.N. peacekeepers rather than resort to unilateral force.

Third, the U.N. secretary general should be given advance authority to deploy peacekeeping forces at any time he or she determines they are needed. Currently, the Security Council delays the deployment of such forces when its members fail to come to agreement.

To overcome this problem, Washington should invite Moscow and other members of the Security Council to agree in advance, on an informal and experimental basis, not to use their veto power to obstruct enforcement undertaken by the secretary general along tense borders and within carefully prescribed guidelines. To prevent injudicious use of these forces, the Council could retain the power to terminate a deployment by a simple majority vote.

A well-trained peacekeeping force bearing the authority of the United Nations could prevent border incidents from erupting into war, discourage superpower interventions, and deter aggression by adventurist smaller powers. Such a force might have prevented the Vietnam-Kampuchea conflict, Iraq's invasion of Iran, Syrian and Israeli attacks on the Palestinian Liberation Organization within Lebanon, violations of the Honduran-Nicaraguan border, and clandestine troop movements between Libya and Chad, Libya and Sudan, and South Africa and Angola.

A successful standing U.N. force, enjoying the legitimacy of the world community, would develop a reputation for greater effectiveness than the armed forces of small countries acting on their own or even backed by an external military power. This in turn would stimulate a powerful new idea: that U.N.-protected countries are a realistic possibility. Rather than maintaining a full-scale national military force with offensive capabilities, countries could avail themselves of U.N. protection. This would pave the way for regional or global arrangements strictly limiting national forces to nonoffensive defense.

Global Monitoring

An international monitoring agency, utilizing on-site U.N. inspectors and advanced seismic and surveillance technology, could further enhance U.N. peacekeeping capabilities. Such an agency would warn of and help deter surprise attacks, collect evidence to confirm or deny alleged border violations, monitor cease-fires, assist U.N. peacekeeping missions and observer patrols, discourage clandestine tests of missiles or warheads, hamper covert operations aimed at manipulating political events in small countries, and reinforce confidence-building measures anywhere in the world.

An international agency, working independently from national intelligence agencies in Washington, Moscow, and elsewhere, would draw on less partisan information to evaluate conflicting claims about violations of arms control treaties or U.N. Charter prohibitions against the use of force.

Domestically, an international monitoring agency could provide a check on the abuse of intelligence reports for partisan political purposes. Additional sources of information could deter violations of U.S. law or congressional intent, such as apparently occurred in the Reagan administration's funding of the Nicaraguan contras. For Congress, U.N.-provided data would also help corroborate or disprove allegations by Washington or Moscow about violations of arms treaties.

Building Support

Multilateralism is too often scoffed at by U.S. officials, except when it involves partnerships within its own military bloc. The early Reagan administration portrayed the United Nations as either impotent or anti-American. The prevailing popular view still sees a beleaguered United States victimized by hostile Third World countries and the Soviet bloc voting in concert against U.S. interests.

But the Reagan administration itself has recently softened its assault on the United Nations, requesting funding for U.N. dues from a by-now reluctant Congress. And outside the United States, support has grown among many Third World countries and middle-range powers for expanded U.N. peacemaking and peacekeeping. More than 120 countries have indicated support for an International Satellite Monitoring Agency. And although there have been no specific proposals for a standing U.N. force, there is growing support for the idea of using multilateral forces in situations such as the Persian Gulf, the Soviet withdrawal from Afghanistan, and any future Palestinian-Israeli settlement.

There is another positive sign: the Soviet Union, which for years viewed the United Nations with deep skepticism, has under Mikhail Gorbachev renewed its financial commitment to the organization and expressed an interest in U.N.-sponsored monitoring and peacekeeping.

Yet many countries look to the United States for leadership on global issues, and it is here that the peace movement must make its case for a stronger United Nations. A post-Reagan administration—Democratic or Republican—will present a fresh opportunity to do just that.

CHAPTER

FIVE

The Movement Part Two:
Transitions 1984–1989

Election Lessons to Build On
By David Corn
December 1984

FOR ARMS CONTROL ADVOCATES, THE REAL DAY AFTER HIT NOVEMBER 7. It wasn't a bolt out of the blue. The landslide that reelected Ronald Reagan, who for many in the antinuclear movement personified the arms race and the Cold War, was long in coming. Still, it crushed the hopes of activists who believed the nuclear issue could help elect a president more sympathetic to their cause.

But while few positive signs can be found in the staggering defeat of Walter Mondale, Election Day did hold some victories for proponents of arms control. In the Senate contests, Representatives Paul Simon and Tom Harkin, Democrats who boast solid records on arms control, were able to defeat incumbent Republicans who strongly supported Reagan's nuclear arms policies. And in the House, most of the representatives who make up the informal arms control bloc survived Reagan's massive victory and won reelection, many in spite of strong and well-financed opponents who had clutched Reagan's coattails. Of the 12 vulnerable incumbents on the American Security Council's "Anti-Defense Dozen" list, for example, only three representatives were defeated.

Though the electorate overwhelmingly endorsed Reagan, no ideology achieved a true mandate. And Reagan, the engineer of a tremendous military buildup, was forced to talk peace to overrun Mondale, who tried, with limited persistence and effectiveness, to turn the freeze and Star Wars into issues.

Damn Lucky
Following the elections, movement leaders began to put the best face possible on the results. The bottom line analysis was that arms control and other progressive forces were able to stem the Reagan tide in Congress. "We are damn

lucky to have done as well as we did, given the presidential campaign," says Mike Mawby of SANE PAC. David Riley of Friends of the Earth PAC notes that the PAC went 17 for 25 in its top priority races. Around 70 percent of Freeze Voter '84-backed candidates who were in "marginal races" won, according to Bill Curry, director of that PAC. And the movement's gain in the Senate may finally produce an anti-MX majority.

But all challengers—save one—in House races endorsed by movement PACs lost. And nationally, the subject of arms control never gained the prominence that many movement activists had hoped to see. In fact, it was Reagan who most effectively manipulated the war and peace issue, as evidenced by the infamous "bear-in-the-woods" television ads.

If one measured the outcome against the movement rhetoric tossed around earlier this year, then the election results can only be taken as disappointing. Bill Curry called for a "congressional build-down," trading pro-freeze politicians for anti-freeze lawmakers. Dr. Helen Caldicott, on the stump, exclaimed last April that the movement had seven months left to save the world—that is, to prevent a Reagan victory. Promises were made about the dramatic effects of registration drives and the gender gap. "I believe the 1984 elections will probably represent the final big test for the freeze movement," Randall Forsberg, the author of the freeze, wrote last January. Yet in the only direct test of the issue, voters in South Dakota rejected a freeze referendum.

So was all the rhetoric overblown? Truth is, it doesn't matter after the fact. "The important message," says Randy Kehler, the national coordinator of the Freeze Campaign, "is that the American people are in favor of a freeze but they don't feel the freeze is an urgent necessity. To them it's not more important than short-term economics or personalities." The same can be said for arms control in general. The movement, despite the hoopla and energy exhibited by some activists, was just not able to push the arms race to the center stage in the national political debate. Some activists who work in Washington, D.C., suggest that given the dynamics of the presidential race, perhaps it was unrealistic to expect this. The movement just doesn't wield such clout yet.

To some organizers who scorned electoral involvement, the results confirmed their suspicions. "This was to have been a watershed year for advocates of a nuclear weapons freeze," says Norman Solomon, disarmament director for the Fellowship of Reconciliation. "Instead 1984 turned into a washout." And what is worse, he adds, is that the nuclear weapons issue "slipped away. . . . In many ways abhorrence of nuclear war and even of its weaponry has become a non-sequitur of American political parlance, which can be pressed into the service of buildups, build-downs, or anything else."

The Cash Crunch

Though claims are made that the nomination of a pro-freeze Democratic presidential candidate, the inclusion of the moratorium concept in the Democratic platform, and even Reagan's swing in rhetoric all represent progress for the movement, activists, asked to cite gains in the electoral arena, usually point to organizational development and local races.

For example, Council for a Livable World and its affiliate Peace PAC raised slightly over $1 million for pro-arms control candidates—just about double the amount it raised in 1982. For Harkin (a member of the board of SANE), it raised $133,600. That's close to the entire amount Harkin received from all of organized labor. SANE PAC channeled $200,000 in funds and services into several campaigns. Freeze Voter '84, according to Curry, raised over $2.6 million, signed up 1,000 full-time volunteers and fielded a paid staff of close to 200. Women's Action for Nuclear Disarmament (WAND) PAC, in addition to contributing volunteers and money, produced radio spots that featured Caldicott endorsing candidates. And the Committee for a Strong Peaceful America, formerly the Peace Media Project, acquired about $750,000 in air time for radio and television commercials that stressed the importance of considering the arms race when voting for a candidate.

So what did all this accomplish? "There is a solid group of peace leaders on the Hill who can now say for the first time that the peace movement really put its money where its mouth is," SANE PAC's Mawby asserts. "When the crunch came, we helped."

Following his victory, Senator-elect Simon noted Freeze Voter's contribution to his campaign. Bob Stein, director of Illinois Freeze Voter, estimates that his group (utilizing over 1,000 volunteers), and other freeze activists identified more than 50,000 pro-freeze Simon supporters for the candidate's get-out-the-vote drive. Kim Tilley of the Simon campaign maintains that all of the arms control PACs were "invaluable for us" especially considering that Simon won by 71,000 votes out of more than 4.5 million cast. A spokesperson for the Harkin campaign also cited a "very active peace constituency" as one reason for Harkin's victory.

Kevin Smith, the campaign manager for Representative Les AuCoin, a leading MX opponent who won a tough reelection fight, maintains that "staff support from the peace movement had a major impact on the outcome of the race." Staffers from SANE PAC and Freeze Voter were at the helm of both the phone banking and canvassing operations of the AuCoin campaign in Oregon. "Because so much attention was focused on this race, by sending Les AuCoin back to the House we sent a message to other members," says Smith. "Those middle-of-the-road members, who watch which way the political wind blows, will see you can be a leader in arms control and still be reelected."

Although freeze and arms control issues never gained great prominence in the presidential campaign, in some states and congressional districts they played a significant role.

The issue appears to have helped Representative George Brown, a leading antisatellite (ASAT) weapons opponent who was targeted by pro-space weapons organizations, for example. According to a spokesperson for Brown, the "defense question" was a big issue in the campaign, with Brown's challenger, John Paul

Stark, lining up with Reagan on Star Wars. Yet in what was expected to be a tight race, Brown, a Democrat, survived the Reagan sweep, beating Stark by a greater margin than in 1982.

Mondale Got Grief

But peace and arms control is far from an automatic vote-getter, as strong pro-freeze Senate candidates such as Joan Growe in Minnesota and Nancy Dick in Colorado discovered. In New Mexico, state senator Judith Pratt, a peace activist, faced Senator Peter Domenici, the powerful Republican chair of the Budget Committee. Pratt hit hard at military spending and highlighted the freeze. Domenici struck back, citing his strong support for the military. Pratt was swamped, winning only 28 percent of the vote. Her campaign illustrates the obstacles peace candidates face in areas where the local economy is dependent on military spending.

"Our economy is not diversified," says Dede Feldman, Pratt's press secretary. "All we have is mining, agriculture, and the military." And a lot of the work on space weapons is expected to take place in the state. So is electoral work in such a situation worthwhile? Feldman notes that the Pratt campaign did mobilize a new constituency in the state. "We raised the issues," says Feldman. "That's a victory in and of itself. We'll take any we can get."

Many other challengers who focused on the freeze went down swinging. In Maine, Libby Mitchell, who made the freeze and PAC spending the cornerstones of her campaign, was soundly beaten by Senator William Cohen of "build-down" fame. In Pennsylvania, state senator Joseph Hoeffel tried to make much of the fact that Representative Lawrence Coughlin changed his vote to oppose the freeze in the last minutes of the 1982 House debate on the freeze. To prove his arms control credentials, Coughlin played up his role in opposing ASATs. "Both jockeyed to be viewed as the peace candidate," says Charlie Kraybill, a SANE PAC staffer who worked on the Hoeffel campaign. Hoeffel lost by 13 percent.

In the presidential race, the Democratic challenger never seemed to find the way to turn the arms control issue into a positive campaign despite his professed support for the freeze and various weapons moratoria. This failure—combined with the occasional hawkish remark, such as his threat to quarantine Nicaragua—turned off some movement activists, who concentrated their efforts on local races. But Karen Mulhauser, executive director of Citizens Against Nuclear War, who took a leave of absence to work on the Mondale campaign, notes that Mondale believed the movement failed to deliver the backing he deserved.

"Mondale and his advisers thought he had taken a leadership role on the freeze," Mulhauser explains. "He talked about it. It was in his literature. And all he got was grief, with people in the movement saying his position was not strong enough, that he's not for no-first-use and that he won't cut the military budget." So Mondale pulled back, and a vicious spiral drove the movement and the campaign apart.

Panacea Later?

As far as lessons go, there are plenty—both positive and negative—to be found. Many activists learned the hard way that in American politics the agendas in national campaigns are largely determined at the top. Influencing the debate, then, is much tougher than some activists presumed it to be. And many canvassers found that there was a good deal of basic education still to be done. They discovered, for example, that a surprisingly high percentage of freeze supporters believed that Reagan had endorsed the freeze.

Another lesson: there are no panaceas. Registration as a partisan tool only works if the other side does not counter. All the talk earlier this year about Democratic, black, and progressive registration drives spurred the Republicans and their allies, such as the Moral Majority, to register their own. In many areas of the West and South, Republican-oriented registration drives found more recruits than those that may have favored Democrats.

And the gender gap, which was once hailed by women's peace groups, was no magic cure for Reaganism. Though it may have played a role in some close House and Senate races, in the presidential contest the gap was only about 4 percent (compared to 10 percent four years ago) with 57 percent of women voters endorsing Reagan, according to a CBS News/*New York Times* poll.

But helping incumbents retain their seats and aiding a few successful challengers has encouraged those working with arms control PACs. They cite their participation in these races, their ability to raise more funds and motivate more volunteers than in 1982 as yet another sign of the ever-growing political sophistication of the movement. And they look forward to 1986—when the Senate class of 1986, those conservative Republicans whom Reagan brought in, face reelection. Of the 34 senators up for reelection then, 22 are Republicans, many of them vulnerable.

But there remains disappointment that the issue—as a paramount concern—never took off on its own. What does that mean for the movement? Representative Ronald Dellums maintains that the movement must stick with the fundamentals. And Randy Kehler notes that the movement cannot simply rely on sympathetic politicians to make its case. Mondale, like many politicians who support but may not understand the freeze, acted "as if the freeze was his soft 'left' plank, which he had to protect at all times," Kehler asserts.

"We need to recreate the climate of urgency regarding the nuclear arms race," Kehler explains. "We have not yet succeeded in conveying that sense of emergency." And to do so requires increased personal commitment. "If we really thought the world could come to an end in a matter of years, why aren't we making larger changes in our own lives?" Kehler asks. "We thought we could stop the nuclear arms race without that—get a majority with us, a few votes in Congress, win some elections and stop the arms race."

That certainly didn't occur in 1984. And the overwhelming message dictated by the electorate is that those who want to end the arms race still have a lot of convincing to do.

Freeze Debates Direct Action
By Renata Rizzo
January/February 1985

FOR THE FIRST TIME IN THE FREEZE CAMPAIGN'S FIVE-YEAR HISTORY THE subject of civil disobedience has been summoned from the periphery of national debate. Randy Kehler may have set the tone for this when, in his welcoming speech in St. Louis, he spoke of "the power of personal example . . . of putting oneself on the line." There is no doubt that legislative and electoral work form the essence of Freeze strategy. But the fifth national convention—sensitive to a political climate where Congress members are being arrested protesting apartheid, and responsive to the months of work undertaken by its own Direct Action Task Force—took a historic step in grappling officially with civil disobedience and direct action.

"What a difference I've seen," said task force member Jim Rice of Sojourners. "In 1981, there was a proposal to start a direct action task force, but it got very little support, and the idea just died. This time the task force was formed, funded, and supported. And people have been talking about the issue all year."

For the ten members of the DATF the convention signaled the conclusion to months of often frustrating work. Their original strategy, which was presented to the Campaign's executive and strategy committees last spring, was a stronger paper than the one that eventually reached the convention floor. Among other things, it called for actions to begin on Martin Luther King's birthday (January 15), a massive August 6 action at the Nevada Test Site involving waves of freeze activists shutting it down for 30 to 90 days, an illegal tax resistance plan, and pressure tactics (such as sit-ins) at local congressional offices. The idea was to construct a series of coordinated, escalating actions that would stir the public's conscience and bring about a national crisis.

But by the time the DATF's third strategy draft was issued, the Campaign's executive committee voted to remove it from the main strategy proposal and offer it instead as a separate report. A statement issued by the strategy and executive committees of the Campaign declared: "We believe that the National Freeze Campaign should not take on nonviolent civil disobedience as part of its strategy at this time."

"There was a lot of conflict over this," task force member Nancy Hale from Oregon says. "The executive committee felt the grassroots weren't ready for it. Our feeling was, 'Fine—let them see it and let them say no.'"

Terms of Debate

At the convention the biggest problem was definition. Much debate—and some confusion—arose over the meaning of the term "direct action." To the task force, it means "taking direct responsibility" for getting a freeze, including lobbying and a wide range of legal activities—as well as civil disobedience (or "CD" as it's often referred to). There was a general feeling among delegates that the real debate—and the one that could be divisive—was over whether to endorse civil disobedience, since the Freeze Campaign had already been engaging in other forms of "direct action."

But Jim Rice and other members of the DATF saw the essential debate lying in the specific strategy proposals—often lost sight of amid larger issues—put forth by the task force. "At issue here is the Nevada Test Site action, at issue here is tax resistance," Rice said midway through the convention. "This is *not* a blanket debate about CD."

But even when the issue of CD was focused on specific actions, was the Campaign ready to endorse it?

As the weekend unfolded, many signs were negative. One argument—which soon began to sound like the convention's Greek Chorus—was voiced by many at the "top" of the organization, and seconded by innumerable delegates: While *I'm* not against CD personally, Campaign endorsement of it will alienate the millions of reachable people out there who *are*.

"People are really afraid the movement will become radicalized," Randall Forsberg, author of the freeze, said. "And the fact is, we haven't exhausted all our other routes yet. In a way, CD is a cop-out—you're giving up on the legislative and electoral channels." And, Forsberg said, CD can foster an unattractive sense of self-righteousness. "Relatively speaking, it's easy to say 'I know the answer and I'm going to do what's *right*,'" Forsberg said, echoing a reservation Kehler—who is personally in favor of CD—raised about the tactic. "Sometimes it's harder to talk to people who disagree with you than to lie down on the tracks."

Many activists, like Mike Kelly of Illinois, who helped introduce an anti-CD amendment at the plenary session, argue that CD would seem like a unilateral strategy to the American public. And, of course, there's the fundamental problem of having no "bad laws"—like apartheid—to confront directly. In the absence of a one-to-one correlation between an illegal act and an unjust law, the chances of public misperception are great.

But the fear of public alienation cropped up so often that several people wondered if the Freeze Campaign is more interested in not offending anyone than in ending the arms race. "It's not just fear of alienating the grass-roots, although that's essential," said Raoul Rosenberg, executive director of the Downstate New York Freeze. "We might also lose some powerful sympathizers—people like George Kennan, who believe we should work through channels."

Alienation works both ways, of course, and CD partisans wondered how Campaign disavowal of the tactic would affect the thousands of antinuclear protesters who were arrested last year, and those who support them. Many were worried that the Freeze Campaign would disenfranchise portions of the religious community, which has taken a leading role in CD. And there are those, like Jane Gruenebaum, one of the Campaign's interim directors, who argue that the Freeze Campaign should encourage all types of citizen pressure. "There's always the potential for a positive effect," she said, "as long as the actions are carried out with a clear moral imperative, dignity, and clarity."

Gruenebaum was probably thinking of the South African embassy protests, which for many people legitimized illegal tactics almost overnight. Some people at the convention remarked that resistance through civil disobedience is becoming more respectable.

"The time is not here yet, but I think it's approaching," Randy Kehler predicts, "when we can ask famous people to join us in CD. We don't have that one-to-one correlation that is so clear with the South African apartheid laws. But we *do* have the advantage of an overwhelming danger."

A substantial number of activists pointed out that even if the Freeze Campaign did endorse CD, local groups would still have the autonomy to do as they pleased. But if the Campaign, in its plenary vote, deliberately excluded the tactic—thus in effect dictating strategy—the movement could become fractured, its strength crippled.

The Vote and Beyond

The running debate over CD continued through the weekend, in formal group discussions and synthesis conferences, and informally over coffee breaks and meals. When the DATF's report finally came up for a vote amid the din of the plenary session, it was no longer entirely cohesive, and it did not call for the National Freeze Campaign to spearhead a single illegal action. But it did include the following proposals:

• to sponsor and help organize the April mobilization in Washington, D.C.;

• to organize illegal and legal tax resistance;

• to encourage national coordinated local activities (with emphasis on nuclear weapons facilities) from August 6–9;

• to endorse the August 6–9 activities, including civil disobedience, at the Nevada Test Site;

• to organize a fall Moratorium Day.

And after all the debating and talk of floor fights and close votes, all but two of these proposals—illegal tax resistance and the Moratorium Day—passed easily. Clearly a lot of opinions had been swayed. In addition, the Central America "contingency plan"—including support for its CD element—passed. In fact, in some instances, proposals were toughened up considerably by amendments passed on the floor. For example, in declaring what tactics might be considered by groups lobbying at local congressional offices, the delegates deleted the deliberately ambiguous phrase "more assertive activities" and replaced it with "sit-ins."

To erase any doubt about the convention's mandate, anti-CD amendments that came up—saying essentially that CD is not an appropriate tactic for the Campaign to either endorse or encourage—were voted down with very little heated debate.

Several clear messages emerged from the convention. An obvious one is that the grassroots want to maintain local autonomy in areas like CD. Another is that the Campaign has recognized the necessity for a variety of tactics—hopefully working in concert—to help bring about a freeze. A third is that Freeze sentiment is moving, albeit slowly, from protest to resistance.

As the DATF continues its work this year (carrying out another convention mandate) it will concentrate on education. The need for it was apparent in St. Louis, where CD was sometimes defined as "throwing rocks," and often fearfully identified with the radical tactics of the 1960s.

According to task force members, their job will also include "wrapping the American flag" around CD, tying it into American history. And they plan to get into the nuts and bolts of the tactic.

In addition to education, the DATF will lobby to place someone on the Campaign's staff in Washington, D.C., to work specifically on direct action. And at next year's convention, the DATF will present a position paper on CD that will establish guidelines and procedures for endorsing the tactic as a truly national campaign.

While many activists came to St. Louis expecting a splintering over civil disobedience, they left with a strong sense of unity. Hale views the outcome as "really supportive" and "a good expansion in tactics." And Harold Nash, author of one of the anti-CD amendments, was satisfied, too. "We did vote against illegal tax resistance," says the former technical director of a major Navy laboratory in Groton, Connecticut. "And we're basically leaving the rest up to local groups. I wouldn't want to be in an organization that *sponsors* CD." But then, in an uncanny echo of Randy Kehler's opening speech, Nash adds, "But I have to say that I respect the commitment of people who feel so strongly that they'll put themselves on the line for it."

Perhaps next year a stronger direct action strategy will reach the convention floor. But for now, few are finding fault with a program that sent both sides home happy. Those who wind up in jail this year can take heart at the surprising level of support for CD exhibited in St. Louis. Those who would prefer to stay clear of the law can be comfortable with the fact that the Campaign won't be organizing or sponsoring CD events of its own. Whether planned or not, it was an astute compromise.

Is There a Peace Candidate? Does It Really Matter?
By Donna Eberwine
January/February 1988

THEY'VE BEEN CALLED BORING, HARD-TO-DISTINGUISH, LACKING STATure. Indeed, until scandals forced Joe Biden and Gary Hart out of the race, they were "the seven dwarves." For the peace movement, however, the Democrats are the good guys. Their Republic counterparts think arms control is a four-letter word.

But is there in the 1988 Democratic lineup a "peace candidate"—someone the peace movement can identify with, rally around, and help put in the White House?

"That's the wrong question," says Chip Reynolds, executive director of Freeze Voter. "The question is 'Who are the candidates we can work with to stop the arms race, and what will it take to do that?'"

The view is one shared by many in the peace movement as the campaign season heats up. Leading peace activists say they are shunning the search for a perfect candidate with the "right" stand on everything from Trident II to contra aid. Instead, they are setting what they see as a broader agenda: to keep peace issues alive in election-year debates, to promote friendly—if imperfect—candidates while trying to influence their positions, and to lay the groundwork for future progress toward peace no matter which candidate wins.

This approach is in part a response to a more favorable political climate. The election season is coming on the heels of significant victories for the peace movement in Congress, including a moratorium on antisatellite (ASAT) weapons testing, cuts in Star Wars funding, and limits on the administration's ability to depart from the 1972 Anti-Ballistic Missile and SALT II treaties. More important, Ronald Reagan's own negotiations for the INF Treaty with the Soviets have given arms control new respectability.

"Our issues have matured and become more mainstream," says Nancy Donaldson, political director of Women's Action for Nuclear Disarmament. "Today the country is behind these issues, not just the peace movement."

That growing national consensus has not fazed the Republican candidates—perhaps in part because polls show arms control, while favored, is low among voters' concerns. But all of the Democrats have responded by adopting what arms control advocates see as basically "good positions—the major reason few activists are urging that the movement latch onto a single candidate.

"The [Democratic] candidates are so close together on our issues," says Dan Houston, SANE/FREEZE political director, "we want to encourage groups to get involved in all the campaigns." "We're working on as many campaigns as possible," agrees Donaldson.

It is not just the absence of an obvious "peace candidate" that has peace activists pursuing this strategy. "Our goal is for each candidate to have the experience of an ongoing relationship with voters and the progressive community on [peace] issues," says Donaldson, "to have influence now and later on their decisionmaking."

On the national level, the strategy means peace leaders are trying to get inside campaigns to influence policy. Donaldson, for example, has volunteered for the Gephardt campaign. She has watched the candidate face strong pressure from advisers concerned with capturing the conservative southern swing vote—expected to be decisive come Super Tuesday on March 8.

"Whenever Gephardt gives a speech on arms control, foreign policy, or military reform, there are people [in his campaign] who try to pull him to the right," she says. By "becoming part of the decision-making process," a well-placed peace activist can help keep a friendly candidate on track.

Freeze Voter is urging activists to use election-year debate to give peace issues a boost, by trying to influence the way candidates shape their positions. Given the Democrats' bemoaned lack of distinction, Reynolds believes the moment is ripe.

"This time around we have the opportunity to help define symbols and images that were already defined for us in 1984," says Reynolds. "The challenge is to shape them in a way that benefits the candidates *and* the issues: defining arms control issues so they resonate positively with American voters; redefining the meaning of American strength."

Freeze Voter is drawing on the work of pollster Stanley Greenberg and others that shows voters today are less afraid of the Soviet Union, less supportive of a military buildup, and more concerned with economic than military strength.

"There's now a strong plurality of the American public that is convinced we cannot continue to increase military spending," says Reynolds. "Large segments of the public are more interested in spending money on domestic needs. The way you talk about this [cuts in military spending] is by pointing out that national security is strengthened by strong education, a strong economy, as well as by maintaining an adequate defense."

If activists in 1988 are less concerned with finding and endorsing a perfect "peace candidate" than with building working relationships with all the Democratic candidates, some say it is a reflection of the peace movement's coming of age.

"The whole movement has gotten more politically sophisticated since the 1984 elections," says Karen Mulhauser, who in December resigned as director of Citizens Against Nuclear War to become more directly involved in electoral politics. Activists who relentlessly dogged the candidates during the last election, Mulhauser says, "marginalized" the peace movement and "contributed to an environment in which a Democrat could not be elected." Now, she says, peace activists are urging each other "to find a candidate who supports your issue and get involved in his campaign and in delegate selection."

While that approach to the 1988 elections is shared widely in the peace movement, it has some observers perplexed.

"If the criterion is who is prepared to take leadership in building a world at peace, it seems to me you have only one choice—and that's [Jesse] Jackson," says Robert Borosage, director of the Institute for Policy Studies and an adviser to the Jackson campaign. Jackson's supporters argue he is the only candidate with grassroots origins, making him the peace movement's natural ally. And beyond having the right stands on arms control, they say he has an entire agenda—nonintervention, respect for international law and promotion of human rights—for building world peace. If peace activists do not endorse Jackson,

Borosage says, it is because they are pursuing too "technocratic" an agenda—or else they see him as "unelectable" and are "picking a winner rather than [a candidate] who represents them."

Some peace leaders admit their strategy hedges bets on who is likely to win. But their reluctance to throw the peace movement's weight behind any one candidate, they say, has more to do with trying to expand the movement's influence.

While Washington activists—the "beltway insiders"—are working on national campaigns, activists at the local level are sticking to other time-tested methods. Some are running as delegates to the Democratic convention—or trying to influence delegate selection—in hopes that peace activists will have some say when the party drafts its platform. Others are combining grassroots organizing with electoral work, emphasizing voter registration and turnout.

"We're connecting issues that affect people daily—farm issues, social security, medicare—to the need to cut the defense budget," says Linda Stout, director of the Piedmont Peace Project, in Concord, North Carolina. When those connections are drawn, "people vote the right way—you don't have to tell them how to vote."

Local activists are also using traditional "bird-dog" tactics at public candidate forums, to keep the issues alive and the candidates honest. "It's critical to pin them down on what they're going to do," says Bob Brammer, a founding member of Stop the Arms Race Political Action Committee, in Iowa. "We're very conscious of the difference between saying lots of very nice things and promises that they would undertake upon taking office."

A year ago, STARPAC sent the candidates questionnaires asking their positions on key issues, with questions phrased in what Brammer calls "promise-language form." "We asked them not 'What do you think about a test ban?' but 'Do you pledge a U.S. moratorium on testing and then to proceed to negotiate [with the Soviets]?'"

The early work has satisfied STARPAC that all the Democrats are "locked into" a comprehensive test ban. All but Gore oppose a ban on flight tests of ballistic missiles. And all are on record supporting cuts in Star Wars funding, reductions in the overall military budget, and compliance with SALT II and the ABM Treaty.

Some campaign aides complain that the process has been precisely one of litmus testing—a charge Brammer denies: "Admittedly, people look very carefully at the issues. But a litmus test implies, if you're wrong on one issue—say Trident II—you're off our list. That's not true. Some may have wrong positions, but sometimes their wrong positions are quite sophisticated. If anything, it's a leadership test."

One candidate who has failed that test is Sen. Albert Gore of Tennessee. Last September, Gore used a STARPAC-sponsored foreign policy debate to attack his fellow Democrats as being "soft" on defense. It was a calculated gamble to win over the southern swing vote, but it cost the candidate STARPAC's support.

Brammer denies that Gore fell victim to any litmus test: "Gore has been pretty good on most of the issues. But when you exaggerate the differences, call others out of the mainstream, and run away from your own record, that's what we don't like."

Others are not so quick to bristle at the idea that they are too tough on candidates. While national peace leaders argue that all the Democrats are "good" on a handful of issues, some local activists say the candidates don't begin to touch the movement's longer-term goals, such as "deep cuts" in nuclear arsenals, a no-first-strike doctrine, or eventual disarmament. While presidential contenders may be unwilling to adopt such policies, some believe grassroots activists should use election-year debates to voice more far-reaching demands.

Randy Kehler, former national coordinator for the Freeze Campaign, calls it "helping to build an alternative, pushing back the parameters of the debate." It is work, he says, that is best done outside campaigns. "Working for a candidate almost by definition puts a straitjacket on you," he says. "Someone has to carry the banner for what we really want, rather than what we think we can get."

Those who have decided to immerse themselves in the electoral process admit they are going somewhat easy on the candidates. Campaign debate may not be "quite as issue-focused as we'd like it," says Ann Edgerton, an Iowa Democratic county chair and member of WAND's board of directors. "But we have to look at electability. We have to deal with the American public, not just ourselves."

Furthermore, it can be easier to achieve progress on arms control with a president who is seen as "tough" on foreign policy. Freeze Voter's Reynolds cites the atmospheric test ban, negotiated by Kennedy after the Cuban missile crisis, and the ABM Treaty, negotiated by Nixon. "If we press hard for all our issues and force commitments from candidates, we run the risk of making them unelectable or unable to push our issues in office," he says.

Unperturbed by that dilemma, groups like STARPAC are already considering turning their evaluations of candidates into endorsements—if not of any perfect peace candidate, of the one candidate they think is best. Endorsements are "the name of the game in politics," says Brammer, and particularly effective in Iowa, where peace activists wield considerable influence in the state's February precinct caucuses—the lead-off contest of the election year.

But given the relatively few differences between the Democrats, STARPAC is proceeding cautiously. Many of its members are leaning strongly toward Sen. Paul Simon of Illinois. But others are equally enthusiastic about Jackson, Gov. Michael Dukakis, or former Governor Bruce Babbitt. STARPAC is trying to solve its dilemma by supplementing any endorsement with a list of other "affirmable" candidates.

At the national level, peace groups are likely to avoid endorsements altogether. "In general, we've tried not to identify ourselves with any one party," says David Cortright, codirector of SANE/FREEZE, which makes endorsements only in congressional races. Some fear endorsements can spark criticism that a candidate is vulnerable to "interest group" pressure. Others caution that being too close to the Democrats can undermine efforts to influence moderate Republicans in Congress.

Congress—and congressional races—remains at least as high as the presidential race among activists' priorities in 1988. At stake is what Freeze Voter's Reynolds terms "the ability to actually stop the arms race rather than talk about stopping it."

Donaldson agrees: "In order for any president to succeed [in advancing peace], we'll need a Congress that will support him in ratifying treaties and in legislation."

Cortright says SANE/FREEZE recommends "a lot of action on presidential races up to the convention, when the primary season has candidates most open to citizen pressure." Then, "it's Senate and House races," he says, prescribing a dose of realism: "In the general elections, we're talking about 60 million voters and hundreds of millions of dollars. It's hard then to have any influence."

What Next?
March/April 1989

THE U.S. PEACE MOVEMENT IS AT A CROSSROADS. GONE ARE THE HEADY days of the freeze campaign, when millions joined its ranks. Today, in the wake of the INF Treaty, it has lost members and visibility.

But the peace movement has also matured—from a chorus screaming "no" at the Reagan administration to a diverse collection of organizations, each working largely behind the scenes and, to some extent, with its own audience and agenda.

Where the peace movement goes from here will be in large measure dictated by the political climate. Internationally, Mikhail Gorbachev set the stage in his speech before the United Nations last December, in which he promised unilateral cuts in Soviet military forces and urged international cooperation to settle regional conflicts, promote development, and address global environmental problems. At home, the Bush administration has signaled it prefers to "go slow" in responding to Gorbachev. But the pressure—both economic and political—to end the Cold War has never been greater.

How will the peace movement respond to these challenges? We asked the leaders of a dozen organizations; their answers follow.

Time for Deep Cuts
"Recent changes in the security policies and domestic economies of the United States and Soviet Union provide a historic opportunity for serious steps toward ending the arms race and the Cold War. Ronald Reagan's about-face on arms control and Mikhail Gorbachev's dramatic proposals have made deep cuts in nuclear weapons arsenals politically acceptable for the new administration.

"The Council for a Livable World believes that the immediate goal of the Bush administration and arms control community in the next six months should be completion of a Strategic Arms Reduction Treaty. Once that agreement has been ratified, the country has an opportunity—unprecedented since World War II—to adopt fundamentally different politics.

"In the next four years, the Council intends to pursue treaties and policies that have as immediate goals:

"• deep cuts in nuclear arsenals, to the point where no country maintains more than a minimum deterrent force of 1,000 or fewer nuclear weapons;

"• a nuclear force reconfigured to provide the least destabilizing posture possible;

"• narrowing the role of nuclear weapons to the deterrence of nuclear attack;

"• an end to underground testing of nuclear warheads;

"• preventing an arms race in space;

"• an international effort to prevent the spread of nuclear and chemical weapons to other countries; and

"• restructured conventional forces so that both NATO and Warsaw Pact forces are in defense positions only.

"In the coming months, the Council will work with other organizations to build pressure on the Bush administration to move aggressively in the directions outlined above. Congress provided an important brake on the worst anti-arms-control tendencies of the Reagan administration. We will continue working with Congress, so that it supports the president's efforts to take advantage of opportunities or takes its own initiatives if he fails to act. Congress can, for example, refuse to allocate billions of dollars to build weapons we hope to dismantle very soon.

"We also hope to build grassroots support for the nearer-term goals of a START treaty, early action on a chemical weapons ban, and sharp reductions of NATO and Warsaw Pact forces.

"Finally, the Council will allocate increased resources and efforts to working with the media to get our message of change to the administration, Congress, and the public.

"Since 1776 the United States has succeeded in turning former adversaries—including Great Britain, Germany, Spain, Japan, and China—into nations with whom we deal on a cooperative problem-solving basis. We must begin to develop a similar relationship with the Soviet Union. True security will come when nuclear weapons are as irrelevant to our relations with the Soviet Union as they are to our relations with Britain and Japan."

—*John Isaacs, legislative director, Council for a Livable World*

You Can't Eat Bombs

"The American public is prepared for a debate about national security—a debate prompted in large measure by the warming of U.S.-Soviet relations and the policies of Mikhail Gorbachev.

"In 1989, Physicians for Social Responsibility will shift its resources toward a revitalized domestic speakers program to address the national security debate in terms of the real costs of the arms race. These costs are reflected in more than the dollar amounts spent on missiles, bombers, nuclear tests, and Star Wars research. Physicians have seen the impact most acutely in the government's declining commitment to public health programs, including care for the very young and the very old. These problems and others, such as rebuilding our industrial base, educating future generations, and reversing the damage we've done to the environment, have everything to do with national—and global —security.

"What Gorbachev offers the United States and its allies is a chance to end the Cold War once and for all, and to begin cooperatively to bring economic and ecological balance to the world. PSR's ongoing series of exchanges between U.S. and Soviet physicians will foster such cooperation while continuing to break down the barriers between habitual adversaries.

"The unfolding scandal at our nation's weapons manufacturing plants leads PSR to believe that unsafe nuclear weapons plants should be closed and stay closed; and that the Department of Energy should release health, safety, and environmental data that have been kept secret for decades to independent researchers who can assess the dangers to which employees and the public have been exposed. We have established a Physicians Task Force, composed of PSR activists and prominent doctors in the fields of public health and radiation, who will work with medical and environmental experts and with Congress to assemble and publish the facts about nuclear weapons production and its impact on public health.

"Beyond the health and safety issues related to existing facilities, PSR is also concerned about plans to construct new DOE facilities for the production of tritium and plutonium at a time when the promise of negotiated nuclear weapons reductions reduces—and perhaps eliminates—the need for such inherently dangerous plants. We opposed such plans.

"In 1989, PSR intends to strengthen its ties with other medical associations and encourage them to investigate the impact of the arms race and military spending on their ability to provide health services in their own specialties. Prevention of nuclear war—which remains the primary mission of PSR and a legitimate concern for everyone—can only be assured if we pay attention to the economic and political causes of the arms race, and to the national priorities that have too often been sacrificed in the name of security."

—*Maureen T. Thornton, executive director, Physicians for Social Responsibility*

She Who Defines, Wins

"Women's Action for Nuclear Disarmament greets the new era announced by Mikhail Gorbachev's December U.N. speech and George Bush's election with a new twist to an old theme: 'Redefining Inter/National Security.' Recognizing that we are at the beginning a long process, we nonetheless believe that we must begin now to create a new understanding of national priorities, emphasizing environmental, economic, human, and military needs. As the old adage so aptly puts it: '(S)he who defines the question wins the argument.'

"WAND's programmatic goal is to create a 'flexible response capability' for local activists, so that they can meet that challenge and participate fully in the process of redefining inter/national security.

"We believe successful programming must engage the head, hands, and heart. Thus, WAND will continue to emphasize strategies and materials that empower as they educate and mobilize. Our programs and projects for 1989 include:

"• The WAND Game, a gaming simulation developed with Prof. Richard D. Duke of the University of Michigan's School of Architecture and Urban Studies. The game, now in prototype, employs concepts of common security and alternative defense, and is designed to get players—especially women—to think about defense in ways that empower them to influence policy.

"• Political skills building, designed to assist local activists in following the activities of elected representatives in Washington. We will provide information on the legislative process and training in communication skills so that participants can effectively lobby members of Congress and their staffs.

"• Electoral action, through WAND PAC, which will be maintained in this off-election year to enhance effectiveness in 1990. We will identify and assist candidates, particularly women, interested in redefining inter/national security and supporting an arms control and disarmament agenda. We will also continue working with candidates, elected representatives, and political parties toward developing a 'peace platform' for 1992.

"• Mother's Day for Peace, a continuing effort by the WAND Education Fund to return Mother's Day to the originally envisioned occasion for speaking out for peace. Last year our TV satellite tour reached 13 million people in 40 countries. The 1989 tour will be hosted by actress Susan Clark and supported by educational materials distributed by 45 groups. Our efforts this year will focus on achieving diversity of cultural and ethnic participation.

"• Network '89, an effort to forge coalitions and joint ventures with other peace groups, such as the recently formed coalition for a comprehensive test ban and a joint project with Boston Women's Fund to put women from the peace community in dialogue with women working on inner-city projects."

—*M. Calien Lewis, executive director,*
Women's Action for Nuclear Disarmament

To Finish START

"Will 1989 be the year of deep cuts in nuclear arsenals and reduced, restructured conventional forces in Europe? The year we clean up bomb-factory waste and reorder our national security priorities to acknowledge the importance of a healthy economy and environment?

"The Union of Concerned Scientists is engaged in a major legislative, media, and grassroots campaign to insure that policymakers in the White House and Congress move to take advantage of opportunities that exist to achieve all of these goals.

"The key to success in each area, we believe, lies in what UCS considers its top priority in 1989: the completion of a START treaty that cuts U.S. and Soviet long-range forces by up to 50 percent.

"Why START? Because a successful START treaty will reaffirm and continue important precedents established by the Intermediate-range Forces Treaty: that *reductions* in weapons, rather than just limits on their future growth, can be achieved; that cuts can be asymmetrical; and that treaties can be verified through on-site inspection. It will also, by increasing crisis stability, obviate expensive new weapons and reinforce the goodwill and cooperation that is growing between the superpowers. After START, the thornier issue of conventional forces can be addressed.

"UCS's Finish START campaign will pressure the executive and legislative branches to eliminate the roadblocks to a START agreement. These include Star Wars, the question of the Anti-Ballistic Missile Treaty, control of mobile ICBMs, sea-launched cruise missiles, on-site verification procedures, and U.S. force structure.

"Key components of the campaign will be a new report detailing these roadblocks and suggesting ways to remove them; monthly mailings to newspaper editors updating them on the status of START and urging their support; expansion of our legislative efforts to involve a greater number of senators in START; and publication of a special study on verification of START and follow-on agreements. UCS's field program will urge grassroots activists to participate in editorial board meetings and lobbying efforts of their own.

"In early March, UCS will celebrate its 20th year of public policy advocacy at our national meeting in Washington, D.C. This event and celebrations in Boston and San Francisco will focus attention on our Finish START campaign.

"As we push for START, we must also address the question of what comes next. Answering this requires articulating a national security vision based on greatly reduced nuclear arsenals. If we fail to allay fears of such reductions, our opponents will be able to block our efforts to move beyond a START treaty to further reductions in weapons and military spending.

"The challenge to UCS and others in the peace movement is to insure that our nation takes full advantage of the currents of change and the resulting opportunities for progress toward peace."

—*Howard Ris, executive director, Union of Concerned Scientists*

Reclaim the Test Site

"The greatest long-term impact of Mikhail Gorbachev's speech may be to assist the American peace movement in confronting the mix of madness and *realpolitik* that drives the nuclear arms race. As the Soviet leader institutes reforms at home and offers disarmament initiatives abroad, the U.S. government seems to respond with no more than cosmetic changes. The rhetoric is different, but the arms race goes on; the Bush administration may give up some specific toys, but it will not likely change the game.

"Yet the arms race is precisely about 'the game' and not about 'defense.' The rules of the game are a mixture of rationality and madness concocted from the supposed imperatives of international power, imperialism, national egoism, and the reciprocal momentum and self-interest of Soviet and American military-industrial-academic complexes. The lack of substantive response from our government—when there is no rational reason to impede progress toward disarmament—is clear proof that the arms race, in E.P. Thompson's words, 'is about itself.'

"In 1989, the work of the American Peace Test will be to take nonviolent action to challenge the inertia of the arms race. Our Reclaim the Test Site II action, April 7–16, will further the resistance to testing where it takes place. The RTS peace camp will continue the process of living our way into a peaceful world. Nationally, we will assist groups to take action against the arms race in their communities.

"We will also focus efforts on working across boundaries, both internationally and within the movement. Internationally, we are calling for a moratorium on nuclear testing by all nuclear weapons states. Nationally, we will seek ways to work with other issue and constituency groups, to facilitate regionally based resistance communities. Finally, this is a time of great creativity and change within the nonviolence community. The APT will contribute to this evolutionary process through discussions, writing, and workshops.

"Whatever the Gorbachev initiative and the new Bush administration may offer, concrete changes will be brought about through the persistent and courageous efforts of large numbers of ordinary people. In 1989 the APT will continue efforts to empower as many folks as possible to wage peace boldly."

—Nancy Heskett, eastern field organizer and
Roy Morrison, special projects coordinator, American Peace Test

Grassroots Mandate

"As a grassroots organization, we at SANE/FREEZE take our mandate from local members and affiliates. At our second national congress, held in December in Atlanta, more than 600 members and chapter leaders gathered to debate and vote on priorities for 1980. The results:

"• Organizing for a 'peace economy' will be the principal program for the year. With a focus on NATO's 40th anniversary, we will begin work on the following areas: SANE/FREEZE will demand a cut in military spending (not just a freeze) and a redirection of federal funds to meet human needs. We will join with other groups and actively press Congress to enact legislation mandating economic conversion. The proposed Defense Economic Adjustment Act, which SANE/FREEZE supports, would create alternative use committees at major military facilities and provide adjustment benefits for workers and communities now dependent on defense industries.

"Beginning on Tax Day, April 15, we will sponsor citizen hearings on the need for reordered budget priorities. These will be followed in the fall with "local accountability" hearings, in which peace activists working with the leaders of domestic service constituencies—trade union officers, senior citizen leaders, local elected officials, and others—will testify before their congressional representatives on unmet domestic social needs and the need for reduced military spending. Through these "peace economy" activities, we will build a broad coalition for reordered budget priorities and economic conversion.

"• SANE/FREEZE also plans to sponsor national and local programs to keep the DOE nuclear weapons facilities shut and begin a major environmental cleanup of these contaminated sites. We believe there is no need for any additional production of nuclear weapons materials, and that we should aim towards arms reductions and disarmament rather than continued weapons production.

"The first activity in this program will be a DOE Lobby Day in Washington, D.C., on April 3 and 4, sponsored by the Military Production Network, a coalition of disarmament and environmental groups including SANE/FREEZE.

"• In keeping with our continuing pursuit of a comprehensive test ban, SANE/FREEZE will also support the American Peace Test nonviolence mass action scheduled at the Nevada Test Site April 7–16. Thousands of SANE/FREEZE members and other supporters will continue the campaign of demonstrations and nonviolent resistance in Nevada. We will also continue our work with the International Comprehensive Test Ban Campaign to support legislation and other policy initiatives that seek a complete halt to nuclear testing.

"The new year is a time of great potential as we continue to mobilize citizen pressure for reduced military spending, an end to the production of nuclear weapons materials, and a nuclear test ban."

—*Nick Carter, executive director, SANE/FREEZE*

War Toys and War Taxes

"The War Resisters League regrets the election of a former CIA director as president. But regardless of the winner, there is not enough difference between the two major parties for us to make a dramatic shift in direction.

"The remarkable changes in the Soviet Union and in Soviet foreign policy are more important for our work. Because of the Gorbachev initiatives, we will pay more attention to the United Nations and strengthen our contacts with the European peace movements, East and West, official and unofficial, to demand that NATO use his proposals as the basis for major cuts in conventional weapons in Western Europe. We hope this is but the first step toward the dissolution of both the NATO and the Warsaw Pact military alliances.

"What worries us deeply is that the sense of detente can lead people to forget that the machinery of nuclear and conventional war remains in place. Historically, WRL has not been content to wait for national leaders to bring peace. We intend to use this new period of detente to urge sharp cuts in the U.S. military budget, including military aid to Israel and other Middle Eastern nations, Central America, and elsewhere.

"Since WRL opposes not only war, but the causes of war, our work reflects a wide range of interests. Some of the major areas WRL will be working in during the coming year include:

"• Stop War Toys Campaign: a WRL project that serves as a national network and clearinghouse for activists concerned about the sale of violent toys for children. The campaign circulates petitions, distributes flyers to parents, provides speakers for public meetings and TV and radio shows, and sells a modestly priced packet of information on war toys.

"• War Tax Resistance: to educate people on how their tax dollars are being spent. We are publishing a manual that explains how to redirect (legally and illegally) income taxes from the military toward socially beneficial causes.

"• Resist Third World War campaign: to highlight the connection between conventional- and nuclear-war planning and weapons systems, focusing attention on the many wars the United States is involved in that get little or no attention in this country.

"• Draft Counter-recruitment: to reach out and involve young people in our work. The centerpiece of this effort is *SPEW*, a magazine by and for high school students, with articles on ecology, nonviolence, racism, and Third World liberation movements. WRL will also provide young people with alternative information on military enlistment.

"• Promote nonviolence: to further one of WRL's major objectives as a secular pacifist organization. We provide training for national and smaller civil disobedience actions. WRL also publishes a highly respected organizer's manual and is producing a nonviolence handbook for use in small- and medium-size actions. In addition, WRL is compiling a national directory of nonviolence trainers."   —*David McReynolds, War Resisters League*

Building a Movement

"Two important developments will shape the American Friends Service Committee's work on disarmament and East-West issues in 1989. The first is the remarkable process of radical change in the Soviet Union. The second development is here at home, where conservatives are formulating a new rationale for preserving U.S. power in the Third World to supplant the waning anti-Soviet Cold War ideology. They are now promoting "low-intensity conflict," covert action, and 'antiterrorist strikes' as the answer to perceived instabilities, local liberation struggles, drug trafficking, and terrorism.

"Our work is also guided by several domestic political imperatives: the necessity of building a strong grassroots movement that unites progressive communities across racial, ethnic, nationality, gender, and class lines; the need for more work on issues of peace and independence in the East Asia-Pacific region; and the importance of developing a new approach to global security.

"As AFSC moves toward a broader emphasis on U.S. foreign policies, it is initiating a campaign to build domestic support for movements to remove U.S. (and Soviet) bases from nations in the Pacific, Europe, and the Third World. As a part of this campaign, AFSC will sponsor a speaking tour entitled 'Voices of Hope and Anger: Women Speak Out for Sovereignty and Self-Determination.' Starting in April, the tour will feature eight women from the Philippines, Okinawa, Honduras, Puerto Rico, West Germany, South Korea, and the United States, who will describe the effects of a large U.S. military presence on their countries. Next year AFSC plans to publish a book on foreign military bases.

"Our East-West Program complements this project. Its staff has organized three seminars for U.S. and Third World peace and justice activists on the connections between the East-West and North-South conflicts. In April, the program will sponsor an exchange between experts from the United States, the Soviet Union, and several African nations on the impact of the two superpowers' policies on African conflicts. Soviet participants will then meet with faculty and students at several black colleges in the American South.

"In our extensive work with European peace movements we have also found a strong common interest in working for the withdrawal of all foreign military forces from both Eastern and Western Europe.

"In all of our work we are struggling to build a movement that unites black, Latino, Asian, Pacific, and Native American activists and organizations with those of the largely white, middle-class peace movement. And through the speaking tour, we are trying to develop stronger bonds with feminists and women's organizations. Such a united movement is necessary to reverse the militarization of our society and the world, and build peace and security on a solid foundation of justice and freedom."

—*Bruce Birchard, Michael Simmons, and Chris Wing,*
American Friends Service Committee

Stop the Tests; Free the Seas

"Greenpeace expects the disarmament talks that began with Reagan and Gorbachev to continue under the leadership of Gorbachev and Bush. But it is not clear in which directions real change will occur. Talks on conventional forces and chemical weapons are important and should be supported. But initiatives must be brought to fruition on the nuclear weapons front as well.

"We are concerned that momentum on this front has been sidetracked by the outgoing administration's intransigence on ending nuclear testing. Discussions have been based on ratifying old treaties (the 1974 Threshold Test Ban Treaty and the 1976 Peaceful Nuclear Explosions Treaty) that limit tests to a ceiling of 150 kilotons, or on the exchange of technical information during nuclear tests. But the United States has thwarted progress toward a comprehensive test ban. The CTB is a top priority for Greenpeace; it is a simple yet significant step towards halting the spiraling arms race.

"In the United States we will be working with a coalition of groups to get

Congress to renew efforts for a CTB, enacting legislation that urges President Bush to resume negotiations and to initiate a bilateral testing moratorium during the talks. As of this writing, we have collected more than 100,000 signatures on a petition toward this end. We will support the upcoming U.N. conference to amend the Limited Test Ban Treaty to make it comprehensive—an initiative supported by 127 U.N. members. In addition, we will begin activities to draw attention to the 1990 Nuclear Non-Proliferation Treaty Conference (as part of its 1968 NPT commitments, the United States promised to negotiate a CTB).

"Internationally, Greenpeace will continue to draw attention to nuclear testing in the Soviet Union, Muroroa and Fangataufa atolls, and China. Our new ship, the Rainbow Warrior II, will be sailing into the South Pacific to continue protests against French nuclear testing.

"As part of our continuing Nuclear Free Seas activities, two Greenpeace ships will be visiting ports on both U.S. coasts, making public presentations that explain the arms race at sea and the role of local naval bases and vessels in the U.S. Navy's nuclear war-fighting strategy.

"With START stalled over the United States's unwillingness to negotiate on sea-launched cruise missiles, we will play an active part in this debate—in Congress, with direct action, and through grassroots pressure. In addition, Greenpeace will try to get Congress to introduce legislation to eliminate all tactical nuclear weapons at sea.

"Greenpeace will also continue its campaign to stop production of nuclear weapons materials. Internationally, we will be working with The Plutonium Challenge initiative, an attempt to get all countries with nuclear weapons (particularly the United States and the Soviet Union) to stop such production. In the United States, we will sponsor petition drives and letter-writing campaigns urging Congress to end the production of nuclear weapons materials and to divert funds to the cleanup of existing Department of Energy facilities.

"Greenpeace, along with other groups, is currently a plaintiff in a lawsuit filed last year against DOE to keep the nuclear reactors at the Savannah River nuclear materials plant shut down pending a complete safety review and completion of an environmental impact statement. Greenpeace will join other efforts by local groups who are organizing around DOE facilities out of concern over disarmament, environmental pollution and public health."

—*Peter Bahouth, executive director, Greenpeace*

Teaching for a Better World

"As educators looking not to the next administration, but to the next *generation*, Educators for Social Responsibility's goal remains relatively constant: to teach young people in a way that develops their social consciousness and enhances their abilities to make the world a better place.

"Still, the national and international environments in which we do this strongly affect our work. As the East-West competition winds down, for example, ESR is finding increased acceptance of its goal of teaching about the Soviet Union and superpower conflict. And with recent signs of peace 'breaking out' around the world, ESR can enlarge its scope beyond nuclear issues to include a host of other critical concerns: ecological dangers, apartheid, drug trafficking, and regional conflicts.

"In 1989, ESR will initiate a National Conflict Resolution Program to survey what conflict resolution programs are currently underway in schools around the country, to study the pedagogical problems in the field and to determine how best to integrate conflict resolution into existing curricula.

"Our Teacher-Veteran Partnership Program is a three-way collaboration among ESR, the Vietnam Veterans of America, and the Center for Social Studies Education. The project aims to expand the scope of, and improve teaching about, the Vietnam War in schools across the country.

"Our Economics and Social Responsibility Project will help students become more aware of the social issues raised by economic policy and of their own roles as consumers, workers, and producers—and as future voters and investors. The Council for Economic Priorities has joined the project's working group; we are soliciting additional collaborators and funders.

"In Portland, Oregon, and in the greater Boston area, school districts are joining efforts to infuse education about nuclear, peace, and conflict studies in all grades as part of ESR's Educating for Living in a Nuclear Age. A three-day conference in Boston in March will showcase materials and approaches developed by classroom teachers in the program.

"New publications for 1989 from our Controversy Series will examine the role of covert action in a democracy, along with drug trafficking, and student rights and the Constitution. In a collaborative effort with the Nobel Prize Committee, we are also producing teaching guides to accompany 'videographies' of Nobel Peace Prize winners.

"Finally, ESR will focus on teacher education seminars for using our new Soviet curriculum and new audiovisual materials. We will also hold our second joint institute with Soviet educators, 'Teaching for Critical Thinking in the Nuclear Age,' in Leningrad."

—*Susan Alexander, executive director, Educators for Social Responsibility*

Too Much is Enough

"As an environmental organization, the Natural Resources Defense Council has been actively concerned for many years about the health and environmental hazards posed by the Department of Energy's complex of nuclear warhead production facilities. Today, none of DOE's nuclear weapons production reactors are operating, and the total cost of cleaning up and renovating the complex is estimated at more than $100 billion.

"One of our main goals in 1989 is to compel the government to fundamentally reexamine the nuclear weapons production complex and its future. We will be responding to efforts by some to rush ahead with the restart of unsafe

158

existing reactors and to authorize the construction of five new ones proposed by DOE. Specifically, NRDC will target the agency's plan to build the Special Isotope Separator plutonium refinery in Idaho—a $1 billion pork-barrel project at a time when former Energy Secretary John Herrington says the nation is 'awash in plutonium'.

"In cooperation with other organizations, NRDC is also seeking to foster a dialogue between U.S. and Soviet scientists on environmental dangers posed by the two superpowers' nuclear bomb-making enterprises. Although little is known about the Soviets' nuclear weapons production, there are indications they are also operating old, outmoded production reactors. We have set forth our objectives in The Plutonium Challenge, issued in late 1987 by a coalition of arms control and environmental groups and more than 30 distinguished scientists and experts. Already possessing vast stockpiles of plutonium and highly enriched uranium, the United States and the Soviet Union should agree to cut off fissile material production.

"At the same time, we must not lose the momentum towards ending nuclear testing. Under the auspices of our Verification Project, NRDC and the Soviet Academy of Sciences have jointly operated sophisticated seismic stations in each other's countries and have established seismic verification networks. This scientific cooperation, in its third year, should allow the Bush administration to make rapid progress in phasing out nuclear testing, or set the stage for Congress—if pushed by a concerned American public—to legislate a low-threshold moratorium as a first step toward a comprehensive test ban.

"Sustained pressure and research in recent years has produced a wealth of information on the superpowers' arsenals—data that have been essential to public participation in these critical policy choices. Now, with the 'new thinking' in the Soviet Union, NRDC and thousands of other Americans are creating new channels for scientist-to-scientist and citizen-to-citizen cooperation. If we stay on course, the prospects for arms control breakthroughs and reductions in the 1990s are bright; informed citizen pressure can make it happen. NRDC looks forward to working with other concerned organizations and individuals in the years ahead."

—S. Jacob Scheer and Thomas B. Cochran, codirectors,
Nuclear Program, Natural Resources Defense Council

CHAPTER
SIX

Access and Image:
Representations in the News Media

Why the Bomb Didn't Hit Home
By Susan Jaffe
March 1983

THE MOST PASSIONATE AND POWERFUL ANTINUCLEAR MOVIE WAS NOT made by a Hollywood producer or an independent documentary filmmaker. It was shot by a special motion picture unit under direct orders from President Harry S. Truman, the only man to initiate a nuclear attack.

Four months after the atomic bomb attacks on Japan in August 1945, a military film crew was sent to Hiroshima and Nagasaki to record the damage. The footage exposed the human toll of the bombings so dramatically that all 95,000 feet of color film (enough for 30 feature-length movies) were classified "top secret" in 1946 and concealed from the public.

Few Americans even knew the footage existed. The film might still be on the shelf gathering dust—still classified for all practical purposes—if not for Herbert Sussan, now retired and living in New York City after an award-winning career in television.

Sussan knew the film existed and he has never been able to forget it. When he was 24 years old, Sussan was the production director for the movie crew sent to Hiroshima and Nagasaki.

For more than 30 years Sussan waged a one-man campaign to get the film released and shown on network television. During the 1950s and 1960s he spoke to Pentagon officials, Edward R. Murrow, Robert F. Kennedy, and President Truman, among others. Repeatedly he was told—sometimes quite falsely—that the footage was still classified.

"I wanted to get the footage," Sussan explains, "so that the American people could see, firsthand, what the effects of the bombs were. And if they saw the effects, I felt there would be a groundswell against ever using nuclear weapons of any type again."

Mindful of this message, top officials in the Pentagon and the Atomic Energy Commission attempted to "have the film buried," according to the air force colonel who handled the footage after it left Herbert Sussan's hands. Until recently Americans were only allowed to glimpse brief, black and white newsclips of the devastation caused by the atomic bombs. Hidden, along with the film footage from Hiroshima and Nagasaki, was the horror of nuclear war, in full color, in real life, with real people.

The 36-Year Gap

During the first Special Session on Disarmament at the United Nations in 1978, the Tokyo-based Hiroshima-Nagasaki Publishing Committee set up an exhibit of photographs taken in 1945 and 1946. Herbert Sussan visited the exhibit, recalls Tsutomu Iwakura, chief coordinator of the committee, which has prepared several books and films about the bombings.

"He noticed some of the photographs," Iwakura recalls, "and explained that he had filmed many of the same scenes himself." Iwakura was surprised to hear that Sussan had, in fact, shot thousands of feet of color film in Hiroshima and Nagasaki, although Sussan wasn't sure where the footage was kept, and whether it was still classified.

Iwakura began looking for the film and in 1979 he found it in Washington, D.C., at the National Archives. By 1981 Iwakura and the Hiroshima-Nagasaki Publishing Committee had raised enough money to begin purchasing a reprint of some of Sussan's footage. Nearly 500,000 Japanese had contributed to the committee's "Ten Foot Campaign"—donating $12 to $15 to purchase 10 feet of film. Iwakura's group produced two extraordinary films from the Sussan footage, which were shown during the U.N.'s second disarmament session last June. Until that time Sussan had seen virtually none of the footage he had shot 36 years earlier.

"It was the first time [American viewers] realized the extent of the horrible damage inflicted by the bomb," Iwakura says, describing the reaction to the film in New York. "It went way beyond what they even *thought* it could look like."

The only American documentary that has utilized any of the Sussan footage is *Dark Circle*, which premiered at the New York Film Festival last fall and will be shown across the country this spring. For a section on Japan, filmmakers Chris Beaver, Judy Irving, and Ruth Landy interviewed survivors of the atomic bombing and juxtaposed it with film (in which the same people appeared) by Sussan in 1946.

Chris Beaver watched all 30 hours of the Sussan material at the National Archives. "The film is extremely gruesome," he reports. "Somebody's lost an eye and they [medical staff] will hold up a piece of glass to show how the injury would have happened. At one point the Japanese doctor takes off his coat and shows you his burns and his cuts. It's horrible. It's upsetting to look at very much of it." The first day Beaver viewed the footage he had to take a break when he started crying.

"You really get a sense of being there," Beaver says. "The color is vivid, rich. A shot might start on a pile of rubble and slowly rise into the air and you just see more and more and more, and you can't believe what you're seeing, how far it went on."

The use of color film was almost nonexistent in that period. "The color seems so much more real [than black and white]," Beaver says, "so much more immediate, that I think the American government didn't want to show it because they were afraid of what the reaction would be to our nuclear weapons policy. I think they didn't want Americans to see what we had actually done in Japan and they didn't want them to think about *themselves* being in that picture. It's one thing to know about that and another thing to see it."

The Top Secrecy Network

Near the end of 1945 a special motion picture unit of the U.S. Strategic Bombing Survey was ordered to film, in 38 days, the effectiveness of American air attacks on 22 Japanese cities.

Air Corps Lieutenant Daniel A. McGovern was in charge of the unit. Herbert Sussan, an air corps lieutenant stationed at a base outside of Tokyo, supervised much of the on-location shooting. (Before going overseas, Sussan had been assigned to a motion picture studio in Culver City, California, producing training films for the air corps. His squadron commander was Lieutenant Ronald Reagan.) Sussan and nine others boarded a special train in Tokyo, which took them to their first stop, Nagasaki. "From that moment," Sussan says, "my life was forever changed."

"We were sent on this trip without very much direction," Sussan recalls. "Nobody had prepared us for what was in this city as we went in. I was shocked. I could not believe what one bomb, what one little bomb could do. I felt that we were here in this moment, which hopefully would never be repeated, and if we didn't get a picture of what's happening—this holocaust—nobody would ever know.

"We weren't asked to cover all the medical effects. But when we got to Nagasaki, I arranged for Washington to be contacted and we were given unlimited time, because I felt we had to stay there as long as we could."

After ordering all of the color film available in the Pacific, Sussan's unit began filming the ruins and the survivors.

"We shot all the burn cases in the Omura Navy Hospital in Nagasaki and we kept logs of who they were, for medical history," Sussan says. "The worst burn case in the hospital was a young man. All the skin of this man's back had been entirely burned away. I never believed that young man would live. I winced when we turned the lights on to take the film [which appears in *Dark Circle*], but I thought we should take it. He was lying in a bed of penicillin. He lay there for over a year. And he did survive.

"We told the people that we'd like them to appear in these films because we hoped it would prove to the world that this weapon should not exist. I was 24 years old and I was very idealistic and very naive, it turns out. I honestly felt that if we brought back these pictures and people throughout the world saw them,

163

never again would anybody consider using this power for destructive purposes. If they [his superiors] had known what my point of view was, they probably would have stopped the project."

In March, Sussan was sent to Hiroshima. "We took pictures in Hiroshima," Sussan recalls, "where vaporized bodies—the remains of people in the bomb shelters—were given back [to relatives] in little wooden boxes. That's what was left of people in the shelters."

When the mission was completed in June 1946 the crew was abruptly ordered to bring the unprocessed film back to Washington "immediately." (Sussan had already been interviewed by John Hersey, who was researching his book, *Hiroshima*.) At the Pentagon, Sussan reported to Major General Orvil A. Anderson, who headed the Military Analysis Division of the Strategic Bombing Survey. "The MPs [military police] came," Sussan says, "took the footlockers [containing the reels of film] and the footage was taken to the Pentagon's basement."

Sussan completed a three-volume photographic report on his Japan mission for President Truman, and left the air force in December 1946. General Anderson, says Sussan, wanted him to stay in the service and make training films out of the footage, but Sussan "didn't like the attitude being expressed at that time." General Anderson, among others, thought it might be a good idea to unleash an atomic attack on the Soviets before they developed a huge nuclear arsenal. He called his strategy "preventative war." (For airing such views, Anderson was suspended from his post as commandant of the Air War College by the Truman administration in 1950.)

When Sussan returned to his home in New York, he discovered that "six or seven months in bombed-out places really affected me. The first year after I came back was horrendous. I could not work. I used to walk through the streets and see keloid formations on people's faces—the scars from burns caused by the bomb. I used to look at buildings and imagine how they would look after a bombing. The townhouses on the East Side are very much like a lot of buildings in Hiroshima."

Allied Occupation officials in Japan were keeping strict control of all media coverage coming out of Hiroshima and Nagasaki; the United States denied, officially, that radioactive fallout was harmful. Sussan felt that there was "very little understanding of what nuclear weapons were or what had happened in those two cities, other than the one picture of the mushroom cloud that people had seen."

Besides concealing the Sussan film, the American government confiscated all of the footage taken by Japanese film crews in Hiroshima and Nagasaki, and declared it top secret. But the Department of Defense did release a 22-minute black-and-white film about the bombing of Hiroshima and Nagasaki, called *A Tale of Two Cities*. According to Tom Greenburg of the Center for Defense Information in Washington, which nows distributes the film, the "sanitized" newsreel footage showed the physical effects of the atomic attack without mentioning human casualties; the film's narrator stressed that the cities returned to normal quickly. This was the official version of Hiroshima and Nagasaki, and the only one the American public would know about for many years.

Evidence Too "Scientific"

In 1947 Sussan learned that Jean Benoit-Levy, a famous French documentary filmmaker who emigrated to America in 1940, was working at the United Nations. Sussan met Benoit-Levy, executive director of the Council of Cinema at the U.N., for lunch, and told him that a film made out of his color footage would be the best way to show the world what atomic war was really like.

Benoit-Levy, according to Sussan, replied that this would be a "mistake," because "worldwide resentment of the United States for dropping the bomb would only be enlarged by releasing this footage." Sussan claims that Benoit-Levy "endorsed what the American government was doing in withholding the material."

In 1948, Sussan joined CBS in New York, the first step in a career that would earn him many top awards, including an Emmy and a gold medal from the Freedom Foundation. Two years later, with Secretary of Navy Francis Matthews advocating a war with the Soviets "to compel cooperation for peace" (as Matthews put it), Sussan decided to write to President Truman. In a letter to the president on September 25, 1950, Sussan suggested that "now is the time" for the "top secret" footage he had shot in Japan to be made into a full-length motion picture. "Such a film," Sussan wrote, "would vividly and clearly reveal the implications and effects of the weapons that confront us at this serious moment in our history . . .The times fairly scream out for release of this motion picture material."

A reply from the White House was written on October 3, 1950. In this letter, Dallas Halverstadt, a presidential assistant in charge of Motion Picture Liaison, told Sussan that parts of his footage had been assembled by the RKO studios into four films. "Because the pictures were made for military training purposes," Halverstadt wrote, "they lack a wide public appeal . . . The Air Force informs me that because of the record and scientific nature of the footage it would, indeed, be very difficult to attempt to remake any of this footage into a film which might have wide public appeal or information value."

At CBS, Sussan met Edward R. Murrow who, as host of *See It Now*, was the most influential journalist on television. Sussan wanted to make a documentary, narrated by Murrow. "I thought it would be particularly valuable if his voice was part of it. With Mr. Murrow's involvement I would also have the kind of person who had the prestige to get the [classified] footage.

"But he investigated and felt, no, it wasn't the thing for him to do. I was shocked by his lack of interest. He didn't have to give any reason, he was the star. CBS News agreed." (One of Murrow's close friends was David Lilienthal, first chair of the Atomic Energy Commission.)

Sussan became senior producer for NBC's heralded *Wide Wide World*, a

90-minute Sunday afternoon program hosted by Dave Garroway, in 1955. He approached NBC News and co-anchor Chet Huntley about obtaining the footage. "I thought Huntley and David Brinkley would be very instrumental in obtaining the film," Sussan says, "particularly Brinkley, who had excellent contacts in Washington. But NBC News felt this was not a subject they wanted to get into.

"You have to remember the period we're talking about," Sussan says. "The United States had been criticized throughout the world for dropping the bomb, and the criticism had not ended. The American government was still very sensitive to this. None of the networks was going to fight what both the military and government said—that the material is classified. That was a different world than today. Whatever the military or the government said, nobody questioned."

Whenever his work took him to Washington, Sussan inquired about the film. In 1956 when he produced *Force for Survival*, a program saluting the armed services, he met the secretary of defense and the joint chiefs of staff. Replying to Sussan's inquiry, Secretary of Defense Neil McElroy wrote that the film was still classified.

When Sussan was developing a television series in 1962 for Columbia Pictures called *The Law Enforcers*, he met Robert F. Kennedy, then attorney general, and asked about his film. Again he was informed that the footage was classified and "the attorney general's office would not or could not get this film declassified," Sussan claims.

Although the answer by now was predictable, Sussan didn't stop asking about the film. As head of international production for Screen Gems, Sussan arranged for the filming of a 39-part series called *The Decisions of Harry Truman*. Sussan and his wife had lunch with the former president several times in New York during 1963 and 1964. "I asked him about this film," Sussan says. "He said he wasn't aware of it but would check on it. Then I was told—it was classified and cannot be declassified."

After all these rebuffs, Sussan was frustrated and disappointed. "I was just a single person, not powerful," he explains. "I didn't have an organization, I was trying to do this on my own. If there was any group, 20 years ago, that I felt would be meaningful in making the film available, I would have gone to them."

Sussan finally got his first look at the footage when a friend obtained from the Pentagon the military training films made in the late 1940s. Sussan watched for just a few minutes before getting "ill." One of the films, titled *Strategic Attack*, showed how to use an atomic bomb in battle, "which is not what I shot the footage for," Sussan points out. Sussan has learned that the narrator of at least one of these films was Edward R. Murrow.

Sealed with Red Tape

Herbert Sussan finally found out, in 1973, where his film was being stored. A friend had heard that the footage was being kept at the defense department's film depository at Norton Air Force Base in California.

On a visit to the base, Sussan visited the office of Daniel A. McGovern, who had supervised Sussan's film unit in Hiroshima and Nagasaki (as well as all of the Japanese newsreel teams). McGovern, a retired colonel working at the base as a film producer, directed him to the area where records on all footage were stored.

Sussan found the card file on his film that indicated, he says, that the footage was still classified. Sussan left Norton empty-handed, unaware that the film had actually been declassified several years before and was sitting in the National Archives in Washington.

A researcher at the Archives, Bob Finley, who managed to track down some records on the film, reports that it was "declassified after 12 years" as part of a group of material automatically declassified after an established period of time had elapsed. The records show that the film's classification status was "downgraded" every four years and that it was declassified in 1959 (long before Sussan's meetings with Kennedy and Truman). It was transferred from Wright-Patterson Air Force Base near Dayton, Ohio, to the Archives in February 1962. But apparently the card files and indexes on the film at the Norton base were never relabeled to denote this change in secrecy status.

Today, Pentagon officials are reluctant to discuss how the film became declassified and why it was ever classified at all. In any event, when it was declassified no one bothered to tell Herbert Sussan.

As a result, the footage remained hidden until 1979 (when it was uncovered by Tsutomu Iwakura), long after it arrived at the National Archives. As Edwin Thompson, director of the Archives' declassification division puts it: "If no one asks for the film it's as closed as when it was classified."

Buried Truth

One person who can speak with authority about what happened to the color footage shot in Hiroshima and Nagasaki is Daniel McGovern, who admits he "had control" of it for many years. A self-described "conservative" who does not fully share Herbert Sussan's antinuclear views, McGovern, 72, left Norton in 1980, and now lives in Northridge, California.

In 1946 McGovern and Major General Orvil Anderson (with whom he served as an aide for three years) wanted to make military training films out of the color footage. But this, McGovern explains, caused "quite a problem." Top brass in the Pentagon and at the Atomic Energy Commission did not want the footage to have even a limited circulation; they wanted the footage "buried," McGovern says.

"I was told by those people that—hell no and damn no—they did not want that material shown," McGovern says, "because it showed the horrible effects on man, woman, and child. They were fearful of it being circulated." Finally, after a strong argument by General Anderson, the Pentagon provided $80,000 so that RKO, with McGovern's assistance, could make the four training films. But first the entire footage was declared "secret."

McGovern has retained a copy of a March 3, 1947 memorandum that explains why the footage was classified. In the document, Major Francis E. Rundell of the air corps notes that the "secret" status was arrived at "after study of subject material, especially concerning the footage taken at Hiroshima and Nagasaki. . . . It is believed that the information contained in the films should be safeguarded until cleared by the Atomic Energy Commission." After the training films were completed, Rundell wrote, the classification of the material "will be raised to 'Top Secret' pending final classification by the Atomic Energy Commission."

The main reason the footage was classified, according to McGovern, was because of its "medical aspects, the horror, the devastation it showed."

One project back by Anderson did not come to fruition. In a memorandum to the commanding general of the Army Air Forces on July 10, 1946, Anderson revealed that Warner Brothers Studios in Hollywood had offered to produce a feature film for public release in this country at no cost to the government. The proposed film, based on the color footage, would "portray dramatically the results achieved by the Army Air Forces against Japan, and is intended for showing to a national audience of 80,000,000 people." (Anderson stated that the Warners Brothers film could be used for "indoctrination purposes." He may have wanted to show Americans what awaited them—atomic devastation—if they did not back his plan for a preemptive strike on the Soviets, McGovern believes.)

But the Warner Brothers project "fell by the wayside," McGovern says. It was the AEC, not the air force, he charges, that kept the explicit truth of Hiroshima and Nagasaki from the public. "The AEC had power of God over everybody," McGovern says. "They did not want that film released. They were the ones that stopped it. At a time when they were working on upcoming atomic tests they didn't want the general public to know what the weapon had already done."

After outtakes from the training films were shipped to the air force's film depository at Wright-Patterson, McGovern spent a year there cataloging the dozens of reels of film. McGovern says that until it was shipped to the National Archives, the footage was under his control within the air force but he did not have authority to declassify it.

"Herb [Sussan] was frustrated that he couldn't get his hands on the material," McGovern says, "but I had been told that under no circumstances would it be released."

Effects and a Cause

Herbert Sussan feels it's ironic that he was sent to Hiroshima and Nagasaki in 1946, while his boss, Ronald Reagan, stayed behind at a film studio in California. "Reagan," Sussan notes, "still doesn't know the true effects of the atomic bomb, obviously."

Sussan may have suffered ill-effects himself. He has been stricken with lymphoma, a form of cancer common among atomic bomb survivors in Japan and soldiers and civilians exposed to fallout from nuclear tests. Sussan feels his illness may have been caused by his months of exposure to residual radiation in Hiroshima and Nagasaki. According to studies of atomic survivors in Japan, lymphoma has an extremely long latency period.

At least two other members of the ten-person U.S. film crew also got cancer; one died last year and McGovern has skin cancer. (The whereabouts of the other seven crew members are unknown.)

"The American government told us when we first went in that there was no radiation, that it was all gone—the bomb had been detonated 1,600 feet in the air," Sussan says. "So we had no worry, we just walked right in, we drank the water"—Sussan laughs—"we did everything, nobody understood the bomb and its potential long-term effects."

Sussan, 62, lives with his wife in Manhattan, where he is working on a book. He has been too ill lately to renew his fight to get some of the footage on network television, but calling attention to the existence of the film remains "the goal of my life," he says.

"All I want to do for the next two to five years, or whatever time I have, is to work to make people understand that this kind of weapon must be erased from the face of the earth," Sussan says. "They must understand the dimensions they're dealing with."

The Sussan footage is still compelling today, *Dark Circle*'s Chris Beaver believes. "When the government is trying to sell the American people on civil defense and that we can survive a nuclear war, this footage," Beaver says "is awfully bad publicity."

Sussan says that he is very happy to see that when parts of the footage are used, as in *Dark Circle*, "they're very effective with the audience, but I would like it to reach a broader audience. I think one of the problems today in antinuclear activities is that they use people who can't back up what they're saying with effective visual material that tells the story. Nobody can visualize 40,000 nuclear bombs. Those discussions of numbers are meaningless. I don't think I'm capable, individually, of telling the story but I think the film is, properly used.

"Eventually the world will finally see a small bit of what the true reality of the nuclear age is. I saw what happened to a little piece of land in Japan. If you can translate that into big pieces of land in the United States and in Europe, and visualize it all happening at once, and then realize after millions of people are destroyed that radiation will keep blowing around the rest of the earth, then you've got a picture of what the world will be like. What do you have when you're finished? What do you leave to your children? No world at all."

Will Millions Get the Message?
By Renata Rizzo
November/December 1983

ON THE EVENING OF NOVEMBER 20, JUST FOUR DAYS BEFORE A THANK-ful America sits down to turkey dinners, tens of millions of people will be gathering around television sets in livingrooms, churches, and town halls—not to enjoy a heartwarming holiday special, but to watch Kansas City get blown off the face of the earth.

At 8 o'clock on that Sunday evening, ABC plans to air what many believe is the most controversial television movie ever made—*The Day After*. Directed by Nicholas Meyer, and starring Jason Robards, the $7 million film grimly— and at great length—depicts World War III, focusing on America's heartland and the losing battle for survival by those unlucky enough to live through a nuclear war.

Airing on the eve of the planned deployment of American nuclear missiles in Europe, *The Day After*—despite ABC's assertions that the film advocates no political philosophy—is being viewed by many as a timely commercial for the antinuclear movement. The film dramatizes two points peace activists have long been making: that the deterrence theory is dangerous and that no one will survive a nuclear war. After a slow start, peace activists are now planning both local and national strategies to ensure that the public not only tunes in to the movie, but into the movement as well.

Right-wing groups are paying attention, too; their accusation that ABC is peddling Soviet propaganda is adding to the controversy surrounding the film. As Theo Brown, deputy director of Ground Zero in Washington, D.C., says, "My organizer's nose tells me that this movie is going to create one helluva hullabaloo, and we better plan on being there for the duration."

From Shopping Centers to Congress

Most antinuclear groups are concentrating on grassroots organizing, encouraging outreach through group viewings. "No one should see this film alone—not kids, not adults," says Wendy Roberts, a California social worker. "It should be watched in the framework of group support."

Ground Zero plans to print 200,000 *Day After* guides to help "walk" viewers through the movie and subsequent discussions. The guides will be sent to schools, churches, and community groups; and members plan to distribute them in shopping centers during the busy preholiday weekend when the film airs, thereby reaching many nonactivist shoppers. A special toll-free number is being set up by activists in New York and Washington, D.C., to match callers with peace groups. Members of Physicians for Social Resposibility throughout the United States will write to their local Chambers of Commerce for lists of for lists of mainstream community groups. "Then we'll write to them and say, 'If you saw the movie and want to get involved, we're here to show you how,'" explains Abram Claude, PSR's associate director.

Susan Alexander with Educators for Social Responsibility is assembling a *Day After* guide with specific suggestions for discussions people can have after seeing the film. And the Center for Defense Information in Washington, D.C., is trying to place ads for their "nuclear war prevention kit" on dozens of ABC stations immediately following the film.

STOP Nuclear War in Northfield, Massachusetts, hopes to flood the White House and offices of all elected officials with letters saying, "I'm watching *The Day After*; I hope you do the same." And, in an effort to supplement a national media campaign, SANE, together with the Freeze Campaign, is sending thousands of activists packets containing a how-to manual for putting together viewing groups, suggestions for doing local press work around the movie, and material urging activists to get out into their communities during the week following the film. Says Randy Kehler, national coordinator of the Freeze, "This movie has given us a fantastic opportunity for growth—now it's up to us to run with it."

The Day After has sparked considerable interest on Capitol Hill as well. "It produced the single most emotional response I've ever had to a movie," says Representative Edward Markey. And Representative Thomas Downey is planning a *Day After* conference for his constituents, and will open up his district office for phone calls on the night the movie airs.

Waking the Movement

Josh Baran, a publicist based in Berkeley, California, is finishing a marathon run with *The Day After*. Months ago he dreamed up a project called Target Kansas City; that, along with a companion project, Let Lawrence Live (Lawrence, 40 miles from Kansas City, is where the film's nuclear war survivors struggle with radiation sickness and social entropy), promises to be at the center of public attention when *The Day After* airs. Organizers there have planned midnight vigils, public rallies, press conferences, forums, and town hall meetings with local congressional representatives. "After the movie, a lot of Americans will be looking to us out here to see what we're thinking and doing," says Allen Hanson, director of Let Lawrence Live. "You can count on us to make a hell of a lot of noise."

Baran, who traveled across the country last summer urging movement groups to use the film as an organizing tool, wants to hear a clamor from coast to coast. "I've been working full-time on getting the movement awakened to the movie," he says. "It's taken a *long* time. For four months I was a lone voice crying in the wilderness. People in the peace movement are ignorant about the media; they have no understanding of how it works and how to use it. They'd rather spend a quarter of a million dollars on a documentary that no one will see than grab the opportunity that *The Day After* presents." However, once ABC announced the November air-date for the film in September, Baran says, antinuclear groups began to get involved in the event.

Previews of the movie also contributed to a sudden increase in movement activity. "We heard about the movie last June, but it was only after seeing it that we began intense work and made it a top priority," says ESR's Susan Alexander. "*The Day After* is very powerful," says PSR's Abram Claude. "After seeing it, I realized that it makes what we're trying to say to the public much more real. It really gets to the heart of the matter."

However, Claude, Alexander, and a number of other organizers are concerned about the film's limitations—limitations that Baran freely admits.

"The movie is a passive-depressive experience and offers no sense of hope or idea about what you can do," Baran says. "That's why it's imperative for groups to relay the message that nuclear war *is* preventable. Groups should get representatives on talk shows the day after the movie. They should hit the newspapers and magazines. Get out there and tell the public what they can do."

Before the Deluge

That is precisely the premise of a project based in Emeryville, California, called The Day Before. Director Wendy Roberts, backed by 12 national organizations, has arranged community gatherings in over 100 locations through-out the United States for the Monday and Tuesday nights following the Sunday night movie to show people that nuclear war is preventable—if they work on it.

"Talking about nuclear fear is almost as taboo as talking about sex once was," Roberts observes. "*The Day After* provides us with an opportunity to break that taboo. We can finally begin to confront what we all know is out there."

The Day Before project is focusing on the mainstream. Field organizers throughout the United States have been instructed to make sure that non-activists comprise at least half of the participants at Day Before gatherings. "We're going after the mainstream people who love their kids, their lives, and their country, and who don't want to see it all blown up," says Roberts. Day Before gatherings are planned for YWCAs, garden clubs, churches, and in one town in Virginia, the local firehouse. All of these people, Roberts says, must be shown that nuclear war is not inevitable. "After we deal with their responses to the film," Roberts says, "we want to get them active. We want them to take their heads out of the sand and do whatever they can do to help."

Janet Michaud, with the Campaign for Nuclear Disarmament in Washington, D.C., hopes to make that first step toward action as simple as picking up a phone. Michaud is finalizing plans to set up a toll-free "800" number anyone can call in the days and weeks following *The Day After*. Callers will then be hooked up to local peace groups and the national antinuclear movement. The number will be advertised in national and local newspapers, and on radio shows, television, and billboards.

But one Washington, D.C., activist already sees problems arising over this area of outreach strategy. "The movie is like a giant rally," he observes, "and we'll all be trying to get the people who come to the rally to join *our* group. Who gets first whack at the names for direct mail membership drives? There are, unfortunately, questions of turf here."

Michaud says that the names will be made available to any group that wants them. But, as one New York organizer points out, "If the list goes to everyone, we'll have chaos. If people start getting letters from four or five different groups, we could end up killing their good intentions with kindness."

Despite the problems raised by such an ambitious media campaign, Michaud believes that the effectiveness of the antinuclear effort depends on this project and others like it. "There is a lack of understanding and commitment to using serious media as outreach in the peace movement," Michaud says. "And there's good reason for it. Organizers are out in the trenches, and they *should* be there. But we've all got to understand that the union of the peace movement and the media is the perfect marriage." Of course, the chronic shortage of capital in the peace movement has severely limited its mass media outreach. That's why Jenny Russell of Women's Action for Nuclear Disarmament in Arlington, Massachusetts, feels that *The Day After* (which cost the movement nothing to produce) is so important. "In order to make a difference, the disarmament movement has got to start talking numbers," Russell says, "and for numbers, TV is the way to go."

Saving the Titanic

Not everyone is sure that they *want* to go with *The Day After*. Although the Lawyers Alliance in Boston is arranging group viewings and working to get members on talk shows in the days following the film, Gail Gallessich, the group's director of public relations, has misgivings about it. "The movie does not address the fact that there are alternatives to the arms race," she explains. "There are no activist role models in the film. It is so negative that if we become overly associated with it, it may backfire on us."

Organizers from Educators for Social Responsibility are concerned about the movie's effect on children, and are recommending that no one under the age of 12 sees it; as Susan Alexander half-jokingly puts it, "They should be torn away from the TV and tied to their beds." (Some organizers, however, fear that if such protective impulses are overly publicized, this may unwittingly play into the hands of right-wing groups who are making the related—but broader—claim that the movie will terrify *all* Americans.)

Leslie Cagan of Mobilization for Survival in New York wonders how to get *The Day After* out of the context of despair and move it into the context of politics. But Josh Baran maintains that it is precisely the movement's job to charge the atmosphere around the movie and turn it into a political event. "We must be there to move people through the experience, catch them the day after *The Day After*," Baran says. "But we've got to stop futzing around here; this is not Never Never Land. We're on the Titanic, and we have to do all we can to break into the control room and turn the ship around. We can't wait around forever for the perfect movie," Baran adds. "We don't have the time."

Whatever the movie's failings, the fact remains that ABC has spent $7 million on what amounts to a powerful indictment of nuclear weapons. Watching people die from radiation sickness can never be a pleasant experience, but when viewed in the context of responsible support groups, *The Day After* could prove to be a landmark political and educational event for the nation. As Jenny Russell said, after leaving a preview of the film, "I kept wondering, 'how can anyone be expected to watch this?' and yet knowing that this is one movie everyone *must* see."

The Media and the Movement
By Renata Rizzo
November/December 1985

ON TUESDAY, JULY 30, 1985, IN A HASTILY CALLED PRESS CONFERENCE AT the Rayburn House Office Building in Washington, D.C., several leading arms control experts, including Senator Edward Kennedy and former CIA director William Colby, explained why the Soviet moratorium on nuclear testing, announced the day before, merited serious consideration by the American public and government. Although nearly 20 print and television reporters, including representatives from the *New York Times*, the *Washington Post*, and national television networks, covered the conference, hardly a word about it appeared in the nation's press or over the airwaves. Movement organizers were disappointed—and frustrated. "The press conference was a first," says Raoul Rosenberg, associate director of Physicians for Social Responsibility, one of the groups that organized the event. "We mounted a fast, professional response [to breaking news]. It didn't seem to matter."

This media boycott illuminates the hurdles blocking the antinuclear movement's bid to be heard. And though those obstacles may seem formidable—the current administration seems to manipulate the news media with unprecedented skill—the movement is at last jumping into the fray. Suddenly, national media projects are proliferating as efforts are made to provide what many term the "missing link" in movement strategy.

"For years, this movement has neglected the media," says Richard Pollock, who heads up the Peace Media Project in Washington, D.C. "Now there are so many campaigns. But I say it's better to have too many than not enough."

Fortunately, since no two are exactly alike, the projects could work well together if coordinated closely (another movement sore point). But do any of these efforts really have the slightest chance of success, given the current structure of the movement, its financial base, and its relations with the American public, Congress, and the press?

Turnabout for the Movement

After over three months of research involving 13 paid associates, Women's Action for Nuclear Disarmament is about to release *Turnabout,* a report on national communications, compiled by strategic planning consultants John Marttila and Tom Kiley. The $160,000 project (financed largely by Joan Kroc) leaves little doubt that the movement has an enormous job ahead of it. Through in-depth interviews with 100 of the nation's top journalists and roughly 40 members of Congress, and a survey of over 1,000 Americans, the report sheds some harsh light on the movement's national profile.

"I can't stress enough that the key, enduring, non-trendy foundation for all communications programs is thinking about strategy that will affect coverage," says John Marttila in his Boston office. "There can be no quick-hit solution through advertising. Advertising can only be used to supplement P.R. initiatives. To think that ads can be used to move American opinion is ridiculous. There will never, never be enough money."

Instead, Marttila and Kiley—and WAND—hope to make people aware of the Reagan administration's superb media manipulation, and of the movement's corresponding failure to communicate its side of the story. Each section of their report offers a series of strategic recommendations for improved relations with the press, Congress, and the general public.

Some of the movement's problems are obvious: Most groups, for example, do not have full-time press secretaries. "We called a meeting for the media directors and press secretaries of 20 national groups in Washington, D.C.," recalls Diane Aronson, administrative director of WAND. "*Two* showed up."

WAND's report shows that this basic, structural disadvantage has taken its toll: The attitude of journalists toward the movement "goes beyond normal, healthy skepticism," says John Marttila, who has run successful political campaigns for Representative Ed Markey, Senator John Kerry, and Madeleine Kunin, governor of Vermont. "They view this as a social movement rather than a movement with good ideas. We were taken aback by their lack of respect—particularly the Washington reporters."

In politics, Marttila points out, the battleground is the press. "You've got to be on the phone all the time," Marttila says. "One NBC newsman told me that there's been nothing but a deafening silence from the progressive community, whereas the Reagan administration is all over them." Marttila also points out that the freeze, based on the report's interviews, is not taken seriously by the press. "There's something wrong," he says, "when so many people and so much effort are going into something that is not highly regarded by the very people writing about it."

A lack of candid communication also exists between members of Congress and the movement, the report says. According to Marttila, several legislators said they held few hopes that the movement would listen to them, even if their voting records were generally favorable to the movement. Other legislators, who believe that the movement is advocating ideas that are politically and substantially incorrect, feel that activists are not at all interested in discussing their differences of opinion.

But Marttila and Aronson do not want to give the impression that the situation is hopeless. "There are many opportunities for the movement to break through on," says Aronson.

Monitoring Mood

People serious about "selling peace" must, before anything else, undertake the enormously complicated task of analyzing the mood of the country. After all, the White House conducts four opinion polls a month.

In the past year, the movement has begun to pay closer attention to polling and poll results. SANE and the Center for Defense Information, for example, recently commissioned an opinion poll showing that the American public favors a U.S. nuclear testing moratorium (as long as it's also undertaken by the Soviets) by a margin of two-to-one. "We commissioned the poll to confirm that the public did indeed support a moratorium" says David Cortright, executive director of SANE. "But—just as important—we wanted to use that information as a media story. A poll of this sort can be a powerful form of political lobbying if used in the right ways." Cortright reports that the poll results were picked up on the Associated Press wire.

As for the ambitious WAND public opinion poll, both Marttila's and Aronson's initial reactions are cautiously pessimistic; with over 500 pages of cross-tabulations to absorb, they are reluctant to jump to conclusions. In fact, they postponed a press conference on the poll in order to step back and analyze the data, which were less hopeful than expected.

"It is very sobering," Aronson comments. "It looks to be more conservative than anyone would like to have seen. The country is more polarized than we imagined. A lot of people seem to be attracted to power and strength—we noticed a lot of 'Rambo' personalities."

Richard Pollock's Peace Media Project recently compiled its own "public attitude" report using existing polls and drawing on interviews with leading pollsters, advertisers, media consultants, and creative producers. (Many of Pollock's recommendations for improving the peace movement's public image, overall structure, and priorities are echoed in the WAND report.) Although Pollock is waiting to see *Turnabout* before proceeding with his own agenda, he is (among other things) encouraging the movement to mount strategic, escalating public relations campaigns around issues that are "value-oriented"—the Geneva Summit and military spending emerged as "salient" themes—using advertising as a final (not a preliminary) tactic. And, Pollock stresses, advertising must ask people to *do* something—support a bill, send money, vote for someone.

Conceptual Thinking

One thing that every peace media organizer has in common: Much of what they know about mass communication has been learned at the knee of such conservative groups as the American Security Council, who typically use "concept" campaigns to win points with the public. Evocative messages like "Peace through Strength" pack a punch with people on a gut level.

It's not going to be nearly as easy, however, for the antinuclear movement—even if it is armed with reams of polling data—to appeal to America's gut. Many recent surveys, including the Yankelovich data, show that most people are turned off to nuclear issues because of terror and a profound sense of personal powerlessness.

"There is enormous hunger for the message that personal involvement *is* possible, and can make a difference," says Gil Friend, president of the Foundation for the Arts of Peace in Berkeley, California. (The group is best known for its marketing of the television show "In Our Defense," which has been aired on over 150 commercial stations across the country.)

Since late spring, Friend's project, "Marketing Peace," has been recruiting advertising executives (who are themselves relieved to be hawking something other than lipstick and cars) to come up with campaigns that will break through the paralyzing sense of helplessness. "We want to touch people very deeply in an emotional way," Friend says. "We cannot continue to tell people how bad things are."

Friend feels that the movement has more than enough polls to work with, and is concentrating instead on carefully designed "focus" groups to round out, with qualitative data, the quantitative data gleaned from polls. From this research, Friend says, he expects several positive, evocative messages to emerge, which will then be used in a nationwide advertising campaign in both the print and electronic media. "We don't know yet what the messages will be," Friend says. "But we do think that themes along the lines of 'It can be done' and 'You can help' will be featured. And there will probably be a sequence of messages that will build, and be demographically different." The ads might suggest groups to join or contact for information. And Friend hopes that they will complement efforts that focus on more specific issues, like the military budget.

Friend envisions getting this "irresistible" message out through traditional nonprofit funding. But he also plans to approach major corporations for financial backing—the "Brought to you by Exxon" route. And he wants to donate the project's creative concepts to selected corporate advertisers for use in their own "identity" campaigns, much in the way AT&T keyed into the LIVE AID concert.

With the marketing of "In Our Defense" under its belt, Friend says the Foundation will rely heavily on television to spread its message, claiming that it's not as expensive as people think. "We've got to use TV more," Friend says. "People in environmental and peace groups are a subculture. Many of them think TV's tacky. We have to decide if we're committed to this subculture or to changing the world. We can't say that television is sleazy. So what? Eighty-four percent of America gets its election information from TV. If we're too holy to get down in the trenches to do battle, we may as well hand it over to the American Security Council. We ignore TV at our peril."

That's no news to Ted Turner, who has given seed money to form the Better World Society, a new organization, based in Washington, D.C., devoted entirely to getting antinuclear, environmental, and population-control programs on America's airwaves.

"We want our programs to serve as mobilizers," says BWS President Thomas Belford. "We'll be pointing viewers to organizations. We'll be providing information on groups. We'll be profiling individuals active in the movement. We'd consider it a missed opportunity to use all this broadcast time and not tell people how to get involved."

While most of BWS's programs are still being developed, Belford says that they will focus on hope. "We believe that everybody can make a difference," Belford says, and "and we hope to relay this optimism to our viewers." For example, BWS will present one of its first productions in mid-November, timed for the Geneva Summit. The show, called "Challenge of the Caucasus," depicts a U.S.-Soviet mountain-climbing team successfully scaling the highest peak in the Soviet Union. The analogy to mutual survival, Belford hopes, will not be lost on viewers.

Shows produced by BWS will be "fair game" for network or public television stations to pick up. But, Belford says, Turner Broadcasting, which reaches 35 million households, is their guarantee for air time. BWS plans to maximize the use of its productions by distributing them to the grassroots through home video cassettes, schools, and libraries, and civic and public interest organizations. "The most important thing we're trying to do, though," says Belford, "is get that long-term, ongoing programming on television."

Another promising television effort is the "Popularizing Peace Task Force," headed up by Norman Fleishman, who, in recent years, has gotten progressive messages on network dramas by cultivating relationships with prominent actors, directors, and producers. (As a result, in some circles he's known as Hollywood's "conscience.") Working with a team of writers, editors, business leaders, and entertainers, Fleishman will appeal to middle America's survival instinct through an escalating campaign involving television programming, advertising, and celebrity spokespeople.

Moving to the Write

There is a growing consensus that without mounting ongoing centralized, focused media campaigns, the movement will continue to be seen as amorphous, with no clear agenda or readily accessible message. "Our whole hope is that groups—by looking at the issue through the prism of this WAND report—will become sensitized to why strategic planning and coordination are essential,"

John Marttila says. "The movement must begin to work together more—to meet every two weeks and decide which issues to hit."

But even before the WAND report is released, steps are being taken to improve movement coordination, both internally and externally. Every media project director hopes to hook up with other media initiatives; tentative plans are being made for a central meeting of all project leaders. There is talk of establishing one movement media center in Washington, D.C., where groups can work together on specific press campaigns. And for the last six months, press secretaries from eight national groups in Washington, D.C., calling themselves the Working Press Group, have met regularly to discuss strategy and share resources.

In addition to coordination, there is a need for spokespersons with strong, clear credentials. This presents an obstacle, since the movement has traditionally been antihierarchical, shying away from cultivating visible leaders. As a result, aside from several arms control experts, there are few accessible movement spokespeople for the media to contact routinely.

But now, the Arms Control Association and the Committee for National Security, both based in Washington, have been given an initial grant of $250,000 by a celebrity funder to constantly brief a large group of experts, such as Paul Warnke, Robert McNamara, and William Colby, who will then be in a position to provide prompt responses and counterviews to administration policy.

"We will brief Washington, D.C., reporters frequently, and we'll be sending regular press advisories to journalists outside of Washington," says Ann Cahn, executive director of CNS. ACA and CNS intend to set up a telephone hotline service to handle media queries. Each group will give two full-time staff people to the effort. "We want to be *pro*active, not reactive," Cahn says. "We'll be thinking ahead to critical decision points."

Another effort, undertaken by the National Communications Consortium, a project of the Tides Foundation in San Francisco, aims to compile a master press list of key reporters nationwide that could eventually—in six to nine months—be shared by the movement. This group plans to coordinate with Cahn's project and supply celebrities and less well-known experts to the CNS/ACA pool.

But a well-run, coordinated media strategy is bound to be a financial drain on the movement. How can it ever hope to sustain a far-reaching, professional public relations campaign?

John Marttila recommends one basic strategy: Make membership recruitment a priority. "The right goes out and says, 'Write a check,'" Marttila says. "They have master mailing lists and computers. Out of the core contributors, or members, come your volunteers. If individual organizations were committed to building a members' base, the funds would be available for media work. There would be movement stability, and an impressive network of people." WAND, for one, has now taken on the goal of going out and launching an aggressive membership drive.

But not everyone agrees that emulating the right wing's strategy is necessarily a strategic stroke of brilliance. "The right wing is successful because it is built on a system of already existing beliefs, fears, and prejudices," says Richard Healey, executive director of the Coalition for a New Foreign and Military Policy in Washington, D.C. "Our task is fundamentally different. We have to *overcome* deepset fears of not just the Soviets, but everything that's foreign. Americans have this 'Back off—we're going to be the toughest kid on the block' attitude." Healey, agreeing with Marttila on at least one point, believes that the movement must grow considerably before it can even hope to compete with the well-established communications network of the right.

Whatever approaches are taken, it's going to take a good deal of national coordination—perhaps even national consolidation—to begin to mount a serious P.R. campaign. It's going to mean dealing simultaneously with the American public, Congress, the press, and each other in a perpetual four-dimensional chess match. The movement must decide now to either forfeit the game—or get serious about media strategy.

How "They" See "Us":
The Military Views Peace Activists
as a Bunch of Crusaders, Criminals, and Crazies
By Julie Morrissey and William Arkin
March/April 1989

ON SEPTEMBER 1, 1987, A U.S. NAVY LOCOMOTIVE RAN OVER BRIAN Willson, leader of a group of protesters who were blocking the railroad tracks outside the Concord Naval Weapons Station in California. The train, operated by civilian navy employees, hit Willson when he failed to move off the tracks, fracturing his skull and severing his legs.

The House Armed Services Committee concluded after an investigation that the accident had resulted "from an overabundance of trust on the part of all concerned": the protesters standing on the tracks believed the oncoming train would stop; the train crew believed that the protesters would move. But this game of chicken seems more indicative of a mutual lack of understanding—the wide gulf between the military establishment and its civilian critics that has both sides thinking in terms of "us" versus "them," with little idea of what makes the other side tick.

For its part, however, the military has made some effort to understand its critics. This has been seen as necessary in recent years, whether to deal with growing local opposition to nuclear weapons in the early 1980s, or more recently, to mobilize public support for military spending at a time of budget crunches and improving U.S.-Soviet relations.

The results of these efforts, as revealed in writings and through recent interviews, show attitudes that are biased by the nature of the military itself: its purpose in "understanding" the peace movement has been to learn how better to fight it.

"Crusaders, Criminals, and Crazies"

Every activist in the country is familiar with the litany of derogatory adjectives used to describe them: naive, misguided, emotional, irresponsible, anti-American—just for starters. Typical of military literature on the subject is the army's 1983 training manual, *Countering Terrorism on U.S. Army Installations*, which specifies three types of radical activists: "crusaders, criminals, and crazies."

Elsewhere, peace movement activists are frequently characterized as floundering fools—crazies in the weird, disjointed sense. A 1983 study by the conservative Hudson Institute for the Department of Defense categorizes antinuclear activists as either "protected"—"those who actually believe that unilateral sweetheart actions will bring like responses"—or "naifs"—"those who believe simpleminded 'peace' slogans." The study's author, B. Bruce-Briggs, refers to these activists as "silly riffraff." Dale Smith, a retired air force major and author of *The Eagle's Talons: A Military View of Civil Control of the Military*, prefers the term "starry-eyed idealists." In a March 1983 editorial, the *Santa Maria Times*, which serves California's Vandenburg Air Force Base, calls antinuclear activists simply "anti-whatevers."

While these analysts are largely dismissive, others stress that it is a serious mistake to underestimate the "excessively or persistently optimistic" viewpoint. "Peacekeeping by wishful thinking" can be subversive, or at best, "dangerously counterproductive," explains James H. Toner, in the September 1987 issue of *Parameters*, the official military journal published by the U.S. Army War College. "Confronted by a popular mythology which often suggests that peace is available virtually for the asking, leaders, sycophantic and saccharine, truckle to Pollyannas in endorsing schemes which sometimes, in their simplicity, may undermine rather than support the structures of peace."

Soviet Tools

At the opposite extreme from irrelevant crazies is, according to the Hudson Institute, a more sinister group: the outright "leftists," "deviants," and "nihilists." These supposedly disaffected activists are seen as the genuine subversives in the peace cause—not least because they are believed to serve as intentional or unwitting agents of Soviet propaganda.

Alleged Soviet manipulation and disinformation of peace groups seems a given for military and right-wing civilian political analysts. In the September 1988 issue of *Army* magazine, Gen. John R. Galvin, commander of U.S. forces in Europe, attributes opposition from the European and U.S. peace movements to "the Soviet effort to prevent deployment of the Pershing II and ground-launched cruise missiles." In an October 1982 column for the *Washington Times*, Patrick Buchanan, former Reagan White House communications director, wrote, "Anyone who cannot see the hand of Moscow and the ugly faces of its odious little affiliates inside the 'peace movement' in Europe and the 'freeze movement' in the United States is simply not looking." There seems to be some disagreement, however, over whether the peace movement is subordinate to, or merely manipulated by, the Soviet Union: when asked in off-the-record interviews about the alleged Soviet link, several Pentagon officers took great care to assure that they don't believe the Soviets actually "run the show," but that they understandably take an interest in it.

Activism and Terrorism

Military analysts reserve a special category for peace activists who engage in civil disobedience and direct action. These "antinuclear extremists," in the words of a February 1982 RAND Corporation report, *The Appeal of Nuclear Crimes to the Spectrum of Potential Adversaries*, represent a special threat. The report describes such activists as "individuals or groups so committed in their opposition to nuclear programs that they would be willing to undertake criminal actions to further their cause." A 1980 RAND memorandum lists "possible" crimes that could be committed by these "extremists" as including "low-level standoff attack," "theft or purchase of information," and taking and holding hostages.

The absence of such crimes in any instances of direct action has not stopped military observers from perfunctorily equating the criminality of civil disobedience with terrorism. Analyzing Nuclear Regulatory Commission data, the army's counterterrorism manual lists "extremist protest groups" in the category of terrorists motivated by politics and ideology.

Similarly, Lt. Col. David Linn of the Office of Security Police, writing in the August 1985 *USAF Security Police Digest*, describes what he calls the "soft-core terrorism" practiced by Western European activists targeting NATO. "Militant protesters vandalizing road signs which direct forces on military maneuvers or cementing demolition shafts can easily springboard to acts of hard-core terrorism such as fire-bombing vehicles and bombing pipelines or communi-cation sites."

Crusaders

While crazies can be dismissed, and "countermeasures" can be taken against criminals, the military is less sure of what to do with a third type of activist, the "rank and file" of the movement: students, professionals, housewives, retirees, and environmentalists. As described in the Hudson Institute study, these are "the concerned," those who "recognize the great problem of nuclear war and have been sold programs that *appear* to deal with it" (emphasis added).

These "crusaders" are generally viewed as well-intentioned, reasonable, and law-abiding. Several Washington-based Pentagon officers we spoke with went so far as to acknowledge a positive role of what they call the "public interest" community—a group most peace activists would consider themselves to be a part of.

Yet for others in the military, it is precisely this group's success that is most alarming. Citing antinuclear activists' ability to draw media attention and embarrass the armed services, and the way they "negatively shape U.S. defense policies," the Hudson Institute concluded that "the concerned are those at whom a counterdisarmament campaign can be directed."

Dealing with Activists

Not everyone in the military holds extremist views of antinuclear activists, and the military's negativism about peace activists has to some extent ebbed and flowed with the movement's own growth and decline. In the heyday of the freeze, for example, some—particularly high-level officers—voiced positive and respectful views of the movement and its participants. In a January 1983 interview with *National Guard* magazine, Gen. John W. Vessey, Jr., chair of the Joint Chiefs of Staff, said, "Those people arguing for a freeze now have their hearts in the right place. But their logic is flawed." General David C. Jones, Vessey's predecessor, asserted in the official DOD publication, *Defense 82*, that "this movement cannot be dismissed as the emanations of a fringe element—it is drawing increasing numbers of very serious-minded concerned citizens."

But in spite of such respectful attitudes on the part of high-level officers, the rank and file of the military—particularly those responsible for physical security and public relations—generally have held more negative attitudes. And because it is precisely these functionaries who have been assigned the task of "interfacing" with antinuclear activists, the military has in a way codified their more extremist views.

In turn, such attitudes are reinforced by the mandate the military has assigned its public affairs and security programs. Rather than emphasize direct debate with critics, the military defines these programs' mission as "confrontation management"—containing the visibility and effectiveness of protesters. The approach means that the military deliberately limits its interaction with questioning citizens. Officers who have contact with an unfriendly public are directed to forego discussions about policy. During the deployment of MX missiles, for instance, Maj. Michael C. McMullin, the official air force public liaison for Nebraska and Wyoming, flatly ruled that "blue-suiters [air force officers] would not enter into a debate, nor share the same platform with someone representing the opposition, i.e., an 'anti-MX' group." Further, the major noted in his 1987 thesis for the Air Command and Staff College that "we did not recognize these types of groups [the MX opposition] as civic groups; therefore, we would not accept speaking requests from them."

In an article entitled "Participatory Democracy: Challenge to Readiness" in the June 1986 issue of *Army*, Milton H. Mater, a retired army colonel, and Dr. Jean Mater discuss "organized civilian efforts to halt, delay, or change military projects." The authors write that, today, peace activists' "battle arenas are the public hearing or public meeting and the courtroom. Their weapons are grassroots groups, coalitions, media-bait slogans, letters to the editor. . . . While adversaries play the game of power politics, the army plays a different game, based on rationality, attempting to resolve the conflict by carefully explaining technology and military requirements."

The Maters' article, although extremist in tone, reveals a subtler, but more fundamental bias that widens the gap between the military and the peace movement. Hiding behind claims of impartiality and rationality—and the declared political neutrality of the armed forces—the military not only excuses itself from real contact with citizens, it intimates that politics is an illegitimate way to make decisions about defense. Here the military itself seems naive. Decisions on competing programs *are* made on the basis of politics, whether those political struggles be interservice or intrabureaucratic within the Pentagon, or in the public domain.

Gen. Galvin, writing in *Army*, appears to acknowledge this at least in part: "Development of the ability to present the military viewpoint will be more critical in the years ahead . . . To maintain support for adequate national and alliance security, leaders at all levels are going to have to become more articulate and more accessible to the press and the public than we frequently have been in the past."

But as battles are fought in the coming years over defense spending and program priorities—and over the very definition of "national security"— the military will have to do more than articulately express its views. It will have to recognize that its opposition is more than a bunch of crazies—it is a manifes-tation of a nation weary of nuclear weapons. It will have to join the political debate as an equal partner—and work *with* the peace movement and the public—rather than merely sharpen its sword for a tougher battle ahead.

Covering the Peace Movement
By Tracey Cohen
Summer 1991

FOR MANY PEACE ACTIVISTS, THE U.S. WAR IN THE PERSIAN GULF WAS A painful and demoralizing experience. A solid majority of Americans supported the war once it started, and efforts at organizing an opposition movement were largely met with derision, hostility, and an occasional threat of violence. "It was a dangerous time to speak out against war," says Meg Gage, executive director of the Peace Development Fund, who received hate mail after publicly opposing the war on National Public Radio.

Reactions of both hostility and indifference to the peace movement caught many activists by surprise. After all, in the months leading up to the war American society appeared to be strongly opposed to a military initiative.

Not surprisingly, the Bush administration, determined to exorcise the ghost of Vietnam, mobilized a major public relations effort to generate popular support for the war. Key to this campaign were strict military censorship of the flow of information from the battlefield and the manipulation of popular symbols at home.

But as activists soon realized, opposition to official government policy had become as much a target of the war as Baghdad was. And the most surprising and perhaps most damaging attack came not from the administration but from the news media.

War Cheerleading

"I feel like there were 100,000 media sorties against the antiwar movement," says Charlotte Ryan, codirector of the Boston College Media Research and Action Project.

When the bombs began falling, journalists were quick to jump on the military bandwagon. But the news media war began well before January 16. In fact, analysts at Fairness and Accuracy in Reporting had noted that in the months leading up to the war, columnists and commentators urged the United States to make short work of the Iraqi army. "Masterful" and "brilliant" were among the adjectives used repeatedly to describe Bush's military mobilization.

A FAIR study of "Nightline" and the "MacNeil/Lehrer Newshour" during the first month of the crisis revealed that nearly half of their U.S. guests were current or former government officials; on "Nightline," not one argued against military intervention.

Both national and local news media downplayed negotiations as a way to resolve the crisis. A study of the print media in Boston, for example, found little coverage of diplomatic activity, even around the January 15 deadline when France, the Soviet Union, and Iran were all making efforts at negotiation. News coverage, says Bill Hoynes, a member of BCMRAP and the coalition that prepared the Boston study, suited the Bush administration's objectives of obscuring these attempts.

"There was very little coverage of the long-term consequences of military intervention for the gulf region," Hoynes says. "In comparison, there was fifteen times as much coverage of military preparation."

When the war began in the gulf, the news media stepped up its campaign at home. Film footage giving a weapon's-eye view of events mesmerized the public. Any pretense of objectivity fell away as military euphemisms permeated the working vocabulary of reporters. News reports unabashedly revealed the fascination and admiration journalists had for "smart" missiles and the "surgical precision" of the bombers. There were tallies of enemy weapons "killed," while injured and dead civilians were discreetly noted as unavoidable "collateral damage." And disclaimers stating that Iraqi censors provided information accompanied the occasional acknowledgement of civilian damage.

Hoynes notes that it was Israeli casualties that were the focus of discussions of death and destruction during the war, even though the number of Iraqi casualties was significantly greater. "Three times as much space in newspapers was devoted to Israeli civilian casualties as to Iraqi casualties," he says.

Delegitimizing the Opposition

While coverage of bombings and the success of military hardware was plentiful, the press marginalized reports on the opposition to the war. FAIR found that in the first five months of the gulf crisis, the major television networks devoted only one percent of their Persian Gulf coverage to popular opposition to U.S. policy. Another FAIR study showed that out of the 878 sources the networks used during the first two weeks of the war, only one source was a representative of the national peace movement.

What coverage there was of the antiwar movement, says Jim Naureckas, editor of the FAIR newsletter *Extra!*, was little more than short sound bites and isolated segments from demonstrations. "They looked for the strangest people, violent behavior, or flag burning," he asserts.

BCMRAP's Charlotte Ryan notes that the news media frequently stereotyped members of the peace movement as being suburban, privileged, and white, in other words, those unaffected by the war. Activists were also presented as unpatriotic and disloyal, deviant hippie leftovers, or naive pacifists hopelessly ill-informed about real-world geopolitics. The effect of such representations combined with constant references to prowar activity as pro-American helped strip the opposition of its legitimacy.

Moreover, the press picked up on the Bush administration's successfully chosen themes of international cooperation and opposition to aggression, which gave moral justification to U.S. military intervention. Given the typical corporate media approach to events, in which history and context are both absent, activists were hard pressed to explain what the war really meant.

The administration was also able to shift the terms of debate away from politics to a purely military viewpoint, asserts Michael Schiffer, an analyst for New York University's Center for War, Peace, and the News Media. "The administration and the Pentagon were very effective in classifying the discourse as military discourse," says Schiffer. "So the only voices who could respond to the military were other military people."

The emphasis on military considerations was a successful stumbling block for the peace movement. The Vietnam War, in particular, became the main antiwar framework. "The peace movement didn't have the sense that there were alternative military scenarios," says Harold Jordan, coordinator of the national youth and militarism program for the American Friends Service Committee. "We got duped by military propaganda about how strong the Iraqi army was. So the movement tried to shock America as to how bad casualties would be."

The peace movement, says PDF's Meg Gage, needed to build moral opposition to war in general because of the incalculable suffering and destruction it unleashes on other people, which shows that it is not the way to solve problems. "Opposing the war on the basis of how costly it would be in lives and dollars was a mistake," she says. "When the war began appearing superficially worthwhile, we appeared to be wrong."

Other issues plagued the peace movement as well. Saddam Hussein's image as a brutal tyrant weakened arguments against deposing him, causing the peace movement, in its calls for a cease-fire and negotiations, to appear as if it were making a pact with the devil.

Says AFSC's Jordan, "the peace movement didn't understand that Iraq and Saddam Hussein were symbols." Some people were fighting an old war. Others were fighting an anti-Arab or anti-Muslim war they felt should have been fought years ago against Iran. Some supporters of the war, Jordan maintains, were simply searching for community and an issue around which Americans could unite.

That elusive unity was achieved by what was perhaps the most damaging issue for the peace movement: support for the troops. The Bush administration, culminating years of historical revisionism by the right wing, successfully argued that Vietnam was lost because the antiwar movement eroded troop morale. Thus the war in the gulf became primarily a question of morale. Media images of hometown boys and girls in the desert and the families they left behind obscured the broader questions of the war. To support the troops, it was not necessary to know anything at all about the issues involved or whether the administration's policy was right or wrong.

"The antiwar movement had the task of severing the connection between support for the soldiers from support for the war," explains BCMRAP's Ryan. "Activists tried to argue that the best support was to bring the troops home." But the Bush administration maintained that the two issues were not separate. Opposing the war would undercut soldiers' morale, thereby prolonging the war and endangering them. Ryan notes that message rang especially true for people with family members in the military.

A Watershed Event

The length of the war was the final blow to the opposition, but NYU's Schiffer points out that some historical perspective has been lost. The huge protests against the Vietnam War came, he recalls, after several years of organizing. "Building coalitions and catalyzing opposition takes time," he maintains.

Other analysts agree. "If the war had dragged on even six months, there would have been an enormous antiwar movement by the summer," asserts Bill Gamson, a BCMRAP codirector. "Bush believed it too; he had to have a quick victory."

One task for the peace movement then, Gamson adds, is to prepare for the fight over the lessons of the war. "The aftermath will be messy," he says. "The United States will have a difficult time extricating itself, and this can be used to draw different lessons than the administration will draw."

Whatever peace activists learn from the gulf war, perhaps nothing is as critical as a clear understanding of the role the news media played. Never before has the press's promotion of official policy and manipulation of public opinion been so blatant. "The way the media were used to promote government propaganda is out there now," says BCMRAP's Charlotte Ryan.

In the past, peace activists have viewed the news media as outlets for free publicity. Now, however, the mainstream media are being seen as yet another arena for struggle.

"Access to the media is a necessary condition for having a movement that reaches large numbers of people," asserts FAIR's Naureckas. And Ryan agrees: "Access to media is beginning to be seen as a democratic right."

The importance of publicity to peace movement organizing is well illustrated by a recent study done by three researchers at the Center for the Study of Communication at the University of Massachusetts in Amherst. Alarmed by the way the media was using public opinion polls to justify the administration's policies in the gulf, these researchers evaluated the relationship between the news media, public opinion, and public knowledge of issues related to the war.

Their report concluded that people who supported the war tended to know only those facts that would not lead them to question the administration's policies. For instance, 80 percent of the people surveyed knew that Saddam Hussein used chemical weapons on the Kurds and in Iran, but only 46 percent knew there were other lands besides Kuwait under illegal occupation in the Middle East.

Support for the war correlated directly with the levels and types of knowledge people had: The more people knew, the less they supported the war. How much television people watched also corresponded to how much they knew about the war and where their support lay. In general, the more television people watched, the less they knew and the more likely they were to support the war. "This is an appalling indictment of an information system and its priorities," says Justin Lewis, one of the study's authors.

"The news media did a dismal job in reporting the war," Lewis maintains. "Television coverage was not only dismal, but very much worked in favor of Bush's policy." He concludes that if people had been better informed and the news coverage more balanced, then there would have been much less support for the war.

Learning Lessons

Around the country, activists have already begun taking this lesson to heart. FAIR has experienced a 20 percent increase in subscriptions to its newsletter, says Jim Naureckas. The organization has also been setting up local offices in several cities. The Boston College Media Research and Action Project has received calls from activists around the country, including San Francisco, Philadelphia, and Hartford, wanting to know how to organize and directly target the news media. The Peace Development Fund has given grants to a number of media-related projects and is considering the addition of a media-training program. And in Boston, an ambitious new project has been launched to hold the press accountable for its biases and distortions and to demand equal access for alternative viewpoints and analyses.

"We'll never get the mainstream coverage that we want or be treated as the equals of the so-called legitimate experts," says BCMRAP's Hoynes. "But once we recognize the possibility of problems with the news media in the same way that there are problems with other institutions, our situation will get better."

CHAPTER
SEVEN

The Academy:
The Growth of Peace Studies Programs

Teaching the Unthinkable
By Paul Loeb
October 1983

The most upsetting letters I receive are from schoolchildren who write to me as a class assignment. It's evident they've discussed the most nightmarish aspects of a nuclear holocaust in their classrooms. Their letters are full of terror. This should not be so ... Our children should not grow up frightened.

—*President Reagan*

THE KIDS ARE LEARNING ABOUT HIROSHIMA. THEIR TEACHER, RONNIE Sydney, explains the word *hibakusha*—atomic bomb survivor—and writes it on the board. She reads an account of collapsing buildings, skin hanging from burned hands, and charred corpses soaked with radioactive rain. The kids look down or watch with wide eyes, sheared of their ninth grade Boston cool, taking in this terrible story not only as a past event, but as a possible future.

The teacher hesitates and interrupts her reading. "I didn't mean to scare you," she explains, "just to give you a sense of what it was like." The kids ask questions—"Were there babies born without limbs?" "Don't we need bombs because of the Russians?" "Would the Charles River be destroyed?"—and the pain of the immediate testament recedes. They begin discussing the size of current weapons.

President Reagan said on July 5 that the nuclear curriculum taught here is "aimed more at frightening and brainwashing American schoolchildren than at fostering learning." Entitled *Choices: A Unit on Conflict and Nuclear War*, the curriculum was developed jointly by the National Education Association and the Union of Concerned Scientists for use in junior high schools. Reagan's charges echoed those of the NEA's rival American Federation of Teachers. AFT president Albert Shanker called the unit "lopsided propaganda" containing "almost no discussion of the near-universally accepted concept of deterrence," and designed to transform innocent students into hardened disarmament cadres.

Is the NEA really propagandizing by addressing the threat of nuclear war? And how can teachers best educate children about the issues?

Breaking the Silence

Aside from the 1950s and 1960s civil defense drills, schools have ignored the nuclear issue. The single best-selling high school history text, *The Rise Of The American Nation*, by Lewis Todd and Merle Curtis, gives atomic weapons one 64-word paragraph, recounting the number of Hiroshima dead and explaining only that "a new force had been added to warfare, a force that would enormously complicate the post-war world." Neither this book nor its major competitors makes more than perfunctory reference to the steady development of weapons since the original devices were exploded. Two of the top four texts fail even to mention the H-bomb. As a result, schools have supported the prevailing silence about nuclear war, and it is just not seen as an appropriate subject for discussion. Although many kids fear a holocaust, they've never addressed its possibility in class. Like the rest of us, they've been assured that the matter is being taken care of.

The new nuclear curricula—the NEA's *Choices* and a variety of others now being developed—confront the issue head-on. They discuss what nuclear war would be like, how the weapons buildup has come about, and our options for preventing catastrophe. In the first lesson of *Choices*, the Hiroshima story gives "the threat" a human meaning through the memories of the *hibakusha*. It acts as a call and a warning, framing the later sections on Cold War history and arms race economics, conflict resolution, and disarmament options—the choices that lead toward or away from its terminal implications. The teaching methods involve kids directly in decisionmaking through games and role playing. The emphasis is on how understanding and imagination can help to make a better world.

The new curriculum does not wholly disrupt school conventions. Kids still ask about tests and requirements, complain about having to keep classroom journals, and do their best to maintain their flip, tough, flirty, punky, or even just doggedly studious stances. But where other courses look toward a time when the kids will leave the world of the classroom and become adult actors and creators, the nuclear lessons warn that their future may be obliterated.

The lessons pass, of course, and the kids go out into the halls, slamming their battered metal lockers and teasing their friends. But they have learned to name previously shapeless fears, and perhaps even to turn them to strength. While many of the kids will still cling to their trust in government leaders or to the fatalism that insists that they are powerless, others will bring up the atomic issue with their families and friends, perhaps for the first time. And some will start high school peace groups, write letters, hold forums, and join the dissent of a broader community—like the Cambridge, Massachusetts, senior who organized a busload of kids to attend the June 12 rally, coordinated a regional student conference, and later cotaught the course that initially stirred her interest.

Is this kind of teaching propaganda? If kids are exposed only to the lessons in *Choices*, they might need the counterbalance of material advocating weapons buildup to help them understand rationalizations of the arms race (such as the deterrence theory). But the nuclear unit does not confront kids in a vacuum. It questions assumptions already created by *Time* and CBS, by history books that explain how Truman had no choice but to drop the bomb, by a web of intimations that our present path is inevitable.

"There is no question about it, the curriculum is biased for a nuclear freeze," said Bruce Feiderstein, a social studies teacher in the Brighton public schools outside Rochester, New York, at the height of the *Choices* controversy earlier this year. "But what's wrong with telling kids that nuclear war is wrong?" Or as Roberta Snow, coordinator of the high school teaching guide *Decision Making in a Nuclear Age*, recently put it, "All we really want is to help kids think critically about the most significant issue they may face in their lifetime."

Resisting the Missionary Impulse

The educators who drew up the nuclear curricula believe that citizen involvement is a good thing. But they are still concerned about the danger of forcing their own beliefs on students. During a two-hour Educators for Social Responsibility discussion in Boston last January, several teachers said they cared too much about the issues to mask their voices in a false neutrality, but also wanted to avoid being missionaries.

As one ESR member explained, "I have a personal desire to do something really quickly on the issue, but also feel it's wrong to enlist young people in the cause. So I use materials from PSR, but also from Committee on the Present Danger. I hope as a citizen they'll choose PSR, but also hope the kids will be able to challenge my assumptions."

Another participant pointed out that strong personal opinions can actually spur discussion and disagreement. "The best teachers I ever had were very committed to a particular point of view, a particular topic or particular authors, but not in a closed way," she said. "They were open to hearing other people . . . and invited students to go through that process with them. . . . If there isn't any commitment, there isn't any education; there's just an accretion of knowledge." In the words of ESR cofounder Shelley Berman, the important thing is not to convey a monolithic viewpoint, but "a way of looking at everything in the world and assessing it and evaluating it." That way, the kids are encouraged to question their teachers' assumptions as well as their own. And the nuclear lessons can be used as a window to broader issues, an entry, as Berman said, "to exploring questions of justice, global awareness, our own aggression, and violence."

Many teachers find that the best way to teach balanced classes without compromising their own beliefs is to bring up contrasting viewpoints in a way that doesn't imply their endorsement. Boston teacher Ronnie Sydney tells her class about an argument she had on the nuclear issue with her father. Others counterpose extra reading material or bring in outside speakers. And all try to create an atmosphere where the kids can express diverse ideas without feeling attacked.

Mid-Course Correction

I saw an example of this in Sydney's classroom when a kid named Keith defended armed strength as the sole path to security. He didn't think we'd see a war in his time, but if we did, he said, we should have a strong defense "so we'd be able to wipe them out." He explained that "a nuclear war and building up arms are two different things." He believed in "peace through competition."

Sydney encouraged his comments, drawing him out, and remarking, "you said it so well." Other students argued back, and Keith held his ground all the more firmly, taking the stance of a patriot besieged by insurgents. He wasn't cowed, and when a CBS crew covering *Choices* came to film a news segment in the classroom, he had another kid wear his red, white, and blue windbreaker with the letters USA, so it would show on television. In his own interview, he told the camera, "If Russia keeps going then *we* should," then added that he liked the class and thought it fair and interesting.

The NEA unit succeeded here both in making room for Keith's beliefs and in encouraging others toward active questioning and involvement. And Sydney's kids rated the *Choices* lessons the highest of any in their semester-long "Law and Society" course. This success was due in large part to her teaching. But the curriculum gave her a roadmap—a tool to begin a new dialogue and discuss what had not been discussed before. Unlike teachers clinging to the objective verities of the three Rs, those involved with the peace curricula do not know all the answers. Given that they are as vulnerable as their students to the threat they discuss, their task is to use their experience and teaching skill to make this common vulnerability a spur to learning and engagement—and to help kids address a world where previous guarantees (for instance, that children of succeeding generations will sit and learn in classrooms such as these) can no longer be taken as givens.

Colleges on the Right Course?
By Cathy Cevoli
October 1983

AS STUDENTS RETURNED TO COLLEGE THIS FALL, MANY FOUND A NEW offering in their catalogs, something that might be called a nuclear war course. It can appear in any of a number of departments: physics, religion, economics, political science, philosophy, English, or math. Even more likely—an interdisciplinary survey. In one form or another, the nuclear question is alive on campus.

A network of students and faculty called UCAM (United Campuses to Prevent Nuclear War) now lists 61 nuclear-related courses on every level and in every part of the country. The trend is almost too young to have a name, but many are calling it nuclear education. Still in the process of definition, nuclear education is already showing great diversity. An American University course explores the links between nuclear power and proliferation; a course at Arizona State is on "the nature of humanity in the atomic age"; and Seymour Melman teaches a course at Columbia on military spending and conversion to a civilian economy. Nuclear strategy is being incorporated into classes on defense policy and the ethics of war, while sociology and history courses are also taking up the subject. Three English courses listed by UCAM use books on nuclear war as a vehicle to teach writing.

The Missile Gap

This sudden explosion rectifies a longstanding shortcoming of American schools. For a variety of reasons—including the Vietnam War's domination of foreign policy discussions and a general unwillingness to confront the end of the world—nuclear issues have been absent on the college level for almost two decades. Arms control itself was subsumed into foreign policy studies (which in turn underwent plummeting enrollments in the late 1960s), where it was taught in a manner most kindly described as traditional.

Some time around the Cuban Missile Crisis, says Columbia University's Seymour Melman, "all the ideas around arms race reversal were caused to go down the memory hold," to be replaced at schools by strategic courses. "As two generations of young people came through the universities, trained [to think] there was nothing around but the arms race, or the regulation of the arms race—arms control—the very *idea* of the *reversal* of the arms race got lost."

Among the consequences of this neglect was a general public ignorant of nuclear issues. For years, says Daniel Ellsberg, no one in his lecture audiences could explain the difference between an A-bomb and an H-bomb. "Until the freeze movement, there was widespread ignorance of the simplest facts of the arms race," he says. "This extends to journalists, congressmen, and people in the antinuclear movement."

The cause of disarmament was also severely hurt. While graduate centers for studying arms control did exist, many feel they functioned, in Ellsberg's words, "to produce more useful components in the arms race"—a bias reflected in the title of a new book by several Harvard professors, *Living with Nuclear Weapons*. Randall Forsberg has said she was the only person in her Massachusetts Institute of Technology doctoral program who even seemed to know the word "disarmament." And while Forsberg's colleagues went off to jobs in the Pentagon and government, peace studies programs lingering from the 1960s were admitting in their brochures that few jobs for peacemakers existed.

Disarmament *is* hard to teach, says Coit Blacker, associate director of Stanford's Center for International Security and Arms Control. "It doesn't lend itself well to instruction," Blacker explains, "partly because there's not much history to go on."

Many other barriers exist to instituting nuclear-ed courses. Since the field is new, faculty members lack basic textbooks and incentive. Teachers must also balance a controversial topic and fend off charges of bias. Limited resources and conservatism inhibit any major new course. And as Stanford's Blacker notes, opening up a topic long viewed as the province of a select group of academic experts means asking that group to yield a little territory.

Above all, the very vastness of the topic hampers growth. A typical nuclear survey—what UCAM calls "a basic course"—would include the effects of nuclear war, the history of the arms race, new weapons and doctrine, and past arms control efforts. It may also touch on the technology of the Bomb and the moral and psychological aspects of the arms race. But where in the curriculum would such a course fit? And who is qualified to teach it? Given their usual sense of objectivity, scientists are often uncomfortable teaching courses with ethical and moral components. Other teachers may not have the time, or inclination, to master technical details.

A Class Bias?

A common solution is for the course to be team-taught. One example on the grand scale is underway at Houston's Rice University, where professor Stephen Klineberg has gathered 15 lecturers "from electrical engineering to philosophy" for a course called "Sanity and Survival: Perspectives on the Nuclear Age." Students originally suggested the course to Klineberg and then helped him recruit faculty. "Everyone we spoke to was delighted about the course and eager to help shape it," he says. As a text, his students will read two *Scientific American* readers, the two Ground Zero paperbacks, and *Living with Nuclear Weapons*.

At the new Peace and Social Justice Program at Tufts, projects include an innovative teaching award to foster faculty interest, and the creation of peace concentrations within departments. Yet director Robert Elias admits he encounters "the sense that such programs are biased and activist in orientation. And in a way they *are* activist, if you think the university's mission is to help solve human problems." About the problem of suspicious trustees, Elias advises: "Get the best and most respected professors involved from the start. Try to get outside funding. And try to avoid discussions about the university's role."

Other helpful tips may come out of an ambitious survey of students and nuclear-ed faculty to be conducted on at least 30 campuses later this year by International Student Pugwash. This organization, which has sponsored several major conferences but is just now forming campus chapters, feels that there has been an absence of discussion about the purposes and methods of teaching nuclear war courses. "We feel it is critical that we not only get the nuclear issue on educators' agenda but that we insure the *quality* of what actually gets taught," says Jeff Leifer, an ISP founder. "And we want to see if the courses are getting so political that faculty and parents can gang up on them."

Even in its infancy, nuclear education is struggling with an image problem. George Perkovich, former executive director of ISP, feels the news media is hurting nuclear-ed—by simplifying it, playing up charges of indoctrination, and linking it too closely with antinuclear sentiment among students. Most professors agree that the commitment of faculty and administrators is more crucial for instituting these courses than student demand. Students may take the issues more seriously once they're sanctified by faculty.

"Undergrad courses are being taken by people who don't know anything and are tremendously anxious to learn," says physics professor Aron Bernstein at M.I.T. "This includes many who support the government position. It's not uncommon in these classes to have very heated debates."

It's also quite common for one of the coteachers to represent military training on campus. "War and Peace in the Nuclear Age," a highly popular course at Cornell, is taught by a government professor, by the campus head of Naval Reserve Officers' Training Corps, and by physics professor Peter Stein, who is also national UCAM chair. "We made a very conscious effort to make sure the course was balanced," says Stein. "After all, there's no admission charge for a Physicians for Social Responsibility symposium, but this course costs students $1,000."

Several groups are promoting this process. Teachers interested in developing peace curricula can turn to UCAM or United Ministries, a group associated with Columbia University's Teachers College in New York, which can provide a core text and a self-assessment kit to help educators evaluate the "peace component" of their existing courses.

There's also an establishment to turn to, housed in the graduate centers funded in 1973 by the Ford Foundation. In the last decade, Ford has spent $17 million to encourage international security and arms control in the United States, with the bulk going to programs at Harvard, Cornell, M.I.T., and Stanford. It's to these schools—which range in orientation from M.I.T.'s defense analysis to Cornell's peace studies program—that students interested in further education will probably head.

A Berlitz Creed

Publication of the Harvard book—which many antinuclear activists feel teaches benign acceptance of the arms race—has fired the debate over exactly what these programs teach. "These schools train people to be hired," says Ellsberg, who has taught on the arms race at Stanford and will lecture this year at Harvard and at University of California at Irvine. "The criticism they encourage is the kind acceptable to administrations. Maybe a student will write on waste in the Pentagon budget. That critique involves the way goals are implemented, but not the goals themselves."

Natalie Goldring, a Ph.D. candidate at M.I.T.'s Center for International Studies, observes: "This is a tough program psychologically for someone who believes in disarmament. There's a continuum in the field—people at one end tend not to believe in deterrence at all, while the other end believes in it very strongly. The arms controllers come in the middle."

Last summer, those in the middle began reaching out to newer teachers, at the Harvard/M.I.T. Workshop on Nuclear Weapons and Arms Control. Attended mostly by teachers from small colleges, this two-week session was designed as a sort of nuclear Berlitz course; its presenters (including several contributors to the Harvard book) spoke from a centrist, "arms control establishment" position.

The problem, according to its executive director, William Durch, is that "a matter-of-fact delivery can come across as acceptance. The people who attended were, for the most part, as disgruntled with academic experts as with the right wing, and worse, lumped them together. So the old-line arms controllers were seen as part of the problem, whereas they've thought of themselves for years as struggling for a solution. You have to know the nuts and bolts to affect policy—there's a tremendous amount of information to digest. Still, there's no denying the clinical approach met with a minor revolt."

Coit Blacker feels anti-arms race sentiment may have an effect on the way graduate courses are taught. "When arms control is in a slack period, it's easier to teach in traditional ways. The students coming in now are forcing us to be more imaginative and comprehensive. We spend more time discussing the psychology of the arms race—that it's not inevitable, that there were and will be points in the process where it could be turned around."

It remains to be seen where the students flooding into these courses will make their impact. Almost no one foresees a repeat of the 1960s protest; Bernstein notes that the weekly vigil at Cambridge's Draper Lab is "marked by an absence of M.I.T. students." And while it's now possible to major in peace studies at several schools, the programs seem directed to the kind of conflict resolution skills equally geared to prison reform and family crisis centers as to arms negotiations.

On the undergraduate level, most educators describe their goal as an informed citizenry, capable of understanding all sides of an issue such as the MX. UCAM director Sanford Gottlieb says that a grounding in history will also help voters appreciate their own importance, since arms control has had as much to do with public pressure as with international tension.

Another common goal is to institutionalize courses as permanent offerings while public opinion, notoriously episodic on arms issues, is still strong. "The hope," says Blacker, "is that study of the significance of nuclear weapons will become an inherent part of any good liberal education."

Will it be possible to emerge from grad school and fight the arms race? "Most of our graduates go to the state department, to Rand, to teach at the armed services academies," says Goldring. Yet Goldring works part-time for the Union of Concerned Scientists and likes to point out that Randall Forsberg plans to return to M.I.T. to finish her doctorate. Bernstein adds that it's possible now for a "small minority" to make a living in the opposition—as a writer or scholar, or within public interest science.

"I know several grad students in the field," says Peter Stein. "One is writing now on disarmament issues. The other has a nice summer job with the CIA."

Peace Studies Comes of Age
By John Feffer
September/October 1988

WHEN BARBARA WIEN ANSWERED HER TELEPHONE ONE DAY LAST YEAR and found that Richard Perle was on the line, it was a sure indication that peace studies had finally graduated to the academic big time.

What did the "Prince of Darkness"—the former assistant secretary of defense under Ronald Reagan—want from a peace studies specialist at the Institute for Policy Studies, that favorite target of right-wing red-baiting? Advice, believe it or not, on which peace studies programs the U.S. government should fund through its Institute of Peace. Perle, who used to sit on the Institute's board, called Wien several times afterward asking for additional assistance, which she has given despite her skepticism of the Institute's political goals.

What's going on? It was difficult enough getting used to Ronald Reagan's newfound warmth for the "Evil Empire." Now, the most hawkish administration in decades is giving peace studies a good name, not to mention a million dollars a year.

With such mainstream benefactors, peace studies has apparently made the successful transition from orphan-child of academia to family member in good standing. Where five years ago, peace studies programs were scrambling for students and fighting off charges of trendiness, today such programs are receiving millions of dollars annually and enrolling thousands of students. The statistics are impressive:

- More than 300 colleges and universities offer peace studies courses;
- 150 colleges offer degree programs and 30 have graduate programs;
- 111 law schools offer courses in alternative dispute resolution compared to only 10 schools a decade ago;
- the Peace Studies Association recently formed to serve the needs of the growing community of peace educators.

Why such success? In part, the flowering of peace studies can be credited to the disarmament movement. The Freeze Campaign of the early 1980s gave nuclear war issues such wide exposure that significant numbers of students were drawn to courses and institutions that taught about those issues. Since the demise of the freeze, peace studies has continued to grow, evolving beyond the study of nuclear weapons issues.

This evolution, however, has triggered a debate within the peace studies community. Has success transformed peace studies into just another academic subject? Has peace studies become *too* respectable?

Gary Weaver lectures like a stand-up comedian. In his graduate class on cross-cultural communication at American University in Washington, D.C., Weaver peppers his presentation with anecdotes about cultural misunderstandings. There's the one about the visitors from Botswana who try to tip the cashier at Burger King and the one about the Muslim farmer who takes religious offense when pressed by an insensitive American official to predict the future of his crops.

Weaver's class is not your stereotypical peace studies course. He makes little mention of nuclear weapons, global security, international law, or nonviolence. It's not "touchy-feely," but it's not heavy on academic jargon either. His syllabus is bulging with books and articles on culture and history. For all of Weaver's funny stories, this is a serious class.

Nor do the students in the class conform to the peace studies stereotype. No tie-dyed Deadheads. No fire-and-brimstone ideologues. Instead, there are a few middle-aged students, conservatively dressed. Several students major in international education, others in international relations. There is even one student who carefully explains during the break that he is in "conflict management," *not* peace studies. Most students stress they are in the class to learn skills, not simply facts and statistics.

With its academic rigor and interdisciplinary spirit, Weaver's class is a good example of the new generation of peace studies instruction, a field now entering its fifth decade. The first peace studies courses, established in 1948 at Manchester College in Indiana, were primarily attempts to grapple with the central paradox of the postwar age: the invention of the atom bomb and the founding of the United Nations. Those early courses, according to Ken Brown, director of the Peace Studies Institute at Manchester, tended to be more philosophical than technical, favoring the study of Gandhi over the analysis of atomic war. During the Cold War, the field barely survived by concentrating on ideologically "safe" topics like world law.

At the height of the Vietnam War protests, peace studies gained new momentum, as activists sought to straddle the gap between ideas taught in the classroom and demands shouted over bullhorns at demonstrations. Programs sprang up at Kent State, Notre Dame, Colgate, and Penn State. When campus activism tailed off, some programs, like Penn State's Center for the Study of World Problems, suffered premature deaths.

A decade later, however, peace studies was back with a new focus: nuclear weapons. The enormous popularity of the Nuclear Weapons Freeze Campaign spread onto campus, and suddenly peace studies—originally conceived as a multi-issue discipline—became linked in the public mind with disarmament studies.

"There was a big surge in the early 1980s," says Michael Klare, director of the Five College Program in Peace and World Security Studies in Amherst,

Massachusetts, "and we thought that it would peter out. But in fact the growth of programs has continued at a steady rate in the 1980s." Klare's office receives notices of new programs at the rate of two or three a month and he estimates that there are at least twice as many that he doesn't hear about.

Unlike those developed in the freeze days, the new programs reflect a trend away from a nuclear weapons emphasis. The very titles of the programs give an indication of their diversity: global studies, conflict resolution studies, peace, and nonviolence studies. As Klare points out, "You can't really find two pro-grams with the same name. The field is really peace studies and then 'fill in the blank.'"

The differences in course titles are also reflected in curriculum content. Where five years ago, Klare notes, courses on nuclear weapons contained mostly nuclear scare literature, a similar course today covers a much wider range of issues: the history of the arms race, nuclear doctrine, U.S.-Soviet relations, verification and compliance, Third World issues. And these new courses frequently offer literature from a pronuclear point of view as well, treating nuclear weapons as necessary evils.

The students who take such courses have often undergone a similar evolution themselves. Initially drawn to peace studies because of an interest in preventing nuclear war, they often end up focusing on another aspect of the field. Dale Largent, a senior at Manchester College, says that he turned to peace studies because of an interest in disarmament. Now, however, he concentrates his studies on interpersonal conflict resolution and the historical roots of war. Deborah St. Claire, a graduate student at Columbia Teachers College, discovered peace studies because of a seminar she attended on arms control. Now she believes "that there is more to peace education than nuclear age education."

Despite the increased popularity and, some say, sophistication of peace studies, old criticisms can still be heard: "You can't do anything with a peace studies degree," "Peace studies is biased," "Peace studies isn't rigorous."

Secretary of Education William Bennett and various right-wing think tanks have attacked peace studies because they say it has allowed leftists to infiltrate American campuses. Leftists themselves criticize peace studies for not being sufficiently advocacy-oriented.

New peace studies programs still have to address these questions. But, as many programs successfully move into middle age, the debate is no longer fueled by outside critics. Peace educators are now beginning to debate among themselves.

The first question debated is a definitional one: what should and should not be considered peace studies. The field, after all, is not an undifferentiated mass. Listed cheek-and-jowl in peace studies course catalogs are classes on arms control and hunger, nonviolence and human rights, women's issues, and the environment.

But it isn't so much the range of topics that causes friction. More divisive in peace studies is the *respectability* of the issues. The field is a continuum,

BETWEEN FEAR & HOPE

stretching from topics offbeat and radical like "future imaging" to mainstream concerns like arms control negotiating.

Colman McCarthy clearly falls in the offbeat camp. As a peace educator and syndicated columnist, he has raised many administrative eyebrows with his innovative teaching style and controversial views on the virtues of nonviolence. At American University in 1986, McCarthy initially let his students grade themselves before the university insisted on the more traditional arrangement. His lengthy reading list, which is virtually all "unrequired," joins Martin Luther King and pacifism together with vegetarianism and anti-abortionism.

Finally, McCarthy encourages his students to volunteer in the community. "High school and college students tend to be idea-rich but experience-poor," he says. "One solution I've found is take them into the community: to literacy programs, homeless shelters, soup kitchens, or homes for the elderly and get them to volunteer there during the semester. They've learned more in one week about the English language while teaching in a literacy program than in majoring in English."

This emphasis on "experiential" education and internships in the community contributes to making peace studies programs unique in academia. But some educators fear that peace studies is in danger of losing its uniqueness. Peace studies at the university level has become "too discipline-bound," says Betty Reardon, a professor at Columbia Teachers College. Contrasting teaching *about* peace and teaching *for* peace, Reardon maintains that peace is a way of life, not simply an academic discipline like political science. The idea of peace studies, she explains, is not simply to establish one little corner of academia that teaches peace. Rather, she argues, peace studies should be spread throughout the entire academic curriculum.

The institutionalization of peace studies in the academy has been accomplished, others argue, at considerable cost to original ideals. "As peace studies succeeds, it get assimilated, co-opted," says Robert Johansen, senior fellow at Notre Dame University's Institute for International Peace Studies. "Peace studies courses get adopted by universities, but the content of the courses gets watered down." The courses that achieve the most success in this context, he continues, "are those that tend to be heavily empirical and do not challenge the underlying assumptions of the status quo."

Those courses most accepted within the university make up the "respectable" end of the peace studies spectrum: arms control or security studies, international relations, and conflict resolution. In some peace studies programs, all three coexist in the same department. But some educators are careful to stress the distinctions, for instance, between peace studies and arms control studies. "People entering the arcane world of arms control lose sight of the fundamental questions," says Barbara Wien. "Arms control studies has done a lot of damage. It has further institutionalized the arms race."

But perhaps the largest irritant to peace educators involved in nonviolent studies or world order studies is the financial support lavished on the three sister fields. Arms control studies receives the lion's share of foundation support. The MacArthur Foundation, for instance, sends the majority of its institutional grants to high-profile strategic studies programs at Columbia University, Stanford University, and the University of Maryland. Conflict resolution programs, like George Mason's in Virginia or Syracuse University in New York, have attracted sizable contributions from Hewlett-Packard's foundation.

Furthermore, the major foundations favor graduate programs, primarily in strategic studies, leaving undergraduate education out in the cold. "We think undergraduate education is very important," says Joel Federman, associate director of the Peace and Conflict Studies Program at University of Southern California. "But the foundations haven't come around to that yet. They want a tangible product, but they don't realize that students are tangible products."

For many undergraduate peace studies departments, the financial situation is precarious. For example, at Berkeley's Peace and Conflict Studies Program— despite some outside funding—the professors aren't even paid for the peace studies courses they teach. Many undergraduate programs "rely on the good will of faculty to do additional work for which they are compensated little," according to Neil Katz, director of the Program in Nonviolent Conflict and Change at Syracuse University. "It's often a way for the university to get more mileage out of faculty because of their passion and commitment."

With major funding sources often inaccessible to them, many programs have begun to look elsewhere. USC has linked up with progressive Hollywood stars like Barbra Streisand, who provided a $15,000 grant through her foundation. At the University of California at Irvine, the Global Peace and Conflict Studies Program funded a chair in peace research entirely through contributions from local businesses. Notre Dame's Institute for International Peace Studies has been blessed with a generous principal benefactor, philanthropist Joan Kroc, the widow of the late McDonald's hamburger chain magnate. Kroc's foundation has given the program $12 million, a figure only dreamed about by peace studies proponents several years ago.

And then there's the U.S. Institute of Peace, established in 1986 to promote peaceful resolution to international conflict. In 1988, Congress allocated $4.3 million, of which at least one quarter must be given to research programs: a cool million for peace research.

Many activists, however, are suspicious of the Institute's goals. "Everyone knows that the deck is stacked against peace studies in terms of getting meaningful support from the Institute," says Robert Elias, founder of the Peace and Social Justice Program at Tufts University.

Why? Some point to a board of directors that consists of *ex officio* members like Lt. General Bradley Hosmer, president of the National Defense University, and Secretary of Defense Frank Carlucci. Others note that the grants are principally directed to large research centers like the Brookings Institution or the Hoover Institution, rather than small, poorly funded peace studies programs.

But even the Institute's harshest critics realize that it operates very much like a foundation, rarely funding smaller programs, and generally going with the institutions with proven track records. And the institute's grants are minor compared to the other money available: one million dollars is only nine percent of what the MacArthur Foundation provided in institutional funding alone in 1987.

So the money is out there for peace studies, but only for a certain type of peace studies: conflict resolution, arms control studies, research fellowships. What about the more visionary peace study programs? "They don't have to be competing factions," says Barbara Wien. "They could be complementary. Some people are trying to bridge the gap, but I'm skeptical. The future of peace studies is up for grabs."

The Peace Movement's New Frontier:
Peace Studies Programs Struggle for Identity
By Elliott Negin
Summer 1991

PEACE BRIGADES FROM COLLEGE CAMPUSES ACROSS THE COUNTRY IN-vaded Washington, D.C., in early April for the Peace Studies Association's third annual conference. Given the timing, one would have expected a slew of activities on the gulf war. Surprisingly, only 20 percent of the events at the two-day meeting, hosted by Catholic University, touched upon the topic— a testimony to the wide range of subjects that make up this relatively new academic field.

Although some educators argue the field's diversity is its strength, others call it a discipline with no discipline. "Peace studies is still struggling for an identity," explains Robert Herman, a doctoral candidate at Cornell and a member of the PSA executive committee. "What isn't peace studies? If you want to define yourself as a discipline, what are the parameters? We want to see ourselves as unique, interdisciplinary, and bring in issues of empowerment, and still want to be taken seriously as a discipline."

Most peace studies programs in the early 1980s were devoted only to issues of war and peace, but the Cold War thaw—and the growing perception that security means far more than military strength—let a thousand flowers bloom. Besides courses on the history of the arms race, nuclear doctrine, and verification issues, programs now include classes on industrial policy, nonviolence, human rights, ethnic politics, hunger, and women's issues. The workshops, plenary sessions, and papers at the meeting, which attracted 120 academics from the United States and Canada, reflected this diversity—or, as some contend, confusion.

"We need to be clear about theoretical constructs," adds Herman. "What are the important questions to be addressed? There is no consensus, and there probably won't be any in the near future."

Bigger Role for the U.N.?

For Lester Brown, the conference's keynote speaker, the environment is the number one issue. Brown, the president of Worldwatch Institute, described how ecological disasters caused by humans, such as soil erosion, air pollution, acid rain, and global warming affect food production and health and can lead to broader conflict over resources. He sees the new emphasis on international cooperation as a potential solution.

"The 'old world order' from 1950 to 1990 was dominated by ideological conflict that defined priorities on the use of public resources and dictated the shape of coalitions among countries," he told the gathering. "A 'new order' is now emerging and the new organizing principle should be environmental sustainability. We see the opportunity for the entire world to pursue a common goal—environmental survival. No single country can do this; it has to be a global effort."

Panelists in the second plenary session echoed Brown's call for collective approaches to world crises. This session focused on the implications of the gulf war. The panelists agreed that the reinvigoration of the United Nations would benefit from international security, if the organization can maintain consistency.

"The present level of attention to international moral and legal norms is unprecedented," said David Little, of the United States Institute of Peace, "but there isn't a total unanimity on how to view these norms or apply them." He pointed out, for example, that while most countries condemned the Iraqi invasion of Kuwait as a violation of international law, the world community failed to respond when Iraq invaded Iran in 1980.

Carolyn Stevenson, a political science professor at the University of Hawaii, said she hoped the new collective process in the U.N. Security Council would force U.S. officials to "reassess the question of whether the United States should be the world's police officer and react unilaterally" and opt for a "multilateral, common security approach in which each nation's security is dependent on the security of other nations." She said this move toward collective diplomacy will have to counterbalance the drive for countries to try to build or obtain high-tech weapons.

Finally, Abdul Assiz Said, director of American University's Peace and Conflict Resolution Studies Program, presented a six-point Middle East peace plan, and said no matter what the U.N. does, nothing will happen without strong efforts by the United States. "We are the heirs of an old order of violence," he said. "We need to become the architects of an order of human decency and justice. Only the United States can make it possible."

A third plenary session featured a panel discussion on socioeconomic security —especially for the Third World—as a crucial element in maintaining peaceful relations among nations. Other conference events covered a range of topics, including workshops on setting up peace studies programs, on writing grant proposals, and on teaching methods. Faculty papers included such issues as "The Bomb and the Rainforest," "State Theory in the Post-Cold War Era," and "Relations Between Nonviolence and Human Rights."

Rapid Expansion

The PSA conference comes at a time of phenomenal growth for peace studies programs. Like the peace movement, such programs have waxed and waned over the past four decades. The first program was established in 1948 at Manchester College in Indiana, on the heels of Hiroshima and the founding of the United Nations. But the peace studies concept barely survived the Cold War and only gained a foothold at a handful of U.S. campuses at the height of the Vietnam War. Some of those programs, however, were canceled soon after the war ended. By the early 1970s, only three remained.

It was the next wave of peace activism—the movement to freeze nuclear weapons—that reawakened peace education. By 1980, there were 30 programs, and today there are approximately 250 undergraduate and graduate programs across the country. This expansion prompted representatives from 23 peace studies programs to form the Peace Studies Association in December 1987. In three years the number of member peace studies programs has jumped to 100.

Even with this growth, PSA Executive Director Robin Crews cautioned in his opening remarks that "the status of peace studies' future is uncertain. The recession is hitting peace studies hard—it's one of the first programs to go."

Peace studies are plagued with other problems, both internal and external. On many campuses, according to American University's Said, peace studies programs are fighting for "recognition and acceptance as a legitimate discipline." Some critics charge that it is too amorphous, while others say it is either too radical, or not radical enough.

Furthermore, there is a debate over content. Said supports the notion that peace studies needs to broaden the parameters of the field. "We must free ourselves from viewing peace studies through the narrow prism of conflict, conflict resolution, and war," he says.

Conversely, Michael Klare, of the Five College Program on Peace and World Security Studies program based at Hampshire College, maintains the peace community has leaned too far from things military. "Peace studies is not environmental studies," he stressed at one conference workshop. "Our job is to understand the dynamics of what causes people to make war on one another. There is an 'allergy' in peace studies to political and military security issues, which are seen as the preserve of national security studies. Peace studies people remove themselves from the debate."

Finally, Said raises the question of pedagogy. Peace studies, he believes, should wed theory with practice. "Peace education has to combine education about peace with education for peace," he says. "It should be about personal and political liberation." Klare also wants peace studies to affect public policy. "Peace studies should be an applied science," he says. "It should grant a professional degree."

Thinking Globally, Acting Locally

Despite disagreements over what constitutes peace studies, rising interest in the subject has spawned not only a national organization, but local intercollegiate associations as well. The Washington, D.C., area, for example, home to two PSA member schools—Catholic University and American University—boasts its own peace studies group. Three years ago, programs at both universities joined with programs and interested faculty and students at four other schools to found Capital Area Peace Studies. Instead of holding conferences to showcase faculty papers, however, CAPS conferences give undergraduate and graduate students the chance to present papers to their peers. The same weekend of the PSA meeting at Catholic University, CAPS held its third annual student conference a few buildings away. The day-long meeting attracted 125 students to hear 30 papers in a dozen workshops.

"The CAPS conference is a unique opportunity for students to participate in academics outside the classroom and integrate their concerns for social justice with their academic work," said Jackie Smith, a graduate student at the University of Maryland and coordinator of the conference. "Students rarely get the chance to get feedback from other students on what they're doing, and given that conference participation is voluntary, students are sharing and learning rather than just trying to get a good grade."

The CAPS student papers were more wide-ranging than those at the PSA event—ranging from electoral politics to sexual violence and the Catholic Church to U.S.-Japanese relations to the civil rights movement. If these students represent the future of peace studies, the future will mean even more diversity. Or, depending on your perspective, more confusion.

CHAPTER
EIGHT

The Movement Part Three:
Moving On 1990–present

Ecology Wars?
By Donald Snow
Spring 1990

If the Pentagon had been put in charge of negotiating an ozone protocol, we might still be stockpiling chlorofluorocarbons as a bargaining chip.
— *Daniel Deudney*

TOM BLESSINGER IS NOT THE SORT OF PERSON ONE NORMALLY ASSOCIATES with peace activism. He is a politically conservative rancher who runs a large cattle operation in the Owyhee Desert where Idaho, Nevada, and Oregon meet. Like a lot of Western ranchers, he counts among his most important neighbors the U.S. Bureau of Land Management, trustee and manager of nearly all of the five-million-acre Owyhee country. Blessinger leases public land from the BLM— lots of land, because it takes a lot to raise cattle on the sage-choked plateaus of the Idaho high desert. His winter range is a 200,000-acre lease he shares with four other ranchers.

For decades, the cattleranchers of Owyhee County, Idaho, have lived in quiet harmony with their federal landlord, but the harmony has been disturbed by the rise of public interest in the federal lands. Lately, Blessinger has found himself competing at a furied pitch with environmentalists, river runners, wilderness enthusiasts, and other recreationists who demand that the BLM manage the high desert much less for cattle ranching and much more for recreational, scenic, and preservationist purposes. They have proposed "Wild and Scenic" designations for several of the desert's spectacular canyon streams, wilderness for some of the same plateaus prized by graziers like Tom Blessinger, and even a national park.

In Blessinger's eyes the environmentalists are a bunch of come-latelies, there to "rescue" the high desert from the Bureau of Land Management and a scattering of cattle operators who have kept the land in agriculture for more than a century. For a long time, he just wished the environmentalists would go back to wherever they came from. If it weren't for the U.S. Air Force, he might have felt that way forever.

It seems that the air force has also "discovered" the Owyhee Desert, but where the ranchers see it as a fertile land for cattle, and the environmentalists have come to secure its solitude and rugged beauty against development, the air force regards it as a wasteland. As part of a $100 million expansion of Idaho's Mountain Home Air Force Base, the Pentagon wants to expand the Saylor Creek Bombing Range out in the Owyhee Desert to more than 15 times its present size—from 102,000 acres to more than 1.5 million—transforming it into one of the largest and most advanced live bombing ranges in the world. The air force has now claimed the entire eastern quarter of the Owyhee—the ranchers' home and the environmentalists' playground—as a place to practice annihilation. And that has turned Tom Blessinger around.

When he stood to testify at an air force hearing in Boise last September, just after the Saylor Creek proposal hit Idaho so suddenly, no one in the room knew what he was about to say. A few dozen of his old enemies, the environmentalists, were there, expecting the worst. They had seen him at hearings before and feared him as an articulate spokesperson for the ranchers who were willing to fight to keep the high desert agricultural. This time, Blessinger got up and said: "I'm used to going to these kinds of meetings and having you all stare daggers at me. Tonight I see friendly faces. We have a common enemy—the U.S. Air Force." There was a moment of stunned silence, then cheering erupted.

In the view of the more than 200 who have now testified against the air force expansion plan in Idaho, the high desert is no place to test so many F-4 fighters and weapons. The rock-walled canyons and free-flowing rivers, the livestock and wildlife, the deep silences of the vast and once-indomitable Owyhee country could not withstand a quadrupling of air force presence. Supersonic overflights as low as 50 feet would terrify animals—Blessinger says it would disrupt their reproductive cycles and drive wildlife away—and shatter the peace of the ancient canyons of the Bruneau River. The constant flyovers, the pummeling bombs and missiles would squeeze out the last bit of wildness from the Owyhee.

The Saylor Creek Bombing Range plan is but one of many proposed expansions of weapons testing sites that arose from Congress's 1988 decision to relocate urban and coastal military bases to rural areas. In addition to the 1.5-million-acre expansion in Idaho, the Pentagon wants a million acres in Montana, a quarter-million acres in California, 900,000 to add to its more than four million acres in Nevada, 600,000 acres in Oklahoma, and another half-million acres in Utah to build a multibillion-dollar electronic battlefield.

Blessinger describes his newfound allies—environmentalists and peace activists—as "strange bedfellows," but enjoys his association with them. "We've been meeting, and it's really improved the understanding," he says. But he still stands by his claims that agriculture remains the best use of the Owyhee country, just as he stands foursquare patriotic. "I'm a dyed-in-the-wool American," he says. "My family's been around here more than a hundred years. I'm for a strong defense, and I know these guys need a place to test weapons, but you look at a map and you can see that they've got plenty of places already. They don't need to take more of this country than they've already got."

The Perpetual Toll of War

The newfound and unlikely allies who are fighting the Saylor Creek proposal are not alone in their environmental opposition to military expansion. They join a growing chorus of environmentalists, agriculturalists, and peace and social justice activists who together decry the increasingly destructive reach of the military and the enormous expenditures of money, human talent, and industrial effort required to keep global arsenals modern while the planetary environment declines. Many question the commitment to the luxurious militarism required to maintain conventional notions of security.

As data on climate change, declining agricultural productivity, deforestation, and the ubiquitous contamination of fresh air and water continue to emerge, the old shibboleths of what constitutes national security lose meaning. Some defense analysts now argue that the deterioration of the natural environment must be numbered among the gravest security threats facing all nations, for it holds the potential to erode the biological foundations of human life, thus threatening economic stability, homelands, and peace across much of the planet.

At the very least, the enormous costs of national defense—now running at about $2 billion a day worldwide—represent resources *not* being spent on environmental protection and restoration or on strategies to achieve economic sustainability. Yet the minute-by-minute costs of maintaining the illusory security promised by militarism pale against the human costs of warfare.

Since the end of World War II, more than 20 million people have died in wars. The share of civilian victims has been rising disproportionately with the death rate. While in 1950 civilians comprised about half of all war deaths, the percentage has climbed to 85 today. The 1980s witnessed 22 wars, the most recorded in any decade. An estimated 13 million refugees now exist—the living victims of warfare, despotic governments, and the resulting economic decline.

Meanwhile, the economic toll of preparing for war continues to wreak havoc, especially in the Third World. While industrialized nations doubled their military expenditures, Third World countries expanded theirs sixfold since 1960, bringing their share up to 18 percent of the world's military spending today. Some 50 million people now hold military jobs, equally divided between soldiers and workers in the arms industries. Since the end of World War II, some $16 trillion have been spent on the world's armed forces. "National defense," says economist Kenneth Boulding, "is now the greatest enemy of national security."

But in many regions of the world, environmental violence now rivals warfare as a major cause of hardship and death. Scientists' predictions of future environmental decline strongly suggest that these regions are not aberrations, but the barometers of future conditions around the globe. Environmental decline is no longer being seen merely as an aesthetic concern of the wealthy, but as a killer and usurper.

The Growing Toll of Ecocide

In addition to the millions of refugees from war and political conflict, there are now an estimated 10 million *environmental* refugees who lost homelands through the collapse of natural systems. Millions have died because of the march of human-induced deserts, droughts, the destruction of croplands, and the floods and mudslides caused by the desperate exploitation of land. Global warming, the loss of the ozone layer, and deforestation promise to kill millions more, as the trends of environmental devastation sharply accelerate.

Tropical rainforest destruction, a post-World War II phenomenon, now impoverishes a billion people. Each year, an area the size of Maine ceases to be rainforest and begins its decline into tropical desert. In Central America, two thirds of the original rainforests have vanished before the march of coffee and cotton plantations, strawberry, broccoli and melon farms, and cattle ranches—all to produce export crops to enrich corporations and wealthy planters, often at the expense of subsistence farmers who lose their land to "progress." The cities of Central America are now bulging with the landless—ringed with concentric circles of shantytowns where lawlessness and unrest fester. The rainforests that have sustained life for millenia now fall to the overblown dreams of oligarchs, often to service national debts to international banks—the bill for hundreds of earlier ill-conceived development schemes.

A United Nations Environment Programme survey estimates that 35 percent of the earth's land is in various stages of turning into deserts. More than 135 million people now live on lands experiencing severe desertification. The African Sahel, which spans nine countries from Mauritania to Sudan, suffers the gravest threats to arable land. Two droughts in the past 20 years killed an estimated quarter-million people in the Sahel, with another two million forced to flee the countryside and into the crowded cities.

The persistent droughts of the 1980s proved that diminished agricultural productivity is no longer a local problem confined to a few unfortunate regions. It is global in scope. Thanks to drought—exacerbated by soil losses and farming practices that deepen its effects—the past two years have marked the only back-to-back declines ever recorded in world grain production. If scientists' predictions of future climate change come true, the ability to feed the world will only worsen, especially if, as some predict, the U.S. grain belt collapses.

Officials from NASA are now 99 percent certain that the temperature increases observed this century reflect the greenhouse effect. The burning of fossil fuels—three fourths of which occurs in the industrialized nations of the North—pumps 5.5 billion tons of carbon into the atmosphere each year, with another 2.5 billion added through deforestation. Ozone depletion, once believed to be confined to the poles, has now been positively measured above the United

States and Europe, which collectively pump 90 percent of the ozone-gobbling chlorofluorocarbons into the air.

These atmospheric assaults, if allowed to continue, are likely to reduce food production, speed up desertification, diminish the efficacy and boost the costs of irrigated agriculture, exacerbate flooding, and cause marine inundation. They will accelerate the pace of extinction, already running at levels not seen since the Cretaceous period, 65 million years ago. Within a scant ten years, 20 percent of all known species will be gone forever.

These declines can be traced in part to worldwide economic expansion. Since 1950, global economic output has doubled, and with it has come commensurate increases in the combustion of fossil fuels and other pollutants that contribute to climate change. Moreover, economic expansion is accompanied by the dissemination of an industrial growth philosophy that pays no heed to the notion of sustainability. And the resources most vulnerable to industrial appetites are the renewables. Industrial economies have proven themselves remarkably able to find substitutes for scarce nonrenewables—plastics and ceramics to replace rare metals, for instance—but remarkably unable to sustain forests, grasslands, watersheds, aquifers—even soils—without depleting them.

With an expected quintupling of world economic output by the year 2050 and a tripling of fossil fuel consumption, the attack on renewable resources is bound to intensify, and the trends contributing to the loss of croplands and forests, clean air, and water will worsen. As these horrifying events unfold, the world of the next century will begin to resemble nuclear winter in the extent, if not the details, of its devastation.

The Costs in America

In the face of these mounting catastrophes, conventional patterns of national security are beginning to appear archaic. Indeed, the very notion of national boundaries begins to lose meaning. Just where are the "borders" of the industrialized countries whose combined pollutants worsen droughts and famine a continent away, or whose vision of industrialized agriculture, masquerading Third World "development," leads to the destruction of the very rainforests that could sustain local populations indefinitely, even as they cleanse the earth's air? Modern militarism as a means to secure nations against threats from foreign powers seems especially outmoded in the face of environmental violence. Nuclear weapons will not stop the rising oceans nor threaten the ozone layer to knit itself back together.

Yet the United States and other nuclear powers continue to gird up for warfare, seemingly oblivious to the environmental devastation that mounts around them. U.S. military spending virtually eclipses the national commitment to sound environmental management. Congress in 1986 appropriated $273 billion on the military, but only $18 billion (with another $60 billion in private funds) on pollution control. Around 30 percent of U.S. scientists and engineers work in military-related jobs, but the much-vaunted "spinoffs" into commercial products are more mythical than actual. In 1982, the Pentagon invested nearly 40 percent as much in plants and equipment as was invested by all private manufacturers combined.

While we have tied up an enormous share of public capital in rebuilding our national defenses against increasingly vague military threats, we have largely ignored the menace of a rapidly deteriorating environment. Our recalcitrance over acid rain regulation and the ensuing tensions with Canada are well-documented. So, too, is U.S. foot-dragging on global warming. A less known but illustrative example is U.S. opposition to a Scandinavian proposal to cut sulfur dioxide emissions 30 percent by 1993. As of 1985, 21 countries excluding the United States had joined the "30 percent club." By 1986, ten had already met the goal and four had committed to a 70 percent reduction. The United States continues to ignore the proposal.

While America's response to the environmental crisis has been dilatory, it must be said that the threats posed by global warming, deforestation, ozone depletion, and other such assaults are speculative as *security* threats in any conventional sense. We know that a rise in sea level of one meter will make homeless many millions of Egyptians and Bengalis; or that a two-degree-Celsius rise in global temperature could cause the collapse of rice production. Such consequences certainly bode ill for international stability, but will these and other forms of environmental decay spark major conflicts?

Of much greater certainty is this: military activity is a clear and present danger to the environment and those who depend on it directly for their livelihoods.

This threat is apparent to Tom Blessinger. As he and his new environmentalist allies point out, the air force's massive land withdrawals for bombing runs will harm the public domain and, if Blessinger's convictions about ranching are true, end agriculture in the eastern quarter of the Owyhee. But the withdrawals are nothing new. They are merely the latest chapter in a decades-long saga of U.S. military escalation against the environment, evidenced by nuclear testing, toxic waste dumping, excessive use of resources and, most egregiously, attempts to revive the dilapidated weapons complex. The last, in particular, revealed the startling price of the "old thinking" about defense, a price that includes not only billions of dollars but radioactive pollution in multiple forms and implicit encouragement for other nations to follow the American example.

What citizens had begun to learn from the Reagan rearmament is that militarism and the conventional mindset of national security underpinning it, aside from the threats they present to peace, cause unacceptable levels of environmental violence. Like farmer and author Wendell Berry, many were beginning to wonder, "who *are* the enemies of this country?"

A Historic Alliance

On April 22, 1970, Earth Day founder Denis Hayes described Vietnam as an "ecological catastrophe." American bombs had already left more than two-and-a-half-million craters in the Vietnamese countryside, while the use of defoliants, at rates exceeding 10,000 pounds per month, had blackened 6,600 square miles of jungle. With this proclamation, Hayes identified a compelling reason for the new environmentalists to remain joined with the American peace community: warfare in any form is environmentally devastating.

Today, with the American public newly stirred by the ecological crisis, it is time for environmentalists to reassess their commitments to peace—to look more closely at what they can do to help link the interests of environmental protection and economic sustainability with the interests of peace. And peace activists must do the same. Neither should have to look very far.

The history of the U.S. Department of Energy is a vivid illustration of how the federal government continues to favor military over environmental security, and how environmentalists and peace activists interact in an ebb-and-flow of activity.

Since the early days of the Atomic Energy Commission, the federal government has been divided between peace and war in matters related to energy. During its first decade, the AEC came under increasingly harsh congressional criticism for neglecting its mandate to develop nuclear power while it provided the brainpower, testing, and production of America's massive nuclear arms buildup. With the emergence of environmentalism and the eventual creation of the Department of Energy in 1977, the tension between peace and war in federal initiatives shifted ground but continued and intensified.

The new environmental activism that Earth Day 1970 symbolized and helped galvanize largely supplanted the antiwar fervor of the late '60s and early '70s. Within that broad movement were those who saw energy as a key ingredient of a new attitude: *renewable* energy, conservation, and appropriate technology rose to the top of the agenda. The new DOE seemed to promise government attention to these priorities, but it failed to deemphasize the "peaceful atom" as an energy source. So nuclear power grew as a pivotal issue for '70s activists; in addition to its environmental and safety hazards, it symbolized increased centralization and decreased public control over decisions affecting human and environmental health.

During the Reagan years, antinuclear activism translated readily into a new antiwar movement. Reagan's twin emphases on rearmament and growth at any cost crystallized the two strains of activism and put them on separate but parallel tracks. Reagan shut down the DOE Solar Energy Research Institute and cut off most funding for alternative energy research, while DOE and the Pentagon proceeded with the largest nuclear arms buildup in years. Near the end of Reagan's presidency, however, an issue surfaced that provided common ground for ecologists and peaceniks—the DOE nuclear weapons complex. Reagan had unwittingly spurred their renewed alliance by calling for a "modernized" nuclear weapons complex—virtually a second Manhattan Project to feed the military's hunger for nuclear weapons and establish the tone and central mission of the nuclear bureaucracy well into the next century.

In its closing months, the Reagan DOE called for new plutonium and tritium reactors to be built in Idaho and South Carolina, a Special Isotope Separator to modernize plutonium extraction, and the phasing out and relocation of both the Rocky Flats "trigger" factory and the Fernald uranium fabrication plant. All of this was to be done, interestingly, under the aegis of environmental cleanup. Some DOE contractors even insisted that cleanup of the grossly contaminated plants could not proceed without the promise of modernization. Said Westinghouse Hanford Company President William Jacobi, "In terms of a major investment in environmental cleanup, I think it will happen only if we can get the defense mission continued."

The Bush administration has inherited, and slightly modified, the nuclear complex modernization plan. As for a peacetime energy mission, DOE apparently will persist in trying to revive the nuclear power industry—once again under the peculiar banner of environmental protection, since nuclear energy will be touted as a solution to global warming.

The dreadful mismanagement of Fernald, Rocky Flats, Hanford, Savannah River, and other weapons plants activated very effective peace-environmental coalitions. Local groups have sprung up near the weapons facilities and, aided by national networks and organizations such as the Natural Resources Defense Council and SANE/FREEZE, have thrown a wrench into DOE's ambitious plans. Front page headlines, official investigations, shutdowns of facilities, and even criminal indictments have resulted from this cooperative work.

But the alliance has not been without friction.

Strengthening the Links

Despite the successes of the coalitions fighting the weapons plants, institutional caution has crept in. It needs to be examined.

While peace activists have loudly denounced DOE's continued commitment to nuclear weapons development, some environmentalists—by no means all of them—have embraced the cleanup plan as a "more realistic" political approach to reducing the egregious contamination of the weapons complex. They stand silent on the issue of whether the weapons complex ought to be restarted at all, let alone modernized, believing that to challenge the need to build weapons would destroy their hard-won credibility before Congress.

In the process, however, these realists, focused as they are on only the environmental component of weapons production, are missing a special opportunity. For the production complex is emblematic of disregard for the environment in the service of decrepit notions of national security. The production of plutonium and weapons-grade uranium also has profound implications for nuclear proliferation and arms control.

In a larger sense, DOE's activities—including weapons-making—demonstrate the relationships between planetary environmental destruction, the growth of Northern industrial economies at others' expense, and foreign and military policies geared to protect such economic policies. In fact, U.S. policy not only allows for but implicitly encourages the continuing devastation of Third World ecosystems in exchange for participation in the global economy. Activists should come to see "political realism" in this new light.

For environmentalists and peace activists both to be effective in helping to stem environmental violence, they must loosen their grip on the institutional borders of their own organizations and of their movements. Environmentalists should consider entering into foreign policy debates. The roots of rainforest destruction in Brazil and Central America, for example, can be traced to over-population, coupled with a desperate need for land and economic reform. Yet U.S. policy prohibits "interference" in population planning and thwarts efforts at land reform, particularly in Central America, often under the banner of U.S. security.

Instead of tackling these structural and political problems head on, some environmental organizations hope to save the rainforests via conventional approaches to land conservation—national parks, nature preserves, and other "wilderness areas" set aside and protected as much *from* people as for them. It's a plan that worked well in the United States throughout the 20th century, but it did not face the civil war, famine, and shortages of resources that plague Central America today. Some U.S.-inspired preserves there have already been plundered. In the next few decades of worsening resource destruction and warfare, it is doubtful that the will can be summoned to maintain parks and preserves as tiny islands of ecological wealth in a sea of devastated rainforest.

Peace organizations can provide leadership by expanding into the environmental sphere their critique of militarism and rigid nationalism. They can enter into the worldwide effort to organize citizens against the onslaught of new "weapons" against the environment—the unforgiving rain of pollutants that increases tension and waters the seeds of conflict.

The links that existed at the first Earth Day between the antiwar movement and environmentalists can be reasserted. Few environmentalists said then that their political capital could not be squandered through opposition to the Vietnam War. And few antiwar activists failed to decry the environmental devastation of Southeast Asia.

The links are evident throughout the world. Now activists can make such links the focal point of strategy.

Emphasizing Sustainability

"Perhaps the most useful outcome of the environmental experience is that it illuminates the relationship between the outward manifestations of the ills that trouble modern society and the common origin of those ills," Barry Commoner writes in his landmark 1987 essay in *The New Yorker*, which summarizes the successes and failures of the environmental movement since Earth Day 1970. But, he warns, there are risks in pursuing that "common origin"—risks that few social movement organizations are ever willing to take. For the illumination of the common threads underweaving our plight—the increase of poverty, homelessness, warfare, and violence—necessarily broadens the agenda and seems to many to divert it from its most gainful course. And, as Commoner points out, it threatens greater numbers who benefit from the status quo.

Commoner closes his essay by recalling Dr. Martin Luther King, Jr., who "died believing . . .that beneath the legal basis of racial discrimination lay deeper problems of poverty and violence; that the root of racial discrimination is also the root of poverty and war." That belief inspired King to lead a march against the Vietnam War. His critics, Commoner reports, charged that King was out of his element, that he had veered dangerously from the cause of civil rights, which could be undertaken more conservatively by defining themes narrowly and claiming victories against discrimination under the law. But King persisted, broadening his work until he died.

Commoner insists that none of the issues-oriented movements of the late 20th century has attempted to follow the lead of Dr. King in exposing the underlying, common roots of violence. For reasons that pertain mostly to organizational business—to the gathering and tending of the membership flock, to the grooming of funders or the cultivating of political influence—nearly all movement organizations reach a point where they feel that they can no longer afford the luxury of a broad focus or the risks of alliances with "radicals." Like corporations that learn how to maximize profits by capturing a significant market share for a single product, some social change organizations have learned to block out all concerns that seem to stand outside of a narrow focus on a single problem.

Still, an increasing number of peace and environmental organizations are together finding common threads in their work toward greater security, nonviolence, and reversing the ecological crisis. They have begun to weave together the fabric of a new vision broader than what either had achieved alone. They are beginning to see that militarism, poverty, racism, the loss of home-lands, and planetary environmental destruction have common roots. The common solution is to identify and eradicate them; the common goal is *sustainability*, which cannot be achieved militarily nor under current patterns of development and consumption.

Sustainability encompasses both economic and environmental concerns, even as it challenges modern industrial societies with a mandate for profound change. Former EPA administrator William Ruckelshaus has said that the movement toward sustainability "would be a modification of society comparable in scale to only two other changes: the agricultural revolution of the Late Neolithic and the Industrial Revolution of the past two centuries." Our illusory cycle of nonsustainable economic growth protected by nihilistic military power clearly stands apart from any vision of sustainability.

As long as Congress and the administration continue to pour resources into the military, the United States will appear hopelessly out of sync with those prepared to participate in a new vision of a sustainable world. With the right leadership—more simply, with the proper response to public attitudes—the United States could both research and promote sustainable technologies and shape a global vision of sustainability and the tools to make it work.

What we now face is a threat to *biological security*. Like nuclear war, it is a threat that exceeds our abilities to imagine. If climatologists are correct, we will soon reach a point when we will be forced to leave the secure and familiar surroundings of our own nationalities, our identities as a people superior, regal and apart, and join in the common plight of all humanity, indeed, of all species. Our weapons, no matter how modern, will be more useless than ever.

The Gulf Crisis and American Activists:
What Should Be Done?
Nuclear Times Roundtable
Winter 1990–91

THE CONFRONTATION OVER KUWAIT PRESENTS ACTIVISTS WITH AN IM-mense challenge. The issues are complex, the public is uncertain, the Bush administration has vacillated between multilateral peacekeeping and unilateral war-mongering. In this climate, the options for activists worried about war and angered by the causes of the crisis are not entirely clear. But the prospect for a large-scale war with many casualties makes it imperative for activists to shape U.S. policy toward a peaceful resolution and new global measures to prevent such crises from rising again.

To address these questions, Nuclear Times brought together four thoughtful people involved in informing and mobilizing the public on the gulf crisis. Gail Pressberg is codirector of the Washington, D.C., office of Americans for Peace Now, the U.S. arm of the Israeli peace movement. Jim Driscoll is national coordinator of Operation Real Security in Tempe, Arizona; a longtime grassroots activist, Driscoll is organizing Vietnam veterans to speak out about the possibility of war. Sherle R. Schwenninger is director of research and policy studies at the World Policy Institute in New York, and is editor of the World Policy Journal. *James Zogby is director of the Arab American Institute in Washington, D.C.*

The four panelists met with Nuclear Times's *moderator John Tirman in Washington on October 24, 1990.*

Nuclear Times: *Do you think that American support for U.S. intervention is strong, and why?*

James Zogby: The reason that it's popular is that it's on the television all the time. Interest is sustained as long as the media sustain interest. If there's an invasion, it's not merely oil, it's not merely the violation of international law, it's not merely the fact that Saddam is simply not a nice person. It really is the issue that the media focused on it and made it a story. I wouldn't take the polls as an indication of anything other than where peoples' attention is.

Jim Driscoll: It seems to me it's real clear that the American people don't support the use of offensive force in the Persian Gulf. So long as you're talking about collective security and stopping naked aggression and defending poor little Saudi Arabia, how can you be against it? But if you ask whether you should use offensive force to clear the Iraqis out of Kuwait, it's like 10 percent of the American people support that. When you ask, "Should they stay there forever?" it drops way down, so Bush has support as long as he doesn't use them, and he doesn't keep them there long.

This crisis has radicalized me a lot. We *were* talking about the end of the Cold War and the dawn of peace. The role of the media has been abysmal, the cheerleading and not asking questions. The number of leaders in the so-called peace movement who in the first few weeks came out publicly and said that they support the deployment of troops is unconscionable to me. Thirty-five percent of the troops on the ground in Saudi Arabia are black or Hispanic; the communities of color in the polls are opposed to this and about the only reliable opponents in Congress have been members of the black caucus. Families of the U.S. troops who are deployed over there are speaking out. Vietnam veterans are starting to come forward and question this deployment. I hope that it will be adequate to prevent the war that I think the president is very likely to initiate.

Gail Pressberg: Some of us are not very sanguine about the new "dawn of peace" breaking out, the end of the Cold War, because we saw a series of conflicts in the Third World that were going to continue. The conflict in the Middle East is the first one, unfortunately, of a series of conflicts over resources. The frustration I've had with the peace movement, which I've been involved with my entire adult life, is the absence of really wanting to deal with the substance of those conflicts. To some degree, one of the reasons our organization has supported Bush has been a sense that sanctions are better than an unchecked Saddam Hussein. That doesn't mean that Saddam Hussein is Hitler, but it does mean that people who follow the Middle East understand the histories of some governments and leaders, and they're worried. And Saddam's military potential is a problem for Arab neighbors as well as a problem for Israel.

There *is* public support in this country for response to Saddam Hussein. Bush would have been clobbered had he sat back and done nothing. I think there is support for sanctions largely because sanctions don't cost the American people anything. And I agree, it gets much more complicated when it comes down to the deployment of a large number of troops over there. I would like to see the peace movement perhaps be skeptical of war, but strongly support sanctions; I have seen almost no mention of that.

Zogby: Not only that, but no dealing with the substance of the issue at all. Kuwait is a real country, Kuwaiti people are really suffering, there is indeed a question of international law and of commitment to enforce it. I am as angry as any Arab and Arab-American that international law has not been enforced on the Palestine question. But that does not mean that I am willing to allow Kuwait to be destroyed and forgotten.

I don't know what prompted the initial motivation for the administration to get into it, but as I look at what they've done, I'm not too displeased. They've succeeded in maybe unwittingly fashioning a new world order, I think they themselves are rather surprised at the consensus that's been built. The consensus now serves as a constraint on our actions. While some chafe, there are those of us who ought to be rather pleased that the United States cannot function unilaterally, because we may be fashioning an international mechanism to resolve these regional disputes.

The test, of course, will be if it gets applied to the Israel-Palestine issue as well. But something interesting is happening out there, and while we have condemned the U.S. double standard on the question of Palestine, I don't want to see it compounded by a double standard coming back the other way—which is to say, it's really just about oil, bring the boys home, and the hell with Kuwait. I find that unacceptable, immoral, and I think that the peace movement has got to be able to be responsible for human suffering, for violation of rights, for the ravaging, raping, and destruction of an entire country. If we can't be, then what are we?

NT: *But isn't this a war for oil? As Gail said, a resource war?*

Sherle R. Schwenninger: One problem with the Bush administration's response is its ambiguity. Bush has defended his policy in different ways at different times—as necessary not only to maintain international order and deter further aggression but also to preserve our access to oil and protect our way of life. Interestingly, basing his case on oil didn't sell so well with the American public. Thus, he was forced to come back to the "maintenance of international order" as the principal justification for his policy. But in committing more than 200,000 troops to the area, far more than what would be required to maintain collective security, he has made this look more like a case of the United States playing world policeman for its own particular reasons. To be sure, he has taken the case to the U.N., but at times it looks more like a cover for U.S. action rather than a step for collective U.N. action.

The peace movement should be pushing the Bush administration to make this a clear and unambiguous case of U.N. collective security, of standing on international principles. This crisis presents an opportunity to reactivate and strengthen U.N. peacekeeping machinery. This means replacing U.S. military forces with U.N. and Arab League peacekeeping forces, activating the U.N. military staff committee, and empowering the U.N secretary general to negotiate with Saddam Hussein. It should not be the U.S. who determines what action should be pursued to resolve the crisis. That should be done through the U.N. Security Council.

NT: *Do you think Americans would support a deal that in some ways would change the nature of Kuwait to avoid war? What some would decry as a new "Munich."*

Zogby: The Kuwaitis have a right to sovereignty. A clear statement came from the U.N. Security Council, which passed right on the heels of the invasion, that contained two parts. The first part was unconditional withdrawal, linked with the second part, which called for negotiations to resolve outstanding claims. What I find from Saddam is an effort to convert it, which is to say, "first I want what I want and then we'll talk about the rest." That becomes unacceptable, because it's an issue of rewarding aggression. It's an issue in the region of resolving the outstanding issue of Kuwaiti sovereignty.

There is, I think, a failure here, not only in the peace movement, but in the country as a whole, to understand the region, the depth of feeling of those who support Saddam on the one side, the depth of fear of those who are afraid of Saddam on the other side. He has tapped a resentment of the West, we need to understand that and deal with it. Dealing with it doesn't just mean bringing the boys home. It means dealing with how badly we have behaved in the region over the last many decades.

We've created Israel as some kind of special surrogate for America in the region and then ignored the rest of the region; allowed Israel to invade and ravage Lebanon, allowed them to occupy the lands of three countries, and ignore it. If we want to understand and beat Saddam, we must deal with that double standard.

On the other hand, we also have to understand the fears of the gulf states. We've not understood Kuwait as a real country. It's important that we take the fears of those people to heart and understand that it's emerged as a real state, there's an internal democratic process that's underway that's really quite advanced in the gulf that's important for us to encourage and support and not allow Saddam to continue to hover over in a post-settlement period with the constant threat that he can do it again any time he doesn't get his way.

Driscoll: It's difficult for me to sit at a table with somebody who would with a straight face endorse the deployment of 200,000 U.S. troops in this situation as somehow in defense of international law and human rights. We're dickering with the Khmer Rouge in Cambodia, we invaded Panama, we supported a renegade army and undermined the government of Nicaragua. This is not an administration that's in there because of human rights and international law. Give me a break. George Bush has defined a set of objectives that aren't perfectly clear, but which at this point seem only achievable by an attack on Iraq. He's demonized Saddam Hussein.

If Saddam pulls out tomorrow, it's described by the administration as the nightmare scenario because that doesn't allow them to get rid of Saddam and the nuclear and chemical capabilities of Iraq. Those are serious long-term problems. How we deal with them is difficult, but I for one don't endorse going in militarily and assassinating the guy and destroying the complex as a way of dealing with it, it's a problem the world community's got to deal with, not George Bush acting *for* the world community. The week Saddam invaded Kuwait, the administration said that border disputes between Arab nations are not our problem. I don't know what happened from that pretty clear signal that it was okay to go in. He was our guy after all, he wasn't Hitler then; the peace movement called him Hitler for gassing the Kurds and the other things he did to his own people. Something happened in between there which was not a newfound concern about human rights on the part of George Bush.

This is a clear line in the sand for the U.S. peace movement. We have two paths that our country can go on. Do we deal with environmental problems, do we deal with our economy, do we become a geoeconomic power, or do we continue as the world's mercenary force? I don't want to trample on the human rights of the Kuwaiti citizen, that's wrong, but how you deal with that is a serious question.

Zogby: It's got to be a little more than writing a letter of protest to Saddam Hussein. But let me just jump on that for a minute. You mention all these other scenarios, and I'm with that ticket. I've been in part of the community that has opposed U.S. behavior. This is the first instance of its type in the post-Cold War period. We do not have the Soviet Union lining up on one side, and the U.S. lining up on the other side and therefore the possibility of a prolonged stalemate or war. He is isolated. While we speak, his weapons rot and rust. He's got to get a message clearly that it's not going to work.

When Baker and Shevardnadze came up with the joint statement, he must have somehow been impressed with the fact that there's something new happening out there. When the U.N. passed the resolution as quickly and as firmly as they did, something new was happening out there. When it began to get the fairly broad support from the world community, that there be a deterrence against Saddam, something new was happening out there.

I think that there are two things that the world's agreeing on. One is that he must be rolled back, and the other is that there really should not be a war. With the exception of Israel and maybe Margaret Thatcher and a few neocons here in America, I think most everyone is committed to the force in the region as a *deterrent* force to send a very clear message that the embargo's going to be enforced, and you've got to get out of Kuwait, and I'm with that. We don't call for a strike against Iraq. We don't want to see it dismembered, destroyed, don't want to see any lives lost; we're committed to a peaceful resolution. I don't think the signal—that there must be a resolution—would get sent as clearly as it is if there were not an effective deterrent force there.

The peace movement has to be talking about making this new world order a reality. That then has us consistent on the human rights and on the respect for human sovereignty, but also really effective on the peace issue.

Pressberg: I totally share the skepticism about Bush having any set of standards on human rights. Nonetheless, it's possible for sanctions to work to implement Bush's stated goals. We ought to be supporting the sanctions. I also should point out that Israel has been remarkably restrained, partly because of the consequences of war for Israel.

The fact of the matter—and this is why I think the effect of sanctions is important—is that Saddam Hussein is going to have to walk away from this with very little if sanctions work. As soon as the United States jumps into war, the alliance in the Middle East might become shaky. Support for the sanctions keeps the pressure on. I think we have to accept the fact that there's not a heck of a lot to negotiate over.

Schwenninger: I do think the Bush administration, at least to some degree, cares about the question of maintaining international order. The position ascribed to by the Bush administration—that it's an unacceptable outcome if Saddam is left in power with his military intact—more accurately characterizes the "hasty hawks"—the A.M. Rosenthals, the editorial writers of the *New Republic.* The administration's position has up to this point emphasized the unconditional withdrawal of Iraq from Kuwait. They seem to believe that if they are successful, if the sanctions are successful, and if the principle of the U.S. military coming to the rescue of the Saudis is established, this will create a new security environment in the Persian Gulf such that Saddam will be effectively constrained in the future. The more cynical interpretation of the Bush policy in this respect is that such an outcome will also be the one that's most likely to legitimate some form of continued U.S. military presence in the region. If they get rid of Saddam then one of the more visible justifications for the U.S. military presence is undercut. It may not be troops on the ground, but an expanded structure of military bases and, of course, a major naval presence.

The U.S.-Saudi relationship is critical to the Bush administration's calculations, since Saudi Arabia, in effect, controls the pricing mechanism of international oil. This relationship is therefore critical—critical for the maintenance of the dollar and our ability to handle our international finances at this point in time. The Saudis are wedded to pricing oil in dollars and recycling petrodollars into U.S. banks, U.S. construction projects, U.S. weapons supplies. As long as oil is priced in dollars, this provides an artificial prop under the dollar, allowing us to repay our debts in our own currency, and allowing us to buy oil in a declining currency.

But this policy may be shortsighted. To have an adequately stable region in the future, one is also going to have to address the inequitable distribution of oil wealth in the region. It may not be exactly accurate to describe Kuwait as an outdated, repressive sheikdom, but it does fit the Saudi regime. In fact, the Saudis at times intervened in Kuwait to try to restrain the democractic process. The U.S. may therefore be creating new conditions of instability with its unqualified embrace of the Saudi kingdom.

Zogby: I don't see how you can say that it will create greater instability.

Schwenninger: In part, it will depend on the evolution of Saudi policy. The Saudis have now decided that it's even too risky to have a lot of Arab migrant workers on their soil. So the process they started a decade ago of replacing Palestinians and other "troublesome" Arab workers with Asians now has further escalated to kicking out workers from neighboring Yemen. If they are seen as unresponsive to the rich-poor issue at the same time that they seem to be dependent on the U.S. for their security, it may create a real legitimacy crisis for the Saudi kingdom. I don't think you can put the issue of the division between rich and poor in the Arab world back in the bottle where it was.

Zogby: And I don't think it will. I have a feeling that we're going to come out of this with an accelerated process internally in each country and also in the region as a whole towards enhanced cooperation, greater pluralism moving towards democracy. That's essential, and that's something that I think we Arab-Americans, for example, and also people in the region, need to be pushing for. But the prerequisite for this process is stability in the region. What retards the process is the continued threat of, for example, the kind of thing Saddam did in Kuwait. It certainly doesn't enhance the process. The two odd men out of this process are Israel and Iraq.

Pressberg: I don't think you're going to get any move, at least on the part of the Israeli public, to question what's going on until the sanctions are allowed to kick in to get Saddam out, and I don't think you're going to make much progress amongst the gulf Arabs that fear Saddam. In other words, I think a prerequisite for negotiations on the other issues is the sanctions working, because as long as people are living in Israel with the threat of gas masks, and Saudi Arabia with the fear of Saddam running across another border, those discussions can't happen.

Zogby: Two interesting observations came out of the briefing we had at the White House. One official said it's essential that the very process we set in place in the gulf to defend a friend and establish security work to create a sense of confidence in the region—that when we say we will defend a friend, we mean it. We can't create the kind of linkage that the people in the Arab world want—to see us say to Israel, you get out of those territories, we'll guarantee borders—if we don't make it stick with Saudi Arabia. If we cut and run, and allow aggression to stand, Israel has absolutely no reason to accept it. So what we're left with is a military confrontation as the only way to get them out of the West Bank and Gaza—one, that's not going to happen, two, that shouldn't happen, and three, it won't work. And so we really have a test here. If the sanctions and if international pressure and the resolve can stick and work, we then have a model we can apply elsewhere.

The second point that was made was also interesting. This issue presents us with the biggest fish we've had to fry yet in regional security in the broadest sense of the term. In referring to the Arab-Israeli conflict, one of the White House people said, if anything, we've learned from this that we don't have the luxury to allow little trouble spots in the region to fester and distract our attention from these major regional issues.

Pressberg: For our constituency it's not a little issue.

Zogby: I think Israelis are really uncomfortable right now. The U.S., Saudi, Egyptian, and Soviet relationship that's emerging in all this doesn't make the Israelis real happy. They've gone from being a strategic ally to a strategic liability. They don't really fit any longer in this, and I think that the Israelis are more afraid right now of the U.S.-Saudi-Egyptian relationship than they are of

Iraq. Because they know how to deal with Iraq, they don't know how to deal with the U.S. having new friends and seeing themselves cast as kind of troublesome outsiders.

NT: *They weren't troublesome outsiders until the Temple Mount shootings, were they?*

Zogby: I think they were troublesome outsiders from the beginning.

Pressberg: Israel stayed out of it because of the assessment of its own interests.

Zogby: It was also told.

Pressberg: But they agreed to that assessment of their own interests. The Temple Mount tragedy has put the Israeli-Palestinian conflict back on the agenda. The United States has got to put a resolution to the Israeli-Palestinian conflict high on its agenda and achieve a solution in which Arab countries recognize Israel, the Israelis recognize the need the Palestinians have to have self-determination, and in which there's a process for how to get from the beginning to the end.

Zogby: We have to have a process that says yes to a Palestinian *state*.

Pressberg: But you've got to have a transition period to get from here to there. There's an urgency to get to negotiations, but the negotiation processes themselves have to be apart—not one big international conference to resolve the whole mess of conflicts, because conflicts have contexts and causes and you can't get to a lasting resolution unless you deal separately with the contexts and causes of each conflict.

NT: *This notion of a new world order, the use of the U.N. and the sanctions as a model—must it include 250,000 troops in the desert? This element of military intervention is troubling as an element of a new world order.*

Driscoll: I guess the particular point when it got hard for me was when Jim made the George Bush-like statement of "we can't cut and run and allow naked aggression to stand." I just want to point out, you're not over there, we're talking about 200,000 20-year-olds who enlisted to get jobs and an education who are going to get chewed up in a vicious, bloody, awful way. And before you use language out of that particularly inflammatory school, I'd like you to think a little. What's at stake here to me is militarism as a new world order. I mean, it's almost enough to wish for the Cold War.

The decision was made unilaterally. There's been virtually no point where this hasn't been a unilateral resort to naked military force as the dominant way to resolve this. I'm all in favor of sanctions. Of course Saddam has to be stopped and sanctions are exactly appropriate. Here is the first crisis of the post-Cold War era, and it was not collective security and international discussions, it was bang, a quarter of a million troops deployed halfway around the world within a couple of months. Every other day, Bush refers to Saddam Hussein as Hitler. Whenever there's any floating of a way to resolve this, it's hammered down. It's made me wonder about the capability of our society to rein in the military.

The peace movement has done a lot of good: we have an infrastructure, there are encouraging new signs, etc., but on the whole, we didn't have the institutional mechanisms or the memberships in place to prevent an awful direction for the "new world order." What is apparent to me is the dominance of the military, and we've got big troubles on our hands if that's the direction of the future.

Zogby: I'd like to respond to that. The first is that Saudi Arabia requested U.S. involvement. We have bilateral ties, and we responded. Kuwait also requested, as they are entitled under the U.N. Charter, that the U.S. or other nations interdict ships leaving Kuwait. Aggression or intervention are two words that do not apply to the U.S. in this instance. It's not intervention when Saudi Arabia requested U.S. involvement.

The word "aggression" means something different when Kuwait says that ship left our port, they stole our country, they stole our ships, and they're stealing our oil; we want you to stop that ship. Would you respond? And the U.S. says yes we will. That's not aggression.

Driscoll: That's going to war.

Zogby: Responding to the request of a country to defend their resources is different. I simply say don't use the word aggression, that's not the right word. I thought it was very appropriate that we sought U.N. sanctions and endorsement for everything else, I simply want to remind you all of the fact of ten U.N. resolutions, the troops of other nations, but also the wealth of other nations in support of this effort, which is exactly multinational. I think that we're all entitled to a healthy dose of cynicism when we come to judge the motivations behind the behavior of any American administration, and the world can be cynical as well. The fact is that, unwittingly or not, something different is in place than we expected. We are now constrained by the consensus that we built. A lively international discussion about where do we go means there is no unilateral U.S. anything. Like it or not, a new world order is shaping out of this international discussion. If this is making a war, it's a hell of an awful way to make a war.

My hope is, and my challenge to the peace movement is that we build on this. How do we make certain this coalition stays in place but avoids war, becomes a truly international, U.N.-led effort, peacefully achieves the liberation of Kuwait, and creates a region-wide negotiating session to reduce the chemical, biological, and nuclear war threat? And then be applied to resolve the other burning issue in the region—the Palestine-Israel issue. That would be a sophisticated movement that is truly worthy of the name peace movement. How do we create real lasting peace in that region?

Driscoll: Next time we have a crisis, send a quarter of a million troops, 400 nuclear weapons, I don't know how many carrier groups, and stand up for peace with Jim Zogby, I like it.

Zogby: Cheap shot. We all get one.

Pressberg: Whether this is going to emerge into a new security framework depends upon what we all do. I don't think the politics are going to come out of the peace movement. I'd first like to see a regional security working group, Arab-American scholars, Jewish-American scholars, people who've worked on arms issues to look at how this fleshes out. The peace movement is mixed, some peace organizations have come close to putting some of these regional concerns into their framework and others haven't. If you want to avoid the use of 250,000 troops the next time around, some of these issues have got to be paid attention to, because post-Cold War conflict might shift to the South. Right now it's in the Middle East; the next conflict could go over to South Asia, the Pacific.

NT: *A concern is that a lesson is going to be drawn from this to send in troops right away instead of dealing with avoiding a crisis by dealing with issues like nuclear proliferation and human rights abuses and . . .*

Schwenninger: One of the lessons being drawn is that this is a dangerous world and that a U.S. military presence is still necessary in many parts of the world if the Saddam Husseins are going to be stopped. But this ignores the extent to which we helped produce the threat. Moreover, it overlooks entirely the question of preventative diplomacy.

The U.S. over the past decade or so had successfully excluded other international powers from exercising any diplomacy in the Middle East. Thus the climate of the region was susceptible to Saddam—he had no reason to believe that his aggression in Kuwait would be met with the type of response with which it was met. It seems, for one thing, that Iraq may have miscalculated the Soviet reaction. If the great powers—U.S., Soviet Union, European—had been engaged in pushing an international peace conference in the Middle East, it's doubtful that he would have felt so unconstrained. He couldn't have counted on Arab support if the U.S. had been engaged with other international powers in a legitimate search for peace in the region and if issues related to the region's economic future were also on the agenda. So, even with all the problems that we had created by tilting toward Iraq in the Iran-Iraq war and by pushing the arms bazaar in the region, even then there was still hope for preventative diplomacy to avoid this crisis. This is where the military mindset of our national security establishment is still very evident. The notion of preventative diplomacy hasn't figured into the Bush administration's foreign policy.

The issue that Jim Driscoll raises is important, because I believe the U.S. still has responsibilities for international order. How do we fulfill those responsibilities without denying ourselves the resources and energy we need to address the very serious questions of our troubled social order and economy at home? I think the answer lies in strengthening U.N. collective security and expanding preventative diplomacy. We could have achieved the same results with a much more modest American military commitment under U.N. auspices that would have provided the reassurance the Saudis needed to move forward with sanctions. But obviously, as I suggested earlier, there were other motivations at play.

One of the things that the peace movement has to pay attention to now is a coalition between the environmentalists, those concerned with energy security, the peace movement, and more importantly, the working and middle class who feel very anxious about their economic future. One thing that's worried me is the extent to which environmentalists advocate major increases in gasoline taxes without explicitly making progressive taxation and jobs and public development programs part of their message.

Pressberg: I agree with you. I think it's important for the peace movement to be putting energy security and progressive taxation on the top of their agenda. I wasn't in New York for the October 21 demonstration, but I would have liked to have seen on the television more posters, more slogans, more demands around the energy crisis. The issue of energy and oil is critical.

NT: *The more immediate problem in resolving the crisis is the status of Kuwait.*

Zogby: It remains a matter of pain to us that for the last 13 to 14 years the peace movement has ignored us. Some of the churches have taken a position, but it's not a legislative or organizing priority for any of them. We cannot get anyone to go to a congressman except us and say cut aid to Israel. Now it's happened to Kuwait. I'm not against bringing the boys home, I don't want any of these kids dying, I don't want any Arab kids dying. I want peace in that region, and I'm convinced that there should be no war.

But I want to ask: What is the peace movement going to do about the fact that Kuwait is occupied, and how does the moral linkage with the Palestinian question affect the peace movement? We ought to have demonstrations by those same thousands and thousands of people, saying no more Israel occupying the territories with U.S. money, no more settlements, and yet they turn a blind eye to that. The same way that my people criticize the U.S. government for a double standard, I have to criticize the peace movement for a double standard. They don't care about Kuwaiti lives, they don't care about Palestinian lives, and they don't care about human rights for Arabs.

Driscoll: Of course the movement cares about Kuwaiti lives.

Pressberg: Let me make another argument. Suppose you woke up tomorrow and Saddam was out of Kuwait, we didn't go to war, troops were coming home. All the other conflicts here remained in the Middle East, but they weren't on the front page. Let's say there was some other military focus for the peace movement. The U.S. peace movement would *still* go on ignoring causes and contexts of conflict, it would *still* go where U.S. troops and money were.

Driscoll: I think that states the obvious. At the moment we have somewhere between 200,000 and 250,000 troops in Saudi Arabia, yes, there's going to be a focus on that. There are many awful human rights situations around the world that don't get the attention they deserve. The United States does in fact wage war on the world in a lot of ways, most recently in Central America. And so it is true that the peace movement tends to focus on those more domestic kinds of levers. You respond to issues that speak to you personally.

Zogby: The issue I really want addressed—and not the way Gail framed it at all. In 1982 Israel went into Lebanon, six days later, at a mass peace march they wouldn't even let us have an Arab speaker and it was holy hell to get it on. It's not an old story, it's a continuing story. We still do not have a peace movement that focuses on the Middle East with anything other than the same double standard the U.S. government uses when dealing with the Middle East. What I want to see is my compatriots in the peace movement be consistent about this one and say Kuwaiti lives count; we have a responsibility to human rights and self-determination and sovereignty for Kuwait, we also have it for the Palestinians and the Israelis to provide them with real security, not the phony security of weapons that will bring about a holocaust for everybody in the region.

Driscoll: I wasn't kidding when I said that Kuwaiti lives count, as do Palestinians and Israelis. That may not make up for past neglects, which I think are real. There has been progress made in the peace movement. I can speak for my organization, I think SANE/FREEZE has done that as well.

Pressberg: I don't want it to be seen as a grassroots versus Washington issue. It's important for people in *Nuclear Times* to recognize that there's a debate within the establishment.

Zogby: And debate in the administration. There are those in the administration that say look, we have a new world order forming, a war will kill it, a war will destroy the coalition we've built. This new world order is something we all ought to be having a stake in. It's making the U.N. real, it's making an international mechanism for peace real. It's moving from unilateral to multinational; it's making international nonviolent efforts real, and I think when all of that's there on the agenda, we've got to strengthen it.

Driscoll: But that *is* the position of the peace movement, it's the position of my organization, it's the position of SANE/FREEZE, it's the position of most other peace organizations. The fact that some groups have refused to condemn Saddam Hussein for invading Kuwait is, to my mind, off the wall.

Pressberg: But it's a real problem for those of us who are trying to work in this peace movement. The broader public I have to deal with in the Jewish community looks at the peace movement now, it looks at how the October demonstration buried this better message. And I think that has to be taken into consideration in terms of strategy.

Driscoll: I see Palestinian students coming forward on universities being deeply concerned. Veterans particularly feel the wounds of this kind of craziness, as do some of the families of these kids stationed in Saudi Arabia. So the next step: we're now calling for teach-ins, partially to remedy what Jim and Gail have appropriately pointed out is decades of neglect of this issue, and to try to get information into people's hands. So the question is, where do you go from here, because unfortunately, right now the energy still comes from people who feel the pain. The great challenge facing the peace movement is how do we move people before the body bags come home.

On Hold: Test Ban Amendment Conference, Conducted in the Shadow of War, Fails to Achieve a CTB but Dodges Bush's Bullets
By Jim Wurst
Spring 1991

ALTHOUGH OVERSHADOWED BY THE OUTBREAK OF THE WAR IN THE Persian Gulf and beleaguered by the United States's and Britain's virulent opposition, the long compaign to enact a nuclear test ban remains unbowed.

To be sure, no one was the unqualified victor at the conference to amend the Partial Test Ban Treaty into a comprehensive nuclear test ban, but advocates of this unprecedented attempt to further nuclear disarmament did succeed in galvanizing diplomats and activists around the cause while showing the depth of U.S. intransigence on the issue.

At first glance, the results of this meeting, which was held at the United Nations from January 7–18, were meager. The initiators of the amendment did table the draft amendments that would, if enacted, add a ban on underground testing to the PTBT's ban on nuclear testing in all other environments—in effect making the treaty a comprehensive test ban (CTB). But they never intended to bring the amendments to a vote since the United States and United Kingdom made it clear two years ago that they would exercise their right as depositary governments of the treaty to veto these amendments.

The specter of veto led to a more ambiguous ending: the conference produced a one-paragraph "decision" that acknowledged "the complex and complicated nature of a CTB" and called on the president of the conference "to conduct consultations with a view to achieving progress" on related issues, including verification of a CTB and sanctions against violating states.

The simplicity of this statement belies its political importance. Even though the United States and Great Britain wanted this entire process buried after January 18, the initiators got what they most wanted—a continuation of the process that will serve as a focal point for CTB advocates. Mexico's ambassador, Miguel Marin Bosch, who has consistently supported the amendment conference, predicts that the increased attention to nuclear testing—one result of the conference—will make the United States change its position to "finally understand that testing only sustains the nuclear arms race."

Evolution of the Process
Officially, Washington is not opposed to a CTB. The Reagan and Bush administrations have made it "a long-term goal." In bilateral talks with the Soviet Union (the only forum where the United States is even considering testing limitations), the official "step-by-step" approach has resulted in agreement on two treaties dealing with irrelevant testing limitations. Those modest talks are now on hold because President Bush "has not identified any further

limitations that would be in the national security interests of the United States." And Washington is adamantly opposed to achieving a CTB through the amendment conference, a line that Great Britain has echoed.

The Soviet Union's views on the meeting were virtually inaudible, even though it was the only depositary to support the amendment conference, and Mikhail Gorbachev was the only head of state to send a message to the conference.

Neither China nor France signed the PTBT and neither sent observers to this meeting. Both have less ambitious testing programs and smaller nuclear arsenals. Still, a CTB where two of the five nuclear weapons powers are excluded will never cap the nuclear arms race. Both countries conducted atmospheric tests long after the PTBT was signed. China, however, has agreed to observe a CTB if the superpowers do.

The United States, Soviet Union, and Britain signed and ratified the PTBT in 1963. These original parties are also the depositary states that have special obligations and rights under the treaty; these include the obligation to call a conference if one member wants to amend the treaty and the right to veto any such proposed amendment.

Since the preamble of the PTBT commits the parties to seek "to achieve the discontinuance of all test explosions of nuclear weapons for all time and to continue negotiations to this end," a group of six nonnuclear states began pressing in 1985 for an amendment that would lead to the fulfillment of this goal. Led by Nobel Peace laureate Ambassador Alfonso Garcia Robles of Mexico, this group of six—Indonesia, Mexico, Peru, Sri Lanka, Venezuela, and Yugoslavia—began lobbying to convene an amendment conference that required the support of one third of the 118 state parties to the treaty. By April 1989, one third of the nations were in agreement, and the amendment process officially began.

At the same time, the six introduced resolutions to the U.N. General Assembly in support of the amendment. Almost 100 nations voted in favor of the process in the 1990 General Assembly; in fact, the United States and Great Britain were the only negative votes. NATO members and other U.S.-aligned countries, such as Israel and Japan, abstained. Five East European countries joined in abstaining after years of affirmative votes.

The Conference Outcome

Traditionally, conferences dealing with arms control try to make all decisions by consensus. Ideally, consensus means all the nations work together to reach a unanimous agreement. In reality, it means one country can paralyze the entire process by vetoing a compromise. U.S. opposition to negotiations for a test ban has stymied the Conference on Disarmament, the only permanent multinational disarmament negotiating body, in Geneva for years. This intransigence at the most logical forum for a negotiated test ban caused the frustration that led to the amendment campaign.

Going into January's amendment conference, there was little hope for consensus—Washington and London despised the amendment. Still, delegates churned out pages of proposals and the president of the conference, Indonesian Foreign Minister Ali Alatas, made a valiant attempt to find common ground.

On the final day of the conference, the six sponsors, joined by Nigeria, the Philippines, Senegal, and Tanzania, offered a draft decision that would have continued the conference through the establishment of a working group to deal with CTB-related issues such as verification and sanctions against violators. The draft called for reconvening the conference by September 1993.

This new draft proposal was unacceptable to the United States and Britain, but at the last minute Marin Bosch of Mexico revised the draft, dropping the working group and the timetable and substituting wording that only called for consultations under the president. This draft was put to a vote and was approved 74–2 with 19 abstentions, and thus it became the decision of the conference.

The continuation of the conference was the core of the sponsors' victory. Additionally, Australia, Ireland, New Zealand, and Sweden, along with NATO members Denmark, Iceland, and Norway, cast pro-amendment votes for the first time after years of abstaining. Aaron Tovish, executive director of Parliamentarians for Global Action and the originator of the amendment plan, sees this additional support as a chance for ongoing political pressure. While it is too early to tell if this change is a one-time vote, Tovish says it "can become permanent and will be one of the main political tasks ahead." He envisions increased parliamentary and public pressure on the governments of these countries to further isolate the hard-line anti-CTB bloc.

Carolyn Cottom, director of the U.S. Comprehensive Test Ban Coalition, says these additional pro-amendment votes are "a very significant development and may influence other areas of arms control." The test ban process, she asserts, "has become a serious arms control initiative."

Tovish also thinks pressure can increase on Eastern Europe. The new governments "have had no chance to think through their positions," he argues, so they just took their cue from the West and switched to abstaining. Now with "the West" in all three columns of support, opposition, and abstention, Tovish thinks the amendment advocates can bring the East Europeans back into the fold.

None of this would have happened, however, if the conference had allowed itself to be held hostage to the veto.

Issues Raised

At the conference, arguments against a CTB sometimes took on an other-worldly quality. Delegates repeated the well-worn arguments that testing was necessary for the safety and reliability of nuclear weapons and questioned whether a total ban could be verified, thus ignoring the volumes of work proving that testing is not necessary for safety or reliability and that a CTB could be verified. Some say it is unwise to try to amend the treaty, but George Bunn—the

233

Kennedy administration's legal adviser to the PTBT negotiations—noted that the potential for creating a comprehensive test ban was the basis for writing the amendment process into the treaty.

Environmental pollution from radiation was the prime motivator behind the original negotiations—the treaty's preamble says that the parties desire "to put an end to the contamination of man's environment by radioactive substances." Although the PTBT pushed testing underground and out of public consciousness, all tests release some radiation into the atmosphere either through deliberate or accidental venting of the test cavities after the explosion. How much, however, is not known.

Attending the conference were 128 nongovernmental organizations representing a spectrum of political and technical expertise. Scientists and former government officials worked with grassroots activists from around the world to lobby the delegates with political, technical, and moral arguments to halt nuclear testing. Among these were the "downwinders"—people living downwind from nuclear test sites who have been exposed to high levels of radiation.

The world's most famous "downwinder," Olzhas Suleimenov, the founder of the "Nevada-Semipalatinsk movement" of Kazakhstan in the Soviet Union attended the conference. As the leader of the movement that closed the Semipalatinsk nuclear test site (see *Nuclear Times,* Autumn 1990), he was one of the most prominent activists at the conference. He is also one of the initiators of a new campaign called the Global Anti-Nuclear Alliance, an international drive to close the test sites in all five nuclear weapons states. In announcing the creation of the alliance, Suleimenov told the audience, "Americans, we've done our bit, we've closed our test site, it's your turn now!"

One of the most difficult issues facing any arms control agreement is how to ensure that parties to a treaty fulfill their obligations. Verification was the only technical issue relating to a CTB that received any attention at the amendment conference, but in light of recent scientific and political advances, worries about verification sound more like excuses than serious concerns.

One draft protocol submitted at the conference called for the establishment of a secretariat that would verify the CTB. The protocol also outlined four systems for monitoring compliance: a permanent global monitoring network, temporary localized monitoring, on-site inspections, and national data provided to the secretariat. This proposal builds on past work of the Group of Scientific Experts, which has been conducting seismic tests for almost 15 years.

A working paper Mexico submitted to the conference estimated that a global seismic network would require 221 monitoring stations at a total cost of $150 million. This amount is minimal compared to the cost of a single nuclear test, which runs between $30 million and $100 million. The independent Verification Technology Information Center of London released a paper maintaining that a credible verification regime is possible with a network of seismic stations, a network of detectors to check for radiation in the air and water, the use of satellites and aircraft, and a regime of on-site inspections.

The other reasons for continued nuclear testing did not come under the same scrutiny as verification at the conference, but there was plenty of expert opinion and research available. The head of the U.S. delegation, Mary Elizabeth Hoinkes of the Arms Control and Disarmament Agency, summarized the pro-testing position to the conference: "As long as nuclear weapons continue to play a critical role in our national security, we must have a sensible testing program to ensure the credibility and safety of our forces."

For years, experts have argued that computers can adequately simulate a test explosion to determine the viability of a warhead. In fact, using computer simulations to check the function and credibility of warheads is apparently so effective that the U.S. government bans the sale of supercomputers to nations suspected of harboring nuclear ambitions.

One argument in support of testing that CTB advocates cannot debunk is that nuclear tests are necessary to develop new nuclear weapons, and that is precisely why a CTB is such an important disarmament measure.

While the gulf war diverted attention that might have created additional public anger over U.S. obstreperousness, Cottom contends that the massive concentration of weapons in the Mideast and concern over Iraq's nuclear ambitions present "a real opportunity, because we have a chance to talk about nonproliferation" and how to prevent it in the future. "The Bush administration helped us out by raising the specter of proliferation," she says. "It raised the question of how weapons proliferate," so pursuing nonproliferation strategies will gain greater visibility.

Nonproliferation will be one of the cornerstones of the growing CTB campaign in the United States. Resolutions in both the House and Senate support all measures to halt nuclear testing, and, according to Cottom, "growing numbers in Congress want cuts in weapons testing budget." Heightening the awareness that a CTB would be one of the quickest and most effective ways of halting the arms race, controlling nuclear proliferation, and demonstrating an unequi-vocal commitment to disarmament will now be a priority for the U.S. movement. Which is why many test ban advocates believe there will finally be a nuclear test ban by the end of the decade.

A Dangerous Victory
By David Callahan
Summer 1991

NINE MONTHS AGO, ONE OF THE MOST FASHIONABLE TOPICS OF DISCUS-sion in Washington was the peace dividend. How large would it be? When would it become available? What should it be spent on? With the Berlin Wall being sold in chunks to tourists, and with the once-mighty Warsaw Pact in shambles, big cuts in U.S. military spending seemed only a matter of course. The end of the Cold War, it was thought, would bring an opportunity to finally put America's economic house in order and address long-neglected domestic issues. There were also high hopes for a more enlightened U.S. foreign policy—one driven by democratic values rather than big-power geopolitics.

In the aftermath of the Persian Gulf War, however, the prospect for such sweeping change seems to be fading. Even before Saddam Hussein's tanks rolled into Kuwait, the Bush administration resisted major defense cuts and any overhaul of American foreign policy. Along with its allies in Congress and a phalanx of conservative policy analysts and commentators, the administration argued, in President Bush's words, that "the world remains a dangerous place with serious threats to important U.S. interests wholly unrelated to the earlier patterns of the U.S.-Soviet relationship." Modest defense cuts could be made, and some peace dividend would be realized, but for the most part the administration's vision of the post-Cold War world entailed few real changes in U.S. national security policy.

Congress and the American public, however, wanted deeper defense cuts than the administration, and it was doubtful whether the Bush team could resist these pressures for long. The administration seemed to be in a losing position in the debate over America's post-Cold War agenda. Unfortunately, this position shifted when the Persian Gulf crisis began last August.

Already, the administration is reaping a massive "war dividend." Republican spin doctors are stressing four points: the crisis reflects Bush's brilliance in foreign affairs; the deployment to the Persian Gulf underscores the need to maintain high levels of defense expenditures; the success of U.S. forces against Iraq buried the "Vietnam syndrome"; and the gulf war reaffirms the role of the United States as the world's leading superpower—a role it should never relinquish.

If these viewpoints are widely accepted, this decade may not see a retrenching of the U.S. military establishment or a peace dividend of any significance. Instead, the revival of American global preeminence may mean more crises and wars in the future—entanglements that could distract the United States from domestic problems and sour the climate for positive international change.

Dubious Leadership

In the short run, no individual or institution reaped a greater war dividend than President Bush. Before the war he was seen as an increasingly ineffectual leader, a president with no clear agenda in either domestic or foreign policy. Bush's greatest success to date had been toppling the Panamanian dictator, Manuel Noriega. A year and a half after taking office, the public perception that he lacked courage and conviction continued to plague him. Political pundits depicted him as a caretaker president who would be vulnerable in 1992.

The war produced a stunning reversal of fortune for Bush. Polls now show him with an 80–90 percent approval rating, some of the highest figures ever recorded for a president. Americans still express doubts about his domestic policy, but in the realm of foreign affairs, Bush is perceived as masterful. This is not surprising since Americans like winners, and for the moment, Bush looks the biggest one around.

Bush's shining image could soon lose its luster, however. Closer scrutiny of the events leading up to the gulf crisis, combined with the negative consequences of the war, have begun to raise questions about the president's foreign policy judgment.

Administration spokespeople like to emphasize American success in the Persian Gulf, but the whole crisis, many experts believe, could have been avoided. The failure lies in U.S. relations with Iraq. Before his invasion of Kuwait, Saddam Hussein was wooed by both the Reagan and Bush administrations. American efforts to strengthen ties with Baghdad began during the early 1980s when Iran and Iraq were locked in a bloody war of attrition. Fearing a victory by Iran's revolutionary government, the United States tilted toward Iraq in the war, providing agricultural loans and allowing Baghdad to buy advanced U.S. technology. The United States orchestrated an international arms embargo against Iran, yet did nothing to stop Iraq from assembling one of the most lethal arsenals in the world.

By the time Bush took office, the Iran-Iraq war had ended and Iran was no longer a regional threat. The rationale for ties with Iraq's brutal government apparently had disappeared. Indeed, with its stepped-up human rights abuses, including the use of poison gas against Kurdish rebels, Iraq was less attractive than ever. The Bush administration, however, made no effort to change U.S. policy. In October 1989, President Bush signed a top-secret review of U.S. policy in the Persian Gulf that called for improving relations with Iraq. Three months later, on January 17, 1990, Bush reaffirmed that position by signing a presidential order declaring that expanded trade with Iraq was in the U.S. national interest.

Around that same time, the state department's human rights office was completing its annual report. Iraq's record was called "abysmal," and the report charged that Saddam Hussein ran a vast police state. "Effective opposition to government policy is stifled," the report said, "the intelligence services engage in extensive surveillance and utilize extralegal means, including torture and summary execution, to deal with antiregime activity."

In the spring of 1990, more evidence of Hussein's malevolence surfaced. In a well-publicized speech in April, the Iraqi leader threatened to incinerate Israel with chemical weapons. The month before he executed a British journalist on trumped-up spying charges, and U.S. intelligence discovered he was building Scud-missile launching sites in western Iraq, within easy range of Israel.

None of these developments, however, changed U.S. policy. Even when Iraq began threatening neighboring Kuwait in mid-July, the United States took no action to review its stance toward Baghdad. Instead, the Bush administration fought congressional efforts to impose sanctions on Iraq. It was still fighting that legislation when word of the invasion reached Washington on the evening of August 1.

Bush showed impressive diplomatic talent in assembling the international coalition against Iraq in early August. He also expressed an appropriate level of outrage against Iraq's brutality. But where was Bush's moral outrage when Iraq was persecuting its dissidents through 1989 and early 1990? Where was his desire to contain Iraq when it was blustering about attacking other nations and building its deadly arsenal? In the months following the invasion of Kuwait, Bush often compared Saddam Hussein to Hitler. But the nature of Iraq's totalitarian rule was known to the president well before Iraqi tanks rumbled through the desert night to storm Kuwait.

Before August 1, Saddam Hussein was a vicious dictator, but one President Bush was willing to do business with because it suited U.S. strategic interests. After August 1, he was the same dictator, only now he jeopardized U.S. interests.

Despite Bush's appeasement of Iraq before the invasion, Americans remain impressed by the president's overall handling of the war. This perception may not last for long, however. In the process of liberating Kuwait, with its prewar population of 1.7 million (over half of which were foreign workers), the United States killed tens of thousands of Iraqi soldiers and virtually destroyed the infrastructure that supports Iraq's population of 18 million. A United Nations team that visited Iraq in early March issued a report on March 21 describing the results of U.S. bombing as "near apocalyptic," and as relegating Iraq "to a preindustrial age." Food, water, and health supplies were scarce, and the report warned of widespread famine and epidemics if "massive life-supporting needs are not rapidly met."

After the release of the U.N. report, however, no international effort was mounted to ship emergency supplies to Iraq. American representatives at the U.N. argued against any relaxation of the embargo against Iraq. While the U.N. finally decided to allow in essential foodstuffs in late March, that move has done little to alleviate a dire situation.

Whether Saddam Hussein, a quintessential survivor, will be overthrown remains to be seen. Whatever happens, stability is not likely to return to Iraq anytime soon. The death count, already high, will continue to rise as disease and hunger take their toll and as civil war convulses the country. The time it would have taken for sanctions to work or the type of diplomatic settlement Hussein might have agreed to will never be known. But with an airtight embargo, denying Iraq billions of dollars in oil revenue, Hussein's eventual reversal of aggression seemed likely.

In the euphoric aftermath of the gulf victory, President Bush has not been compelled to answer difficult questions about his rush to war, nor has he been heavily criticized for the needless U.S. destruction of Iraq's civilian infrastructure. But as the costs of war mount in the months and years to come, questions about the wisdom of Bush's decision to abandon sanctions and diplomacy will grow more persistent. In time—perhaps sooner than expected—Bush's handling of the crisis may no longer seem so masterful to the majority of Americans.

Preserving the Peace Dividend

While Bush's boost from the war may prove ephemeral, the Department of Defense is likely to achieve lasting gains. Proponents of sustained high defense spending could not have asked for a better answer to their post-Cold War prayers. Over a half-million troops and dozens of naval vessels were deployed to the Persian Gulf. Nearly every weapon in the U.S. arsenal was used. Many of the most advanced weapons performed as planned, despite the doubts of the military's critics. Best of all, from the Pentagon's perspective, was that U.S. military action in the Persian Gulf suppressed precisely the sort of new threat that administration officials had been advertising.

How could the United States slash its defense budget, Pentagon officials asked, when Saddam Hussein had so vividly proven that the world remained "a dangerous place"? How could the United States scrap weapons and troops that it might need for another Third World hot spot in a few years? "The peace dividend?" asked New Jersey Senator Frank Lautenberg in August. "It looks like it's evaporating in front of our eyes."

Lautenberg was right. In the wake of Iraq's move against Kuwait, the Bush administration knocked aside a House Armed Services Committee plan to reduce defense spending to $283 billion in early fall 1990. The final Pentagon budget for fiscal year 1991 totalled $288.8 billion, eliminating the few billion dollars in peace dividend funds many had hoped for.

This budget increase is only the beginning. Over time, the gulf war will undoubtedly bolster the administration's case for high defense budgets.

The Bush administration's plan is to reduce defense spending by a mere 2 percent a year over the next five years. This overall spending cut of 10 percent by 1995 would entail a reduction of U.S. forces by 25 percent during the same period. Defense Secretary Dick Cheney claims that these cuts would be dramatic and painful, but to many critics they are paltry. Independent experts, such as William Kaufmann of the Brookings Institution, believe that the end of the Cold War makes spending cuts of up to 50 percent possible.

Before the gulf war, the shifting of the debate toward deeper defense cuts seemed likely. The further the Cold War receded into the past, the more difficult it would become for the administration to justify mammoth defense budgets.

Now such a shift is unlikely to occur. Fresh from victory in the Persian Gulf, the Bush administration is well positioned to defend its plans for only modest cuts in defense. The peace dividend—spent a thousand times over in the minds of so many—could well be one of the chief casualties of the gulf war.

This needn't be the case, however. A first step in salvaging the peace dividend is to recognize that the Persian Gulf War does not alter the reality of declining

U.S. defense needs. A look at Pentagon spending plans confirms this point.

As in previous budgets, this year's Pentagon pie will be divided in the following fashion: about one half will be spent on forces designed to defend Western Europe; roughly 18 percent to maintain and modernize U.S. strategic nuclear systems; and the rest on a range of Pentagon programs, from keeping America's vast naval fleet at sea, to developing exotic new weapons.

But with the reuniting of the Germanys, the disbanding of the Warsaw Pact, and the growing independence of Eastern European countries, along with Mikhail Gorbachev's preoccupation with the Soviet Union's internal problems, even the most conservative assumptions would allow for the possibility of Pentagon budget cuts.

Additionally, the huge U.S. force in Europe—initially deployed in the days of Stalin—has also lost its mission. Cuts in these forces could save tens of billions of dollars annually. Moreover, amid a declining Soviet threat, the United States can move to a purely retaliatory strategic posture. Some estimate that such a posture would require no more than 3,500 nuclear warheads, in contrast to the 12,000 the United States now deploys on bombers, submarines, and land-based missiles. Here, too, billions of dollars could be saved.

Even if the administration's assumption that the United States must be prepared to wage war in the Third World is true, it requires a leap of faith to accept that the United States must keep 1.5 million troops on hand for this reason, as Defense Secretary Cheney says. Military leaders always cite the last war in preparing for the next one. Yet it is unlikely that the unusual situation of the Persian Gulf crisis will be replicated. No other Third World country deploys armed forces comparable to those that Iraq had and is as well-poised to use them against vital U.S. interests.

Despite claims to the contrary, a powerful case still exists for deep defense cuts. Many in Congress know this, of course, and while it will be difficult at first to continue the fight for a large peace dividend, the Bush administration's position on defense is likely to weaken over time. Sheer logic will see to that.

The Vietnam Syndrome: Alive and Well

Whatever the outcome of the defense debate between Congress and the Bush administration, one thing is clear: sixteen years after the fall of Saigon, a new confidence has arisen about America's ability to win wars. "By golly, we've finally licked the Vietnam syndrome," Bush said ecstatically after U.S. troops liberated Kuwait.

This assumption is off the mark. Vietnam taught the United States some bitter lessons, none of which will be forgotten because of events in the Persian Gulf. One lesson was that the United States should not fight wars that do not have clear objectives or that are not likely to be won. Another lesson was that U.S. troops should not be sent into combat without the full backing of the American public. Vietnam was a deadly hall of mirrors for the United States, a confused world of needless human carnage and conflicting aims. Many who lived through the war, particularly the U.S. military officers who fought in it, were determined never to repeat the experience.

The loss in 1983 of 241 marines in Lebanon reinforced U.S. caution about sending troops into combat zones. The marines had no clear goals in war-torn Lebanon. They were not there to win anything, and the American public did not support them.

Following the debacle in Lebanon, Defense Secretary Caspar Weinberger issued a set of guidelines for the use of force that encapsulated the lessons of Vietnam: "Before the U.S. commits forces abroad, there must be some reasonable assurance we will have the support of the American people and their representatives in Congress." And when the United States did commit forces, it "should do so wholeheartedly, and with the clear intention of winning."

General Colin Powell, chair of the Joint Chiefs of Staff, and General Norman Schwarzkopf, commander of U.S. forces in Saudi Arabia, each served two tours in Vietnam. Both learned the lessons of that ugly war and live by Weinberger's guidelines. In the Persian Gulf, they encountered a situation very different from Vietnam. The liberation of Kuwait and destruction of Iraq's military machine was a clear objective. The American people were divided about the use of force, but Congress backed President Bush's request to attack Iraq. Also, the international community was far more supportive of U.S. action than it had been in Vietnam. Weinberger's criteria, by and large, were fully met.

All this does not signify, however, that the legacy of Vietnam has vanished. Far from being "licked," the Vietnam syndrome is alive and well. The essence of the syndrome continues to be that neither the U.S. public nor its military will support deep American involvement in civil wars or guerilla conflicts. As one observer said: "If it looks like Vietnam, smells like Vietnam, and walks like Vietnam, the public will not want the United States to get involved."

In the years ahead, it is hard to imagine another villain as evil (and as stupid) as Saddam Hussein, an outrage as clear-cut as the invasion of Kuwait, or a jeopardized interest as vital to the West as oil. What the United States is more likely to confront are messy wars fueled by explosive poverty and linked to ethnic conflict and ancient struggles over land or resources. These conflicts, with their imperviousness to quick outside resolution and moral ambiguity, will resemble Vietnam far more than the situation in the Persian Gulf. American intervention in these wars will remain, as before, unpalatable to both the U.S. public and military leaders such as Powell and Schwarzkopf.

The danger lies in political leadership that fails to recognize the impact of the Vietnam example. President Bush has now discovered twice—in Panama and in the Persian Gulf—that there are distinct benefits to launching American troops into combat: popularity ratings soar, Americans become more patriotic, domestic problems are temporarily forgotten, and Democrats are put on the defensive.

"The presidents we eulogize are those who acted dramatically in crisis," observed Bush's aide Roger Porter, a scholar of the office of the president. "We have tended to equate success with action. We sometimes confuse action with accomplishment. A president is instantly under enormous pressure to 'do something'. It is vitally important to have his emotions under control."

Vietnam, the graveyard of Lyndon Johnson's presidency, will remain a powerful counterweight to the interventionary impulses of Bush and future presidents. The lessons of that war, rather than those from the Persian Gulf, will continue to be relevant in the 1990s and beyond as the United States confronts the violent consequences of unaddressed problems in the Third World.

The Price of Hegemony

For much of the postwar era, the United States could afford to protect its allies abroad and foster progress at home. Now, with America's well-being jeopardized by a far-reaching social and economic crisis, such an ambitious agenda is becoming less tenable. While the United States' western allies accumulate huge trade surpluses and take the lead in numerous areas of technology, the United States spends vast amounts of its national treasure to protect them. During the Cold War, that protection came in the form of U.S. forces positioned to repel communist aggression in Europe and Asia. Today, the Persian Gulf is the focus of security concerns, and while President Bush has talked about a "new partnership of nations" emerging from the gulf war, the United States is once again footing most of the bill to maintain collective security.

This imbalance does not bother the Bush administration since the revival of America's superpower status has been a source of pride. "Recent events have surely proven that there is no substitute for American leadership," said President Bush in his September 11 address to Congress.

Before the war, the administration sought to preserve U.S. global power but found the case for hegemony difficult to advance. Now, they can point to Iraq's defeat as an example of why America should remain a superpower. High defense spending and a willingness to use force are part of the package, of course, but to the administration the cost in money and lives is a small price to pay for a new Pax Americana.

Others disagree. Over the last several years many scholars and policy experts—including most notably the historian Paul Kennedy—have argued that the United States must reduce military spending if it hopes to become more economically competitive and tackle its domestic crisis. These thinkers believe that the chief threat to America's well-being is not security issues overseas, but the deterioration of U.S. economic power at home.

What is so dangerous about the gulf war is that it may strengthen the illusion of American omnipotence that was the trademark of the 1980s. In an atmosphere of optimism about American power generated by the gulf war, the pressure to begin making hard choices about U.S. national priorities could subside, and the day of reckoning with the realities of a changing world—avoided so far under presidents Reagan and Bush—could be pushed further into the future.

242

A New World Order?

Despite the many reasons for concern in the aftermath of the gulf war, there are also grounds for hope. President Bush has repeatedly claimed that a new world order has been forged in the showdown with Saddam Hussein. Even though this claim is little more than rhetoric, it is extremely significant. If the United States adheres to the principles of international law it embraced during this crisis, if the U.N. emerges from the war with new influence, and if a formula can be devised for equally sharing the burdens of collective security, then a new world order will indeed have dawned.

Under this new order, American policymakers would have to play by a new set of rules. Decisions long made in secret by U.S. officials about how to protect American and Western interests would have to be coordinated with actions by the U.N. Security Council. U.S. vendettas, such as those against Nicaragua, Libya, and Panama, would be awkward, to say the least. The United States could still maintain preeminence in the realm of military power, but its exercise of that strength would be restrained.

To foster an improved system of international security, the United States would, for example, have to reevaluate the manner in which it cultivates regional allies. As the gulf crisis illustrates, the new threats to international security are not related to the Cold War, but are likely to stem instead from local sources of enmity and instability. Far from promoting U.S. security interests, arms transfers and support for undemocratic regimes, once the basis of U.S. global strategy to limit Soviet influence, may now have a negative effect on international relations, especially in volatile regions.

Reconceptualizing America's global role involves far more than accepting the limits that internationalism imposes on the exercise of U.S. military power. It means relying on a new set of nonmilitary instruments to implement U.S. foreign policy objectives that reflect the realities of a changed world. President Bush has rightly stated that the crisis in the Persian Gulf provides a "rare opportunity to move toward an historic period of cooperation." The challenge in the aftermath of the war will be to display the courage that is needed to seize that opportunity.

NINE

How They Saw It:
The Internal Debates

We Need a Common Voice
By Randy Kehler
June 1984

WE WHO MAKE UP TODAY'S RESURGENT DISARMAMENT MOVEMENT, loosely defined, have scarcely begun to realize the incredible potential that we have for stopping the arms race—really stopping it, between both superpowers and eventually among the other nuclear nations.

Realizing the potential that we have, however, is going to require a far greater level of unity and collaboration than perhaps we have ever thought about. I have this growing sense that we cannot continue working separately, each within our own institution or organization.

We are not, in fact, a disarmament movement. We are a collection of disarmament organizations (or organizations whose programs include major nuclear disarmament components). It is true that there are generally good relations among us. It is also true that many of us have participated in collaborative projects on a sporadic basis, not to mention some important ongoing communication mechanisms.

Nevertheless, most of us operate most of the time within separate organizational frameworks. The result is that funders, the media, most politicians, and the public tend to see us, at best, as fragmented and uncoordinated, and at worst as competitive and self-serving. I am increasingly convinced that we cannot continue this way.

I am not suggesting that we disband all of our separate organizations or nuclear disarmament programs and form one "super organization." I am quite sure that such a plan would never work, not to mention that it runs hard against my decentralist grain. We do still need a healthy diversity of viewpoints, styles, tactics, and strategies. And I am not sure what more "collaboration" and less "institutocentricity" means in any kind of specific way. I have some hunches, but these are the kinds of things we all need to talk about together.

One hunch, for example, is that we need a comprehensive plan for stopping *and reversing* the nuclear arms race, a plan that not only shows the strategy by which we intend to do this, but a plan that also shows how the efforts of particular organizations fit coherently and cohesively into the overall picture.

If we see congressional elections as a critical element in our comprehensive strategy, for example, what does that mean in terms of various field organizing efforts? If we have a profreeze president in 1985, what will be the most effective methods, locally and nationally, for assuring that he really follows through? What groundwork needs to be laid for electoral work in '86 and '88? If the regular institutional channels (legislative and electoral) fail to respond to the nuclear peril, how do we expand the role of citizen protests and nonviolent direct action?

In addition, I would like to see us think about ways to address grassroots and disarmament workers, the media, Congress, the funding community, and the direct-mail audience in a unified way on some level.

Can you imagine the message it would send to the public-at-large if all or most of the disarmament groups in this country really got their act together and began acting in a coordinated, coherent fashion? Not only would *we* be taken more seriously, but "the problem" would be taken more seriously. In fact, it might begin to get the seriousness it requires if life on this fragile planet is going to continue.

Freeze Faults

When I first got involved in setting up the National Freeze Campaign, it was my hope and expectation that the freeze would become a kind of "orchestra" made up of a large and broad spectrum of organizations, all working in harmony to produce a rich, magnificent, and beautifully powerful "sound." To some extent, this *has* happened and, in a sense, beyond my original expectations. That is to say, at key moments—for example, when Kennedy and Hatfield first introduced the freeze resolution in Congress, and later when the House of Representatives debated and voted on that resolution—there was a strong collaborative effort on behalf of the freeze proposal. But in between those moments, and since the last one, it seems to me that the disarmament movement settled back into organizational business-as-usual.

The Freeze Campaign bears a great deal of responsibility for this. Rather than vigorously pursuing the creation of a solid freeze coalition of national organizations, in which all of us were united behind the top arms control priority of a bilateral halt to the nuclear arms race, we have directed our attention primarily to the necessary work of encouraging, coordinating, and facilitating the rapidly growing network of local freeze groups around the country.

The National Freeze Campaign is indeed a strange beast. It began primarily as a coalition of national organizations, and now has become primarily an organization unto itself made up of local, regional, and state freeze groups. This situation must change. The Campaign should never divorce itself from or become less dependent on its local base of support; the U.S. government will never be serious about stopping the nuclear arms race until there is a massive grassroots mobilization all across our country. But the essential complement of an aroused citizenry must be a clear, visible, unshakeable alliance among national organizations.

We in the Freeze Campaign could and should have done more to make this coalition, or alliance, a functioning reality. But for various reasons, we concentrated our energies elsewhere.

Coupled with lack of attention to national coalition building on our part, was the partial inadequacy of our national strategy. Others in the disarmament community were critical, and rightly so, of a strategy that placed so much emphasis on what was, in effect, a nonbinding resolution that, even had it passed, would have been easily thwarted by an intransigent administration. One of the results of not having a truly functional national coalition was our inability to consult more closely with regard to possible changes in strategy.

While we in the Freeze Campaign were trying to figure out what we were and what our strategy should be, other disarmament organizations tended to slide off the mark (except during the key "moments") in two ways. First, instead of doing what they could to participate more fully in the National Freeze Campaign and all its activities and deliberations (or at least raise a stink about the difficulty of doing that), their own institutional needs led them to regard the Freeze Campaign, explicitly or implicitly, as just another disarmament organization—and, in certain areas such as direct mail, foundation solicitation, media, and field work, as a "friendly" competitor.

Second, and far more important, it seemed that many disarmament groups tended to forget the meaning of the freeze itself as an arms control objective. As each organization in its own way responded to horror stories coming out of the Reagan administration, many lost sight of the overall, compelling requirement that the nuclear arms race as a whole be stopped. In part due to each organization's need to carve out its own niche in the disarmament field, it seemed as though they forgot that "the freeze" was not just a neat slogan that happened to arouse a lot of people but was (and is, in fact) a viable and essential arms control proposal, a proposal synonymous with stopping the nuclear arms race—which, after all, is what all of us have been talking about.

Surrendering Ego

But, of course, this is all hindsight. We called them as we saw them (or didn't see them) at the time, as best we could. The point is, where do we go from here?

Before we can go forward, however, two questions jump out. Does everyone, in fact, really agree that the achievement of a U.S.-Soviet freeze, as an essential first step toward nuclear disarmament, is or should be the number one arms control objective for the disarmament movement as a whole? And, if the answer is yes, is the Freeze Campaign, in its present or some revised form, the appropriate vehicle or framework with which to coordinate freeze work?

I myself feel certain that the answer to the first question must be a resounding "Yes!" (What other objective is large enough to be worthwhile, modest enough to be achievable, and clear and dramatic enough to arouse the necessary public support?) And I feel reasonably certain that the answer to the second question is also "Yes." But in both cases there may be good arguments to the contrary. If there are, I and others in the Freeze Campaign need to hear them.

The real point is not what particular objective or form our collaboration assumes. The *collaboration* itself is the point. We simply have to get our collective act together far more than we have. And that probably means laying all our institutional cards on the table. Which in turn means being willing to surrender our institutional egos for the sake of something far, far more important.

For starters, all of us together should simply try to imagine what kinds of increased collaboration might be possible. Here is my own list:

• A comprehensive plan for stopping and reversing the nuclear arms race.

• Cooperative approaches to funders, based on our "plan."

• More integrated field strategies, a more focused unified lobbying effort in Washington, D.C., and coordinated approaches to national and local media.

• Some, at least minimal, organizational framework within which we can all work, and through which we can speak to the world as one voice or chorus of voices, but which also allows each of us to retain our separate organizational identities to whatever extent is appropriate.

If we should succeed in taking some significant steps in any of these areas, I think we would be a far stronger disarmament movement for it. It would be our way of saying to the world, "Guess what? We care more about stopping and reversing the nuclear arms race than we care about our own institutional turf." I am convinced it would also usher in a whole new level of effort and commitment. It might even constitute the extra weight that finally tips the scales in our favor for the first time.

My own timeline for this imagining/discussing process is from now through the November elections. Anything significant we might come up with will surely take some time to put into place, and in the meantime we do have our work (the nationwide public referendum coming up November 6) cut out for us. This is a perfect time to start thinking about next steps. I know that to some these ideas will sound totally unworkable and thus unthinkable. But stopping and reversing the arms race, to others, seems equally unthinkable. This is what I call rising to the occasion.

Coming Alive in '85:
New Plans and Renewed Vision
By David Cortright
October/November 1984

AS WE IMMERSE OURSELVES IN ELECTORAL WORK IN THESE COMING WEEKS, it is not too soon to begin thinking ahead. What challenges and opportunities will we face after November? How do we move toward freezing and reversing the arms race in 1985 and beyond?

The answer will depend to a considerable degree on the outcome of the presidential election. If Reagan is reelected, the arms race will continue to accelerate and we will face a heightened threat of war. U.S. military intervention in Central America will also deepen, perhaps leading to direct combat intervention. If the Democrats win, we can expect the arms contractors to descend on the White House like vultures to sweep aside all promises for peace.

No matter who wins the presidency, a strong and lively peace movement will remain a vital necessity. We must prepare now for a creative and forceful response to the challenges of next year.

In recent years, SANE and other groups have focused on the MX as the most winnable nuclear arms issue and as a vehicle for mobilizing political opposition to the Reagan arms buildup. Thanks to years of effort by tens of thousands of people all over the country, we are gradually winning this fight. The MX has been scaled back considerably and it is unlikely that it will ever become the kind of massive first-strike nuclear threat it was initially planned to be.

While we're winning this skirmish against the MX, though, we're losing the larger struggle to halt the arms race. We've concentrated on winning the MX campaign, while failing to slow the larger momentum of the arms race. If we had applied a similar effort on behalf of a broader approach, we might have achieved greater progress toward real arms reduction.

As we look beyond the MX to a more comprehensive approach, our first task is to develop a strategy for implementing the nuclear freeze. The freeze is our very best hope—perhaps our last hope of stopping the first-strike momentum of the nuclear arms buildup. The question is, how do we achieve this goal? We need an approach that can recapture the spirit of the freeze and fire public imagination. We also need to show that peace is possible—that even under a second-term Reagan administration, we can take steps toward halting the arms race. We need both long-range vision and a plan for immediate victories.

Last year, the National Freeze Conference addressed these concerns by voting for a partial or "quick" freeze. The quick freeze legislation that emerged in Congress this year calls for a halt to nuclear testing (specifically, underground warhead testing, ballistic missile flight tests, and antisatellite testing), and it uses a congressional funding moratorium as the means of enforcing this demand. This attempt to halt nuclear testing through a suspension of funds is, in my view, correct. It should remain the centerpiece of our legislative strategy.

Unfortunately, while the aim is right, the vehicle for implementing it is wrong. The quick freeze has generated considerable criticism and controversy because it fails to address the critical question of the cruise and Pershing 2 missiles. The bill puts us on record as approving funds for nuclear testing if the Soviets don't respond in the specific way demanded. (Is this really what we believe? Aren't we opposed to nuclear testing and space weapons regardless of what the Soviets do?) The certification process contains major loopholes.

How do we get beyond the problems with the quick freeze? How do we resolve the debate over limited versus comprehensive freeze? I believe there is a simple answer: We should support both approaches. We should formally adopt a two-track strategy: 1) pursue the original goal of an immediate, *comprehensive* freeze on all nuclear weapons, and 2) at the same time attempt to stop nuclear testing through a moratorium on funding. The two approaches are mutually complementary. By stopping nuclear testing we would pave the way for a complete halt to the arms race and make the adoption of a comprehensive freeze more likely. In place of the complicated formulations of the quick freeze, we could raise two simple and clear demands: FREEZE THE ARMS RACE. STOP NUCLEAR TESTING.

The demand for a halt to nuclear testing should become a major new focus for our work in 1985. As the world observes the 40th anniversary next year of the Hiroshima bombing, it is eminently appropriate that humankind declare an end to nuclear testing and make a new beginning for peace and arms reduction.

As the first step in this direction we should demand that whoever is inaugurated as president in January immediately suspend nuclear testing and challenge the Soviets to follow suit. Mondale has pledged to adopt this course, and if he is elected we should demand that he fulfill his pledge promptly. If the president refuses to take such action we should mount an all-out effort to achieve this goal through a congressional suspension of funding. We should press for a moratorium on nuclear testing—applied initially to underground warhead testing and ASATs and then extended to ballistic missile flights and other components of the arms race. This testing moratorium approach builds upon our experiences this year in the House of Representatives, where moratorium amendments were attached to the MX, ASATs, and sea-launched cruise missiles. What I am proposing is that this approach be continued and extended, and focused on nuclear testing.

The approach I am advocating differs from simply supporting a Comprehensive Test Ban. The CTB is a desirable goal, but it is not likely to happen soon. Such a treaty depends on compliance by not only the United States and the Soviet Union, but other nuclear powers as well. As such, it gives the two superpowers a convenient excuse for not stopping tests. Also, merely advocating *negotiations* for a treaty can be a futile and demoralizing process. For example, the Senate's recent passage of the Kennedy-Mathias CTB Resolution has had no impact on moving us closer to a test ban.

If we really want to have an impact, we should focus on cutting funds. We should demand that Congress use its power of the purse to initiate a testing moratorium. Specifically, we should propose that funds for nuclear warhead testing and ballistic missile flight tests be suspended for a six- or nine-month period and that no funds be permitted after that, provided the Soviets also refrain from testing. This would follow the example of the Kennedy administration in 1962, when the United States suspended testing, the Soviets followed suit, and the two sides quickly signed the Atmospheric Test Ban Treaty.

This stop-nuclear-testing proposal avoids the problems of the quick freeze while remaining true to the position adopted at the December 1983 Freeze Conference. It is a first-step approach that focuses on the most verifiable components of the arms race and seeks to achieve this result through a congressional suspension of funding. As noted, this demand for a halt to nuclear testing should be coupled with support for a comprehensive freeze. Whatever plan we develop, the goal of a *complete* halt to the arms race must remain a top priority.

The two-track strategy I am proposing allows us to take practical steps toward slowing the momentum of the arms race, while remaining true to our original vision of a comprehensive freeze. The choice should not be either/or, but both.

●　　　●　　　●

What are the organizational means needed to achieve our goals? We should recognize that the peace movement remains relatively weak institutionally. No progress toward a freeze and reduction of arms will be possible without a quantum leap forward in the organizational clout of the peace movement. Our strategy must include a long-term effort to expand the organized constituency for peace. This must include a consolidation and coming together of existing organizations both nationally and at the grassroots level.

We must also recognize the importance of coalition politics—of overcoming the racial barriers that still divide us. During the presidential primaries, for example, Reverend Jesse Jackson provided the clearest stand on peace issues, yet few of us supported him. We should recognize who our allies are and bring the peace movement into the Rainbow Coalition.

Are we ready to link our concern about nuclear war to broader peace issues? I believe we can and must do so. In particular, we should work for reductions in military spending and a noninterventionist foreign policy.

Let our imaginations be bold enough to envision a *radically* different security policy. We should remember that just 20 years ago, the United States and the Soviet Union came to a preliminary agreement on a plan for general and complete disarmament. The McCloy-Zorin Agreement of 1962 called for a mutual, phased reduction of all nuclear *and* conventional armaments by both sides. If these questions could be considered in the 1960s, why shouldn't they be addressed now? And isn't it time that we press for a *comprehensive* economic conversion plan that can redirect our industrial resources toward peaceful purposes?

The program of the peace movement must be both visionary and practical. Our long-term goals and short-term objectives must be tied together in a series of steps that lead steadily to reduced levels of armament. For the long run, we need a motivating vision that goes beyond our immediate goals and allows us to maintain the commitment of our supporters for sustained peace activity. We also need practical goals that can be won in the short run and that build momentum for our larger aims. Both are necessary if we wish to draw in new people and inspire them to greater levels of commitment and action for peace.

Blind Men's Bluffs
By Daniel Ellsberg
July/August 1985

A PUBLIC OPINION SURVEY IN THE SPRING OF 1984 SPONSORED BY THE Committee on the Present Danger confirmed previous findings that roughly 80 percent of the public favored a U.S.-Soviet nuclear weapons freeze at current levels. Yet Ronald Reagan continued to denounce the idea of a bilateral halt to the arms race and refused to explore it with the Soviets.

He maintained this stand up to Election Day. The day after, it was apparent that half or more of the 80 percent who favored the freeze had voted for Ronald Reagan.

No doubt a number of factors went into this result. For one, Mondale's own "commitment" to the freeze—and to the moratorium on warhead and missile testing promised in the Democratic platform—was almost inaudible in the fall campaign and in the debates with Reagan. But the Reagan landslide has been followed by apparent public acceptance—at any rate, lack of outraged protest—of Reagan's Strategic Defense Initiative, his persistently nonnegotiable positions in Geneva, and his success at winning congressional support for destabilizing strategic programs.

It is difficult to believe that 80 percent of the citizenry, or any large fraction of that, shares with freeze activists a sense that ending the nuclear arms race by a comprehensive freeze or a moratorium on missile and warhead testing is a matter of urgency or high national priority. We have, it would seem, a lot of convincing left to do. But how, exactly, to proceed?

Talking and Arming
Our movement began to roll toward those perplexing opinion poll majorities in 1981 when there were no strategic talks going on with the Soviets, and none scheduled. I now think that most of the people favoring the freeze in polls and referenda were simply telling President Reagan that they wanted this situation

to change—i.e., to change *back*. They wanted him to overcome his reservations about the SALT process and get back to negotiating some kind of arms limitations with the Soviets. They expected him to do his best to arrive at agreements, but whether successful in this or not (they no longer expect success but don't hold it against him) they wanted Reagan "talking to the Russians."

Reagan got that message, and responded. He sent delegations to INF and START. Instead of talking about the need for superiority, he outflanked the Freeze Campaign by talking about "reductions," and lately, "abolition." None of this has impeded Weinberger's buildup program, and in fact it amounts to nothing—nothing more was demanded, apparently—than a formal return to the arms control approach of Reagan's predecessors, which was always good enough in the past to keep the arms race going. Reagan's one innovation is the SDI, designed to assure nuclear testing forever and to preclude any risk that the Soviets might accept proposed limits on offensive forces.

Further inducements to the rapid growth of the antinuclear movement in both Europe and the United States in 1981 were the colorful statements on nuclear war by Reagan officials. They claimed to believe that nuclear war could be limited, won, and survived. So Reagan induced his officials to stop saying these things, to Robert Scheer at least.

As with his shift on negotiations, he then found that to agree with the mass of the public that "nuclear war cannot be won and must never be fought" he need not slow down any of his first-strike weapons programs. For the formula does not insist—nor does the public, it seems—that nuclear war must never be credibly *threatened*, hence prepared for.

The logic of Reagan's policies did not, in fact, depend on any of the "crazy" Reaganaut notions that were publicly retired. After all, the same strategic logic, policies, and weapons capabilities have been pursued by every president for the last 40 years. (The notion that "war-fighting strategy" or counterforce targeting, or first use threats, or plans for preemption, were invented under Reagan is simply a delusion.) Nor have the types of weapons needed to implement these traditional (secret) policies changed recently. With the exception of the B-1 and SDI, every single weapon that Reagan is now pursuing is a Ford-Carter weapon.

Weinberger's predecessors did not program these particular weapons because they feared a Soviet surprise attack on the United States, nor because they looked forward to winning nuclear wars with the Soviets. These weapons are designed to strengthen the ability of American expeditionary forces to avert, or defeat, nonnuclear challenges to U.S. and allied interests far from our shores. They are to do this by enhancing the credibility of U.S. threats to initiate "limited" nuclear war.

Of course, in addition to overseas interests, there are domestic incentives that are also critical to sustaining the programs. The three services all "need" new missiles, the producers need contracts, unions need jobs, congressional and presidential candidates need votes and contributions. All these needs can be satisfied by weapons programs that are compatible with any of the current "arms control" programs—except for the freeze. Both these external and internal considerations explain why the freeze is not perceived by the foreign policy and military establishment as "serious arms control."

It is true that public support for the freeze in polls has held up, despite competition since 1982 from Reagan's various INF and START proposals, renewed interest in SALT II, and congressional formulas for build-down and Midgetman-as-stabilizer. But, in truth, we lack opinion data suggesting that the public prefers the freeze to any of these other proposals (now including SDI), or even recognizes a sharp and significant difference between the freeze and all of the others. I conjecture that most of the public does not.

From my point of view, that is awful. I see all the difference in the world. The freeze would stop the arms race; the other proposals would not. The freeze would halt further testing or deployment of all the impending U.S. and Soviet first-strike (or unverifiable) weapons that raise the risk of nuclear war. Every one of these weapons is compatible with—is permitted and likely to be pursued under—each of the "official" arms control alternatives to the freeze. If the public doesn't see that as a vital and urgent difference—and I'm afraid it may not—then our message needs a good deal of sharpening, and most of our work remains to be done.

Better Threats Than Red

The study last fall by Daniel Yankelovich for the Public Agenda Foundation found that a consensus of 77 percent of Americans, asked what U.S. policy should be by the end of the decade, rejects the first use of U.S. nuclear weapons under any circumstances, even against a nonnuclear "Soviet invasion of Europe or Japan." Seventy-six percent say it should be U.S. policy to use nuclear weapons against the Soviet Union if and only if they attack the United States first with nuclear weapons. (Eighty-one percent mistakenly believe this to be U.S. policy *now*.)

However, the Public Agenda poll did not ask what people thought about threatening nuclear war. But another study did. The 1984 poll for the Committee on the Present Danger, conducted by Penn and Schoen Associates, asked the question: "Do you favor or oppose *telling* the Soviets that we will not respond with nuclear weapons if they attack our allies?" (emphasis added). Only 20 percent favored telling the Soviets that we would not respond with nuclear weapons; 66 percent were opposed.

The CPD summarized this result, reasonably: "A substantial majority of Americans . . . support the *threatened* use of nuclear weapons to deter a Soviet attack against U.S. allies . . ." (emphasis added). A longer summary adds: "Interestingly, the college educated citizens were most opposed to the actual use of nuclear weapons. This same group was the most in favor of keeping up the threat of their use to defend our allies."

It is good news, from Yankelovich, that the majority of Americans do not want nuclear weapons "actually used" (first) by us in combat. They don't want nuclear threats to be implemented if they fail; they want the threats to be just bluffs. But, according to the CPD poll—which I find all too plausible—they do think that threats are needed, to protect our allies and overseas interests. They want the "bluffs" to be made.

This is bad news—worse than it may appear at first. For it would follow—and the political behavior of voters is regrettably consistent with this—that they would be receptive to buying the kinds of weapons for first use, escalation, and preemptive first-strike that are designed to enhance the *credibility* of such threats. And that is essentially what the current, dangerous arms race is.

Higher Education

Freeze Campaign literature asserts: "We have convinced the American public of the risks of the arms race." On the basis of these and other public opinion data, I would say, "That's wrong." We have convinced them of the risks associated with a nuclear war. We have not convinced them of the risks associated with acquiring new nuclear weapons—risks of testing them, deploying them, threatening with them.

Many people see the ongoing arms race as wasteful, but not enough yet see it, as we do, as adding immediately, on balance, to our overall danger. Nor have we convinced them that threats are not necessary, or not safe. That means that we have not convinced them that the means to make threats credible and effective ought to be strongly opposed. We have not taught them that Reagan's arms race is an unacceptable approach to peace.

It is simply the other side of this that stopping the arms race, even to those who see it as desirable, does not necessarily appear as a means to higher security. The pollsters for the Committee on the Present Danger found that "the freeze is seen more as a budget-cutting measure than an answer to the country's defense problems. Only one third said that a nuclear freeze would reduce the chance of a nuclear war, while 55 percent said it 'would only reduce the expense of continuing to develop nuclear weapons.'"

The main argument of the Freeze Campaign itself encourages this evaluation, perhaps inadvertently, with its emphasis on halting all weapons, without focus on qualitative differences. Earlier campaigns that stressed "overkill" and redundancy may have had a similar effect. The Yankelovich survey asked what difference it would make to national security if both the United States and Soviet Union cut their nuclear arsenals in half (George Kennan's proposal). It found that 61 percent said it would make no difference. Fifty-two percent said it wouldn't matter if the two countries "froze all nuclear weapons at present levels." Seventy-one percent felt it would make no difference if both *doubled* the size of their nuclear arsenals (the current direction).

These attitudes correspond to the 90 percent consensus Yankelovich finds among Americans that "we and the Soviets now have enough to blow up each other several times over." In the context of political mobilization and action, emphasis on this familiar "overkill" perception can be seen to cut two ways. It points toward the infeasibility of achieving a meaningful superiority, on which Americans are now nearly unanimous. But at the same time it undercuts any judgment that achieving a mutual halt is a matter of grave urgency or priority; the chances are, as people see it, that it would make no difference to national security, only to spending.

Such judgments make a freeze look "permissible"; they do not make it look strongly necessary. On the contrary.

Speaking from a background as a weapons analyst and war planner for the Rand Corporation and defense department, what concerns and frightens me about the current arms race is not the number or the cost of the weapons that are multiplying, but the type of weapons that are being added on both sides, the functions and strategies they serve, and the effects of their interaction. I am well aware of the complexity and unfamiliarity of these arguments, and the contrary need for simplicity in political communication. In the past I myself deferred to these considerations. But to communicate the awareness of urgency that is appropriate and, it now appears, politically essential, there may be simply no substitute for moving beyond gut generalities to the daunting educational task of preparing more Americans to feel confident in making critical judgments on specific weapons systems, political/military strategies, and negotiating proposals.

Let us not be too hasty, this round, in judging that to be infeasible; if that is so, our experience so far suggests that real change, and survival, could be infeasible.

Thus, we need to criticize the Strategic Defense Initiative not mainly in terms of its high cost or the probability that it won't work. The key objection is that it guarantees the continuation of an offensive and defensive arms race that is bringing us weapons—including the SDI systems themselves—that make the world even more dangerous than it is today. And we have to oppose those other weapons—MX, ASAT, Trident II (D-5), Pershing 2, and SLCMs—along with the whole new round of Soviet counterparts, for the reasons that they lower our security and that of the world.

These weapons are not, primarily, for fighting but for threatening. That type of use is not less dangerous but its dangers need to be explained. It is one thing for Americans to accept in principle the need for nuclear first use "bluffs" (primarily to defend Europe). It could be quite another thing for them to discover just how close we have actually come to initiating tactical nuclear war a dozen times in the past—mostly against Third World opponents with links to the Soviets—and how far our current threats are from being pure bluffs.

These new weapons coming along markedly strengthen the deadly connection between interventions and the actual first use of nuclear weapons in combat. They increase the likelihood of nuclear escalation, and of full-scale preemption once any nuclear weapon has exploded. They encourage leaders to continue to make first use threats, to use their nuclear weapons by pointing them at others in confrontations. At the same time, the mutual buildup is making it more likely that such threats will fail, and that someday one will be carried out, at the risk of our world. These reckless programs are pushing ahead year by year, gathering momentum that makes them progressively harder to halt. Probably only a new president—rather than Congress in opposition to Reagan—could achieve a comprehensive freeze, with its requirements for negotiated verification. But Congress can and must slow down and halt individual weapons systems before that time, and could go beyond that to institute a *de facto* moratorium on the testing of warheads and flight testing of ballistic missiles— both now thoroughly verifiable without further negotiation—by making funding for such testing conditional on Soviet testing.

We cannot afford to freeze the arms race only after both sides have acquired these new weapons. We need, by every means, to stop these new developments (essentially through Congress) on the basis of a newly committed and informed public mood, and by nominating and electing a candidate in 1988 far different from any we have seen so far in dedication to protecting us from the dangers of the nuclear arms race. We have a lot of educating—of ourselves and the public— ahead of us.

Toward a New Patriotism
By Randy Kehler
November/December 1985

WHY IS IT THAT A LARGE MAJORITY OF OUR FELLOW CITIZENS SUPPORT important objectives of the peace movement—for example, freezing the nuclear arms race, and establishing peaceful relations with Nicaragua—but seem not to support the peace movement itself? It may be that many Americans feel caught in a bind between conscience and culture. They genuinely believe, for instance, that nuclear weapons are highly dangerous as well as morally repugnant. But they also share the prevailing cultural attitude that protest and dissent are "unpatriotic."

The bind is paralyzing, and it constitutes a major obstacle to the peace movement.

Recently, on a beautiful Sunday evening, I found myself sitting among a crowd of 4,000 people assembled on the bank of the Cumberland River in Nashville. The largest peace gathering in recent Nashville history was just getting underway: a commemoration of the 40th anniversary of the atomic bombings of Hiroshima and Nagasaki. One of the organizers leaned over to offer some advice about the short speech I was about to give.

"I know you're going to emphasize the importance of the Soviet Union's unilateral testing moratorium," she said, "and I think you *should*. But I just want to remind you that this is Tennessee and not Massachusetts. Most of these people here are pretty conservative, and patriotic." I swallowed hard and told myself that this was the time to say something I'd never said before, something that had been welling up inside me for a couple of years.

After Rosanne Cash and several of her country music friends led us in singing "This land is your land, this land is my land," it was my turn. I told the crowd the Soviet moratorium was probably the most significant initiative either country had taken in over 20 years. "But let us be perfectly clear," I added. "When we protest our government's initial rejection of the Soviet initiative, it is not because we are against our country. It is because we are *for* our country, because we *love* our country. 'This land *is* your land and my land,' and we have to protect it. Perhaps this is the meaning of patriotism in the nuclear age—recognizing that the interests of the whole world can no longer be separated. And so when we protest a particular policy of a particular administration, let no one call us 'unpatriotic.' We are true patriots of the nuclear age." The crowd roared its approval.

Like most of us in the peace movement, I used to feel patriotic toward my country. The Vietnam War—and the two years I spent in federal prison for noncooperation with the draft—changed all that, as it did for many others of my generation, and left a permanent scar. The American flag became an intolerable symbol, the "Pledge of Allegiance" an impossible oath.

Although the issue of patriotism came up often during my four years with the National Freeze Campaign, we ourselves never raised it. Our opposition did. Many people considered (and possibly still consider) us "disloyal" and "anti-American." Our response, was, of course, that stopping the nuclear arms race was in the best interests of the United States, the Soviet Union, and the whole world. But we never really went so far as to speak of "patriotism."

•　　•　　•

We in the peace movement tend to see the problems and obstacles before us largely in political and organizational terms. Yet we often speak of the seemingly inexplicable gap between citizen awareness and citizen action and wonder how people can understand the danger and immorality of the arms race and yet not get involved in actions to halt it. This suggests that the biggest obstacle to the movement's growth may be cultural.

Most of those who know, or at least sense, that things in this country have gone awry—some things dangerously so—continue to find many things about our country that are valuable and ought to be appreciated. The fact that this tension or dichotomy is deliberately and cynically promoted by individuals in power makes it no less real and no less an obstacle.

It is tempting to think that we can bridge the "patriotism gulf" that seems to separate us from so many of our fellow citizens, most of whom do share our basic values (and many of our political objectives), simply by hiring a public relations firm to re-package the peace movement in red, white, and blue. If we just change our language, "clean up" our appearance, and adopt familiar symbols, perhaps the problem will go away.

I am convinced that this would be the wrong approach, or at least it is the wrong place to begin. If we really want to bridge the gulf we have to start with ourselves, by painstakingly examining our own thoughts and feelings about our country. The "P.R." approach will ring hollow (like George Bush pretending to the far right that he's a macho Texan) if it doesn't come from the heart. As some of my religious friends would say, "There's no such thing as cheap grace."

In my own case, it has been very hard to think, explicitly, about "loving my country." Those words never even came to mind. It was almost as though in order to remain true to the genuine feelings of horror and revulsion I experienced during the Vietnam War—or to similar feelings I now have regarding, for example, U.S. aid to the contras—I had to repress any positive feelings I had toward this country. Now, however, I am slowly realizing that in fact I do love my country—in the sense that I genuinely appreciate and care for many aspects of it.

I find that I am able to love my country despite its monumental failures just as I am able to love particular individuals whose flaws are sometimes enormous. In neither case is this the love of blind allegiance ("my country right or wrong") nor does it require being better than everyone else ("USA—Number One!"). To a large extent it is a love born of familiarity, which may breed contempt on occasion, but over time usually produces a deep affection and attachment.

Looking back, I can see that one expression of this attachment was my firm decision to stay in this country and face prison during the Vietnam War, rather than flee to Canada; I couldn't stand the idea of the war perpetrators forcing me to leave my own country.

More and more this kind of attachment, and affection, translates for me into particular people and places. When I think about "my country," the country I love, I can't help but think of the rolling hills and old country roads, the historic villages and feisty Yankees of western Massachusetts where I've now spent nearly half my life. In recent years I have also come to love the little farmhouse and piece of farmland that we have been trying to care for and make habitable and productive again. In a recent talk on national security, Kentucky poet and farmer Wendell Berry touched on the meaning of this kind of affection when he said, "Any people who hope to be capable of national defense must love their country with the particularizing passion of people who love their homes and land."

There are other things I care about. I very much appreciate the optimistic, "can do" idealism that runs all through our history and is still evident today. I admire the spirit of practical ingenuity and self-reliance that is especially strong in rural parts of this country. I also appreciate the political freedoms embodied in our Bill of Rights (and I know how easy they are to take for granted). The very fact that we can have a Freeze Campaign or a Pledge of Resistance network, openly protest government policies, and organize opposition gives testimony to these freedoms. So does the fact that we have such a thing as a Freedom of Information Act, which, as British journalist William Shawcross put it in his book *Sideshow*, "recognizes rights of citizens that are hardly to be conceived anywhere else in the world."

While our system has major flaws (the disproportionate influence of wealth on public policy is no small defect), I also know how important and valuable is our constitutionally anchored commitment to democratic government.

We in the peace movement are frequently accused of being "against" everything and not "for" anything, but I can say that besides being "for" a halt to the arms race and to military interventions I am very much "for" democracy. To date we have made far too little of this. Connecticut author and freeze activist David Keppel argues persuasively that the Freeze Campaign's organizing tactics—town meetings, local and state referenda, signature gathering, and so forth—"are not just ways of achieving the freeze: They are exercises for a [democratic] society."

Our efforts to revitalize American democracy should not pit citizens against their government (the hollow Reagan theme), but should insist that citizens be involved in and take responsibility for their government—through protest and resistance as well as legislative and electoral activities. The central problem is not that government is "too big" (although that may be true), but that it is largely unaccountable. Democracy cannot be a spectator sport; it works only if we get in there and make it work.

Common Defense

There is another aspect to patriotism, however, besides loving one's country and being "for" various things one's country stands for. *Webster's* defines a "patriot" as "a person who loves his [sic] country *and defends and promotes its interests*" (italics mine). The essential questions are, What *are* its interests? And by what *means* does one defend and protect them?

My own evolving answers to these questions have not only to do with certain moral imperatives but, increasingly, with the survival imperatives of the nuclear age. In its preamble, the U.S. Constitution lists as one of the Constitution's purposes, "To provide for the common defense." Whereas 200 years ago "common" referred to all 13 colonies, it now must refer to all people everywhere. And the armed violence by which the Constitution's framers meant to defend and protect their fragile and imperiled republic must now be replaced by a no less active or ambitious *non*violence capable of defending and protecting our fragile and imperiled planet.

The single most important axiom of the nuclear age is this: No people or nation can be secure as long as others are insecure—we must strive for common security for all, or else there will be no security for any. This is especially true among nuclear-armed nations. But because more and more nations are acquiring nuclear weapons, and because the affairs and well-being of those who already have them (the East-West powers) are increasingly intertwined with the affairs and well-being of those without them (the Third World nations), the axiom must apply to all.

The implications of this common security axiom are far-reaching. Certainly it requires alleviating some of the major causes of conflict in the world. Specifically, the poisonous and artificially inflated East-West enmity must be overcome, and the inequitable, exploitative relationship between North and South must end. These goals point to what I consider to be the paramount "interests" of my country, interests I believe in "defending and promoting," interests for which I am prepared to make personal sacrifices and take personal risks. It is in pursuit of these interests that I believe I can best protect my country and all those things I love about it.

Common Sense

Despite all this, I confess to a lingering malaise concerning the word "patriotism" itself. Its patriarchal roots I find offensive, especially in light of our long, sad history of wars, violence, and oppression so often conducted under its misguided banner. I must also say that the American flag, like the wrathful bald eagle, still arouses in me as many negative emotions as positive. And I'm still not sure I could stand with my hand over my heart and recite, with seeming obedience, the "Pledge of Allegiance" (despite my belief in "liberty and justice for all").

Is either the word or the concept redeemable? I don't know. But it seems worth a try. Not as a gimmick or ploy, but as a genuine, heartfelt effort to communicate with our more mainstream neighbors and fellow citizens, and more broadly, to begin the kind of transformation of cultural values that is required if all that we love and cherish in our country and the world is to survive.

I have a hunch that if we could somehow eradicate or at least diminish the apparent contradiction that so many Americans feel between protesting what they know to be wrong and remaining faithful to the country they love, an unprecedented new social force for peace might be unleashed.

We must aim to create what Lawrence Goodwyn (author of *The Populist Movement*) calls "a visible new public ethic." The essential underlying principles of this new ethic, this "new patriotism," must be two-fold. The first principle is inward-looking, toward our own country: In a democracy, protest *is* patriotic. The second is outward-looking, toward the world: common security or no security.

Is today's peace movement capable of initiating this new public ethic? I think we've never been in a better position to do so. To some extent, the process of initiating this new ethic has already begun. Important discussions are taking place all over the country concerning the necessity and implications of a world "beyond war," and peace advocates are involved in a growing number of efforts to find "common ground" with people of opposing views. But for the most part this process—particularly as it relates to the question of patriotism—is not explicit, and rarely is it the dominant theme of our work. I am convinced that it must become so.

The first step, however, is for us as individuals, and for the peace movement as a whole, to come to terms with not only our unpatriotic public image, but, more importantly, our personal feelings that are at least partially responsible for that image. We need to set aside time to talk about this, to write about it, to discuss its implications for our work.

It has been said many times, particularly by revolutionaries, that it is impossible to change your country if you do not love it. In fact, this may be our single most important lesson as we dig in for the long haul. I hope the day is not far off when we will be able to declare, publicly and proudly, our love for our country and our allegiance to the principles of democracy upon which our country was founded. Then we will cease being apologetic about our protest, defensive about our dissent, embarrassed to be "disturbing the peace." I am not arguing for less sensitivity as to how our words and actions affect others—just the opposite. I am arguing for a "public relations campaign" that is rooted in a new boldness, a greater self-confidence, a genuine and radiating pride in knowing that, despite all our mistakes and unanswered questions, we are working to improve and protect the country and world that we love.

Post-Election Plans:
A Veteran Peace Activist Charts a Political Strategy for the Next Decade
By Pam Solo
November/December 1988

WITH A NEW OCCUPANT IN THE WHITE HOUSE NEXT YEAR, THE $64,000 question is, of course, "What's next for the peace movement?" As of this writing, George Bush and Michael Dukakis are still slugging it out on the campaign trail; I don't have the benefit of knowing who won on November 8. But it really doesn't matter as far as the peace movement is concerned. Regardless of who won the election, our agenda remains much the same.

Sure the Democrats may be more receptive to peace politics for political and philosophical reasons, but the essential agreement between Cold War liberals and conservative hawks provides continued momentum for the arms race and a static foreign policy. They will disagree about specific weapons systems or certain actions in Nicaragua. But until the underlying politics of the Cold War are challenged, the peace movement will continue to play the role of Sisyphus, pushing the rock of incremental change up Capitol Hill.

The peace movement needs to redefine the larger security agenda, fight to give legitimacy to our ideas and push back the boundaries of what is now considered reasonable or politically possible. We can shape the terms of the U.S. security debate in the next few years by advancing policy proposals to end the arms race, restructure U.S.-Soviet relations, reduce military spending, and create a U.S. foreign policy dedicated to resolving regional conflicts and global problem solving. In order to turn such proposals into policy, however, the movement must articulate a persuasive new paradigm that moves beyond the logic of the Cold War as the context within which legislative, electoral, and nonviolent direct action campaigns are conducted.

What Is the New Framework?

The fundamental principle of "common security" is that no nation can ensure its own security at the expense of another. Put another way, the security of one cannot be rooted in the insecurity of another. A policy based on common security would require real steps toward nuclear and conventional disarmament, economic and social development, and active conflict resolution.

Common security is guided by the following principles:

1. All nations and peoples have a right to security.

2. In the nuclear age, national security cannot be achieved through unilateral action.

3. True security derives not from military forces but from economic prosperity and justice, vibrant social and cultural life and freedoms, the affirmation of human, civil, and political rights, and full ecological integrity. Massive spending for military forces drains societies of needed financial, technical, and human resources.

4. Military force is not a legitimate instrument for resolving disputes among nations or promoting national interests. National military forces must be confined to strictly defensive, nonthreatening postures.

5. U.S. policy toward the Soviet Union must reject confrontation and promote cooperation, trade, cultural interaction, problem solving, and peacemaking.

6. U.S. allies are autonomous and should define their own security needs.

7. U.S. relations with Third World nations must respect different paths of political and economic development. The United States should support global efforts to transcend poverty, repression, and environmental degradation throughout the underdeveloped world. Local conflicts in the Third World must not be used as theaters of East-West confrontation.

8. International security leadership and direction must derive increasingly from transnational institutions devoted to conflict resolution, peacekeeping, verification and monitoring of military forces and agreements, problem-solving research, and development of international standards of economic, social, and political rights.

What Are the Policies?

Common security policy options can be grouped in three categories: restructuring the military and reducing reliance on nuclear deterrence; broadening the security agenda to include international environmental and economic development challenges; and advocating political agreements to resolve conflicts, eliminate intervention, and increase cooperation and confidence in the United Nations and other international organizations.

• Restructuring the military and reducing reliance on nuclear deterrence. One of the most difficult tasks will be to move away from military definitions of security, restructure military forces, and redirect the resources now devoted to them toward other threats to common security. Reliance on military strategies to achieve security cannot be changed without the assertion of other threats, nor can the habitual reliance on expanding military power be abandoned easily or quickly. Military doctrines and force structures must be replaced by defensive defense. Two parallel paths must be pursued in restructuring the military.

The first path, denuclearization, involves reducing and eliminating reliance on nuclear weapons, ending the qualitative competition in new weapons systems, and reducing the number of nuclear weapons.

The second path, nonprovocative defense, involves reducing and restructuring conventional military forces to smaller, purely defensive, nonthreatening defenses.

• Broadening the security agenda to include international environmental and economic challenges. The international security agenda must be expanded to include global environmental threats, economic challenges posed by a global economy, and critical social and economic development problems in the Third World. Clearly, the peace movement has less depth of understanding and experience in environmental and development policy. Here, new alliances and coalitions can be built with environmentalists and with international development and domestic-community-development activists.

• Advocating political agreements to resolve conflicts, eliminate intervention, and increase cooperation and confidence in international organizations. Restructuring political relationships is as important as restructuring military relationships. These political agreements can be reached bilaterally and multilaterally. New bilateral contacts should be encouraged between governments and citizens movements and between citizens of all nations.

An urgent task in the restructuring of international relations is the conclusion of a nonintervention regime. Such as regime would end and delegitimize the use of military force as a tool of power by initiating regular discussions among major powers on military forces and doctrine, arms reduction, and confidence building; end all current military interventions; and increase reliance on international mechanisms to resolve conflict.

Citizen peace initiatives are also critical. Peacemaking and the building of alternative security systems cannot be left to governments. Citizens need to build their own networks and international organizations.

In addition, it is important to make a point that cannot be fully developed in such a brief essay. When planning our strategies, we must distinguish policy proposals requiring popularization before they become politically viable from those that can gain a credible hearing because they are being considered by Congress or have been raised by allied or Soviet initiatives.

Lastly, political strategy cannot be implemented with weak organization. And right now the peace movement continues to struggle for organizational survival. Organizations cannot be built without a compelling, visionary, and practical political strategy. Funds seem to be drying up and morale in national offices is at an all-time low. Funding and participation will increase when we get our political program back at the center of our daily work.

It is time to turn our attention toward generating and shaping the new security debate. As we do this we can rebuild our movement and move from protesting policy to shaping it.

The Civilization Crisis:
Activists Voice Their Hopes for a New Era
Facilitated by Andrea Ayvazian and Michael Klare
Spring 1990/Summer 1990

WORLD EVENTS AT THE END OF THE 1980S LEFT PEACE ACTIVISTS AND THE general public both breathless and speechless. Within a matter of months, China was convulsed by mammoth demonstrations and bloody repression, Eastern Europe experienced an unprecedented political transformation, and the United States invaded Panama. And 1989 was just one year in a decade of sweeping change. As suggested by Richard Falk, "The 1980s have been a period of exceptional political creativity, probably ranking in their eventual historical significance with such cataclysmic upheavals as the American, French, and Russian revolutions."

Given the dramatic sweep of events, it is hardly surprising that the American peace movement experienced a loss of focus at the end of the decade. Moreover, the apparent progress in nuclear arms control significantly eroded the sense of urgency that had gripped peace activists early in the decade, and produced a noticeable falling off in funding and volunteer support. The Nuclear Weapons Freeze Campaign, which mobilized thousands and thousands of peace activists in the early 1980s and provided a shared national agenda, has given way to a more diffuse movement with many issues competing for activists' attention.

Social movements are always in a state of flux, experiencing periodic bursts of energy followed by more introspective periods in which the groundwork is laid for the next period of growth. Clearly, the American peace movement is currently in a state of transition—seeking both to assess the meaning of recent world events and to identify the issues that will merit its concern and attention in the 1990s.

This process of reassessment is a natural and necessary step in the life of our movement, and one that will lead to greater clarity in the years ahead. To facilitate this process, in November Nuclear Times brought together a group of nine activists from a cross section of U.S. groups working on peace, justice, and environmental issues to examine the state of the peace movement and to discuss future directions for our work. Each began with a statement. Part one of the edited transcript follows; the second part will appear in the next issue of Nuclear Times.

Roz Spier, *associate director of Connecticut SANE/FREEZE: Campaign for Global Security:* From 1980 to 1985, the greatest sense of urgency among the upper-middle and middle class was attached to the nuclear arms race. Today the attention of upper- and middle-class groups, including students on college campuses, is shifting to the wreckage of the Reagan administration: what's happening in our cities, AIDS, drug abuse, and the increased destruction of the environment.

For Connecticut SANE/FREEZE, a grassroots organization that originally was devoted exclusively to working on the nuclear arms race, there have been some immediate consequences. What we feel most is the decline of heavy-duty volunteers. In local groups, the activity level is down and it's hard to find people to take leadership. The weaker groups have folded. There has also been a decline in income from a high in 1986.

Attention to social issues depends on a very delicate balance between fear and hope. The fear of nuclear exchange that was whipped up by President Reagan and Secretary of State Haig in the early 1980s has largely subsided, for good reasons. Fear can also be blunted by disinformation, and we've seen that. Hope, on the other hand, depends on appropriate vehicles for action; the nuclear freeze proposal was that vehicle for a long time, and had a reasonable expectation of success. Hope can be shriveled by the apparent strength of the opposition, and it can be drained away by the experience of failure. I met a former freeze activist who all but sneered at me, "Stopped any nuclear weapons systems lately?"

The positive things that have happened in the past ten years include the tremendous growth in the professionalism of the peace movement, and the increased institutionalization of the work of the peace movement in churches and schools and other enduring institutions, and I see that throughout Connecticut.

There are three new things I see that are very encouraging. One is connections, one is coalitions, and one is internationalism. People are turning from a tight focus on so-called single issues to articulating the connections between them, and the peace economy project of SANE/FREEZE is a conspicuous example. Coalitions grow rather naturally out of a union of concerns. The groups I work with seem to be increasingly secure in their individual identity and quite willing now to join coalitions that they might not have been five years ago.

I also see growing internationalism. All sorts of people are going to Eastern Europe. Many of the people who went to Russia went on to Central Asia and Siberia, places we hardly knew existed ten or twelve years ago. In communities throughout Connecticut, people are going to Central America, either with sister city projects or with Witness for Peace.

Jeffrey Richardson, *director of the Pittsburgh Jobs with Peace Campaign:* The work of peace and justice activists today takes place within a civilization crisis, a dying world order, which forces all of us to make some choices between imitating that dying system or liberating ourselves through the creation of a new one. Perhaps we face today one of the greatest challenges in world history: the forces of oppression and exploitation are threatening us and the environment that sustains us. The problems are global in scope.

There are three areas of decline in the peace and justice community. One is the failure to deal with the movement at the grassroots level. Two is the failure to forthrightly address the racism, classism, sexism, and other "isms" that are part of the movement, as they are in society as a whole. And three is the lack of clear goals, long-range planning, and a sense of program.

The movement for peace and justice is, in most cases, more form than content. I think of a movement as a powerful organized reality that moves people and moves through people in communities all across this nation, involving poor people, African-Americans, Latinos, Asians, Caucasians, the working class, unemployed, single heads of households, despairing youth, the homeless. However, often the movement has overstepped those people, gone around, or not included them. But you can't move without a base.

Second, the movement for peace and justice has not effectively addressed internal inequities. As an African-American, I am sometimes repulsed by the vulgar racism and classism of this movement. Poorer people and people of color are frequently viewed as objects to be molded and shuffled about to meet the political ego needs of middle-class or wealthy whites. We serve the function and pose for the pictures, but our voices are stifled. If we call for sheer power, we are often driven out of the very movement which claimed to represent justice, equality, and peace. This must cease.

Finally, the peace and justice movement seems to have no real program. We need vision to think through the big questions of global peace, national and international economic equality, and justice. But we also need concrete local linkages, the steps to reach our goals. Some of the failure to develop effective organizing initiatives is the result of inadequate or nonexistent long-range planning. Without such planning, our days may be filled with activity but lack progress toward a new economic order or power to control and humanize the institutions that have used us. If we don't plan for a new society, how can we replace it?

Fortunately, there are also rays of hope. I am pleased with conferences that I have attended over the last two years where there is a massive recognition of the need to return to basic grassroots organizing and door-to-door house meetings around a host of issues. The movement is most powerful when, through our joint work, we acknowledge the complexity and interrelatedness of the world's current situation. I'm happy to see a recognition of the need to develop basic skills in the movement, which are the tools of our work.

I am also pleased by the new and diverse leadership at the meetings I have attended recently: people of color from most of the nation's communities, women in greater positions, people of color as directors. Those changes are important, but the push must continue; the barriers must be removed.

Finally, there are a few more examples of organizations that are working, to use Randy Kehler's word, with "intentionality," to develop democratic organizations at the local level. I am inspired by these hardworking and committed leaders, who represent the real movement.

Virginia Baron, *director of publications for the Fellowship of Reconciliation and editor of* Fellowship: A week ago, a homeless woman said some things to me that seem pertinent to today's discussion. The woman is an artist and a writer who publishes a monthly newsletter for and about homeless people in New York City. Because she's been unable to find a church or printer in the city willing to back the paper or place printing facilities at her disposal, she travels to a church in a northern suburb where she can use their rather old-fashioned mimeographing equipment. The woman is a squatter in a building on Manhattan's Lower East Side. I had arranged to meet her to see her artwork with a view to using it in the December issue of *Fellowship*.

The woman was obviously feeling pressured and tired, as she sets high standards for herself. She was hand printing 5,000 issues of her newsletter. But I had selected several drawings that I thought we might use, assuring her that they would be returned to her after the issue was printed, along with a small fee for permitting us to print them. "Look, you may be a perfectly nice person," she said tensely. "But I have no reason to believe you. I have no use for anybody in the peace movement, no matter what organization they come from.

"What has the peace movement ever done for us? Whenever we've asked people to join us in protests or do anything to help us they never show up. I don't trust you anymore than I would trust anybody else from any peace organization. Since my friend asked me to let you use my work, I'll do it, but I'm not happy about it. Other so-called religious or peace groups have ripped me off in the past." I don't think she's alone in her feelings. Poor people's confidence in us, if they ever had any, is at a low these days. Whether it has declined or whether it actually existed is hard to say.

The following ways in which the peace movement seems to have declined and grown has been developed from interviews I've conducted with several members of the Fellowship of Reconciliation staff and with one member of War Resisters' League. The list represents the thinking of peace activists whose ages and experience cover a wide range.

On the decline side of the ledger are interest in Central American and South African issues, a leveling off of U.S.-USSR work, and a waning interest in civil rights and women's rights. The Freeze as a concept was considered totally irrelevant today. Somebody commented on how unfortunate it was to have that word attached to an organization's name, now that Gorbachev has made the term obsolete. There is a lack of interest in disarmament issues because the public believes recent agreements have solved the problem.

On the growth side, issues thought to be gaining more attention are housing and homelessness, civilian-based defense, environmental threats, animal rights, the Middle East, and Eastern Europe. It was thought that more young people are getting involved, that the movement is making more connections between peace and justice issues, and that there is some positive envisioning of the future. The peace studies departments in colleges and universities are increasing. Grassroots networks have been growing, but so has apathy and passivity among the largest sector of the population.

All of us in the nonviolent movement have had our spirits buoyed by the growth in nonviolent actions throughout the world. We're amazed to see the acceptance of nonviolence as a desired and chosen form of action and protest in most national movements. We're bemused that Americans still don't seem to understand how much the world has changed, that they're so busy cheering what they consider to be capitalism's victory over communism that they haven't taken note of the sweeping antiwar feelings rising around the globe.

What are the reasons for the decline of interest in the above-mentioned issues? We, as a movement, seem to have great trouble sustaining long-term commitments. Our attention span is short. We jump on and off bandwagons, influenced too much by the media, which seem to drive us in whatever direction they choose. We ride on the shirttails of other movements when they achieve success, such as environmental groups. We go where the money is, just as the rest of the country does. If there's no more money for disarmament, we jump to another issue more appealing to our public, upon whom we depend. We have not learned to plan, especially for the long haul. We can mobilize, but we can't organize.

Too often we're a cheering squad building negative momentum instead of leading the way. Without our favorite enemy, Ronald Reagan, we're stranded on our high ground, not knowing how to regain the interest of the crowd. When there's positive momentum, as was let loose by Gorbachev and Reagan, and now with Gorbachev and Bush, we stand on the sidelines, jaws hanging open with nothing to say.

Some organizations have been successful in appealing to the popular culture, such as Amnesty International and Greenpeace. This has probably influenced the rise in campus activity. In other parts of the world there are mass marches, civil disobedience, tax resistance, boycotts—all superb examples of active nonviolence. Meanwhile, back in the U.S., we watch in awe, wondering what we can do to regain for ourselves, as a people, a sense a power over our destiny, as others appear to be doing.

Mary Butters, *director of the Watch in Moscow, Idaho:* From the small rural towns in the West where I am called an organizer, I find myself one of many people, in true western fashion, riding with the pollution posse. We are called the Watch, members of the Palouse-Clearwater Environmental Institute. Groups like ours are sprouting up all over rural America, resisting assaults on our lives created by the production, use, and dumping of deadly substances. But something different has begun to make itself felt: a movement that is community-based, pulling together people who have been poisoned. These are people who know firsthand about plutonium, toxic waste, and the contamination of their drinking water, as opposed to traditional environmentalists concerned about instream water flows, or national peace groups who talk about ratification of the SALT II Treaty. Peace for us is an acronym meaning People for Equality and A Clean Environment.

Over the years, mainstream environmentalists have relied on lobbying, litigation, and science, creating a kind of technical peace-environmental expert able to use government acronyms, facts and figures, and pieces of legislation. I call it toxic talk; it stifles discussion. Two-and-a-half years ago, the editorial page editor of Idaho's second-largest newspaper wrote a column about my work entitled, "Somewhere She Lost Her Native Tongue." He said that I no longer spoke English because I'd been fighting bureaucracy. "She has been arguing with the Feds for so long that she has been infused with their jargon and can no longer speak anything else." Toxic talk intimidates the very people who, in large numbers, are out there and need to stand up and sound off.

Suppose I'm a victim of radiation; I grew up in Utah, downwind of the Nevada test site, where atomic blasts covered us with radioactive dust. I suffer; I feel very alone. All the big-name professional peace and environmental groups are meeting frequently to strategize how to stop the SIS and the NPR, acronyms for the factories where nuclear weapons are manufactured. I need to talk about my feelings, my emotions, and I need support. Everyone there is saying ERDA, RCRA, programmatic EIS, the 2010 Report, the Clean Air Act, vitrification, and vaporization. My health is talked about in terms of studies that will take years and cost millions of dollars. So even there I am still alone.

Across our country, poisoning for profit escalates. More people get sick or die. Most do not say, "They are killing me," but, "I am sick now." We begin to stand together, seeing the connections that bind us: the same poisons, corporate citizens, regulatory denial, and interests who profit from the poisons and the poisoning.

I am now meeting with other community organizers. I've been in Tennessee with a woman dying because Louisiana Pacific is killing her. I sang songs with a coal miner in Virginia who helped organize a strike. I've cried with a mother from Ohio who unknowingly gave her child uranium from their well water. I've been with Cherokees from Oklahoma where Kerr-McGee spreads radioactive waste on the land, calling it fertilizer. I work with farmers and their families in Idaho who drink well water laced with farm chemicals.

Gandhi said that if you want something really important to be done, you must not merely satisfy the reason, you must use the heart also. The appeal to reason is more to the head, but the penetration of the heart comes from suffering; it opens the inner understanding.

People who have been personally affected by the arms race—by toxic pollution and human injustice—have the strongest, most motivating voice on these issues. We're beginning to stand together, joined by families and friends and others in our communities. Voicing our pent-up feelings does not require expertise. Our numbers have grown, one by one. We identify who poisons us in a tangible fashion: this community is poisoned by this company, and these people suffer. We build friendships to help build our spirits. We have fun. We realize we're not alone. We talk in our own language without embarrassment. We build hope and community. Establishment environmentalists needn't be embarrassed by our lack of scientific knowledge.

In order to stop the poisoning of our bodies, we need to clean up the pollution of our minds. We need to find and help others—people who suffer, people who cry, people who are afraid—and that will be our final common ground. Our community group, the Watch, has reached out and joined up with farmers poisoned by the chemicals Monsanto sells them. Folks looking to join up with the movement for ecological and human justice are tired of social change professionals and experts in science. We want to work on issues that affect our communities and the qualities of our lives in a straightforward, simple fashion, speaking in our native tongue.

Nick Carter, *executive director of the National SANE/FREEZE: Campaign for Global Security:* First, I want to say we're growing up and I'm optimistic. We've been through our early adolescence, a period of naivete and enthusiasm and eagerness, and we've bumped headlong into a cynical, difficult world and had our dreams popped. But we're growing up, just as a young child moves through that period of confrontation with the real world and begins to recapture her dreams and is able to now have the tools to work toward the accomplishment of those dreams.

There are hard realities of having been co-opted by Washington over the last five or ten years, shifting public opinion, and inconsistent leadership within the movement. It has been a difficult time. I know of at least six national peace organizations and scores of locals that were in existence five years ago that are no longer so, and at least another four national organizations that are on the brink. I know of a host of analyses that talk about how naive we were, and some who believe that we still are.

Folks who once were eagerly involved in peace work have now shifted their alliances, mostly it seems to environmental work, and with good cause. And many funding dollars have gone with them. There's a feeling that peace is at hand in many quarters, and plenty of negative analysis to feed the hungriest of our critics. But while the temptation is great to dine with them, I think it would be a grave mistake to do so.

I look at a couple of indicators; first off, public opinion. It's interesting that through all of the failure that's associated with the freeze, the American public still supports the idea of a nuclear weapons freeze beyond the 80 percentile. In this day and age, when peace is at hand, the freeze movement has pointed to and exposed the question of military spending in a way we've never been able to in the past. And interestingly, it now puts all of us hip-deep in the mainstream after having spent years at the periphery.

If anything, people want peace more now than they did ten years ago. Many of the locals have changed, or changed their names, but those that are there are committed. We're also seeing some interesting areas of rapid growth. While our growth rate may be flat in Massachusetts, we can hardly keep pace with the growth in Texas, Georgia, Tennessee, Hawaii, and Alaska.

We are far more mature now. We've learned some important lessons about the political process, about being co-opted and tricked by pieces of legislation and superficial gestures. We've also learned how to diversify our funding base. And we're getting more sophisticated in our analysis and beginning to deal with where the power really lies. We not only know our issue, but we're able to begin to see the world in a different way. We're not just marching in with a laundry list of which weapons systems we're against, but beginning to move to another level of analysis of what we're for.

My second analogy is one of the boat. People have said that the peace movement is sinking or sunk, and I reject that altogether. This boat that's been launched in the search for peace and justice in this world is a fine ship. It's still afloat. We've been through some difficult storms, and in the midst of it the crew didn't always know how to set the sail. And we managed to find ourselves in irons, where either the winds weren't blowing our way or we couldn't catch them. And people mistook that for the boat sinking. Not at all. As I look at it from my perspective, it seems that things are getting organized on the deck, people are sharing the load, the sails are getting set the right way, and I'm pretty excited about where the boat's going. There's certainly reason for caution, but I think the opportunities are greater than they've been in a long time.

Bruce Birchard, *national coordinator of the American Friends Service Committee Disarmament Program:* The peace movement, however we define it, has a history of going through cycles of gaining strength in crisis situations and then seeing that strength decline. I remember, in 1975, organizing what was a fairly good-sized demonstration of people against the B-1 bomber and in favor of peace conversion in Philadelphia. A reporter from the *Inquirer* covered it as a human-interest story. Her key question to me afterward was, "So is what we're seeing the last, weak hurrah of the antiwar movement?" And I said, "No, what you're seeing is the beginning of the next movement."

But the 1970s were a time in which the B-1 bomber and peace conversion campaign was indeed one of the first efforts, after the almost total preoccupation with the war in Indochina, to build a new peace movement. Clearly we've come off the high point of protest of the early 1980s. But the structures have been built, the organizations and the level of general public awareness and concern all have been pushed up several notches. Now there are hundreds of groups across a wide range of constituencies, and we're so much stronger at the grassroots level. I'm sure that newspaper reporters are asking the same kinds of questions they asked me in the 1970s: is this the dying whimpers of the Freeze movement?

And I'm sure, in a few more years, there will be another crisis, and at that point we'll be a much more mass political movement, and very visible again.

The peace movement is like a whale; it suddenly breaches and everybody sees it and says, "Oh, my God," and then, of course, it sinks under. The rest of the public figures it's gone, but we're really underneath. We're feeding and eating all those little plankton.

What's AFSC doing? We're much more focused on Third World conflicts than on nuclear weapons. I look around at regional offices and see more focus on the relationship between foreign policy issues and economic issues at home and abroad, and also on issues of sovereignty and self-determination, both for countries abroad—Third World and European—and for peoples within the United States. AFSC offices are responding to local conditions and opportunities: Frances Crowe in western Massachusetts is taking on the University of Massachusetts for its biological warfare research; in Colorado, they're still working on Rocky Flats; in Portland, Oregon, they're working with Belauans to support the struggling people in Belau to keep U.S. nuclear weapons and bases out of their little island.

In the national office, out of our interest in the common security approach, we've focused on the question of foreign and military presence in foreign bases. We did a speaking tour of nine women from countries where there are foreign military bases in Europe, Latin America, and the Pacific, including a black woman from the very militarized southern United States. All of this is part of a struggle in favor of a withdrawal and demobilization of everybody's troops, at least getting them out of other people's countries. There's a focus within AFSC on the Pacific and East Asia, an area we've too long neglected in favor of Europe. AFSC is also continuing its programs in the Middle East, South Africa, and Central America.

Damon Moglen, *coordinator of Greenpeace's Military Nuclear Fuel Cycle Campaign:* Greenpeace's strength, and perhaps one of our weaknesses, is the specificity of the work that we do. Our kind of global orientation toward environmental and nuclear issues seems very specific in some ways. We are also experiencing a staggering growth. In the United States, Greenpeace is growing by 50,000 members a month. New offices will be open in Japan and the Soviet Union. Offices have opened recently in Latin America, and campaign activity is beginning to stretch into Africa and many Asian countries.

I'd like to talk about the arms control and disarmament movement in this country, which I see as perhaps two different movements, moving within the same stream but at different speeds and levels of eddy. We clearly have a visibility problem. We are not perceived as raising a ruckus or forcing a national debate and agenda. The same problems which, three years ago, would have sent a large proportion of the country into paroxysms of fear and anger are still happening every day. But something has changed to make us less vocal and less visible.

What's changed is that the nuclear issue is not being perceived now as a front-line issue. The INF treaty is an interesting example of this phenomenon. INF was vaunted by so many in the arms control and peace community as being this wonderful step that we all said is the right step—to be followed by the left step, followed by the next step. And as far as any of us can tell, we've gotten bogged down. We were not able to articulate the next step issues. In a strange way, a lost momentum from Mr. Reagan's administration appears to be overtaking us.

Inasmuch as START is the next step, I think we've got a warm, fuzzy feeling and a mild sense of familiarity about it, but we're not really thinking about what this means for our work within our respective organizations. What are the obvious latch-ons to major disarmament agreements? And what is the obvious next step? Just as the INF treaty got rid of a miniscule number of weapons, they were immediately replaced with other new weapons within a few months.

We also have a problem of inadequate interaction with the international movement, which is one of the most important ways that we—as local, regional, and national activists—can realize we're part of a global movement which is articulating an antinuclear position.

I would redefine growth as a question about our maturity, because many of us would say that we haven't grown much in this arms control and disarmament movement. But I think there are some very significant indicators of maturity. To go from Mr. Reagan's Evil Empire to a world in which the INF treaty and START were possible is a remarkable indication of the effectiveness of the antinuclear movement in this country. I think the freeze has often been discounted, and yet it was the articulation of a message that said to people that we can address this staggering problem in an understandable way. Congresspeople can laugh at us for saying that, but they didn't laugh at the polls and when they got reelected.

There has been an increased breadth and depth within the movement, as well as a growing number of arms control and disarmament groups in the 1980s. Some of those groups have disappeared, but some have coalesced from multiple organizations into a single organization. And the growth of professional organizations within the movement is important in a country, like our own, in which professionalization is seen as such a virtue. That professional organizations have taken up the banner of nuclear disarmament as part of their professional responsibility is significant. When nuclear abolitionism is attacked as being an idealistic and therefore vapid position, we are able to counter that by pointing to those people who have committed themselves, not only spiritually and intellectually, but also professionally to this issue. That's a very powerful indication that the movement is here to stay, because it has been adopted as part of the professional attitude.

The downfall of the Department of Energy and its inability to do its dirty business in nuclear and military facilities without the public looking through every single chink in every single fence is a real indication of the effectiveness of our public information and congressional lobbying campaigns. And weapons programs like the B-2 , Trident, and Star Wars are no longer programs that can simply be conducted in a secretive way. Instead, these programs are being seen from a public perspective which has drawn off the lid of secrecy. This is very much a part of the work of the 1980s, and I hope it will become part of the work of the 1990s.

Michael Klare, *director of the Five College Program in Peace and World Security Studies:* I think this is a time in which there are some things moving us forward and others that are holding us back. One thing that's holding us back is the "U.S.-government-is-the-bad-guy" attitude that was so strong in the early 1980s. That the problem was the U.S. government, it was Ronald Reagan, it was the White House, it was Washington—we're very set on that. We're a protest movement that likes to protest Washington, but I think it makes us unable to see injustices and wars that happen elsewhere that are not America's fault.

That's connected to the second thing that I think is holding us back, what I might call East-Westism, that the problem is the U.S. and the Russians, and if we sat down with the Russians, with people of good will on both sides, we could solve the problems of the world. If white men from our side and white men from their side sit down, the problems will go away.

What we fail to see is the scale of violence and warfare and deprivation that's growing on a worldwide basis. I do feel that violence outside of the East-West conflict is growing, and the poorest people are the ones who are being victimized. As many as half a million people died in the Sudan and Ethiopia last year, which is more than Hiroshima and Nagasaki put together. And I have yet to see anyone in the peace movement say, "Hey, people are dying on a scale that we should do something about."

What's moving us forward? Internationalism is something I see a lot of, with young people in particular. Students are very interested in the issues of famine and hunger and underdevelopment and gender on a global basis. Students want to go to Malaysia, Sri Lanka, Africa, and the rainforests to see what's going on, and to help if they can.

Another area that's pushing us forward is the new thinking that's developing. There's a reservoir of new ideas coming forward that can contribute to the search for peace worldwide. The growth of peace studies in colleges and universities, and increasingly peace and conflict resolution education in secondary schools and below could also make a big difference.

Andrea Ayvazian, *trainer and consultant based in Northampton, Massachusetts:* Some of the decline in the peace and justice movement in this country today is somewhat the result of being the victim of our own success. We're suffering somewhat from having succeeded, and I don't hear enough people in the movement pointing to the changes that we helped create. The 1980s were a period of tremendous growth and dramatic changes in the world, some of which we had absolutely nothing to do with, and some of which we just applauded, but some of which we had impact and an influence on.

Roz talked about the delicate balance of fear and hope. We helped reduce the level of fear when we sent delegation after delegation to the Soviet Union and to Central America. We prevented an invasion of Nicaragua. Of course, we had nothing to do with Mikhail Gorbachev rising to power, but we helped shape his agenda. We've had a tremendous impact on national and international history.

We're in a period of some decline, because no movement in history—look back on the women's movement, the labor movement, the gay rights movement —knows what to do when they win. People know about the struggle, the protest, and the fight, but they don't know about winning.

Although we were talking about decline, in my experience of traveling around the country, there is still tremendous activity in this nation. There are a lot of groups doing wonderful work, it's just that nothing is coordinated anymore. There's this group doing Middle East work, and this group doing something on apartheid, and this group working frantically on weapons facilities. It's like a huge orchestra and all the sections are playing different melodies, but they are playing. Or they're tuning up.

The image I'm carrying to the peace and justice movement in this country today is a huge map of the U.S. with separate spinning tops all over it. None of the tops are spinning together, but they're all spinning. Sometimes they bump into each other, and they either both spin or they collapse, but there is a lot of activity.

A few of you said we've lost our visibility, but I don't think so. I think we've lost it in the *Washington Post*, the *Boston Globe*, the *New York Times*— we've lost it on that level. We are not on the front page of anything except the *Cleveland Plain Dealer*, the *Des Moines Register*, and the *San Francisco Chronicle*. Local papers are covering peace and justice activity. I was at the Peacemaking on the Prairie conference in Davenport, Iowa that drew people from four midwestern states; 200 people, lots of activity, and we were beautifully covered by the media.

I also don't think our movement is fickle or jumps on and off bandwagons. I think it's a movement with a remarkable level of stick-to-itiveness. A real backbone in this country are people of faith who are doing peace and justice work, who are committed to it for the next 20 years and have done it for the last 20 years. I would not characterize us as a movement that's fickle.

What is a bit of a problem in the movement today is that there is no shared national focus. I think people wish it were the time of the early days of the freeze again, when 1,100 local groups nationwide were working on the same campaign. It was a remarkable time of energy and activity. My guess is that there isn't going to be a second coming of the freeze movement for years to come, and some of us long for it. It was nice knowing that when you were going door to door with your freeze petitions in your hand in 1982 that people were doing it in all 50 states.

More than a movement in decline, we're a movement in transition, trying to figure out how to respond to a very rapidly changing world. We are changing and reassessing what our boundaries are, what our work is, and how we promote leadership and programs that we believe in.

Baron: The Fellowship of Reconciliation is celebrating its 75th year, and from my memory of the peace movement in this country, it started with the Quakers. When talking about the peace movement, we have to keep that in focus. The peace movement is still going to be here—if the country is—100 years from now. It didn't start with the freeze and it's not going to end with it; the peace movement is here forever.

Birchard: I really agree with Andrea's point about the success we have had. That isn't to say that we didn't also fail. Like so many things in life, there is a lot of complexity here. We failed in our very specific demands, even the rather simple one of the freeze, but we won in terms of setting the agenda and forcing the people in power to respond. It's terrible that we can't win faster, and that we can't get our specific demands met. We've never been able to actually taste power and negotiate the agreements, and my guess is that we probably never will.

The last thing that Ronald Reagan and George Bush are going to say is, "By gosh, you folks really affected us." The *New York Times* is not going to say that either. That maintains the myth that grassroots people do not have power, that it's just going to be left to the experts. Unfortunately, a lot of our spokespeople are complicit in that conspiracy of the powerful to discredit or ignore the power of the people.

There are four areas we need to be working on in the next few years that are essential to the continued development and growth of the peace movement. One is research and discussion about the institutions and mechanisms that can lead us to a more cooperative and just world in which people are free and at peace. Second, we need to be doing education within our organizations. We need, thirdly, to build political power, and that involves the development of coalitions and the linking of foreign policy to domestic policy issues. We must stand with poor, with working people, with black and Third World people of this country.

And finally, we need to enable people to get direct experience of the conflicts and the violence we're against. Despite our slow progress in integrating our movement, we're still a middle-class movement of people whose hearts are in the right place, but who have almost no experience with what it's like to be a Salvadoran peasant or a Filipino church worker—those who are the victims of low-intensity conflict. We don't have the experience of what it is like to live with the drugs and the crime of our inner cities. The experience we had in citizen diplomacy, through East-West delegations and Witness for Peace, has to be multiplied many times over. People develop not only their knowledge but their commitment and inspiration by meeting the people who are suffering from this system of militarism, violence, and profit.

Carter: One of the things we've hinted at is the sense in which we're getting close to the source of power. And when you get close to the source of power, it has a way of creating a negative atmosphere. Things are comfortable when you're not close to the source of power, but when you really get close, it gets hot. We shouldn't always see the negativism that surrounds this as a bad thing.

We're not going to be the ones who negotiate treaties, and we shouldn't desire that. I like Bill Coffin's classic definition of grassroots activity, which looks to Congress to ratify only what it can no longer resist. It's really important for us to have a good sense of history. We need to reread, or read for the first time, the history of the abolition movement and the women's suffrage movement, and watch what happened to them over the decades in their attempts to deal with entrenched power and moral issues in this country—their successes and failures and splits and funding problems. There's great inspiration for us in that, and a lot of wisdom.

Klare: Jeffrey said that there's a civilization crisis, and I share that sense. Francis Fukuyama is getting attention for the "End of History" thesis, and a lot of people share that view. They're calling it the Bush Doctrine now in Washington—the notion that we've won the Cold War, that perfection has come to the world. I see quite the opposite.

I see power and wealth being concentrated in fewer hands worldwide and more people being excluded from power and the things they need to live. And that's going to create violence among people, like the Shiites and Sunnis fighting each other while both groups are excluded from power. Nick was talking about getting closer to power, but I think if you look at the world, power is evaporating. It's being broken down into fiefdoms, corporations, and power centers feuding with one another.

Look at what's happening in Eastern Europe and the Soviet Union; they have exploded. I certainly don't want to go back to Stalinism, but we have to face the fact that Eastern Europe and the Soviet Union proper could explode in terribly devastating ways, and China, too—all empires. Ethiopia, Sri Lanka, and Lebanon have all disintegrated. What's our position on the Baltic republics if they decide to break away from the Soviet Union and the Soviets send in troops? All of these things are going to produce tests for our movement that we're not even thinking about.

Moglen: Respectfully, inasmuch as our movement does address those issues, we're in great trouble. We must think globally, but we must act locally. I don't think civilization is collapsing any more than it did in 1212 or 1381. What we see is the train of history moving along, and it's traveling through some very strange places. When I hear about children in Ohio drinking uranium-contaminated water, I'm not sure that the problem ahead of us is the Baltic republics. We oftentimes have a sense of having an impact on an issue that we're working on, and then we become disjointed from that, because we think another issue has suddenly become more prominent. There's a real necessity in sticking with what we have in front of us.

Richardson: I think it's important in our work, our discussions, and specifically in our education to look at what is happening as a civilization crisis, in the sense that civilization is crumbling, like the Roman empire. We can look at our work in the context of putting civilization back together, but we're not recreating that which is falling apart before us. It has be something totally new. That includes values, the way we perceive life, religion—everything. That's what I see crumbling before me, which potentially will take everybody with it.

If you are under the influence of a major power, you will go down with it—not because you want to, but because in some ways you are connected to its economic system, political institutions, and military. Obviously you've been educated by it, so you even have some of that civilization in you. Look at the dangerous potential for this crisis, because people will try to prop it up, which they're doing now. I think it tends to make people become very reactionary because they feel the reality they have based their whole existence and world on is crumbling. And that to me is something that needs to be considered as we do our work, particularly as people of color. We want something totally new, because what we're dealing with is on the way out.

Carter: I resonate well with what Damon said. Global talk takes people's concerns away from what's right at home in their own communities, particularly issues of how toxic wastes affect the poor in this country. And yet we *are* really concerned about global issues, but there's a risk of classism in encouraging global thinking. It doesn't mean that we shouldn't do it, but we need to make sure that the white male rural farmer realizes that he has something bound up with the black woman in Philadelphia, who has something bound up with the people in El Salvador and Southeast Asia. Our analysis and plan of action should make the necessary links and not allow people to escape one concern for something that's a little easier. That sort of Peace Corps syndrome, of bringing the goodness of America somewhere else, is not what we want to do.

Klare: What Damon said sounds wise, and yet I feel I have to push my point a little further, because I'm worried about global violence. I ask myself where American soldiers are going to be sent to fight, kill people, and die. The most likely places, I think—after seeing U.S. troops sent to Panama in December—will be against the Sendero Luminoso in Peru, or the poor people of Medellin, or the New People's Army in the Philippines. We haven't the faintest notion of who those people are that we might be sending troops against. We do actually have military people in Peru, shooting at Peruvians now, and I think that's only going to increase in time. We have a military base there. And we're involved in the Philippines. We do have to worry about these places, because that's where our military is going to be. It's going to be an interventionary force that gets sent to fight poor people in these places.

And I think we do have a stake in the Baltics and in Eastern Europe. If Gorbachev is forced to send tanks into one of these countries, which I think is very possible, detente is going to go out the window in a matter of moments. And that's what the people in the Bush administration who really want to get the arms race going again are waiting for. And if Soviet tanks go into Estonia or Latvia, our disarmament movement will be instantly affected by that decision.

I'm not actually saying that I disagree with you, but that as a peace movement we do have a very big vested interest in the decay of global order and the violence it produces.

Baron: I agree with Michael. It proves the need for tight connections, because if something like that were to happen, I think that all of us who have had connections with the Soviets would be over there, on the phone, in contact, and we'd be ready to start moving on whatever the next step would be. We have to continue our connections with people.

Moglen: Chernobyl proved that the earth is a very small place and any political conflict has repercussions. At the same time, here I am, a white guy who goes to Columbia, South Carolina to organize the Savannah River nuclear plant, and what I find is that 85 percent of the blacks in the state of South Carolina live in a community where there is a hazardous waste dump. We can talk about the problem of dumping chemicals in Third World countries, but if we can make people understand that we're doing that in our own country, to our own population, those people will better understand why they must not allow it to happen in other people's countries.

Carter: "Crisis of civilization" is an interesting phrase. It seems to me that what's in crisis is the sense in which we all seek a certain set of definitions to make us feel secure and help us understand our world, so that we feel comfortable and able to function. What's happened in recent years is that most of those definitions have been thrown up for grabs. Defining what an enemy is, what security is, what a good life is, how the world is pasted together and how nations interact, what the definition of liberal and conservative is—all of these definitions have gone haywire.

Nowhere is this more clear than when the Bush administration tries to cram the current international realities back into the old assumptions. Their poverty of thinking is evident when you take a look at how they approach the questions of NATO and Europe. It's happening so fast they don't know what they're supposed to do. So they cram it back into these old definitions. They're totally incapable of coming up with their own new thinking that can adjust to the world.

I think that's where one of our biggest challenges comes. The greatest opportunity we have is to begin to articulate a new set of definitions and a new set of assumptions that are appropriate to the world as it is and as it might be.

Moglen: One of the issues that Greenpeace works very hard at which needs to be addressed by the larger community in the next few years is that of nuclear weapons and reactors at sea. Some one third of the nuclear weapons in the world and a tremendous number of nuclear reactors are at sea, and these weapons have not been covered during arms talks. We also need to confront the nuclear industry and military around the world, who are fighting a last-gasp effort to bring back nuclear power as the answer to global warming.

The Non-Proliferation Treaty conference is going to take place in 1990 and, perhaps for the last time, in 1995. South Africa is armed with nuclear weapons, as are Israel, India, and potentially Pakistan. Argentina and Brazil have budding nuclear weapons programs. That's only going to get worse if we see the demise of the Non-Proliferation Treaty.

We've only begun to see the tip of the iceberg of the impact of over 45 years of nuclear weaponry on the environment and our public health. And it should not be thought that the United States leads the way in environmental degradation. There are significant problems in the Soviet Union and a budding movement there to stop nuclear testing.

Birchard: We can expect to see a very modest decrease in military personnel and in the military budget over the next five to ten years. I think this will come about due to both economic and political pressures. I hope our movement can escalate that process. *Fortune* magazine advocates the need to cut back military spending over the next ten years in constant '89 dollars from roughly $300 billion a year to $200 billion a year. That's a more radical proposal than many peace and arms control groups are pushing right now.

In Europe, we'll continue to see gradual demilitarization and reduction of military forces in offensive weapons. The issues in Europe, east and west, will increasingly be economic, political, and cultural—not military. The possibility of a major war, either conventional or nuclear, starting in Europe—or even spreading to Europe from a Third World crisis area such as the Middle East—will probably decline.

In Eastern Europe and the Soviet Union, there is the realistic possibility of civil war, pitting different nationalities or ethnic groups against each other. Hopefully, such conflicts would be met by international efforts for conciliation and conflict resolution, rather than by attempts to escalate the conflicts and exploit the situation, the way the U.S. might have done ten or twenty years ago.

In the Third World, U.S.-sponsored low-intensity conflict will increase—not using massive American forces, but using American advisors and technologies, which are supplied not just to regular military forces, but to paramilitary forces as well. El Salvador is cited as the model for low-intensity conflict, and that model is being followed in the Philippines, where so-called "Civilian Armed Forces Geographical Units" do a lot of the dirty work. In addition to these local militias, vigilante groups are killing hundreds of people—peasants, religious and community workers, union members, health workers—whose work for the poor makes them "politically suspicious." Some victims are beheaded and disemboweled in attempts to intimidate the people. This is the reality of war in the 1990s.

Carter: Concerns of "good old business" may seem mundane, but I think we need to hold in front of us mundane subjects like finances. We will be eternally poor, but we can be much more efficient about the way that we deal with the money we have. In the future, I see us engaging funders much more creatively than we have in the past. We must find some way to prioritize our thinking and engage them in prioritizing theirs. Often the twain never meet. It's always a guessing game for activists to figure out where the funders are going to put their money.

I also think that we need to be far more sophisticated about our own finances and about investing it in ways that will make for sustainable futures for organizations. That means looking at other mechanisms of raising money, hanging onto money, helping money to grow, and helping people to help each other.

I'd like to raise one question—what do we do with anger and outrage? I think of Helen Caldicott, who was rather notable for the degree of outrage that she could engender. Is there a place for that in our future? If not, what will take its place? If there is, how will we use it? How will we channel it?

On the political side, I'd like us to focus on the military industry and budget, which will be a donnybrook of *major* proportions, if we do a good job of it. But we need to be far more bold than we have been. If Robert McNamara and General Goodpastor can talk about cutting $150 billion from the military budget, why aren't we asking for $250 billion?

Butters: I want to point out that closing bomb plants is a back-door approach to stopping the arms race, and it's a good focus for anyone concerned about peace anywhere in this country. We all recognize that jobs and money fuel the arms race.

Our government's agenda for Idaho is to make it the principal home of the nuclear weapons industry. That will have global consequences. If Idahoans say yes and accept those jobs, we will have the arms race for another 40 years. That's what fuels the arms race. So it's important that we say no in Idaho and that we get help saying no.

The reason they picked Idaho is because we're a redneck state. In Grangeville, where both my children were born, we have bumper stickers that say, "Sierra Club, Kiss My Ax." It's what the DOE calls a rainbow community: it's really easy for them to find and take their pot of gold from us. But I think the soft belly of this issue for Idahoans is the health effects—scaring people about what has happened near other DOE facilities. That's what is really is going to motivate and grab people.

And I would like to see radiation victims given more funding. Foundation money goes to organizations and never to radiation victims, who can do powerful things when they are gathered together.

Baron: What are the major issues facing peace and justice groups in the future? For the long-distance runners of the peace movement, the pacifists, the problem is the age of our members. Can we replace the good old staunch backbone of our movement with new blood, in time to keep us in reasonably good health?

Can we as the peace and justice movement learn to be effective communicators? When we wake up from being stunned by the Gorby momentum, we will have to renew our push for unilateral initiatives from our side. We used to talk about this all the time, before the Soviets picked up the ball and ran with it.

We need dramatic new ideas to keep the public from being conned into thinking we've left the era of militarization behind.

Some of the issues we'll have to deal with are: U.S. materialism, the passivity of the public, rising fear and insecurity among all who are employed as well as unemployed, illiteracy, the growing income gap between rich and poor, the social costs of the budget deficit and military spending, drugs and drug wars, AIDS, low-intensity conflict, continuing U.S. intervention in the Third World, and national military service for the poor as the result of the failure of the volunteer army to enlist enough men and women. We will have to stop asking the poor to join us and find ways to join them.

Instead of leaping from one reactive movement to another, we could try defining our goals and planning to meet them. At a time when demonstrations throughout Eastern Europe are calling for democracy, without really knowing what is meant by the term or how to achieve it, we must also ask the same questions here. We must make stronger, more effective links with our counterpart peace and justice activists in Europe and throughout the world. We may be at a turning point in history, and we should make every effort not to blow our chances of creating real global partnerships.

Richardson: As movements begin to grow from the grassroots, people begin to push and demand, saying, "What we're asking for is not a little bit of change, but we want the whole thing." In finances, we have to push for the development of moral commitment through trust funds, grassroots fundraising, and utilizing all the training and experience that we have to be more efficient in developing and sharing resources, buildings, printing, and equipment to reduce our costs.

The intense competition between various groups of color will be heightened by the increase in the population of people of color by the year 2050, when people of color will be a majority. I can see people, based on skin color, being pitted against each other when there's still a very tight, white ruling class in control. I look at the November 1988 elections in Chicago and Los Angeles and see that trend beginning to develop already. That destroys the movement for all of us.

There is a dangerous tendency to lump all groups and issues together uncritically. Similarity is important, and that helps us to work and develop commonality. But groups have different histories, cultures, and political realities, which must be respected so we can work together better.

We have to concretize our movement. Will we always be on the outside, just pushing? Will we ever take power, or will we always be governed by others? We have to look at forums like the Rainbow Coalition, which is an idea in need of a body that we have to form at the grassroots level. We won't find the leadership that we need in the Democratic and Republican Parties. It has to come from somewhere else.

In our communities, I see increased racism and oppression of all groups. Look at the movies about rape—I don't know whether they're meant to educate people or to encourage rape, they're so sensational. Vigilantism is being fostered, particularly in the "inner city," as it's called. Outside of Pittsburgh, Mel Blount, a former Pittsburgh Steeler, has opened up a youth home that Klan rallies have protested against.

Many communities are calling for the use of the National Guard and opening up military barracks that have been closed to use as holding centers for criminals. Because of the fear of violence, crime, and the drug war—literally a war that's going on because of the other social problems—people may consider these measures. And it's not just the African-American community that will be affected.

Spier: We need vision, leadership, responsiveness, empowerment, and persistence. An ongoing challenge is to stay focused and specific, and still have a broad, integrated, and unified vision. We want to be flexible and receptive to new energy, new ideas, and new openings and, at the same time, maintain some stability and persistence. No one who was active during the Vietnam years would have dreamed that physicians or churches were going to be the leadership in the next wave of the peace movement. I want to be sensitive to where leadership is coming from next, but not neglect the base we have built.

We can be smarter about democratization of the movement. Two groups have been terrific models: 20/20 Vision and Haymarket People's Fund. 20/20 Vision is a letter-writing network of local groups that use the advice of experts in Washington, but make their own decisions as to what issues they will write about each month. Likewise, the Haymarket People's Fund provides guidelines and training for local boards that make grant decisions for applicants from their own communities. That kind of decisionmaking is a good example for the rest of us.

Above all, we need to persist. We need to hang in for as long as it takes to see the changes we are looking for. I am impressed with the campaign put on by Greenpeace to halt radioactive dumping in the North Sea. It took seven years of going to sea in rubber rafts to confront, film, and finally stop the dumping of 50-gallon drums of waste. If Greenpeace had given up after five years or decided that they were using the wrong strategy, there would still be radioactive waste being dumped into the North Sea.

Finally, we have to recognize the power of the opposition and not blame ourselves for the difficulty of the struggle. The military-industrial-academic complex has a lot of clout and a lot of money. If we have any success, we'll know it when we start feeling the heat from those institutions. They will get into high gear if they think we're going to put a dent in their pocketbooks.

Ayvazian: What are the issues, in the next few years, that the peace and justice movement *won't* have to contend with? I think that defining our boundaries is going to be a real issue for our movement. How are we going to limit our focus so that we make an impact and don't become a movement that is a mile wide and an inch deep?

A centerpiece of the work that's waiting for us to look at is the division nationally and globally between the haves and have-nots, the rich and the poor.

I think that the next ten or twenty years is going to show a widening of that gap, which the peace movement is going to have to address.

The peace and justice movement has been operating on the axis of war-peace—issues around pacifism and war and nuclear weapons facilities—which has mainly been the axis of white, middle-class North Americans. I think we're shifting the axis to become one of oppression-liberation—issues that speak to the poor, communities of color, economic injustice, the poisoning of our families, and the disenfranchised. Looking at our racism and what fuels the war machine and roots of violence is where we are moving. And until we make that shift, we're going to stay very white.

Klare: While people have said that the American public has become rather resistant to military activities, as soon as you cross the line into the area of drugs, crime, and terrorism, the gauge goes in the other direction—kill them, use capital punishment.

Intervention is justified on that basis. If there's going to be another Vietnam, it's going to be fought against coca growers in Peru or Colombia, or against the narcoterrorists—as the military now calls them—who, in the U.S., are mainly black and Hispanic male youth who can't get employed elsewhere. The same solution is going to be proposed: sending in military forces to get them.

I don't think the peace movement has really grappled with these issues. We're so happy there's detente internationally that we're not addressing intervention issues.

Birchard: Mary talked about the way in which community-based groups grow in response to locally based issues like toxic pollution and the suffering of downwinders and radiation victims. The gulf that exists between so many of those people and those of us in the more traditional peace movement has a lot to do with class and style. Many of us approach issues in a more analytical way. There are also clear gender differences, to the extent that parts of our movement remain dominated by men who take this very rational and analytical approach. I think it is a terrible tragedy that men cannot accept other approaches to issues that begin more with personal experience. I'm struck by the importance of bridging that particular gap—still another gap that divides and weakens us.

Butters: I would like to ponder how, from my side, I can bridge that gap too.

We work a lot with young people. We have an office that accommodates children, with a TV, playroom, and kitchen, so that mothers can stay with their children. We have our own grade school, and high school students who keep regular office hours. They call themselves the foambusters. They've gotten the school board to ban styrofoam, and they're on the verge of a county ordinance banning it in 1990. They have their own educational programs, sanctioned by the school, where they actually teach, with regular class time set aside to save the world.

I feel that the high school students can come along and replace me, and the younger students that are learning can replace them. The three things that are important to have are fun, music, and kids, and I think we have those three things.

Ayvazian: Jeff said that the peace movement, at least over the last several years, has invited poor people and people of color in, but has not been willing to share power: "Welcome to our movement, with our norms and our values." And then we have the audacity to think that the peace movement, run by white, middle- to upper-class people, is somehow a culture-free zone, which it isn't.

Carter: We set people up for leadership only to knock them down. We don't trust people in positions of authority. We don't want them there. We deeply suspect their motives, and in the process we end up doing enormous violence to these people such that we burn them out and chase them away.

People have a death lock on power in our organizations. They're not willing to step back and give it up, to nurture others, and actually say, "Here, you take my place." People can't learn to be leaders until you give them a chance to lead. And I've been amazed that every time I've been willing to step back from a position of leadership, not only do terrific people come forward, but the organization does fine.

Butters: A lot of us come from dysfunctional families, we come from a dysfunctional culture, and we form dysfunctional organizations. To heal ourselves is an amazing process. I don't think we can go forth and change the world at large until we do that right at home.

Birchard: Andrea said that the peace movement has been moving from a war-peace axis to a liberation-oppression axis. I think we're really adding an axis, and many of us are not giving up on the war-peace axis.

But there's also another axis I want to suggest: the democratization-centralization axis. Throughout the world, from China to Chile and the Philippines to Peru, there is a commitment to resist the global trend toward centralization of power, and to empower people at a grassroots level. Bringing together antimilitary bases activists from the Philippines and members of the new opposition movements in Eastern Europe with people in Idaho could be very worthwhile. Whether we work on crime in communities or low-intensity conflict or nuclear weapons, we believe that power, as well as wealth, needs to be shared.

Richardson: I have a lot of agreement on Mary's point about dysfunctional families, a dysfunctional society, and dysfunctional organizations. I think it's critical that we look at the human side of the work that we're doing. Often the models that we use are, in fact, dysfunctional. I've seen some of the most devious, underhanded, vicious meetings on how to get people out of an organization. This kind of treatment will self-destruct the movement, and there will not be any young people to take over.

We have to discuss spiritual renewal as well, whether it's praying or playing music. We need to nurture each other as human beings more than as a movement.

Moglen: There have been some comments about the importance of play and fun, and one of the contradictions is that doing antinuclear work isn't really fun; it stinks. But Greenpeace's approach is through mischief, which is essentially playful. There's a tremendous amount of time spent thinking about mischief. The "subversive" kind of mischief is very invigorating and empowering, and it gives lots of people vicarious pleasure, especially when it's against the military.

Ayvazian: We've talked about our dysfunctional society, dysfunctional families, and creating dysfunctional organizations despite our best wishes, and we've also talked about the need to nurture ourselves. Christopher Titmuss, a Buddhist teacher and peace worker, said: "Always remember that we are human beings, not human doings." We need time to be who we are, to enjoy our lives, our kids, our music, and to have fun!

Where Did We Go Wrong?
Activists Reflect on What the Peace Movement Overlooked
Spring 1991

"FOR MANY YEARS, THE U.S. PEACE MOVEMENT HAS AVOIDED THE HARD issues of the Middle East. By and large, we sat out the Iran/Iraq war. We stood by silently while Iraq (among others) was armed to the teeth. We failed to notice the construction of military bases throughout the Middle East, designed for use by U.S. troops. We did not press hard enough for active U.S. diplomacy to resolve the Israeli-Palestinian-Arab conflict.

"We have failed on other fronts too. During the oil glut of the 1980s, we let down our guard in the struggle for conservation and renewable energy. In the absence of a draft, we ignored the military's increased emphasis on the reserves. Lulled by the end of the Cold War, many of us overlooked continuing strife in the Third World.

"We need a peace movement that is not focused on only one big issue at a time: nuclear disarmament, Central America, or for that matter, the Persian Gulf. We need a movement which keeps track of developments in many parts of the world, and recognizes the patterns."
—*Denis F. Doyon, American Friends Service Committee*

"Iraq is one of the most ferocious police states in the world, where the slightest opposition is met with maximum brutality. Whatever the Iraqi people might have thought, there was probably little they could do to restrain Saddam Hussein short of dismantling his regime root and branch.

"But in the U.S., which is not a police state, there has also been precious little to restrain Bush. The Democratic Party? In the November elections, the gulf crisis was strictly a non-issue. And when two days later, the deployment became clearly offensive, while polls showed a majority opposed to war, congressional Democrats were virtually silent. In December, Foley, Mitchell, and the rest of the Democratic leadership refused to convene a special session of Congress when public opinion was still strongly antiwar and congressional action might have made a difference.

"The antiwar movement has brought hundreds of thousands into the streets. Perhaps nothing could have prevented Bush from launching his blitzkrieg, but if anything can make him stop, there will have to be bigger marches, more protest, and massive civil disobedience. All this is indispensable—but it is not enough. During the 1960s, the antiwar movement never succeeded in translating protest into political power; today it *must* find a way to do so.

"A new political party would be the only effective way of challenging and ultimately replacing the war makers—including the Democratic party."

—*Thomas Harrison and Joanne Landy, Campaign for Peace and Democracy*

"Activists are no more nor less than citizens fulfilling their highest role in a democracy by participating actively in critical decisions. The case for continued sanctions and military restraint was a strong one.

"I think that citizen activists could have made this case more effectively to the president, Congress, middle America, and the media if they had joined in asserting a more reasoned position—analyzing the limited benefits and major costs to the country of proceeding to war. Unfortunately, the media focused on oversimplified slogans such as 'no blood for oil' rather than reasoned arguments for continued military restraint."

—*David Krieger, Nuclear Age Peace Foundation*

"The Bush administration had decided on the military option from the beginning. Having chosen not to negotiate and to treat Hussein like someone who had already lost a war, they didn't give sanctions or diplomacy a chance.

"We alerted public opinion and lobbied Congress—neither of which could be strong enough to stop an administration bent on war. We did underestimate the power of the political and economic forces propelling this country towards using its vast military machine.

"When the Cold War ended, we turned our attention to lowering the military budget and using the money for rebuilding American society. Perhaps we were naive not to expect a major war within a year. How we conduct ourselves now is very important."

—*Sayre Sheldon, Women's Action for Nuclear Disarmament*

"We could have responded as strongly to the doubling of the forces of Desert Shield in November as we did when hostilities began. We also need more effective networks and channels of communication to the U.N. if we expect it to use such peaceful means of resolving conflict as negotiation, mediation, and arbitration, even under the pressure of the past months.

"We must keep a strong focus on peace, even when peace is breaking out and even when environmental activism is at an unprecedented high. Peace issues must be brought to a focus in ordinary national politics, with insistence on, and education in, preventive diplomacy."

—Psychologists for Social Responsibility

"Our biggest mistake was not to educate the public better on the effectiveness of the economic embargo. In only five months, the Iraqi GNP was lowered by 45 to 50 percent. If the goal was the removal of Iraq from Kuwait, strong arguments could have been made that it could be brought about more effectively by embargo than by war.

"If the U.S. population truly understood the full cost of a war and the almost insignificant cost of maintaining an effective embargo, very few citizens would have chosen war. Unfortunately, because we were not prepared, the president was able to convince enough people in Congress and the media that the embargo had failed, and war was the only option."

—Doug Hostetter, Fellowship of Reconciliation

"Peace activists have contributed to Middle East instability through their consistent and conscious avoidance of tackling U.S. Middle East policy.

"America's Middle East policy consists essentially of an exclusive focus on Israel, with little regard for or understanding of the problems and potentials of other countries in the region . . . Peace groups have consistently refused to tackle the aid issue for fear of offending or alienating their Jewish constituency. The minority of American Jews who have had the courage to call for such a debate have found themselves ostracized and isolated. So politically intolerable is discussion of the aid issue that the charge of anti-Semitism is regularly leveled at non-Jews who raise the issue.

"Yet because Israel will not negotiate without U.S. aid becoming a question rather than a certainty, the aid issue is the one that defines commitment to peace or not. When it is raised, more often than not peace activists take refuge in the nearest political bunker."

—Helen H. McCloskey, Council for the National Interest,
advocacy group for balanced U.S. Middle East policy

"We have much growing and learning to do. While I'm hesitant to criticize a movement based on the predominantly volunteer efforts of principled people, there's no progress without reflection. We could have been more aware of the likelihood of regional conflicts erupting in a post-Cold War world. Once the crisis erupted we could have been more forceful in articulating the devastating consequences of using war as a means of resolving the conflict.

"But I must also say that the peace movement responded profoundly enough to come very close to having Congress oppose U.S. initiation of conflict."

—Ira Shorr, SANE/FREEZE

"The churches . . . did not fail their responsibility. We were among the first and only to raise the moral issues about this war. We were persistent and we were consistent.

"[But] as much as we tried to shape the discussion within a moral frame, the president's agenda became the national agenda. The argument was carried out on his terms and his assumptions. The ability of the churches and peace organizations to affect the debate was limited by the nature of our access to the media. We were heard, but we were heard as marginal 'curious' voices.

"As long as the media is structured in the way it is now, it will be difficult to prevent a repetition of this kind of thing in the future. As long as the administration has unfettered access to the media, we will have to work at a great disadvantage: our views will be filtered through a system that assumes that unless proven wrong, the president is always right."

—*Dale Bishop, National Council of Churches*

"For many years, Mideast organizers warned that the peace movement ignored the region at its own peril. The peril has arrived, with a vengeance.

"The peace movement has finally, if belatedly, gotten serious about the Middle East. By and large, people have responded to the crisis in the gulf both creatively and thoughtfully.

"Existing organizations have been joined by an array of new groups, most of whom have not previously participated in any kind of protest activities. Constituencies who have too often found themselves at odds with 'peace' groups—veterans, families with members serving in the military, communities of color—have provided strong leadership and direction for the movement, and student activism has been reignited across the country.

"Sadly, these efforts were not enough to keep us out of war. . . . Who knows what might have happened if the movement had really addressed Middle East issues a decade ago."

—*Dan Petegorsky, Peace Development Fund*

"The general American antiwar movement made four important errors in responding to the gulf crisis: one, treating the oil question as merely a ruling-class mystification; two, edging its way only slowly and reluctantly, to support sanctions against Iraq; three, committing itself to "bring the troops home now" as a politics and a slogan; and four, letting its opposition to the Israeli occupation of the West Bank/Gaza color its response to the invasion of Kuwait and to the Palestinian support of that invasion.

"What connects all these mistakes? The general American antiwar movement let its opposition to the global oil empire and to the Israeli occupation of the West Bank/Gaza distort and delay its recognition of the fascist character of the Iraqi invasion. That was a milder—but still unhealthy—version of an old failing of American progressives: assuming that "the enemy of my enemy is my friend." In one of its earlier forms, it was "if the USSR is against American capitalism, it must be socialist." It is important to root out this wistful, wishful thought that just because we do not like the grass here, it must be greener somewhere else.

"The peace movement's self-distortion and delay made Bush's job easier. Perhaps Bush would have won anyway, even if the antiwar movement had been more clear-headed. But he might have had a much harder time."

—*Arthur Waskow, Shalom Center*

What Do We Do Now?
By David Cortright
Summer 1991

THESE ARE DIFFICULT TIMES FOR THOSE OF US WHO BELIEVE IN PEACE and the power of nonviolence. Antiwar groups that grew rapidly in December and January are now reeling in shock. The human suffering, the scale of destruction, the shift of opinion toward the war—at times it's been overwhelming. Despite our sadness and feelings of futility, we must not give in to resignation. The peace movement is needed now more than ever. We must rebound to face the enormous challenges ahead.

We should not be in awe of Bush's accomplishment. The administration has shown that the U.S. military can kill efficiently, but it has not proven American military policy right. The problems and contradictions that existed before the Persian Gulf War remain, and in some cases have grown worse. Iraq has been pushed out of Kuwait, but little else has changed. The unjust legacy of colonialism, the disparity between rich and poor, conflicts over the pricing of oil, the denial of Palestinian rights—these and other root causes of violence remain. And now new seeds of conflict have been sown in the humiliation and devastation Bush has imposed upon Iraq.

As we develop the next stages of peace movement activity, the realities of the current political climate must be faced squarely. We cannot do anything about the victory parades and celebrations—trying would be foolish as well as counter-productive. Rather we must develop creative new approaches that chip away at the opposition and that place roadblocks in the path of future military adventures.

Here are some possibilities that may help infuse doubt into the apparent wisdom of Bush's war and sustain and build the antiwar movement.

Humanize the War
Bush's offensive attack was not a model of surgical precision, as military spokespeople claim, but a horrifying exhibition of technological barbarism. Iraqi casualty figures are not known yet, but as they become available the number of dead may reach 100,000 or more, most of them killed within a few days. Thousands more may die in the weeks and months ahead from dysentery and

other diseases resulting from the destruction of Iraq's water, power, and sewage systems. These victims won't even be counted as "collateral" damage. The human cost of Bush's war must be exposed.

One way to reveal these atrocities would be through a humanitarian relief and political education campaign. Local and national groups could begin efforts, as many are doing already, to raise money for the victims of the war in Iraq as well as in Israel, the occupied territories, Jordan, and Kuwait. Delegations should visit the region not only to deliver aid but to observe the devastation wrought by Bush's war and to publicize their observations on their return home. Such efforts have been effective in building the Central American solidarity movement and could have a similar impact on the broader antiwar effort. The Fellowship of Reconciliation has already sponsored such delegations and is establishing a new Civilian Casualty Fund.

Focus on Domestic Needs

As the afterglow of victory fades, questions will arise about the quality of a society that can send a half-million troops around the world to wage war but cannot solve its own problems of homelessness, crime, drug abuse, and unemployment. Budget cuts at all levels of government are intensifying, and poverty and human hardship are increasing. Many Americans, even those who supported the war, will respond to appeals for reordered budgetary priorities. It's not enough to increase bonuses and benefits for returning soldiers; their communities also need support.

In a school system in Michigan, for example, a program to place computers in schools is being cut, forcing local school districts to choose between raising taxes again or removing the computers. Isn't it more important to have smart children instead of smart bombs? Let's put the issue in human terms and demand increased investment in education, health care, housing, and the environment.

Liberate Palestine

Bush claims that the war was fought over the principle that one nation may not invade and occupy another. This principle should be applied uniformly. Certainly it must include Israel's occupation of Gaza and the West Bank, where some 800 Palestinians have been killed since the beginning of the *intifada*. The opportunity exists now to exert pressure on Israel to negotiate with the Palestinians for an equitable solution. If Israel does not change, the United States should cut the $4 billion a year in economic and military aid it provides.

Even the Bush administration now feels the pressure to discuss the Palestinian issue. Change in U.S. policy will not come, however, unless there is a groundswell of pressure from the American people. For the sake of peace in the Middle East and for the long-term security of both the Israelis and the Palestinians, we must mobilize to demand a negotiated political settlement.

No More Fuel for the Fire

Arms transfers by the Soviet Union and the Western powers were blatant factors in contributing to the Persian Gulf crisis, and under Bush administration policy they will continue to fuel conflict. While insisting on an arms boycott of Iraq, the administration is proposing a whopping $23 billion in arms sales to Saudi Arabia, plus an additional $1 billion in sales to Israel and Egypt.

An arms embargo is needed for the entire region, not just for one nation. The administration should also propose, as the Carter administration briefly attempted, a negotiated agreement among the major arms suppliers to limit and reduce arms transfers throughout the world.

Oppose the Next War

If, as Bush says, we've kicked the Vietnam syndrome, is there now danger of the spread of the Iraq syndrome? This was a war to make the world safe for war and to tell other nations that "what we say, goes." The war managers now feel unrestrained and may attempt new military adventures elsewhere. For Bush, it's been two years in office and two wars. Will year three bring another conflict? Which nationalist government in the Third World will be the next victim?

The peace movement must criticize the policy of America as the world's police officer. We should also warn about the increased threat that may now exist for Cuba and other developing nations. Solidarity with the Third World has suddenly taken on new urgency. We must build a movement that can challenge the policy of imperialist intervention at its core.